MODERNIZING PEASANT SOCIETIES

A Comparative Study in Asia and Africa

The Institute of Race Relations is an unofficial and non-political body, founded in England in 1958 to encourage and facilitate the study of the relations between races everywhere. The Institute is precluded by the Memorandum and Articles of its incorporation from expressing a corporate view. The opinions expressed in this work are those of the author.

The Overseas Development Institute (ODI) is an independent, non-government body aiming to promote wise action in the field of overseas development. It was set up in 1960 and is financed by donations from British business and by grants from British and American foundations. Its policies are determined by its Council. Opinions expressed in the publications of the Institute are those of the authors concerned.

MODERNIZING PEASANT SOCIETIES

A Comparative Study in Asia and Africa

GUY HUNTER

Published for
the Institute of Race Relations, London
OXFORD UNIVERSITY PRESS
NEW YORK   1969   LONDON

© Institute of Race Relations 1969

Printed in the United States of America

CONTENTS

Preface and Acknowledgements   ix

PART I   THE STARTING POINT

Chapter I	The Nature of the Problem	3
Chapter II	Background and Change in Traditional Economies	30
Chapter III	Status, Power and Politics at Village Level	55

PART II   AGRICULTURAL DEVELOPMENT

Chapter IV	General Strategies	81
Chapter V	Technical Factors	107
Chapter VI	Structure, Tenure, Institutions	139
Chapter VII	Contact with the Farmer	172

PART III   THE GROWING SOCIETY

Chapter VIII	Administration	191
Chapter IX	Politics	218
Chapter X	Education	240
Chapter XI	Economics	260

PART IV   CONCLUSIONS

| Chapter XII | A New Path | 281 |

Index of Authors and Works quoted in the Text   299

General Index   302

LIST OF TABLES

TABLE 1	Agricultural Administration in Indian States	57 and 209
TABLE 2	Alternative Uses of Land by Size of Holding	142
TABLE 3	India: Enrolment at Different Educational Levels	249
TABLE 4	Educational Progress of a Single Age Group—available to enter Primary School in 1961–2 (Tanzania)	254
TABLE 5	Educational Status of two Groups of Children in 1969 (Tanzania)	255

PREFACE

This book is the outcome of two and a half years' work on a project sponsored jointly by the Institute of Race Relations and the Overseas Development Institute (both in London), and financed by a grant from the Ford Foundation. The purpose of the project was to inquire more deeply into the effect of 'the transfer of institutions from developed to developing countries'.

In October 1967 some preliminary thinking was published, by the Oxford University Press, under the title *The Best of Both Worlds?*. That little book dealt almost wholly with Africa.

But as the work proceeded, it became increasingly clear that to concentrate wholly on 'transfer' did not provide an adequate basis for explanation of the problems and performance of developing countries. These problems arise not only from the fact that ideas, institutions and technology are borrowed from countries at a different stage of development and with a different cultural background. They arise also because developing countries are seeking rapid economic growth in a wholly different total environment from that in which the main thrust of growth took place in the West. They can neither recapitulate the sequences of growth in Europe between 1700 and 1900 nor take the full modern equipment of institutions and technology of the 20th century. Their path of development must be, in many senses, unique. This constituted a challenge to adopt a wider framework which I was forced to accept.

The second challenge, equally unavoidable, was to find a way of writing which would be genuinely 'inter-disciplinary', that is, which treated developing society as a whole, not as a series of separate abstractions (economic, political, administrative, moral, and so forth). It is clear, for example, that the political dimension of development cannot simply be tacked on as a separate item but helps to shape every problem and policy even at farm level. I am only too well aware how imperfectly I have achieved this—the book does not provide a neat and elegant theory: it can at best claim to keep more factors simultaneously in focus than most of the writing on these subjects.

The third challenge was to deal with parts of South and South-East Asia as a comparison with Africa. My wife and I were able to travel in North India and Pakistan in the winter of 1966–1967 and in South India in the early months of 1968; from these journeys a great deal of the material and judgements in the book is drawn. Perhaps even more of the general background comes from work in eight South-East Asian countries for UNESCO-IAU in 1963 and 1964, more recently in Thailand and Fiji, and over the last ten years in Africa.

On so wide a canvas and at any reasonable length it is of course impossible to avoid using general terms which any scholar would question as inapplicable to some local situation: a term such as 'village' has had to do duty for a great range of local settlements, each of which, in a work of narrower scholarship, would need precise definition. The use of the words 'peasant society', in the title and constantly in the book itself, is particularly vulnerable to attack, especially in Africa. African rural settlements are not, in general, peasant societies as they could be strictly defined: tribal societies would be a little nearer. But they are *becoming* something much nearer to peasant societies as customary tenure changes towards individual ownership in a mixed subsistence and cash economy. If the book was to be written and readable at all, these shorthand methods had to be used.

I have not repeated here much of the argument, or the quotations in support of it, which is set out in *The Best of Both Worlds?*—the two books should really be read together, but I hope this volume is intelligible on its own.

Finally, the book is addressed to the informed reader, whether in government or industry or Aid agencies or private institutions or the academic world, who is interested in the practical task of development. One critic of *The Best of Both Worlds?* complained that 'the model' was not accurately set out or 'proved'. I must disclaim at once any attempt to set out a 'model', or to give strict proof of this argument; much of it is not susceptible of 'proof' in any case.

ACKNOWLEDGEMENTS

My first debt is to the two Institutes and to the Ford Foundation for making this work possible. My second is to the Governments of India and of Pakistan for their generous help in making the fieldwork possible. I cannot speak too warmly of the generosity in time and trouble that a very large number of officials showed to my wife and myself in organizing field visits and interviews and in shepherding us on our travels. Although evidence is drawn from many other countries in Asia and Africa which we have visited, the Indian and Pakistan visits were particularly made for this work.

Next, I would like to acknowledge personally the very special debt which I owe to a few books and authors constantly referred to in the text. Notable among these is the splendid collection of articles in Herman W. Southworth and Bruce F. Johnston's *Agricultural Development and Economic Growth*; the work of Bruce Johnston on Japanese development; J. W. Mellor's *Economics of Agricultural Development*; the work of F. G. Bailey in Orissa, and of Mrs. Epstein and Margaret Haswell in South India; and the collection of essays on *Politics in the Indian States*, edited by Myron Weiner. The work of many other scholars is acknowledged in the text, and most gratefully.

I would like to thank Philip Mason and Tom Soper for their kindness and care in reading through the first draft of the book and making many comments, almost invariably accepted as improvements: to read so much so carefully is a heavy burden. I also owe thanks to the editorial staff of the Institute of Race Relations in finally preparing the typescript for the Press.

Finally, like so many authors, but in this case in an exceptionally high degree, I owe an immense debt to my wife, as my constant companion and helper in all field-work over the last ten years, my chief source of suggestions and of informed criticism, and co-worker in the long task of shaping and pruning and checking a fairly long manuscript into a presentable form.

GUY HUNTER

November 1968

PART I
THE STARTING POINT

CHAPTER I

THE NATURE OF THE PROBLEM

This book is about the nature and speed of growth in the peasant societies of Asia and Tropical Africa in the environment of the modern world.

It is not simply a study of agricultural development. Agriculture does indeed occupy the central place in these countries, since 70–90% of their populations live out their life in the villages or more scattered settlements and homesteads, whether working with land and animals directly or serving those who do. It is rather a study of agricultural society regarded as a living whole. For a study of agricultural change is inseparable from other non-economic elements in social life—its history, beliefs, institutions, education, politics, administration, ambitions and ideals. All these elements, so often studied separately as 'economics', 'sociology', 'politics', go together to form the long groundswell of social and technical change which we call modernization. And if indeed this wholeness is taken seriously, then we must expect to find, as wave succeeds wave, that every element is changing, both actively and passively. For a new technique may call forth a new institution, a new institution make possible a new technique: both together may alter the balance of political power. Because of the importance of agriculture, the point of entry for this study is through the farming and village community. If it is possible to make some sense of the process of change there, in all its dimensions, it will go far to make sense of society as a whole. For towns, trade, industry, politics and government itself, however independent they may seem to be, must in the long run be intimately related to the great mass of the rural population.

It is natural to look for guidance in the experience of other peasant societies in the past. Historians can describe how such societies in mediaeval Europe grew, through stages of craft production and merchanting, to their modern industrial form. The problem now is to find some reasoned theory of how Asia and

Africa can achieve far faster sequences of growth in the new environment of the modern world. In this search it is easy to fall into one of two contrasting mistakes. The first is to believe that a set of modern institutions and techniques borrowed from the developed countries, and the laws of economic and social growth evolved from their circumstances, can be applied forthwith. I have tried elsewhere to suggest some of the awkward consequences of this attempted transfer.[1] The second is to look back to the peasant phase of now developed countries, to watch the steps by which they grew and changed, and to deduce from them the sequences which Africa or Asia could best follow today.

The second course is perhaps the more beguiling—indeed, I believe it leads to less ruinous consequences. At least it regards society as in some way organic, and respects the style of organic growth rather than mechanical construction. But it must be largely mistaken. For while the transfer of modern institutions neglects much of the internal social environment of a peasant society, the attempt to repeat history neglects the changes in the external world. The peasant societies of 15th-century Europe were surrounded by 15th-century Europe, with some marginal contacts with overseas societies not much more advanced than they. India and Africa today are surrounded, limited, inspired, almost conditioned by the influences of 20th-century industrial civilization.

Yet history must have some useful message: its very selection from the multi-billion events of the past implies a theory of significance, of sequences which have some logic and meaning. Some of these are political sequences—what is apt to happen to dictatorships or aristocracies; and on these political theory has been based. Some are economic sequences—the effects of transport on the growth of markets; and from these economic laws have been developed. Some are technical—the effects of mechanical power. Yet all must be handled with extreme care. For their validity rests upon the environment of the past, and the theories are always apt to outlive the conditions from which they were deduced. Thus, as the outer environment of local events changes over the centuries—nowadays, over the years—history is hard-pressed to find exact parallels. It might be well enough to compare sequences from two similar starting points, within a single culture,

[1] In *The Best of Both Worlds?* (London, Oxford University Press for the Institute of Race Relations, 1968).

within a single period. But if we take as one element of comparison an English Tudor country town and put alongside it some busy market centre in the Gangetic Plain today, the deductions which can be made are very limited. Certainly, the two towns look alike in many ways. The same crowds jostle in narrow streets, lined by open shops with their baskets of grain, rolls of cloth, clanging workshops, carts and barrows. But the starting points are really very different (one is surrounded by the 16th century and the other by the 20th), and the sequences which follow will be different too.

Even if we narrow the focus to one subject, and ask the economic historian for purely economic parallels, will his rules hold good? A place with no road to it was isolated from the market in 1500; power needed local wind or water; news was at the speed of a man on horseback. In the peasant societies of Asia and Africa the aeroplane comes where there is no road, the pylons carry power, the radio speaks to the peasant when he comes home at evening from the fields.

Nevertheless, between the developed countries of today and all peasant societies, whether of 1500 or 1969, there lies a gap which has many common features. So many of the same things have to be done. Skills must be learned: the skill of the engineer, the factory manager, the modern administrator; institutions must be formed capable of mediating the needs of a commercial and industrial society; a political and administrative framework equal to modern tasks must be evolved. History, if it cannot give recipes, can give suggestive hints of the order in which such changes flowed easily in the past; social anthropology is beginning to show, in modern conditions, modifications and side-effects of that order by the study of the impact of modernity on the traditional societies of today. It would indeed be as great a folly to throw away all that we have learned of human behaviour in social groups —even if we could, for our minds are conditioned by it—as it would be to demand precise parallels from the past. The method of progress must be unique, in new conditions; the speed of progress can be much faster; but much of the journey to be covered is the same.

2

Let us measure at least some main dimensions of the difference which separates the historical conditions of Western economic growth from the conditions which face Asia and Africa today. Leave aside, at least for the moment, the longer history of Western culture and concentrate on that special explosive phase between A.D. 1600 and 1900. Even as far back as 1600, we find that Europe was in many respects well ahead of some developing countries today. England, for example, with a population of less than 5 million in 1600, was already far more differentiated in occupation and skills, in the range of mining, manufacture, shipbuilding, internal and external trade, than most of the countries of Tropical Africa and some of those in Asia when they gained Independence.[1]

In the next 300 years an almost unbelievable area of the globe became open to these small European populations. The whole of Canada and the United States, Australia, New Zealand and South Africa were captured for their use. South America, India, South-East Asia and later Africa were fields for commercial enterprise, local settlement, and administrative vocation. This immense opportunity was both opened and made profitable to them by a sudden technical advantage. It enabled them to absorb into higher productivity almost the whole of their increasing populations.

These populations were growing relatively slowly—Great Britain never exceeded a 1·4% per annum demographic growth at the height of 19th-century expansion; the revolution of declining mortality had not yet been achieved. Industry was not held back by slow growth in purchasing power of the agricultural community, because the expanding export markets supplied the outlet and stimulus. There was indeed some movement from the rural labour force into industry and trade, from the time of the Enclosures and the agricultural revolution of the 18th century, but it was spread over a long period. It was not, as has been thought, entirely the displaced cottagers and farmworkers who supplied the labour force for the new industry, but to a considerable extent the existing and naturally increasing urban population, moving

---

[1] For quick reference, see E. M. Carus Wilson (ed.), *Essays in Economic History* (London, Edward Arnold, 1954), and particularly Wilson, 'The Industrial Revolution of the 13th Century', J. V. Nef, 'The Progress of Technology and the Growth of Large-Scale Industry in Great Britain, 1540–1640', and F. L. Fisher, 'Commercial Trends in Sixteenth Century England'. For distribution of occupations, see Peter Laslett, *The World we have Lost* (London, Methuen, 1965). For a later period, see G. D. H. Cole and Raymond Postgate, *The Common People, 1746–1938* (London, Methuen, 1938).

from superseded crafts or services to the new factories.[1] Short-term unemployment was locally acute, both in the troughs of the trade-cycle and from structural changes in industry; but both unemployment and the population increase were eventually swallowed in the larger wave of overall expansion.

It is necessary to stand far back from history to see the larger pattern which stretches over some centuries. There is little doubt that these advantages of Western Europe—the huge opportunity for territorial expansion, the technical superiority which made it possible, the resulting markets which stimulated industry far beyond the restricted demand from internal agricultural consumers, the fact that the main population growth came late, and (by contrast with rates of growth in today's developing countries) relatively slowly—all helped to ease the absorption of a growing labour force into full employment. Yet it is also horrifying to see how this long-distance view misses the tiny overlapping patterns and colours of which the larger design is made up. It misses, in fact, the human reality, the gross suffering, pauperism, exploitation of children, years of heartbreak which locally and temporarily fell to the lot of the unfortunate. And in missing this, something is missed which is neither local nor temporary. For not only does the memory of those wrongs live on and profoundly influence the social life of industrialized countries today: the story has also strongly moved the developing countries to search for a path of development which is not so disfigured by abuse and suffering. This search is a most significant element in problems of growth which we are studying here. The remaining chapters of this book will be close to the detail and human reality of the present. With this warning of the dangers of the long and broad view, we can turn back to it more safely.

Contrast now the situation of peasant societies in the 20th century as they face the task of social and economic change. First, there is no more world left for their territorial expansion, save for the Arctic icecaps, the great deserts, the Amazonian forest. Some countries, it is true, including many in Tropical Africa and Latin America, and a few in Asia, have land to spare if capital could be

---

[1] See M. M. Postan, quoting also Professor Chambers, 'Address to the Second International Conference of Economic History', Aix-en-Provence, 1962, published in *Second International Conference of Economic Histories*, 2 vols. (New York, Humanities Press, 1965).

found to develop it; but it is mostly the more difficult land which the colonizing nations rejected or could not use.

Next, there is no technical superiority among the peasant societies of today, by which they could capture, even without territorial expansion, a huge external market such as that which fell to Europe. Indeed, the reverse is true. They seek to enter, as latecomers, an already highly competitive and exclusive system of world trade in which their armament, in almost every field except that of tropical agricultural products, is inferior.

Next, the population explosion—2% to 3% per annum—has come before the growth of economic opportunity and employment openings. Unemployment is the universal threat, both as a social problem and as a gross waste of human capacity for development.

Next, although a high technology exists for the borrowing, it is a technology often unsuited to their needs—designed for large-scale production when their markets are small, requiring both capital and sophisticated skills, of which they are short; economical in labour of which they have a surplus, and often ill-adapted to their climate, their land tenure, their social pattern.

This is a formidable list. Almost every major advantage which pushed forward European growth is negated in Africa and Asia. It is true that today's developing countries have some advantages which Europe lacked. Scientific knowledge is available; some technologies at least, such as electric power, are easily borrowed; the means of speedy mass-education are vastly improved. This very combination of handicaps and aids emphasizes again and again how different their path of growth must be. Yet a part of the present difficulties overseas arises just because these fundamental differences have not been genuinely taken into account. Partly through the thoughtless application of economic and social theories derived from Western experience,[1] partly from the demonstration-

---

[1] The trouble lies in inadequate or wrong description of the *data* on which theory is constructed.

'The followers of all disciplines need to be aware that most of the literature they have studied requires re-interpretation in application to the developing areas of the world. In the last analysis, those who are developing must re-write the sciences in their own contexts.'
Introduction to Herman M. Southworth and Bruce F. Johnston (eds.), *Agricultural Development and Economic Growth* (Ithaca, Cornell University Press, 1967).

'Theories which, because of their high degree of abstraction, look perfectly

effect of rich societies which has led poor ones to adopt their ways, the early stages of development in many peasant countries have been distorted and disrupted by borrowings unsuited to the real stages and sequences of their own path of growth. Not only is this true in economic terms: it is the whole matrix of society which has to change—politics, administration, institutions, education. In these fields too the example of Western development has too often been misapplied. Before we can see a better path ahead, it is necessary to signpost more clearly some of these false trails.

3

The first of these confusions concerns the relationship of industry, agriculture and employment, and it has already been foreshadowed. It springs from a careless application of two apparently self-evident truths: first, that demand for food is relatively inelastic—a man can eat only so much food, but the man with one car can demand a second and a third. Thus in the long run wealth must come through industrialization. Second, that in a closed economy with a static labour force, expansion of industry and services must mean release of labour from agriculture. The second proposition needs some care. For in an economy with a 3% population growth, the labour force will be big enough to expand in both the industrial and the agricultural sector; and in a trading (open) economy the allocation of the labour force will depend on whether agricultural or industrial goods can more profitably be sold abroad, that is, on comparative advantage and the terms of trade.

The special case of Britain's economy did indeed stress the supply of labour from agriculture to industry. The agricultural revolution of Britain's 18th century was useful both as a source of labour for industry, and of more food, and of capital. But by the mid-19th century cheap foreign food was available in plenty and capital was being generated by the profits of industry and

---

"neutral" as between one kind of economic system and another often are primarily relevant to the conditions under which they were conceived. . . . For, as we have become used to looking at reality through certain theoretical glasses, we may for a long time be unable to see it as it really is.'

Albert O. Hirschman, *The Strategy of Economic Development* (Yale University Press, 1958).

commerce catering for foreign markets. Thus the role of agriculture as a supplier of labour was emphasized, but its role in supplying food, or capital, or a market for industrial output was minimized.

In contrast, in today's developing countries the precedence of agriculture rests on a quite different balance of argument. In general there is not a shortage but a surplus of labour, though local seasonal shortages can always occur; there is no question of squeezing labour out of the rural sector to man industry and towns—quite the reverse. It is the two other needs of industry— for capital and for markets[1]—which make an agricultural revolution imperative. The small industrial sector in most developing countries does not have a large external market—it is far from easy to sell industrial output to other peasant societies, and harder still to sell it to the industrial giants. A really prosperous agriculture can provide both internal savings and (by the export of tropical crops) foreign exchange, the two vital sources of industrial capital; still more important, it can provide the main and often virtually the only market for industrial output.[2] The only alternative source of capital and consumer demand is the other great primary industry—mining for export, as in Zambia.

Thus the argument, so often expressed even in 1968,[3] that the 'role' of agriculture is to provide cheap food and surplus labour to a growing industrial sector was only partly true in Britain and is grossly misleading in most of Asia and Africa today. Of course, in the long run there must be a structural change towards secondary industry and tertiary services—some advanced industrial countries have less than 10% of their labour force in agriculture.[4] But to say this is the 'role' or 'function' of agriculture in developing countries today is to anticipate development by at least a generation; it is also to diminish the importance and urgency of agricultural

[1] For a recent treatment of this argument, see John W. Mellor, *The Economics of Agricultural Development* (Ithaca, Cornell University Press, 1966). He speaks of 'Agriculture's dual potential as contributor of capital and creator of market'.

[2] Clearly, the two sectors will grow in mutual interaction. There is a limit to agricultural productivity unless it has an industrial base (chemicals, power, transport) and a growing urban market. But the argument here concerns the starter-mechanism for this mutually stimulating system.

[3] See, for example, papers by Sir Joseph Hutchinson and by Professor Jacoby to the Ministry of Overseas Development Conference on Agricultural Development, Cambridge, March–April 1968.

[4] Britain just over 5%; U.S.A. 9%.

development in its own right. It has encouraged a premature and sometimes disastrous investment in industries which have no market, and a neglect of the agricultural sector. It would be far more true to say that the role of agriculture in India and Africa today is to raise the incomes and consumption of the great majority of the population who are farmers, to earn foreign exchange, to supply internal savings (capital) through taxation, to provide a livelihood for a *larger* labour force by intensive use of land. With 2–3% population growth, the point at which there is a shortage of labour for industry, or falling absolute numbers in the rural sector, is certainly nearer fifty than thirty years ahead in many developing countries.[1] The problem in this study is how peasant countries can give a rising standard to an *increasing* labour force in agriculture and its associated services, until a growing industry and a falling population growth-rate make it possible to relieve the pressure.

4

A parallel set of confusions has arisen in the relationships between economic growth, employment, and education. For many centuries in Europe the main function of popular education in schools was to maintain the Christian order and tradition, with literacy used for that purpose and for the simplest needs of everyday life—to read the Bible, to count. Economic skills of production were learned almost wholly from father to son and by apprenticeship outside the school system. By the mid-17th century England had attained a very great range of craft production by this means, with only about 2,000 schools (one for every fifth parish) and two Universities for the elite of Church and State. Technology was empirical, for although the main growth of science springs forward in the 17th century, science did not actually catch up with and start to guide technology until far later—almost the start of the 19th century. Mass Primary education did not become universal until the 1880s. Certainly in the 19th century not much connection between mass education and economic growth was felt to exist.

But from then on the importance of formal education has been stressed more and more, in two respects. First, in industrialized

---

[1] This argument is developed in Chapter IV.

countries relying increasingly on science, competition demanded higher and higher educational levels. Second, the growth of democratic ideals gave education a special halo as a universal Human Right.

In colonial administration the Missions, which played such a huge part in Africa, at first concentrated on the older tradition—the Christian order and literacy.[1] As the Colonial Governments were forced to take a greater part in educational development, they decided to expand somewhat a 'grammar school' type of education, leading to a University for a very few. They did so with misgivings, because they were unable to see what opportunities could arise for more than a tiny proportion of children to use such an education in practical employment. They questioned the relevance of education (of this type) to economic need; they feared the disturbance of traditional values and disciplines; they feared the economic costs of massive provision in poor countries, and they feared the frustration of educated unemployed.[2] The bitter criticism, from Africa in particular, that colonialism restricted educational opportunity reflects these fears.

But the developing countries, who saw industrialization as one cause of Western wealth, saw education as the other. As Independence came, international idealism, the idea of education as a Human Right, the apparent correlation between education and wealth and power, pushed open the floodgates of expansion. Real, though limited administrative needs supported the argument, and the privileges in employment which education gave at first pulled parents (now voters) behind the insistent demand for more schools.

In consequence, the developing nations are faced, at the very start of their desperate race for development, not only with the financial burden of a mushrooming educational system, but with the hopes and ambitions and the bitter dissatisfactions which education can arouse when it is not matched by economic opportunity. In country after country children from 10 to 18 are pouring out of the schools into a world which can offer only to a tiny

---

[1] Some Missions in Africa did endeavour to base education on craft skill. See particularly Roland Oliver, *The Missionary Factor in East Africa* (London, Longmans, 1952).

[2] See, for example, Philip Foster, *Education and Social Change in Ghana* (London, Routledge and Kegan Paul, 1965), and Richard Symonds, *The British and their Successors* (London, Faber and Faber, 1966).

proportion of them any opportunity beyond the unchanged pattern of family and village and subsistence farming. The International Labour Organization[1] has calculated the net increase in the labour force in developing countries as about 162,000,000 in 1960-70 and 226,000,000 in 1970-80 (against 50,000,000 and 55,000,000 respectively in the developed world). What proportion of these will have wage-paid employment? The estimate for Latin America is 9%; in many countries it could well be lower. More than half of these new citizens will have been to school, and children under 16 make up 50% of the total population in many developing countries. This immense problem of half-educated, half-employed young people is, after the demographic explosion which exacerbates it, perhaps the gravest which developing nations face. It is not solely a problem of high population growth: it is a problem of education as yet unrelated to economic life.[2]

What exactly has gone wrong in this adoption of 20th-century Western standards of education needs a far more careful analysis of real needs and resources, and for this reason the chapter on Education is placed very late in this book. It is clear already that one factor of supreme importance in European growth—the early development of widespread and skilled technology outside the schools—has been missing, especially in Africa. It is clear that, if the relationship between education and economic opportunity is awry, the fault may lie on the economic as much as on the educational side. It is clear, as unemployment comes back again and again to the centre of the argument, that even to speak of rapid growth is futile unless some way can be found to use these enormous and half-wasted human resources. If that way can be found, there will be little difficulty in seeing what education is needed; it is not likely to be identical with the European or American systems of 1969.

---

[1] I.L.O., *Report to the Commission for Social Development of the United Nations Economic and Social Council* (E/CN5/422, November 1967). This is a most valuable source of global employment statistics. Developing countries include Asia except Japan, Africa except southern Africa, and Latin America excluding countries in the temperate zone.

[2] The belief that a large educational output is of high value to economic growth 'is based on the assumption that the educational output is based on the needs of the economic system . . . and that the graduates can make a proper contribution to national production'. Hans W. Singer, *International Development: Growth and Change* (New York, McGraw-Hill, 1963).

5

As a third illustration of the confusing impact of modern ideas we may take the tangle of intertwined values associated with political democracy on one hand and with the liberties and rights of the individual in economic organization on the other.

Political democracy grew slowly, step by step, in Europe—some of its history may concern us later. But it started far earlier in America, and the immense economic success of the United States has been there to prove that rapid development from simple beginnings can be carried through under a fairly radical democratic constitution. From both Europe and America the idea that the 20th century was the century of the common man had become the dominant political orthodoxy some time before the eventual Independence leaders in developing countries appeared.

But both in Europe and America political democracy was associated with a private enterprise system in production, and to a considerable degree those who supported the freedom of the individual as entrepreneur sought to bring it under the umbrella of public approval which covered other 'democratic' liberties, such as free speech or free elections. In doing so they followed a considerable tradition of political philosophy, notably exemplified in John Stuart Mill, which saw the interference of State power in the 'private' business of the individual as a major threat to liberty.

In fact, however, private enterprise produced 'the managerial society'. This society never conceded democratic principles in productive relationships—'democracy stops at the factory gate' is an old Trade Union cry. The free craftsmen and cottagers who entered the ranks of industry entered a contractual relationship to obey orders in return for pay. Management was forced to recognize a legitimized opposition (the Trade Unions), and it sought to soften resentment by 'Welfare', both in the factory and in the Welfare State. It was this managerial society, modified by political democracy and by welfare, watchdogged by Trade Unionism, enshrining private enterprise as the mainspring of its energy, which formed the dominant industrial environment of the early 20th century.

The fact that at the very heart of industrial civilization there lay a relationship which was basically authoritarian and non-participatory has caused a bitterness, now perhaps a sourness, which has been, and still is, at the root of social tensions in the Western world. Seen through the eyes of nations struggling against authoritarian colonial rule, it was bound to be an object of suspicion or hostility, increased as the history of 19th century abuses became better known. The Russian Revolution of 1917 suddenly gave a public focus to this hostility. And indeed it was not only that the Bolsheviks bracketed colonialism and capitalism as the objects of hatred which naturally appealed to developing countries. The Soviet Union had managed to steal the stirring vision of both the French and the American Revolution, and project it so powerfully that the authoritarian nature of its own regime could be overlooked as a temporary, wartime, necessity. Ideas of popular democracy and of State Socialism, of participation by the common man in the management of economic as well as political life, spread like wildfire round the world.

Although these ideas had been generated through a political evolution which most developing countries had not lived through and from an industrial system which (save in India and Pakistan) they had not themselves experienced on a large scale, they became, and still are, of tremendous political and economic importance. On the political side they caused great difficulty for those countries in particular where the native tradition was in fact authoritarian. In the Muslim States, and some others in Africa, and in most of Asia, Emirs, Sultans, Maharajahs, kings, landlords, caste systems, and indeed the authority of colonial rule, represented the immediate past. In some degree the whole social order—the piety of family, reverence for elders, religious respect, systems of landholding, the ladder of obligations (service from below, protection from above), all this was utterly alien to the levelling democratic ethos: it was, in these cases, as though feudal England had suddenly been invaded by the values of the Laski school of economics and the B.B.C. Even where there was a natural democracy of elders and family heads, as in some African situations, it was not really a 'democratic' system *sensu moderno*, in which a young man's vote counts as much as an elder's, nor had it the sinews or technical competence to sustain a nation-state rather than a clan council.

Some of the traditional rulers could see what was happening and raised a note of protest. 'Why are you so anxious to hand us over to the *canaille?*' one educated African ruler asked of the British Government. The Emirs of Northern Nigeria and the Sultans of Malaya, the Tutsi of Rwanda, the Ganda, the Lozi of Barotseland, many Indian Princes—all had doubts or worse than doubts. But not only were their voices often drowned by the younger nationalists, they usually had little sympathy from the departing Colonial Power, anxious to leave a progressive democracy in control, both as less vulnerable to subversion and as a memorial to their own progressive rule.

In contrast, the more revolutionary leaders of independent Africa and Asia, who had already used universal suffrage as a weapon with which to gain freedom, were in any case committed to a democratic, participatory philosophy. But they had to translate ideology into real and workable constitutions and policies. It is no wonder that we find a Nyerere or Kaunda or Senghor talking of Fundamental Human Rights or the Nature of Man, or Indian leaders seeking in their own traditions a thread of continuity to bind the future to the past. For the old questions of Plato and Hobbes and Rousseau are being asked again in these societies, who feel, as the Founding Fathers in America felt, that history is offering them the rare gift of a new start. What is justice? Who is to govern? How is government controlled? Above the level of village democracy and clan organization, in which they have a rich and varied tradition, there are no acceptable answers to these questions in their own past; and they are hardly likely to find solutions by persisting with the model constitutions which the departing Colonial Powers somewhat hastily negotiated.

They have been given—or have chosen of their own will—political systems and social institutions which grew out of wholly different societies, in a different stage of growth—Trade Unions, Land Grant Colleges or European model Universities, Rochdale Co-operatives, County Councils, two-Chamber Parliaments, universal adult suffrage; they have been urged to choose free enterprise systems, State socialism, Israeli *moshavim* or some other of the systems which rival each other in the Cold War. Many are now turning away from foreign models, and are looking inwards to observe the real structure of their own society, the locus of power and the resources of leadership, so that some system can be built which rests upon realities and yet has the potential of growth. In their search they have, I believe, in Africa and Asia, accepted in principle the profound demand for social justice and human dignity which has become part of the world environment of thought.

The more idealist solutions have much in common, whether in Africa or Asia:

> The ultimate aim ... is to move towards the attainment of an Islamic social order. This term is almost interchangeable with a Welfare State. In addition to the familiar Welfare goals, an Islamic social order implies that the cultural and religious heritage of the country should not be destroyed in the ruthless pursuit of economic development.... The Government is committed to providing all the facilities which are by now a common feature of the Western world.[1]

This speech of Pakistan's President combines both the search for indigenous tradition and the acceptance of Western welfare standards. But welfare costs money. The high-grade medical services of the West, the model of which has been so widely adopted, are vastly expensive. Health, social insurance, universal education—these are the products of the richest countries in the world, and the adoption of these standards is crippling many a poor country—or would do if they were extended beyond a miniature scale. President Nyerere of Tanzania is both more idealist and more realist, putting the vision firmly above the material gain:

> The growth must come out of our roots, and not from the grafting on to those roots of something which is alien to them.... It is a commitment to a belief that there are more important things in life than the amassing of riches, and that if the pursuit of wealth clashes with things like human dignity and social equality, then the latter will have priority. ... There are certain things which we shall refuse to do or accept, whether as individuals or as a nation, even if the result of accepting them would give a surge forward in our economic development.[2]

These simple words express movingly the dilemma of the poorer countries. There is, first, some disillusion with the borrowing from developed countries which has filled the last decade—not merely that it leads to increasing dependence but because it does not always even work; some revulsion at the materialism and

---

[1] President Ayub Khan, 'Pakistan's Economic Progress', in *International Affairs* (Vol. 43, No. 1, January 1967).
[2] Arusha Declaration, 1966.

'ruthlessness' of Western standards; a desire to turn back to native energy and resources,[1] even at some sacrifice; and a concern for welfare—it must mean health and education and a spreading decency of living standards, perhaps at the expense of consumption of the multitudinous array of manufactured goods which characterizes the affluent world.

No doubt nothing so clear-cut will be achieved. Natural economic motives, the human appetite for power, the ordinary fact that most men cannot live at a high pitch of idealism for more than a moderate fraction of their time—all this will modify the vision. But it does represent a direction of thinking and it does evoke a response.

Yet this is in many ways reactive thinking—a reaction not against the real condition of peasant societies but against the blemishes and discontents which have marked development among the rich nations. One might ask if the response is not strongest among the somewhat Westernized young educated groups (and among foreign sympathizers) rather than among the peasantry themselves. The real crunch will come at the point of detailed action. Later in this book, as we look at the real social structure of the village, at local leadership and farm innovation, at the institutions for production or marketing or credit, at the balance between local democracy and central administration, at the realities of village power, these issues of social philosophy will constantly demand an answer. Is free enterprise to be excluded? Are Co-operatives not only admirable in theory but both admirable and effective in practice? Is the rich and enterprising farmer a development hero or a social menace? Are the philosophies genuinely related to the real situation? Are they compatible with the kinds of growth and change which are in fact open and necessary?

6

It may be helpful to summarize here very briefly what has been said of the situation which faced most developing countries at about the time of their Independence.

First, they start (almost by definition) with largely pre-industrial

---

[1] The Cambodian slogan for development was in 1963 'Le Camboge s'aide lui-même'.

economies, social structure, education, political experience, values. They are, as it were, out of step with time, if we compare them with developed countries, since they are surrounded by the 20th century, not the 16th. They can neither follow a growth-pattern into an 18th century of their own, nor borrow wholly modern institutions and technology without grave risk of distortion.

Economically, they find severe difficulty in industrializing, having neither a technical advantage, nor new countries to expand into; the markets for industrial products have to be found largely internally. Their population explosion, more violent than that of Europe, has come before the development of large-scale employment outside agriculture. The worst symptom of this difficulty is found in the under-employment of their human resources, made perhaps more anguishing by the large expenditures on mass education. They will be forced to find employment and livelihood for an even larger total labour force in the rural economy[1] by more intensive land use and by raising farmers' purchasing power to generate employment in the services, supplies, processing, distributive, construction and consumer goods industries attendant upon a modernized agriculture. The whole of Part II of this book is devoted to this agricultural problem. Chapter XI in Part III reverts to the wider problem of international trade and aid.

Socially and politically, they have been in part bedevilled by inheriting or adopting ideas and standards developed from the quite different experience, circumstances and needs of the world-dominating industrial civilization. It is not only that economic theories have been carelessly applied, or that 'developed' technology does not always suit their needs. Systems of education developed from past experience and current needs of very different societies have been introduced; standards of welfare from the richest countries in the world have been adopted. Above all, political ideas have been lifted which were generated as a reaction to the more brutal aspects of development in Europe and America but which are often not related to the actual situation of developing countries themselves.

There is increasing evidence that many developing countries are aware of these results of borrowing and of outside pressure, and

[1] Even if there is a slow drop in the *proportion* of all labour which is in the rural economy.

sense the mass of Hindu and Muslim society, living as peasantry within ancient socio-religious systems, was very far from it indeed.

In some ways the African situation is easier to change, nearer to a *tabula rasa* upon which new political and social systems can be written. In India, because the old ways were half-adapted to the new and able to continue through the modernizing context, change may be harder.

Again, Asia is in a significant sense more developed. Statistics may prove that Kenya has a higher per caput income than India; Zambia nearly treble; Ghana quadruple. The Indian average is weighed down by the vast mass of peasantry, as the average of Tropical Africa would be if it were treated as one country; Kenya, Zambia, Ghana are high spots. In some degree the potential of a nation can be measured by its high quality striking force, not by the sheer number of untrained foot soldiers. If we look at the education in Asia, at the range of manufactures (including heavy industry), the communications, the irrigation systems, the craft production, the merchanting, the law and administration, and the skill and quality of the farming—all this provides an energizing force of skill and resources and capital assets which will penetrate even India's peasant masses at a speed which is likely to outrun that of Africa. From the Khyber Pass to the southern tip of India, the ox-plough is in use to till the fields; in Tropical Africa it is mainly the man or woman with a hoe. The vast expanses of levelled and 'bunded' fields, with not a square foot wasted, testify to the care and experience of the Asian farmer, whether in India or Thailand or Java; only in the rarest patches of Tropical Africa can anything be seen which compares with this standard.

The very sophistication of Asian life and the antiquity of its culture; the existence of a large middle and lower-middle class, with vested interests in maintaining both an economic and a social status; the elaboration of economic and power relationships right down to the village makes India and most of South-East Asia harder to change. There are landlords and merchants, bankers and entrepreneurs all over the rural and market-town economy; compared to Tropical Africa the whole system is already more deeply commercialized, more strongly graded by class (and caste) and economic interest; and political organization is more solidly rooted in these economic and social interest-groups. Nyerere in Tanzania is speaking to a nation and economy still malleable, not yet set in either a political or social or economic mould. The Indian Prime Minister surveys a huge organism, pulsating with life within quite hard-set traditions, power structures, financial interests, partly sanctioned by ancient religious and cultural beliefs. To swing this system towards even a few broad policy goals is an immense task.

It seems likely therefore that in politics the ideological experiments in Africa will be far more clearcut, the extremes wider. It is still not too late for a small band of leaders to swing an African State of a few millions into a sharply-defined political pattern. There is a chance to experiment with many new institutions and to invent channels of action which may suit this strange phenomenon of a peasant world in the 20th century. Certainly in terms of agricultural experiment the field is clearer than in Asia. There may be traces of a caste system in Senegal; vested interests of the marabouts in Muslim West Africa; a strong touch of the entrepreneur-landlord-capitalist in Ghana's cocoa farmers; the beginnings of an industrial African middle class in the Copperbelt; a sophisticated commercial and credit system in West African trade; a combination of wealth, landownership, education and political power in Buganda which has a somewhat Indian ring. But in huge areas, in East and Central Africa particularly, the great mass of farmers are potentially malleable, and indeed both socially and economically mobile through the operation of Secondary and higher education. The fathers of highly-paid civil servants in Nairobi may be simple farmers; the homes of smart young girls reading Biology in the Sixth Form of an elite school may well be mud huts.

In Asia, change must be more complex. The extraordinary amalgam of interests which may come together behind the Democrats or Republicans in the U.S.A.—Southern landowners, Trade Unions, the Jewish vote, the Catholic vote, States' Rights men, Wall Street or the mid-West farmers—gives some hint of the political problem of a major Party in Federal India, juggling with the linguistic vote, the Hindu religious conservatives, Nehru socialists and secularists, caste, regionalism, the Muslim minority, big business, peasant farmers. Politics which must spread the net so wide can seldom enshrine a clearcut ideology. The problem at village level, which later chapters will show, is almost as confused. Yet against these very different backgrounds there remains the same common task, whether in Uganda or Mysore: to bring the simple farmer out of his ancient poverty into the modern world.

8

Finally, a word is needed on the method of approach to this huge subject. That it is complex, because social change is being studied in five or six dimensions simultaneously, is an unavoidable problem which the book must struggle to handle as best it may. A more serious difficulty is the immense variety of conditions which are found within 'peasant societies' in two continents. Yet in some degree the challenge of this very difficulty suggests some approaches and 'answers' which together form some of the fundamental propositions of the whole study.

It is by no means enough to point out a very few broad differences between two continents. Each contains within it societies in widely differing stages and types of development. There are highly traditional tribal societies in the very centre of India, in the hills of Burma, Thailand, Malaysia, Indonesia—many of them very similar to tribal groups in Africa. In both continents, there are areas of nomadic pastoralists, areas of dense agricultural settlement, areas of highly developed commerce and areas still barely touching the cash economy. Clearly, some method of grouping similar types or stages of development is needed as a basis for any coherent argument.

This is a familiar problem. Some years ago Rostow[1] produced a theory of five stages in economic growth. A little later Harbison and Myers,[2] in an endeavour to make sense of manpower policy, used a multiple factor index to divide countries into four groups or stages, for each of which manpower policy needed to be adjusted. On the purely agricultural side, Clifton Wharton[3] has synthesized three triple stage systems for classifying the state of agricultural production. Although all these 'stage' theories take a

---

[1] W. W. Rostow, *The Stages of Economic Growth* (Cambridge, Cambridge University Press, 1960).

[2] Frederick Harbison and Charles A. Myers, *Education, Manpower and Economic Growth* (New York, McGraw-Hill, 1964).

[3] Clifton R. Wharton, Jnr., *Research on Agricultural Development in Southeast Asia* (New York, Agricultural Development Council Inc., 1965). The three 'Stage' theories summarized are those of Perkins-Witt (1961), Johnston-Mellor (1961) and Hill-Mosher (1963).

fairly wide range of factors into consideration, each is really concentrated on covering a specific field—economic growth (the widest of them), manpower policy, or agricultural development. For example, Wharton lists ten factors which enter into the three stage agricultural analysis. The stages are: I Traditional, II Transitional, III Commercial,[1] and the ten elements considered are: 1. General attitudes and motivations; 2. Goals of Production; 3. Nature of decision-making process; 4. Technology, state of the arts; 5. Degree of commercialization of production; 6. Degree of commercialization of inputs; 7. Factor Proportions and Rate of Return; 8. Infrastructure institutions affecting agriculture; 9. Availability of unused agricultural resources; 10. Share of agricultural sector in total economy.

This kind of analysis can be extremely useful and stimulating, but it is clearly not broad enough for the purpose of this study. It is mainly economic or technically agricultural, save for the useful cover-all element of 'general attitudes and motivations'. But agricultural development, being the growth and change of a whole society, must include social factors, value factors, political factors, education, administration. Further, there is great danger in taking whole countries as the unit for analysis. For even in quite small countries all three 'stages' can be represented, with a hill tribe not thirty miles from a group of mixed cash-and-subsistence farmers and, twenty miles on, a group of highly sophisticated, capital-intensive, cash-conscious horticultural or dairy farmers serving a town or an export market.[2]

I have therefore used in this book three very broad and ill-defined 'stages' of development, which are essentially social and (in a broad sense) political, in that they reflect the changing attitude of farmers and villagers towards each other, towards their local leadership, and, above all, towards the greater, outside society which surrounds them, including both local and central government. This certainly has not the precision to be called a theory. But it has practical advantages, in that the stages can, I believe, be related to many dimensions, and have policy implications in each dimension—dimensions of economic action, of politics, of educational policy, of democratic forms, of administrative methods. It

[1] This is the Hill-Mosher terminology.
[2] Exactly these conditions can be found, for example, in a radius of fifty miles from Chiengmai in North Thailand.

emphasizes strongly the danger of 'national' policies in societies which are so unevenly developed as to require different policies for different zones and types of social evolution; and it emphasizes that growth is multidimensional.

Further, it has led me to emphasize timing and sequence, rather than alternatives; to avoid the questions 'Government *or* private enterprise?', 'Administration *or* elected local government?', 'Doctors *or* medical assistants?'—and to put in their place the sequences of development which lead from one policy to the next. And because these sequences are a matter of hard practical choices by farmers—dare he risk a new crop, dare he desert the money-lender for the Co-operative, dare he vote against the landlord or disregard a religious custom—the whole discussion is seen, not in global or national terms, but from very near the ground, and as far as possible in terms of the hard realities which surround the peasant and his family, and especially the social, political and economic realities.

I have said that the method is imprecise. This is not only because the task is so large, and my own knowledge inadequate, but also because not enough work has yet been done on some vital aspects of it. The problem is to make sense of a total change similar to that which took place in, say, English society between the Middle Ages and the present day, but carried through in the 20th century and therefore subject to very different environmental factors, and proceeding at a far higher speed. It is in understanding both the similarities and dissimilarities in the process of change, and the nature and limits of the accelerators that the task lies. But it can be approached at two different levels. The gross economic and other changes can be described from above, such as the growth of industry, urbanization, trade, skills, technology, institutions and so on. On the whole, there is no lack of argument and expertise here.

But change also has its impact, social and psychological, on the individual. The total transition at this level requires a different type of description. For modernization implies for the individual a transition from security, based on his plot of land, to the insecurity of employment or of production for a changing market; from the security and imprisonment of a poor local community to the risks and freedoms of a larger richer society; from reliance on superstitious observance to the burden of rationalism and religious freedom; from the security and arbitrariness of authority to the freedoms and possible disorder of self-government, that is, from imposed to self-imposed disciplines; from the simple patriotism of an ethnic group to the more complex loyalties of a nation. These aspects of change have been studied for individual groups, usually in an early stage of development, by social anthropologists; but their work has not been integrated with modern economic and political theory, partly because economics, sociology and politics have not, until very recently, been near enough to the fine detail of life in developing countries.

What is needed urgently is widespread and professional study, in which every branch of social science is involved, to analyse the real situation of peasant societies, and to propound and test solutions. In this there will not be time for idle academicism, to which the social sciences are peculiarly prone. It must be professional study in terms of needed and relevant action. It is remarkable in this age how little is accurately known and meaningfully arranged about this issue. Many development economists now confess that an adequate theory has not been worked out. Sociologists and agricultural economists are now carrying out, year by year, detailed studies of farm management and village organization which reveal (on far too small a scale as yet) facts and relationships which have been smothered under broad generalizations, or interpreted wrongly by the use of theories thoughtlessly transferred from experience of the developed world. The laws of social science for modern peasant development, taking into full account their real situations (the nature of their politics, the capacity of their administrations, the contribution of education, the economics and sociology of the farm and village), and above all the nature of the outer environment of the developed world, have not yet been fully studied. A new set is needed, and its formulation is delayed by every repetition of old, inapplicable theories.

The kind of analysis required, if a society is to pass through many stages quickly, is analogous to the 'Critical Path' method in project planning.[1] It is necessary to work out just which stages

[1] For example, for construction of a steel works, it is possible to work out which stage must be completed before the next can start, and what is the minimum time-period for it. By linking together these minimum and necessary time sequences, the minimum time—or critical path—for the whole project can be worked out. Types of work which are not involved in this critical path are planned to continue alongside and simultaneously with the critical series.

must be included—for some can be skipped;[1] which *must* be completed before another can start, and what is the minimum time-period for each. But while the final form of a steel works, and the method of its construction, are known in advance, this is not true of the growth of a society. There must be some fairly precise definition of the target of growth, including a realistic assessment of what must be sacrificed to keep within financial resources; an assessment of timing; an order of sequences; a decision on standards; an estimate of how much government must supply to the structure and how much the spontaneous energy of the community can contribute on its own.

Decisions of this type need, first, a far more detailed and accurate knowledge of the working of the economy at its roots in the farm and village store and carpenter's yard. It is here that the professional effort I have referred to must go on. Those who work in this field need a conscious and sustained effort to question the model from developed societies, the style both of its economic and social thinking, and to develop a style at once historical and new, to correspond with the two time-dimensions—the 16th century and the 20th—in which so many peasant societies live.

Let me end with an analogy, however dangerous, for the stimulation which perhaps it is worth. Over millions of years, animals—the human animal is one—have developed the physical organs and organization which is embodied in them today. The human embryo in the womb hints at these stages as it develops from a complex speck of proteins through a fishy stage, a furry stage, to the 9-month child ready to be delivered. These hints are given at an incredible speed—a few days to cover a stage of millions of years of evolution. No stage is completed—a baby has never been a finished fish; some perhaps are bypassed, and certainly those which led some human ancestor to a dead-end and extinction are not repeated. What we are asking of Nigeria or of India is a similar acceleration. Now that at least an intermediate 'end' is known, they must foreshorten the evolutionary stages by which that end was reached by others in the past. Some stages, which proved unprofitable, may be left out; but not all. It is not necessary to spend fifty years learning to develop Co-operatives and fifty more learning when to discard them: it may be necessary to

---

[1] An African, complimented on his well-cut suit, remarked: 'If I'm going to have a suit at all, I don't need to have a badly cut one first.'

spend ten. It is not necessary to teach doctors on the Equator the diseases peculiar to the cold temperate zones. It is not necessary to live through the century-long sequences of aristocracy, plutocracy, bureaucracy, democracy, dictatorship and its sequel, but it will certainly be necessary to use in controlled form the vital qualitative contribution which each of them made. It is necessary to pick up the hints, but not to pursue them.

Is there any possibility that such a path can be followed? That is what the rest of this book must attempt to answer. The experiment of writing in so many dimensions must be tentative; it is impossible to suggest either clear-cut theories or precise solutions. But if in the smallest way it is able to suggest certain methods of thought which will help towards a better approach to these problems, it will have been worth while. A recognition of the uniqueness of the situation of modern peasant societies; a search for the acceleration of change which modern knowledge and modern technical power should give; a recognition of the sequential nature of growth and change, as against the attempt to reach foreseen objectives in a single bound; a full acceptance of the wholeness of society as an inescapable measure of change—these will be the themes which recur.

CHAPTER II

BACKGROUND AND CHANGE IN TRADITIONAL ECONOMIES

The primary unit of rural development, whether in agricultural, pastoral, forest or fishing societies, is the smallest group which feels itself to be a viable whole for most social and economic[1] purposes of its daily life (all will have at least some outside contact). The most familiar unit is the 'village'. But, especially in pastoral societies, the primary group may be a clan or a series of kinship groups and adherents. Settlements are not always 'villages'—for example, in East Bengal, the village boundary is largely an administrative fiction, dividing a series of hamlets, each with its shade trees and tank, dotted endlessly among the open paddy fields. A tremendous variety of social conditions governs these different primary units, and is of great importance for particular studies. But for our purpose there are certain common pressures exerted upon the vast majority of them—their narrow margin of survival, and the relative weakness of their integration with an outside economy and a larger pattern of institutions. To avoid constant qualifications, 'village' is used to typify this situation, as perhaps the most widespread type of primary unit.

This chapter is concerned with the ways in which change can flow most easily through these primary units in both Asia and Africa. If it seems to be cataloguing mainly the difficulties, it is because in all societies there is some resistance to change, and the more abrupt it is, the higher the resistance. Yet in fact we are dealing with societies which are already changing very fast; a natural emphasis on the traditional background must not obscure the extent of modernizing influence which is already working: here and there it has already transformed the older pattern. This is obviously true as between countries, but it is also true within

---

[1] Both political and religious aspects often embrace a wider aspect—a village may be part of a tribe or ethnic group; religious obligation may stretch out to larger units.

varied areas of a single national unit. The equivalent of centuries of change, in the historical timescale, may lie between tribal primitives in the jungle and a rich modernizing peasantry an hour's drive away. Although, in our telescoping timetable, this differential may be reduced to decades, it cannot be neglected; to these different stages of development quite different approaches will be needed, even within a single district.

In the roughest way it may be useful to think of three main stages of modernization. The first is the traditional society in its fullest sense—groups within which traditional religion, social relations and methods of agriculture seem to stretch back virtually unchanged into history. Stage II represents societies which have already been drawn quite far into a modern economy but are yet strongly held in traditional ways and values: they may grow a cash crop and use fertilizer, but magic, social hierarchy, tribal customs, traditional land tenure, the values and instincts of the past still have a strong grip. Stage III will stand for the modern, commercializing farmers who increasingly have accepted a modern outlook and are finding ways of evading traditional restraints which no longer have binding force upon them.

This unevenness of culture is inevitable today, where grossly unlike civilizations are intermingling—it was not so true in earlier centuries in Europe where change was generated more slowly from within. Policy must take account of it. Land consolidation pressed upon a Stage I group will probably be violently rejected; in the transition from Stage II to Stage III it may be importunately demanded, as the economic opportunities which it offers are seen and the social inhibitions are weakened. Perceptive timing of such changes may save a government many bitter disappointments.

Unevenness exists, though in a different sense, even on the village scale. All descriptions of dominant, majority attitudes at some point of time tend to mask the existence of suppressed minority feelings. Yet some relaxation of social pressure, some offer of security outside the traditional rules may enable these hidden aspirations to appear. If the climate of social approval changes, or the force of disapproval weakens, the progressives can dare to show their heads. In Asia caste, purdah, the ban on cow-slaughter have had this masking influence. In the descriptions which follow, these reservations as to the range of stages and as to suppressed variants in attitude are constantly required. The range is, of course, continuous; 'stages' are artificial divisions which mark noticeable differences, the colours of a rainbow which merge at their margins.

Despite great variation in many particulars, traditional[1] peasant economies in large parts of Africa and Asia have much in common. Perhaps their outstanding characteristic is their emphasis on security. The first concern, for the group as a whole, is not prosperity but survival; it is naturally most marked in the more precarious economies, where the margin between survival and veritable famine is most narrow. Security for the individual is sought by spreading the risks over a whole family or kinship group in the first instance, and over the whole community for certain purposes where only total effort is adequate.

In the simplest situations, quite common in Africa, virtually the entire community has access to land. There may be community effort for certain purposes, particularly land clearance, house building or harvesting, and there will be sharing of both effort and supplies on a family basis: individuals, and even the nuclear family, could hardly exist successfully by isolated effort in these conditions.

But in more complex and differentiated societies the mechanisms for ensuring at least the barest minimum of food supply for survival are also evident. In many types of Indian village there will be a number of different means of access to food. Substantial landowners obviously have it; but there will be a variety of what may be called tenancy or crop-sharing arrangements which spread access to food far more widely. These range from farmers who have their own draught animals and implements and supply their own seed and fertilizer, paying to the landlord around 50% of the crop, to 'tenants' for whom the landlord supplies all these and takes a higher percentage, to men in a serf condition who work the owner's land for the barest minimum payment in kind and are in effect bound to him virtually for life. All of these are assured of at least a starvation ration provided that total crop failure does not strike both the whole local community and neighbouring communities

[1] I have used the words 'traditional economy' to mean the way of life, with some emphasis on economic factors, of rural settlements ('villages' for short) where at least the most important elements of customary life and organization still persist, despite even quite a long contact with colonial and post-colonial influences. This is probably a slightly more practical definition than 'subsistence economies' because neither pure subsistence nor pre-colonial economies exist.

within the range of supply. Some, in bad years, will have to borrow and incur obligations which may involve a step downwards in the scale from farmer to bond-labourer, but they will have at least this chance of survival.

Apart from all these who have access to land, there will be the craftsmen and those who give services—the carpenter or potter or washerman. And they will be bound to give these services to the farming community not against cash but against a share of the harvest and traditional payments, mostly in kind, often paid at feasts and festivals and, of course, at harvest. There will be also the Brahmin or Muslim priest, whose services are needed for many purposes and who are rewarded; and there will be household or village servants, who are also included in the security system. This is a simple division of labour, reinforced by the caste-system in Hindu society, which allocates fairly permanent roles in society, though variegated in certain ways—for example, the craftsman may also hold land. Cash circulates in the Indian villages, and the money-lending system acts as an additional security-insurance, since money is at least to be had—though possibly on terms so harsh that it involves enslavement for more than one generation. If a man's pair of oxen die, he can borrow to buy another pair, and will often do so, cost what it may.

Once again, the whole situation is simpler in most of Tropical Africa, where land—it may be very poor, uncleared 'bush'—is allocated to community members on customary tenure. It is only where land of any kind is strictly limited and densities are high— as in parts of West Africa and some areas round Lake Victoria— that a comparable complexity grows up.

It is the community which gives security; to retain good standing within the community is therefore of supreme importance. It means, in effect, that a man fulfils his customary obligations and inputs to community life, and will therefore be entitled to the reciprocal support of the community to him. The feast and presents for a daughter's wedding may cost a poor man a vast sum in relation to his annual earnings: it may—more often than not it does—entrap him in debt which may take years to pay off. It would seem to be a custom of extraordinary improvidence in a society living so near the margin that providence in every other way is imperative; but in fact it is a social insurance which means that others will ask him to their feasts and pay their dues to him:

he remains an honoured member of the community, and to be such is the best and only insurance which he has. It is sublimated to a sense of a man's 'honour' and as such is of key significance in his whole life. This will be true in much of Africa as in Asia.

The same emphasis on security will be found in the process of agriculture itself. It is notorious that the varieties of crops grown in much of peasant farming are low yielding; and that they are often sown in poor conditions. Yet a higher-yielding variety, even when grown on a demonstration farm, may be refused. The native variety is known; food habits are adapted to it; in all but catastrophic drought it will give some yield, however poor. It is resistant to most local diseases, whereas the new variety may collapse altogether in drought, be subject to new and unmanageable disease, yield only with assured fertilizer and water (the demonstration plot will, of course, have all that is needed). Moreover, a man must borrow to buy the new seed and the fertilizer it needs. Failure will mean not only hunger but also a cash debt. These are risks upon which livelihood may depend.

Further, initiative in new crops and new methods has many difficulties in a communal setting. If a man grows a new, early-ripening variety on his little strip, every bird in the village will feed on his grain; and how is he to get access for harvesting when other crops are not ready to cut and there are no pathways through the strips to carry the crop? A strip system will hold down farming practice to the pace of the slowest.

This 'conservatism' as it is so often called—it is in fact a cautious weighing of real risks—is exactly paralleled when questions of social rather than crop changes are in issue. The Indian Government tells the peasant that caste-discrimination is now against the law; or an African Party member encourages a tribesman to neglect his old-fashioned Chief or Elders and do things the modern way. But the risk may be too great. Caste exists, and will exist tomorrow, when the Government inspector has gone back to town; the Elders may be able to block a marriage or impose a heavy fine. Unless the modernizer can offer a cast-iron and a continuous security, the poor man will not leave the only shelter he has for fair words and promises: they have too often proved worthless. Here is an Indian writer, speaking of a peasant's calculations:

His close contact with the Patel[1] and other official dignitaries had given him an inkling of the genuine and unchallengeable power of the Patel and the Patwari.[2] He knew that short-circuiting them got one nowhere. He knew too that you might give petitions to the Ruler himself but ultimately they came back to the Patel for report and 'necessary action'! He was not angry at this: he accepted it. This was the order of nature and of the gods. After all, if you bypassed the goddess Maisamma you got smallpox.... These sahibs came and they went, but the Patel was here always. He could drive Baliga out of the village. No, he would play safe. If and when the Patel was made powerless, he too would take his case and get it settled; but until then he would wait: after all, he had waited so long....[3]

Although the system looks and is in many ways so rigid, there is constant movement within it. Families with few children to support, or who have inherited from a childless relative or made a lucky marriage, will go up. Others, through bad luck, disease of cattle, the depredations of wild boar or elephant, sickness, a costly lawsuit, will go down. There are limited but real elements of hope and advancement within the system—even more limited by caste in India, but still existing—which keep men calculating and striving, even though they accept failure as the most probable result. It is not a system of total resignation but one of conditional resignation while circumstances remain unchanged. Because each man knows that ill-luck can reduce him to pauperism, he is to that extent willing that there should be security even for the poor.

And even in a system so near the edge of survival, there is still room for the very poor, by the most thrifty use of all its traditional elements. This is both another sign of its precarious balance and another reason why it is hard to change. Cow dung is used for fuel—the slow heat is just right for making curds—and for plastering walls and floors; a little milk from a starveling cow—there cannot be oxen without cows—makes a vast difference to diet, or perhaps a little cash by sale of ghee: how will a tractor replace the dung, the plaster and the milk? Weeds grow between the lines of grain—and are allowed to grow and are cut from time to time (not uprooted) to feed the cattle. Undigested grain is

---

[1] Headman.
[2] Clerk of the Revenue Service.
[3] Zaher Ahmed, *Dusk and Dawn in Village India* (London, Pall Mall Press, 1965).

picked out from cattle-dung and eaten; rats, snakes, white ants, locusts—all may be sources of food. There is also, as there was in England, the reserve factor of the 'waste'—the jungle or the bush, or the odd piece of common land or the road verges where an animal may graze. There is a season for gathering wild honey—in Tanzania whole villages neglected to pick the cotton because the annual honey expedition had fallen due; there is a season for edible fungi—even in Sweden today this means an annual exodus to the woods; there may be a little hunting, or edible caterpillars, or white ants in the bush, and they are worth having.

It is not the bigger farmers who depend on such trifles. But a change of crop and system, enclosure, mechanization, clearance of the waste, almost any progressive action may be cutting away an element of livelihood from the poorest. Peasant society keeps this poorest section in being by a hair's breadth; change will throw it on to the economy in search of wages unless the poor too can be brought in a single stride into a more productive system. Backing the best farmers, with the changes which that will mean, may also mean ruining the weakest.

Conservatism has also behind it a deeply felt religious feeling. A crop which has sustained all the long line of ancestors, grown by careful, important rules, is felt to be in some ways God's provision for the group. It is for this reason that the staple crop, whatever it may be, is often the hardest to change; for it will be surrounded by the maximum of customary and religious rules. Rice in much of Asia is in a sense a sacred crop, the symbol of continued life for a whole community: the inheritance of rice lands, the time for sowing, the time for harvesting will often be guarded by custom and religious feeling. But any staple crop may attract this feeling. In the dry areas, where only the drought-resistant millets will grow, a high level of emotion and social control may centre on this one life-giving crop. In the Kumaon hills of North India a young man adopted the new method of transplanting paddy, without previous sacrifice to gain divine approval: a few weeks later he died of snake-bite. A man planted berseem to feed his cattle—a new crop: a little later his buffalo broke its leg. In both cases divine wrath was assumed to be the cause.[1]

It is with new and at first subsidiary crops that free experiment

---

[1] B. M. Pande, 'Paddy Cultivation Practices', in *Community Development Journal* (Vol. 3, No. 2, April 1968).

is much easier. Thus, in parts of Malaya rice land is inherited through the female line, and dealings in it are highly regulated by custom; but rubber land, a new crop, is a marketable commodity which men can acquire or sell outside the customary rules. Fruits, fibres, cottage industries which women handle, a new crop introduced by government advice may all be wholly or largely free of custom, and here the opening for innovation is greater. Dr. Swift's[1] study in Malaya has shown how the rubber economy brought the modernizing agencies of central government into contact with the village, gradually breaking down the self-enclosed customary system based on rice; Bailey[2] in Orissa shows the effect of the spreading trading frontier in raising the economic status of castes who benefited from it as against the paddy-growing castes; smallholder tea or fruit-growing for a market opened by a new road has opened up the farming economy in parts of East Africa so that it is suddenly receptive to innovation in ways far outside the actual husbandry. These open doors may be of great importance in accelerating change and specialization.

Although there is thrift in peasant life, in the sense of using and re-using every scrap of material which can be found, there is seldom (save where the village is well on the way to modernization) a monetary thrift in saving for future investment. For the poor this is not surprising. Any cash they may have, at least in India, is probably owed to a moneylender; in both continents it will in any case be needed by a relative[3]. Crops usually cannot be stored away from pests for any length of time. Social expenditure will also mop up cash—one of the few forms of monetary saving is for a marriage. And because the future is so uncertain, because an 'investment' in next year's crop may so easily be swallowed without trace of benefit by natural catastrophes, there is a tendency (especially in some parts of Africa) to have a feast when food is plentiful and to starve patiently when a crop fails. Thus almost every attempt at progressive innovation will find the smallest

[1] M. G. Swift, *Malay Peasant Society in Jelebu* (London School of Economics Monographs on Social Anthropology, No. 29, London, 1965).
[2] F. G. Bailey, *Caste and the Economic Frontier* (Manchester, Manchester University Press, 1957).
[3] As Sir Malcom Darling observed in the Punjab, it is the bigger farmers who are usually most heavily indebted. The smallest 'cannot afford to borrow'. *The Punjab Peasant in Prosperity and Debt* (London, Oxford University Press, 1925).

farmers without spare capital. If a new tool is needed, or a new cart, or seed, and fertilizer for a new crop, it may all have to be provided through private or public credit or by subsidy.

With the landlords and rich men it is different; but, in the traditional situation, the money they have will not normally go on productive investment: it will go on jewellery, as a store of money capital, or on marriage feasts and social display of various kinds, including a bigger house of permanent materials, employment of wage labour to save a man and his wife from working in the fields; on more wives (in Africa); on more cattle (in pastoral societies), although they may be economically disastrous in overgrazing. In India particularly money makes more money, or makes power; and the man with some cash resources may well use much of it for moneylending or for patronage which will buy him priority attention in many ways or votes if he needs them. Jewellery, moneylending, social display and patronage will use up much of the free cash-capital which might have gone back into farm improvement. Only where prospects are really improving will it go to a tractor or a tubewell or a large supply of expensive hybrid seed.

The other drain on capital, especially in Africa, will be the payment of quite high school fees. There is virtue in this, both that the need to earn them may increase productivity and that the State is relieved of social costs; but it is draining resources from potentially productive land to an education which, too often, is inappropriate to the real conditions of life which the pupil must meet. I have seen an African farmer's budget in Kenya, on a farm designed to yield £100 of cash income, in which £60 had already been paid for one year in schooling for eight out of twelve children.

And, indeed, saving may not be intended for productive investment in many peasant societies, which are in some senses less materialist than our own. We are apt to misuse words in speaking of 'investment' in status—it is a way of buying honour or perhaps the favour of God. Traditionally a Burmese man who comes by some wealth will give it to build a temple rather than invest it for making yet more wealth. It is probably true that it is the immigrant in a strange land who is the chief saver and investor—both in remitting cash to his home village (the Chinese in South-East Asia or the 'Asians' in East Africa), or in re-investment in his business;

and thus the immigrant peasant seems, in contrast both to the local society and perhaps to his brother at home, a more thrifty person. For status in a strange land, among folk who do not recognize its meaning, is not the same thing as the daily gratification of being honoured among kinsmen and lineages at home. Chinese remittances from Sabah and Sarawak to their home villages in China were partly to show their success where it would be appreciated and partly to ensure burial in the family grave.

Social life and leisure will also have a higher value in peasant societies than in those where it is a short interval in the concentrated drive for higher earnings. For a small-holding peasant, who seldom hopes to be much richer when he is 50 than when he is 30, what counts is the enjoyment of a life which runs roughly to a level. To have health, strong sons, honour among his peers, not too many years of drought or catastrophe, and to enjoy the recurring festivals and feasts; to work hard in the hard-working seasons, and to go visiting and to marriages, or hunting, or talking in the evenings in the off-season will be the philosophy of the good life. Catholic England of 1400 had enough Saint's Days to do the same. It is in part for this reason that the institution of double or even treble-cropping, the speeding of harvest by machines so that the labour of a new cultivation and a new crop can be squeezed in, may meet resistance. Generosity in social life—the man who helps his family, who will give a good feast and pay musicians, who will help his village and the temple of the village gods—counts high in honour; and honour, in Africa as well as in Asia, is the greatest single reward of peasant life. Here is a description of a 'big man' in a Yoruba town of Nigeria:

Some of the bigger traders in a town such as Ado—a commercial centre with a population of 17,000—probably have an annual income exceeding £2,000. It is these men who build the finest houses, own cars and entertain lavishly. Most of these men are from humble origins; those who are now in their fifties have probably not been to school; many are remembered as being poor men in their youth. They have built up their businesses by their own industry. Almost all are working in their own towns and thus have close kinship ties with their neighbours; many continue to live in their family compounds and their elegant two-storey houses rise above the thatch roofs of their relatives. Since they observe the tribal customs of generosity towards their kinsfolk and strangers, these men are highly regarded as assets belonging to the whole town. They have usurped many of the functions of the chiefs, for people will admire their sagacity and wealth and bring to them their disputes for settlement.[1]

If patience, endurance and the highest sense of family and social obligation are among the great virtues of traditional village life, suspicion, faction and fear are on the reverse of the coin. Village societies are levelling societies, in which attempts by equals to gain individual advantage are constantly suspected and bitterly resented. No doubt this springs from fear that the fundamental security of the village will slowly be lost if one individual after another can reach a platform of prosperity from which he might not need the help of the community and could therefore excuse himself from helping them.[2] There are terrible weapons against this offence—social ostracism, and witchcraft of various forms. To be a 'model farmer', by currying favour with the officials, men will say, or to set yourself up as superior in any way is to risk unleashing this social attack; and thereafter if a cow dies or a crop is trampled by wild animals, the thought of malice and even witchcraft will quickly be aroused. Those who have traditional status, by lineage or caste or long-established wealth, can escape this; and these are the men who will chiefly appear as 'traditional leaders', because they can be seen to lead without attracting this penalty. If, in the face of modernizing efforts from outside, they are resistant, perhaps because they have a vested interest in the status quo, there may be the greatest difficulty in finding the 'young, enterprising leadership' for which the agents of development are always searching.

Because the village is so enclosed and so intensely interdependent within the web of family, caste, service obligations, religious observance, ceremonies for puberty or marriage or death, its most deadly and yet common disease is faction. It cannot be ignored, as a townsman can ignore his enemies by avoiding them. Week by week the quarrel is freshly stimulated and deepened as

[1] P. C. Lloyd, 'The Integration of the New Economic Classes into Loca Government in Western Nigeria', in *African Affairs* (October 1953).

[2] For an exact example of this from Rhodesia, see Chapter III, p. 74. In Fiji, a man can contract out of certain obligations and rights by a payment to the community. He becomes an individual cash farmer. This is a very unusual arrangement though with some similarity to commutation of feudal obligations for cash.

some link or obligation is denied by it. Blood feud, its most dramatic form, is getting rarer, though is by no means dead; in 1967 the single hospital in Peshawar was still dealing constantly with gaping gunshot wounds (even in young children) caused by such feuds. But in the normal village a small slight or wrong can grow quickly to a divisive faction, with families or whole caste groups ranged in daily enmity. The arrangements which every village culture has for resolving these quarrels—through the headman's council, or the Chief in Africa, or the Caste councils or the Panchayat—do not always work, and faction can continue unabated over years—some villages are widely known for it over the surrounding countryside.

Faction is not only damaging; it presents the agency of change with constant difficulties. If one faction-leader is receptive to new crops and methods, his opponent, perhaps carrying with him a large section of the village, will oppose and sabotage it. Until the faction is healed the whole village can be frozen into immobility, each initiative checked and blasted by the hostilities which it attracts.

Faction and the fear of it, a levelling jealousy, the sharp eye, long memory and bitter tongue which arm the women in their doorstep quarrels—these are the penalties of a face-to-face society built on this miniature scale, a society deliberately and intricately designed to survive in isolation. In Asia particularly, from centuries of bureaucratic rule which Africa did not have, and in a strongly hierarchical society, the psychological enclosure of the village is at its height. The study in North India by the Wisers[1] brings out, perhaps to an exaggerated extent, the suspicion of outsiders, the fear of anyone who has official or financial power, inside or outside the village, the inability to trust fully anyone who is not a family or clan member.

By excluding any dangerous dependence on the outside world fear excludes also the scope, the tolerances, the freedoms and initiatives, the opportunities for creative change which that contact could bring. Brewster has well described this crippling situation, in terms of the need for larger contacts and groupings if economic progress is to take place: 'The endless chain of reciprocally useful service exchanges is possible only for people with

[1] W. H. and Charlotte Wiser, *Behind Mud Walls* (Berkeley, Los Angeles, 1963).

a large capacity for dealing as fairly with any other as with friends and relatives.'[1]

2

This has been, deliberately, a static picture—and therefore, partially false. All villages change, though sometimes slowly. But there is a crucial difference in the types of change. As many anthropologists have stressed, traditional cultures at any cross-section of time are composed of many borrowings from outside influence. A new type of crop, a new skill, defeat or victory in some local war, a host of accidents in the passage of centuries may have brought in these additions to the old culture. In the traditional stage, these new influences which become part of life—many are rejected as incompatible—become indeed a part of local culture and therefore within its enclosing walls. Traditional systems are not like a clockwork mechanism, where one broken part stops the clock: they are more like a number of elements suspended in a viscous medium which, under heat or pressure, can rearrange themselves. But change is of a quite different order where it breaks through the walls of the traditional cell and establishes a pathway, regularly and increasingly used, to some outside world beyond the village system and perhaps conflicting with it.

It is this second type of change which modernization must bring, linking the village through politics, through economic exchange, through education, through the impact of a modernizing administration to an alien world beyond its walls.

As Bailey has shown,[2] conservatism is not at first so easily defeated by these new intrusions. The village has, of course, known of the outside world—the tax man, the police, the administrator have visited and gone away, leaving usually a sting behind them. The Chief or headman—whoever the deputed leader may be—has been held responsible for these dealings and expected to temper or diminish their unwelcome impact. But when they multiply there may be others in the village—'brokers' as Bailey

[1] John M. Brewster, in Southworth and Johnston, op. cit. For a description of a village faction-quarrel, finally resolved at one of the necessary ceremonies at which village unity is re-emphasized, see Alan R. Beals, *Gopalpur—a South Indian Village* (Stanford University, Holt, Rinehart and Winston, 1966).
[2] F. G. Bailey, 'The Peasant View of the Bad Life', in *The Advancement of Science* (Vol. 23, No. 114, December 1966).

BACKGROUND AND CHANGE IN ECONOMIES 43

calls them—who may be needed to stand between the outer world and the inner, the real world of kinship and custom. They will have to be paid for their services, as an illiterate will pay a letter-writer; but they will be despised too, as men who have ceased to identify with the community or to share fully its view of the world. By this means the hard core of peasant conservatism is protected. In Africa too, in colonial times, when the (ignorant) White government bore down upon a tribal community, demanding change, it was not uncommon for a dummy chief to be put forward to receive the impact, while the real Chief remained hidden and uncommitted.

Nevertheless, the walls do get broken, and eventually in the only decisive way—that is, by willing initiative from within. The way in which this happens is of great importance.

We can distinguish, as it were in pure form, three major types of change—in practice they are often overlapping and confused. The first is an organic change in the whole local society, in response to some new factor in the environment which creates, on a fairly wide scale, new opportunities and new roles. Here, over a period of time, it is possible to watch a whole number of social and economic adaptations which may run right down through the social hierarchy. The second type is essentially produced by one, or a few, individuals, usually of some education and usually with some capital, who start a series of major farming and commercial innovations, not necessarily in response to any environmental change but basically from the availability of new techniques and from market conditions. The third type is change, probably initiated or at least stimulated, by government, by the creation of new, participatory institutions on a wider scale.

To illustrate the organic change arising from a new environmental factor, it may be best to use an illustration, admirably recorded by T. S. Epstein[1] in two villages of Mysore, the one directly covered some years before by an irrigation scheme, the other just beyond the fringe. The results are of extreme interest. For the irrigated village increased its emphasis on a now more profitable agriculture; the social structure and traditional rules were re-confirmed, the prestige of landholding further increased, the customary system enabled to work more fully. But in the

[1] T. S. Epstein, *Economic Development and Social Change in South India* (Manchester, Manchester University Press, 1962).

second village, as the prosperity of their lucky neighbours increased, the effect was opposite. There was money to be earned by establishing a mill for the new sugar production, by acting as carters for the irrigated crops, by finding jobs in the nearby and now more prosperous town. Men grew richer in new ways through off-farm employment, and the symbols of prestige began to be those things which could be displayed, not in the village but outside it in the town—a transistor or a bicycle or a new style of clothes. While the village on irrigated land retained a traditional pattern of house, new types, half-urban, began to appear in the other, and new types of men—not farmers but entrepreneurs—began to be prominent and to disturb the balance of village power.

The significance of this story for our present purpose is twofold. First, that there are reserves of initiative which major change can evoke even within the traditional economy, and that it has, without overt and sudden violence to its fundamental rules, a fair range of adaptability when outside pressure is applied. The second lesson is more complex. Investment which simply enriches the existing tradition, by making the same type of farming economy more profitable, may tend to reinforce the customary rules. If the result is increased density of population, this may be a merely temporary benefit in terms of individual incomes and may well freeze the social situation in ways which will make change more difficult later on.[1] Thus one might conclude that 'more of the same', without structural change, is not a long-term policy by itself. Nevertheless, the connection between the two villages illustrated must be stressed. Higher earnings in the first village, although 'more of the same', assisted town growth, and gave new opportunities to the second. The broader conclusion is that any increase in purchasing power, if it is not buried in hoarding or eaten up by population growth, will diversify employment and encourage initiatives in the region regarded as a whole.

The coming of water, of a road, a factory, electric power or the growth of a small town will start this process of social and even structural change. Even the barber in the first village sought permission from the village elders to give up his customary duties,

---

[1] See Takeshi Matooka, 'The Conditions Governing Agricultural Development', in *The Developing Economies* (Vol. 5, No. 3, September 1967). 'The stronger the communal institutions of the village, the more immobile labour there becomes.'

which were paid for in kind, and to start a barber's shop in town; and although he was forced to find a substitute in the customary role, he found a new living in cutting hair for cash in the town. Such change goes at its own pace, and a slow one; because it is adaptive and slow, it is the less likely to cause acute distress.

Change of the second type, initiated by enterprising individuals, is apt to have a different effect. In India or Pakistan or Thailand, or Ghana—it is much less common in East or Central Africa— there is a scattering of men of some education, social standing and capital resources, over wide areas of the rural economy. Such men are indeed part of the village system, primarily as landowners and landlords, often as merchants as well. But from their contacts with a wider world they stand also outside the village, beyond its haunting need for security and above its cruder superstitions; by their power they are, in large degree, relieved from the fetters of dependence on others. They will live in a bigger and better house than the villagers, sometimes indeed in a neighbouring town, they are sure at least to have connections with the town, perhaps a brother who is a lawyer or in business. They are big men in the village, though by no means rich as riches go in Asia. Sometimes they are youngish men—a son who got to College and came back to farm, with just a little capital, and a sizeable holding of good land. Some, though by no means all of these 'middle-class' men have realized that there is money to be made from the new varieties of crops, by sinking wells and irrigating, and by using the technical help of the extension service or the specialist from a local Agricultural University. Even in our short travels in India we met many such men—a doctor in Krishna District (Andhra) who had started a tobacco co-operative with a few friends; youngish men outside Hyderabad or Bangalore, one with a Biology degree, one with General Science, one recently returned from East Africa, growing perhaps five acres of grapes (with an investment of £700 per acre and a gross yield of £1,200 per acre per annum), growing high-yielding rice, running a Certified Seed factory, or running a modern poultry unit with imported stock. In the Pakistan Punjab and down towards Sind there were plenty of these bigger, enterprising men, owning from 40 acres to 500 or more, with a manager in the bigger units. The Government added to them by giving large blocks of land to senior officers as a retirement pension.

By no means all of the bigger men are enterprising in

agriculture itself: some prefer to keep their tenants farming in the old ways, to draw their rents and interest on their loans, and to concern themselves with other things—perhaps merchanting or a small business, or politics. Some still fill the picture of the old rapacious landlord. Some, in contrast, have assumed agricultural leadership, forming Co-operatives among the villagers, using their land for demonstrations, becoming Chairman of the sub-District Committee—and no doubt causing some jealousy and even faction. Where necessary, most have easily and openly evaded the Land Reform legislation which may limit ownership to thirty irrigated acres in India, by registering different parcels in the names of relatives. Some will have displaced their tenants and re-engaged them as farm labour, again with any necessary bow to the law. The amount of farm land which these commercial farmers work in India is now very great. If we take into account the smaller men, 'big' peasants owning from ten to fifty acres, one estimate[1] is that as much as 65% of cultivated land is in their hands. Undoubtedly, the medium-sized farmers in the Punjab and the old Canal Colonies, and the bigger landlords of West Pakistan, have played a dominant part in the steep rise of output, based on tube-well irrigation, which is again turning the North of the sub-continent into the wheat-granary and the cattle-breeding centre for the whole.

There is a distinction between the two groups. The big peasants, with twenty to forty acres, may not be much educated, though the younger ones will be increasingly so. They are indeed peasant farmers, part of the village in all respects, traditional in their ways, recognizably a part of the system described earlier in this chapter, though a prosperous and powerful part. The bigger, more educated men have in many ways transcended it. They are not outside the system, for in some ways they may dominate it, but they are not exclusively of it: they belong to an educated commercial world, though still enjoying, in the village, a traditional authority and respect.

This increasing emergence of middle and lower-middle class modern farmers greatly modifies, if it does not altogether invalidate in some areas, the concept of 'stages'—traditional, transitional, modern—which I suggested earlier in this chapter.

[1] Hla Myint, *The Economics of Developing Countries* (London, Hutchinson, 1964).

The stages can be found—many tribal areas in India and Pakistan and whole tracts of poorer country still exist where the dominant farming and social pattern is still virtually in Stage I; an even larger area is transitional in the main. But the coexistence of commercial farming, modernized in equipment and methods as far as capital will allow, alongside unaltered traditional systems, does indeed produce a kind of dual economy at the village level. This analogy is not too farfetched: for the commercial farmer in some areas is drawing away faster and faster from the surrounding peasantry, just as the industrial and urban modern sector has drawn away from the subsistence sector all through the developing countries.

This development raises issues of political purpose and philosophy, and of development strategy, which must wait for a later chapter for discussion. At this point it remains to stress that change of this type, in its pure form, represents a drawing-away of better equipped individuals from the peasant pattern and is profoundly different from the organic change described by Mrs. Epstein in Mysore. It is different also from the 'broad-front' advance, through extension and co-operatives, which is the third, and normally government-favoured, philosophy of rural change. In many cases it does little to affect the surrounding traditional pattern, except perhaps to downgrade small tenants to labourers and to make land more expensive and harder to lease in small acreages.

Little of this type of change is to be found on a wide scale in East and Central Africa—as yet. The larger landlords in Uganda, and a few young educated men, are moving fast in that direction. On some of the settlement schemes in Kenya, on ex-European land, larger farms have been deliberately made available to Africans, and some are bought by the politicians or civil servants, with a wife or manager to run them. In West Africa it is rather a different matter: the big cocoa farmers of Ghana are indeed entrepreneurs, though in a different context. But in general the pattern of farming in each tribal area tends to average out locally as a widespread and fairly similar norm, some areas highly traditional, some progressive, some already moving fast into pure commercial farming; and the areas of progress in the main have responded to intensive stimulation by government or by the public or private enterprise of the tobacco or tea or sugar corporations with 'outgrower' or similar systems. The 'stage' division is fairly easily applicable to large groups.

This situation in Africa is certainly unstable at present: the middle or big commercial farmer may emerge far more strikingly where governments allow or favour him; and we have not yet seen the full results of giving a mass of small farmers freehold, consolidated farms—the creation of an open market for land, in which the successful may add to their acres and the failures may lose all.

Finally, this whole phenomenon of the emergence of individuals with modernizing ideas inside the primary units emphasizes the danger of too wide generalization on 'peasant attitudes' or 'primary units'. The peasant world is becoming diversified even within the intimate structure of village life. In India there are at least three horizontal layers in much of village life: the poorest, including the smallest tenants, labourers, servants, Harijans[1] and the group of craftsmen paid in kind; the emerging number of bigger peasants who are modernizing farming methods and rapidly increasing cash earnings; and the big men, landlords, entrepreneurs, wealthy farmers, some modernizing, some enjoying traditional rents and interest. In parts of Africa a similar polarization can be found.[2] This unevenness, mentioned earlier, presents both opportunities and dangers to the policy-makers of economic progress.

3

'Change' has been used without much qualification, mainly with the suggestion of modernizing methods. But it is necessary to look for a moment at the structural effects which it may—or may not—have; by 'structural' is implied a change in the pattern of occupations (for example, more industrial, less farming employment) and in the pattern of social relationships (such as was starting in the 'dry' village of Mysore quoted above).

It might seem that the description of a rural community so enclosed and under such pressure reflected very high density

[1] Harijan is the modern name for 'untouchable'.
[2] See, for example, the classification of farmers into 'large farmers (2%), well-to-do peasants (19%), middling peasants (27%), poor peasants (32%), landless labourers (20%) in Buganda', in C. C. Wrigley, *African Farming in Buganda* (E.A.I.S.R. Conference, 1953). Southern Ghana or Southern Nigeria would provide even more striking examples.

smallholding areas, with a hierarchical society, typical of some parts of Asia, and that a quite different situation would prevail in much of Africa, where the density of settlement is so much lower and the social pattern different. If there is more uncleared land to be had for the asking in Africa, surely the pressure, both social and economic, is less? Indeed, it is widely believed in India that Africa has much easier problems because 'there is plenty of land'. There is, of course, some unreality in *average* density figures in Africa, which are apt to include such areas as vast uncultivated desert or semi-desert zones, swamps, tsetse country. The whole of the old French West Africa had an average of below ten people per square mile. In fact, the settled and cultivated areas are of course far more thickly populated. There are, indeed, many differences in detail if we look at an African area of shifting cultivation with a very low density of population to crude land area.[1] Nevertheless, there are essential similarities, the chief of which is that in both Asia and Africa, whatever the density, we are dealing with communities where the margin of survival is often extremely narrow, where the individual feels forced to stay within the protection of the community, and where risk-taking faces great penalties.

The contrast is apt to be emphasized through a confusion between population pressure on land and achieved density of population. As Allan[2] has shown in his detailed analysis of shifting cultivation systems in Africa, there can be great pressure of population on land even with very low densities in a purely spatial sense. Indeed, we are really faced with a Malthusian situation in which, if population tends to grow faster than the provision of opportunity outside agriculture, pressure on land will create the maximum density which land can support. Population growth in an area where a twenty to thirty year fallow is needed to restore fertility—a common situation in, say, North-East Zambia—will result in a shortening of the fallow period and eventually a lowering of yields to a point where population is checked by malnutrition and finally by starvation. In this way the green orchard bush of much of the Zambian plateau is no more able, without

---

[1] An African cannot just take up a large area of uncleared land. What he can manage is limited by family labour and hand tools, for both clearance and cultivation.

[2] W. Allan, *The African Husbandman* (Edinburgh, Oliver and Boyd, 1965).

major investment, to carry a dense population than is the Sind Desert—indeed, the potential of Sind soils, with investment in irrigation, is generally higher.

With the same limitation on outside opportunity, fertile soils—or fertility created by investment—will attract a maximum density of population, in this case very high, in a pattern of tiny and fragmented holdings, until the final saturation point is reached. This intensive pattern may evoke very high agricultural skills, at a given level of equipment and technology, and will be marked by complex arrangements of subdivision and tenancy, to use every foot of land, such as are not called for in a shifting cultivation society. Yet, because in both systems saturation has been reached, essentially similar pressures mould the social attitudes of both types of community.

There is a clear danger, on this Malthusian argument, that, unless other factors are brought in, massive investment in improving the potential productivity of poor land will simply shift the situation to that of Bengal—to dense instead of extensive poverty and saturation. The high density system is a terminal one. At present the tendency is in this direction: even in Bengal, irrigation of winter crops by investment in pumps and water control could increase densities even further, yet without decreasing poverty for more than a few years.

It was, indeed, such a policy which created the situation in parts of Java,[1] where densities are among the highest in the world. The estimated population of Java was about 6 million in 1800, 28 million in 1900, 40 million in 1930, probably around 60 million today, and on the margin of subsistence. The logical end of a land-focused security system, where land was limited, population increasing, and no fundamental technical or structural change taking place, was further fragmentation of land and a system of 'shared poverty', such as that which grew up between 1900 and 1930 during the Dutch 'ethical' policy. Peasant production became more intensive, more land was taken into the system of tiny holdings, everyone must share the available food. At harvest every

[1] Cf. W. F. Wertheim, *East-West Parallels* (The Hague, S. van Hove, 1964). Wertheim calls this 'static expansion', an expansion of intensive minuscule holdings without structural change. See also Clifford Geertz, who calls it 'a kind of supersaturated solution of land and people sustained at a level only slightly above subsistence'. *The Social Context of Economic Change* (Manchester, Manchester Institute of Technology, 1956).

woman in the village was by custom entitled to take her place in the rice field and cut her tiny section, severing each head of grain separately with a knife between the fingers—for a landlord to use a combine would have caused a revolution. Population-control could, of course, have alleviated this situation; but today the evidence is that it will be slow in action, and perhaps all the slower in so far as investment staves off the point where starvation intervenes.

It is clear, therefore, that in addition to any contribution which family-limitation may make, structural and technical changes must be achieved which reduce the pressure on land (though not necessarily the density of rural population) by reducing the proportion of cultivators to those in other occupations. In areas such as Java or Bengal, where the process has run virtually to its final limit, this must involve either urbanization or emigration; in areas not yet fully saturated it implies vigorous steps to prevent investment from simply increasing the number of cultivators to the same terminal point. The lesson of Mrs. Epstein's Mysore villages—one reinforcing the traditional structure, and doubtless on the road to fragmentation; the other responding by structural change—admirably illustrate these choices.

4

The purpose of this chapter is to lay down a provisional foundation for much of the argument of this book. It will, I hope, have drawn out some of the basic attitudes and a hint of the major social problems which are involved in the attempt to achieve accelerated change. From it, I think, emerges a sign—and perhaps a threat—of the growing divergence between the culture and attitudes of the great mass of the poor peasantry and the relatively small proportion of individuals, who are being drawn into the rapid development of a modern, commercial agriculture.

The first emphasis has been on the conservatism of peasant society, based on a land-focused security and a desperate need to retain mutual support within a tightly-knit and largely closed community. Progressive change must break through these enclosing walls, whether through the organic operation of external environmental change and opportunity, or through the emergence of more powerful modernizing individuals (in practice, by both,

primitive; nor is it greatly ailing. The immense festivals (for example, Puri's Jagarnath festival) are not historical tourist attractions but of the very life of India, which is lived daily and hourly as Hindu or Muslim life. It is probably strong enough, even today, to rise up and crush beneath its enormous weight a progress which leaves out too many tens of millions of India's people.

CHAPTER III

STATUS, POWER AND POLITICS AT VILLAGE LEVEL

Any attempt to influence village life from outside, to use the existing leadership or to evoke a new one, must rest on an understanding of its values—who has power, who has influence, what is the ranking system, who commands respect: there are shades of difference in these questions which are sometimes important.[1] There are, of course, many specific differences between local cultures, both within Africa and Asia, and especially differences between Hindu, Muslim, Buddhist and animist societies. There is also a wider difference between Asian and African culture which will be suggested later. Hindu society, because of the institution of caste, is in a sense a special case, although shadows of the caste system are strong in Muslim Pakistan and there are very partial analogues in other societies, both in Asia and in Africa. But because of the complexity of Hindu culture, the great importance of India, and the particular difficulties which it causes, it is perhaps the best starting point. It might be argued that, if Hindu society can change or be changed to admit of modernization, then any other society can be changed more easily.

Within modern Indian society, at the rural level, there are a number of different focal points. There is the power and influence of the big landlord; the moneylending system; the village headman; the lowest layers of the revenue system, represented in the village by the *patwari*, who might be called the clerk of crops and assessments, and higher up by the *Tehsildar*, covering a large section of a District. Also in the government sphere will be the lowest officer of the Agricultural and of the Community Development services—the *gramsewak* or Village Level Worker, supported by a government hierarchy of many Departments stretching

[1] For example, the landlord and moneylender have power; the schoolmaster may have influence; the formal ranking system may be religious; the successful farmer commands respect.

upwards through the 'Block'[1] and *Tehsil* to District, to State, and to the All-India services which spring from the Federal Government in Delhi. Table I gives a rough visual picture of the official hierarchy and the Panchayats. In the old Princely States and Feudatory Areas there will be at least the shadow of the Raja or Maharajah, sometimes still influential through wealth, or political standing, or inherited respect. In modern India there will also be the statutory elected Village Council ('Panchayat') with its President and members, and the President will usually also be a member of the next higher council (the 'Panchayat Samiti') which covers a 'Block'. There may also be a District Panchayat, often called *Zilla Parishad*. Finally, there will be the caste system and the related system of religious observance, custom and festivals which together make this a Hindu culture. Some of these points of power or influence need closer examination.

2

Because of its importance in almost every action of village life, the caste system may best be dealt with first. It is not necessary here to give either an academic definition or a full description of the working of caste. In crudest outline, a caste (*jati*) is a hereditary endogamous[2] group, with a ranking system in relation to other castes by which the lower can accept food from the higher—but not vice versa. Castes are almost mythologically grouped in four ranks (*Varnas*)—the Brahmins (priests), Kshatryas (warriors), Vaisyas (merchants, etc.) and Sudras (manual workers), with the out-castes—untouchables or Harijans—lying outside and below the whole caste system, although by law discrimination against them is forbidden. In fact and practice, only the Brahmins at one end and the Harijans at the other are unquestionably and throughout the Hindu world the top and the bottom. There is argument and variation in different regions of India as to which castes are really in the Kshatrya or Vaisya or Sudra groups, although locally the castes and sub-castes in these groups will be clearly ranked.

[1] A Block in India covers from 60,000 to 100,000 population—there are about 5,000 Blocks altogether within about 325 Districts. The Block is a development unit; the Tehsil or Taluka a revenue unit; the two do not always correspond: there may be 1 or 1½ or 2 Blocks to a Tehsil. In some Districts a Tehsil is also called a Sub-Division for administrative and judicial purposes.

[2] Endogamous within the caste: exogamous in the village—i.e. wives will come from the appropriate caste in a neighbouring village.

Table 1

Agricultural Administration in Indian States

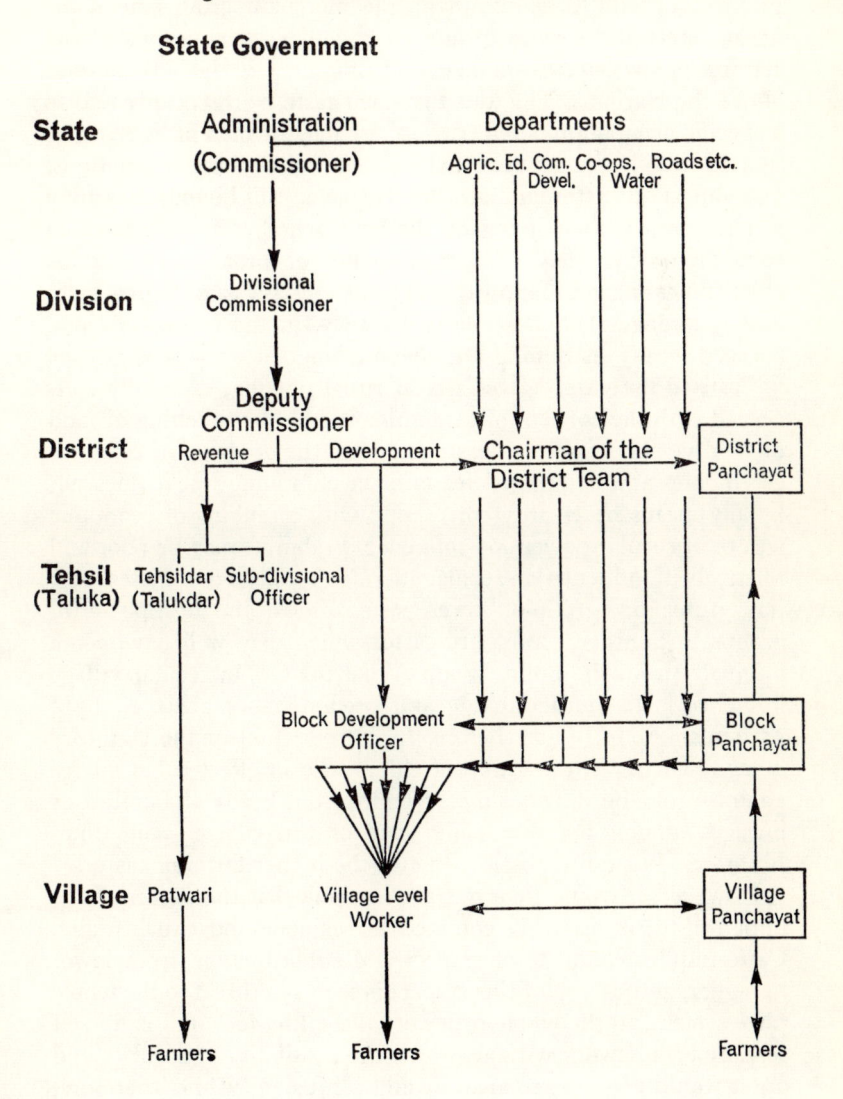

State	State Government → Administration (Commissioner)	Departments: Agric., Ed. Com. Devel., Co-ops. Water, Roads etc.		
Division	Divisional Commissioner			
District	Deputy Commissioner — Revenue / Development → Chairman of the District Team			District Panchayat
Tehsil (Taluka)	Tehsildar (Talukdar) / Sub-divisional Officer			
		Block Development Officer ↔		Block Panchayat
Village	Patwari	Village Level Worker ↔		Village Panchayat
	Farmers	Farmers		Farmers

Excluding Brahmins—of whom there are also different subvarieties—it is very broadly true that the landowning and farming groups will tend to be dominant, the merchant groups next, the 'clean' craft and service groups next, and certain groups giving services of low esteem—tanners or drummers—in the lowest group above the Harijans. The idea that each caste is irrevocably tied to a specific occupation is not true—there may be men of 'weaver' or 'potter' or 'oil-presser' castes who do not follow these occupations, and almost all castes, and also the Harijans, will be found earning at least part of their living by the land, whether as owners or in some form of tenancy. It is not possible for a man to change his caste (unless he goes far away and seeks to 'pass' as of higher caste among strangers), but whole castes may, in the course of time, succeed locally in gaining a higher ranking.

Caste in the village gives a clear ritual ranking, especially concerned with the concept of contamination by the touching of food or food vessels of a lower caste and with the ordering of religious ceremonies and communal feasts or celebrations. But it does not by any means necessarily correspond with a ranking of economic wealth or secular power and influence. Brahmins may be poor and relatively uninfluential in secular affairs in a village dominated by a powerful landed group of 'lower' caste: some of the most powerful groups in Southern India are castes which may well have come originally from the Sudra group. What matters in secular village influence is the local ranking and predominance achieved by a particular group. Thus, before the introduction of the statutory village Panchayat, the group of elders who in effect ruled village affairs would be drawn almost wholly from heads of families or lineages among the dominant caste of the village—sometimes Brahmins, but quite possibly one of the higher farming castes.

However, it would be a mistake to think that the power of the upper castes is narrowly confined to religious and ritual affairs. Caste implies elements of respect and subordination from lower to higher, and breach of this respect is seen as a threat to the whole caste system, to the whole order of village life, to Hinduism itself seen as a framework without which the possibility of security and order would give way to anarchy and confusion. While, therefore, the economic power of a lower caste member may earn him influence and even power in many secular affairs, this power can be exercised only on condition that it does not challenge caste on its own ground. Bailey[1] records in Orissa the occasion when a young man, returning at dusk from the forest, met an older man of lower caste on a narrow path between flooded paddy fields: a misunderstanding, a brief tussle, and the young man was in the muddy water. The village was immediately alarmed by drumbeat, the council summoned, the police warned of the imminence of a riot. Mrs. Epstein[2] records two cases in Mysore. In one, a man was notoriously committing adultery with the wife of a man of lower caste. One day the husband surprised him with her and struck him. There followed a tremendous factional battle, which left traces for years in the village; but in the outcome the husband was severely punished. In another village, a traditional dramatic performance, normally attended by the whole village, was to be given, as was customary, by Harijans. A local politician encouraged them to break with custom and allow one of the actors to sit on a chair during the performance, thus having his head higher than those of the caste Hindus squatting on the ground as audience: as a result, the performance was boycotted by the upper castes, and moreover all traditional services and payments were broken off between the two groups, to their great and mutual inconvenience. The politician failed to make good his promises of support from government officials in the neighbouring town, and the Harijans capitulated completely, with severe penalties.

What is impressive in these stories is the immediate and passionate reaction in defence of the caste order, overriding 'natural justice'—for young men should not jostle old men on a path, or commit adultery; and caste discrimination is officially illegal. But *salus populi suprema lex* is in effect invoked, because in the village the security of the people is felt to depend upon the traditional order.

Yet the order is changing and weakening in many ways—perhaps this increases the violence of its defenders?—and in ways which the caste leaders themselves recognize and tolerate in certain circumstances. In the bus to town it is impossible not to touch a Harijan and impracticable to insist on immediate ritual purification. In the cafés of a town it is illegal to refuse to admit lower castes and impracticable to demand that the cook should be of equal or higher caste—though there are restaurants with an all-Brahmin kitchen staff. In the factory men of different caste work

[1] *Caste and the Economic Frontier.* [2] Epstein, op. cit.

next to each other and will use the same canteen, though with the option of vegetarian food. By the roadside, out of sight of the village, men of different caste will rest and smoke together. Finally, in the sophisticated and educated world of towns and government offices, caste is far below the surface for much of the time and even cross-caste marriages take place, though not without pain and difficulty for the parent generation. In a word, modernization and urbanization are making great inroads into the caste order outside the daily life of the village. But the man who breaks a caste rule at midday in the town will probably observe and support it in the evening in the village; for one thing, village women, with fewer outside contacts, will usually be far more conservative than the men. Indeed, one reason for taking work outside the village, and for living away from home, will be to escape both the social and the economic restrictions; a man can make money in trades and occupations in the town which would be closed to him in his home village. One can see a parallel escape in Africa, where the younger educated African will seek to escape the demands of the extended family, the restrictions and the observances of lineage and age-group hierarchies, by finding work in a distant area where he is more free.

Thus there are opposite streams of influence affecting caste. Urban-industrial development and education weaken it; the need for security strengthens it. While in some parts of South India Brahmins themselves may be joining the development drive and modernizing,[1] other castes are changing to vegetarianism and other forms of 'Sanscritization'[2] in order to raise their status in a system which they must consider valid. It is development itself which will drive caste at least back into a purely ritual and historical backwater, not the head-on intellectual attack upon it.

3

Perhaps the greatest and most confusing impact on the traditional structure of the village has been the introduction of the new form of statutory Panchayat, the Village Committee, to be formed by

[1] Even riding on bicycles with leather seats!
[2] M. N. Srinivas suggested this phrase to describe the process of approximating lower caste customs to the Brahmin standard—e.g. a caste which previously ate meat will become vegetarian, etc. See *Caste in Modern India* (Bombay, Asia Publishing House, 1962).

free elections on universal suffrage, and to include two seats reserved for Harijans,[1] and one for women. In the first place, the idea of a public contest within the village is extremely disturbing, and for good reason: for contest will lead to faction, and faction is recognized as a curse to village life. The pattern which was so common in Africa, for all parties to state their view until the chief or elders felt that a sufficient consensus could be felt, and for the decision then to be made, which all must accept, rested on the same insistence that unanimity must somehow be restored. If it was not, the continuance of an 'opposition' would end in rival claimants to power, civil war, fragmentation and secession imperilling the entire group. In wide areas and particularly in the early days of Panchayati Raj, intense discussion and lobbying would take place before the election, and agreement was often reached on the Panchayat members, who became sole candidates for the seats, making election unnecessary. Another method, recorded by Mrs. Epstein, was to comply with the Ordinance (for perhaps the Government should not be flouted) by hastily drafting members—selected by the existing village leaders—on to the new Panchayat, which was in fact not used for any worth-while business. In the case quoted the result was a strange mixture of names, some chosen for their real influence and respected position, some drafted to serve in case it should prove that the work was unpleasant, unpaid, time-wasting and liable to attract hostility or quarrels, a penalty to be inflicted on chosen victims.

Another variant, quoted by Mayer[2] in Madya Pradesh, is to divide functions, allowing the new Panchayat to do certain things, mainly those related to the development policies of government, but to use or invent other committees for other, usually more traditional, purposes. In any case, the caste councils (also called Panchayats locally) used for settling caste disputes will continue alongside the Panchayat in areas where they were important. In Mayer's case, in addition to the Village Panchayat, of which an oil-presser was elected President in a village dominated by Rajput farmers, the Rajputs formed a 'Comprehensive Committee' which contained no less than forty-three members (one-sixth of all men

---

[1] In some cases, only where Harijans represent 5% or more of the local population.
[2] Adrian C. Mayer, *Caste and Kinship in Central India* (London, Routledge and Kegan Paul, 1960).

in the village); this Committee, formed partly from jealousy of the oil-presser's position, was concerned with resolving disputes and the general welfare of the village on a basis much nearer that of seeking unanimity by wide discussion. It was nearer to the old Headman's council in some States, which the Panchayat system is destroying, just as it is greatly weakening the position of the Headman himself as arbiter and organizer of village affairs.

Election is naturally an extreme disturbance of the hierarchy. If unanimity cannot be achieved, often owing to quarrels between rival lineages, the candidates will have to canvass votes, even from their Harijan clients as well as among the lowest castes. Retzlaff[1] quotes a case (Khalapur, Uttar Pradesh) where rivalry between Rajput lineages resulted, by accident, in a Harijan coming second in the election—and not far from first—because of the cancelling effect of rival Rajput candidates. Indeed, it is clear that the Panchayat elections are altering the power balance, on the whole in favour of leaders who prove good in two respects—first, in their success in relations with government officials, so that the village is favoured with development funds; secondly, in their tact in conciliating village faction.

In villages where two or three elections have already taken place there has often been a change of chairman on each occasion, with a tendency for members of less dominant castes to emerge, through dissatisfaction in the village with the old leadership. That this dissatisfaction dares to find expression is due to the nearer approach of modernizing government to the real concerns of village life, and to the emergence of economic power among castes other than the Brahmins and landowning groups—among merchants, entrepreneurs and modernizing farmers. In the old days the village was largely a closed, self-regulating system, with which government had contact mainly as a tax-collector. But modern government has agents and policies of development, concerned with land consolidation and Co-operatives and fertilizer and Community Development and Panchayati Raj, which brings it into the arena of village politics. It enables the dissatisfied and the progressive to have a court of appeal against the caste leadership, to bring in the law on the Harijans or the orders of the Agricultural Officer as an outside ally in the internal struggle in the village.

[1] R. H. Retzlaff, *Village Government in India* (Bombay, Asia Publishing House, 1962).

This is an unsettling situation. André Béteille[1] has put the underlying issue in exactly the terms of institutional transfer which I have used in this book:

Independent India has decided to adopt political institutions which emerged under specific historical conditions and in the context of a specific ideology. To what extent is this ideology consistent with the basic structure of Indian society?

The weakness of the Village Panchayat seems to arise from the imposition of a democratic formal structure on a social substratum which is segmental and hierarchical in nature. Although the formal structure of power is democratic, the value system within which it operates is inequalitarian.... The effectiveness of the *Cheri Panchayat* (a separate committee of Harijans in this, a Brahmin-dominated village) follows from its social homogeneity and the pervasive nature of the moral bonds which unite its members.

To what extent is the egalitarian and consensual ideology of Panchayati Raj compatible with the segmentary and hierarchical structure of the Indian village?

These analytical statements are helpful, but do not, of course, answer the question of what will emerge from the clash of incompatible systems. In fact it seems likely that the new democratic system, despite weakness in the first years of confusion, will emerge more strongly because it has heavy governmental support and is a more obvious channel for the modernizing effort which should bring great economic rewards to the village. But it is not likely to deal a real death blow to the hierarchical leadership, partly because caste and land ownership give that leadership other means of support; moreover, the old leaders can often capture the positions of leadership in the new system. S. C. Dube[2] puts this situation very well:

Yet the institution (Village Panchayats), democratic in conception and not foreign to village traditions,[3] was adopted by the people as an

[1] André Béteille, *Class, Caste and Power* (Berkeley, University of California Press, 1965).
[2] S. C. Dube, *India's Changing Villages* (London, Routledge and Kegan Paul, 1958).
[3] But I would prefer the view of Béteille, op. cit., that these *elected* bodies were essentially foreign, although Panchayats as village councils for traditional purposes existed before.

instrument to rework the power alignment in the community. Through it the dominant families and factions attempted to stabilize their position, rival families and factions wanted to assert their claims, and hitherto underprivileged groups sought to make a bid for gaining a position of power and wealth in the community.

Thus the traditional hierarchy, based essentially on caste and land-ownership and the Hindu joint family, is under attack from several different directions, and it may be useful to summarize these at this point. First, the new economic opportunities, including both the introduction of new non-hallowed crops and of new trading or industrial opportunities, tend to weaken the traditional dominants. Bailey points out that men in client or service relationships to the farming dominant castes tend to break away and find new opportunities, and this is confirmed by other investigators.[1] Second, the political innovation of statutory elected Panchayats gives a chance to suppressed elements to exert influence. Third, towns and the style of life of a modernizing and industrializing society make strict caste observance difficult and evasion of it easy; and to this may be added the effect of secular education and sophistication. Fourth, the more active interest and closer approach of government servants and policies to the detail of village life provides a court of appeal against traditional authority, particularly to Harijans but also to many of the lower and middle castes. As Bailey remarks, 'Caste is no longer a complete reflection of economic realities nor an adequate means of ordering political relations.'[2]

4

But these four tendencies to weaken the traditional hierarchy may be counterbalanced by a manœuvre which strengthens it. The fact that Panchayats at village and Block level are officially set up and supported, that development funds are channelled through them, and that new economic opportunities come their way can have the effect of strengthening the old magnates even further, by putting

---

[1] For example, the team of Japanese sociologists who made a study of the decay of the Jajmani system in two contrasting villages—see Tudasche Fukatake, Tsutomu Onchi and Chie Nakane, *The Socio-Economic Structure of the Indian Village* (Institute of Asian Economic Affairs, 1964).

[2] *Caste and the Economic Frontier.*

official funds and authority behind them, provided that they make sure of being elected.

The political implications must be pursued a little further. Partly because the Panchayats at all three levels (Village, Block and District) have close contact with the development activities of government, the position of the chairman, at Block level particularly, is one which can give him considerable power and opportunities for patronage. If he is felt to carry a solid block of votes, the Congress or other party leaders in the District will cultivate his support and be prepared to pay for it by securing administrative or other favours for his area, by which he in turn can gain supporters who will vote for him again. André Béteille[1] points out that: 'the power of village leaders such as the Panchayat President derives only partly from support within the village. To a considerable extent it is based on the strength of ties with influential people outside the village.' And again: 'Members (of the Block Panchayat) have at their disposal large sums of money, which can be used for giving contracts to the right kind of people, from whom favours can then be asked in return.' Thus the Panchayat chairman is in a position of strength which, with luck, may be self-perpetuating. Because he controls votes, influential politicians will woo him; because he controls public funds, contractors and others will woo him; and, since he can pass down these favours which he receives from above, he may well be able to continue to control votes. He must, however, be sure not to lose his own local election for the chairmanship in his village; and, since this is by universal suffrage, he can seldom rely on caste or economic dominance altogether. He must get the votes of low castes and Harijans; and this does give them an element of democratic power which before was lacking.

Caste will play an important part in this political game, especially in South India, where a few very large agglomerations of kindred castes may have an almost complete dominance—the Reddis and Kammas of Andhra Pradesh or the Okkalingas and Lingayats of Mysore. So great is this that no political candidate outside these castes is likely to win a State election, and even the Communists have been forced to choose candidates from these dominant castes despite their bourgeois and even 'exploiting'

[1] Béteille, op. cit.

background.[1] However, in Central and Northern India the effect is not so marked. Bailey's[2] study of politics in Orissa pointed out that, in the dispersed villages of a constituency, without these caste amalgamations, appeals to individual caste interests village by village was almost impossible and ineffective; they are also, technically, illegal under electoral law. Studies by Brass in Uttar Pradesh[3] confirm that, although caste appeal is important for certain blocks of votes, it is not decisive.

In many States of India the President of the Village Panchayat, and even more the Chairman at the level of the Block, is thus becoming a person of some political consequence. He is likely, but not certain, to be one of the existing village magnates, and must have some education. He is now the main channel from village to government on matters of great village concern—the building of a road, the siting of a school, the establishment of a Co-operative (of which he will quite probably be chairman). The Block Chairman will have a government jeep—a matter of great prestige and also a tactical advantage: important visitors will be brought to his house; he will be seen hobnobbing with members of the State Legislative Assembly; he will command a good block of votes in the village and have the means to reward his followers with valuable help—a licence from some local Department, an allocation of subsidized fertilizer, support in a dispute over land. In many cases he will not shrink from tougher methods, and his opponents might meet with a beating—village affairs in India have had a streak of physical violence for long enough, and even a powerful physique and a hot temper are significant factors; combined with a band of followers they are formidable.

Thus, if we look at the growing linkages between village or higher-level chairmen and the candidates and agents of the main All-India parties, it is clear that a type of politics which uses village concerns almost purely instrumentally is beginning to penetrate deeply into it. It is a politics not of policies but of power-getting, and each party agent will calculate what combination of appeals (however varied and irreconcilable) will bring home the vote—linguistic, caste, economic, factional, regional, personal. The

[1] See especially Srinivas, op. cit.
[2] F. G. Bailey, *Politics and Social Change* (London, Oxford University Press, 1963).
[3] Paul K. Brass, *Factional Politics in an Indian State* (Berkeley, University of California Press, 1965).

village is well aware of this cynicism and meets it with an equally hard-headed response. Bailey[1] described a meeting of the village in Bisipara (Orissa) to consider what to do about various political candidates: 'Let's get something out of this', they said. Elections, with a good pile of rupees on offer from rival candidates, do not come every year.

5

The third main institutional factor which is of increasing importance in Indian village life, alongside caste and the Panchayat system, is the influence of government officials. The supreme power is, of course, 'the administration', headed at District level by a Deputy Commissioner, a member of the elite Indian Administrative Service. Revenue collection, the magistracy and a general control of the whole District, including development, are concentrated at this point, and 'the administration' has very much more prestige than the special Departments, Agriculture, Education, Engineering and others, which are represented at District and Block level too. At Block level the Block Development Officer will have an increasing standing as a focus of development effort; but his rating is more as the king of these minor Departments. At the village level government naturally peters out, though there are two figures to be mentioned—the *patwari*, the last link in the Revenue service, who records the details upon which the land revenue is based; and the *gramsewak*, or Village Level Worker, usually covering about ten villages, who is the spearhead of the Community Development and Agricultural Extension services— a maid-of-all-work for government Departments but now concentrated mainly on agriculture.

The standing of these two, and the village attitude towards them, is very different. The *patwari* has behind him the shadow of authority—the all-powerful 'administration'. Because he holds the records of boundaries and crops; because he is answerable to the Revenue service at higher levels, he is a person of some significance: it will be useful to have him on your side. But he is not always a rich man, or a creditor in the moneylending system, or a magnate in any sense: indeed, he may well fall under the influence of the bigger landowners and become a slightly sinister

[1] *Politics and Social Change.*

influence in the village.[1] There are constant accusations of falsification or 'loss' of vital details in the Register when the big men of the village are facing a lawsuit or Land Reform legislation: 'We find it inconvenient to face the unholy alliance of the landlords and the Revenue agency, neither of whom is prepared to be dislodged from a vantage position without a stiff fight.'[2] Administration can only be as good as its local tools, and their performance is dependent on the energy and integrity of their immediate superiors.

The Village Level Worker, or *gramsewak*, in contrast, is a figure with virtually no power. He is paid about the same as the village schoolmaster,[3] and his job is to introduce to the village the torrent of development suggestions which pours in from Block level—hybrid seeds, fertilizer, a new plough, the Japanese system of rice-planting, and so on, not to mention Young Farmers' Club, village hygiene, school gardens, Family Planning, and much more. A good V.L.W. will be regarded with some affection in the village because he does endeavour to help the smaller farmers, because occasionally his suggestions are practicable and actually work, and because he represents the benevolent and nursemaiding aspects of government rather than its authority. But he is a poor man, and he is faced by the fact that the actual cultivators are often tenants, share-croppers, or clients in one form or another of the bigger landowners. Much that he recommends can only be done if the landlord consents. It is all too easy for him to accept food, or lodging, from the big man and to become almost wholly dependent upon him. Dube[4] prints a diary of one such V.L.W. in Uttar Pradesh, and it is interesting to see the rather cynical sympathy with which he was treated by the villagers. Obviously they say to each other, this new way of planting maize is quite ridiculous, but the government wants us to do it, and the V.L.W. has walked all this way to give a demonstration, so we had better co-operate.

This is, on the whole, a favourable picture. But it omits the fear and suspicion which form part of the attitude of villagers to

[1] In some areas he is certainly sinister, and relatively rich through his extortions. See particularly the description of the *patwaris* in Karimpur, near Agra, by the Wisers, op. cit.
[2] S. K. Dey, *Panchayati Raj* (Bombay, Asia Publishing House, 1961).
[3] About £7 to £10 per month, according to local rates and seniority.
[4] *India's Changing Villages*.

government (almost all over the world) and also an attitude of passivity and dependence—'if the government wants this, let them do it'—or, 'why doesn't the government provide it free?'. The increased flow of subsidies and free samples (such as seed, fertilizer, instruments on trial) is greatly increasing the second of these responses. Although a valiant effort has been made to elicit spontaneous action from the village through its own leadership, it is inevitable that most of the effort which flows through the V.L.W. is the old pattern of 'drives'—to establish Co-operatives, or make compost pits, or adopt Family Planning, or line-sowing of crops. The V.L.W. must somehow meet his target of 100 farmers converted, and within limits the villagers will help him to do so—and perhaps expect some help from him in return for their good nature.

There is thus a certain reservoir of goodwill towards Government, more particularly among the poor, because Government is sometimes their only ally against the oppression of circumstances or bosses. But it is mixed with cynicism, not least because so much of the benefit of government action seems to come to the bigger men—some say 70% of the effort of Extension Services never gets past the richer farmers.[1] Where government policies are subversive of the village order—land reform or the ban on caste discrimination—it will be deeply disturbing, arousing in the less privileged groups a mixture of hope followed by the fear of friction and faction in which it will be hard to choose sides.

6

This sense of a growing need to choose between an old world and a new is a source of mounting tension. The old 'Zamindari' system, by which the 'Zamindar' (landlord) was responsible to the Revenue service for a total assessment of tax over a wide area, recovering it from his tenants and share-croppers by his own means, has been abolished—it only applied in certain States in any case. But there are still landlords and tenants, and the relationship between them is ambiguous:

There are horrifying accounts of the brutality and avarice of some of the Zamindars. But, even if they were all bad, they performed a service for

[1] Dube, op. cit.

their tenants which the bureaucracy, from its very nature, found it difficult to perform. The essence of their role was that it was personal and direct and paternal. A good Zamindar could remit the rent, if he wished, without looking up the regulations. He lent money and grain. He was not surrounded by a host of clerks and intermediaries through whom the peasant had to find his way to reach a source of power. He was not an impersonal regular machine: he was a man and he was accessible. In other words, though the peasant undoubtedly paid him through the nose for the services he got, he did get something.[1]

Some would paint a picture of oppression and physical violence in even stronger colours; but the conclusion is true—the tenant knew his man, and if he did not cross him, he could manage. He might prefer this harsh but personal relationship to one with officials; for, before the V.L.W.s came, arrogance, ignorance and venality characterized petty officialdom; it was almost as hard to bear and often failed to give results. What is said of the Zamindar as landlord could also be said of the moneylender: he was a ravening wolf, but he lent, and the Co-operative, bound by its own regulations, will not always lend, or lend enough, or lend in time.

Thus, if we look round the world through the peasant's eyes, we see the old world, unjustly ordered but at least ordered by caste, by the landowner, by the moneylender; and the new world, promising more freedom but more risk. Perhaps the heart of his relationships will still be within the old world; but he will see the Panchayat, he will hear of new government rules in his favour, he will see younger men of progressive ideas breaking through to prosperity in new enterprises, he will be tempted to join factions and political groups, he will test out the V.L.W.'s new ideas, provided they do not get him into trouble. For somehow he must reach out and get a handhold on the new world without losing that foothold on the old which may save his life if things go wrong. He will divide his respect and allegiance essentially locally—perhaps to a landlord if he is reasonable and progressive, perhaps to the government if the local officer is honest and effective, perhaps simply to a lineage or to the patron who seems to know his way to success and is worth serving. If he is a small man, and a caste member, he will probably support the caste institution because it

[1] *Politics and Social Change.*

spells a certain stability, because it does not seem to stand between him and his main objectives, perhaps because it is so familiar and natural that it seems one of the laws of life. If he is a bigger peasant—a Punjabi with thirty acres and irrigation—he will trust no one but his own right arm, and he will listen eagerly to those who can offer him a better method or a better tool which is within his means: such men are the backbone of stability and progress, but they are the minority of India's peasantry.

It is to this world that the development effort of Indian policy has to be applied.

Much of what has been said of India, except as to caste, would apply to Pakistan and indeed to the majority[1] cultures of South-East Asia: Muslim in the Malay Peninsular and most of Indonesia, Buddhist on the mainland (Burma, Thailand, Cambodia, Vietnam). Although caste is no part of Islam, something very like it exists in Pakistan, and there is a strong Hindu influence persisting in Indonesia; the strength of social ranking can be seen every time greetings are exchanged in Buddhist Thailand or in Burma. But throughout the whole area the same essential choices face the mass of peasants—to cling to the static security and poverty of a religious and social framework in which he may occupy a low rung, or to risk committing himself to the modernizing bureaucracy, sometimes inefficient and corrupt, through which the offer of new opportunity is likely to be made.

7

The pattern in Tropical Africa is significantly different, though many of the same elements are to be found. It is, in essence, simpler, and particularly so in East and Central Africa where the indigenous economy was less commercialized and less sophisticated than the systems of the West coast. It is not that the cultural systems were less complex—a glance at the anthropological literature is enough to show this. Lineage systems, land tenure, religious and magical systems, structures of government are not only infinitely varied but individually complex. There are systems of subordination of whole ethnic groups—the Hutu to the Tutsi in Rwanda for example—which would find parallels in

[1] That is, excluding the hill-tribes and the immigrant Chinese cultures.

India; there are ranking systems; there are age-grade systems; there are elaborate kingdoms and there are segmentary societies where it is hard to find a system of central government or administration at all.

Yet the problem is simpler because (for manifold reasons) the cultures of the interior of Tropical Africa, at the time when Europeans took effective control (1890-1900), were mainly tribal, in small units, outside the main world stream of craft and commerce, with systems of administration suited to their needs and highly idiosyncratic but never geared to the ordered hierarchy of a major empire or reflecting the common values of a single and major religious system. This statement would have to be modified for certain areas—parts of the Arab and Indian-influenced East coast strip, Ethiopia, the Fulani empire, and some of the most developed forest zones on the West coast, such as Ashanti or the Yoruba Chiefdoms. But in most of the interior there was not a major culture strong enough, sufficiently developed in technical or economic growth or in widespread administrative tradition to absorb into itself the invading European system and subordinate its new elements to an older cultural pattern.

It is easier to see this fact by contrast with Asia. When an 18th-century Europe was gripping India and South-East Asia—quite a different Europe from that which gripped Africa a century later—it was entering civilizations long used to far-flung trade, craft production, the wide administration of central empires, the long-established order of a major religious and cultural system. The European entry was not altogether an abrupt break with the influences from the north-west which had entered India long before and the influences from China which had coloured South-East Asia for centuries. British administration took over from the Moghuls (the I.C.S. learned Persian); the Dutch found a Muslim and Hindu culture in Indonesia; Indo-China betrays its parentage by its name. Asia was able to absorb the new techniques and institutions more gradually, so that towns, commerce, industry, education were bathed in an unmistakable Asian culture. Above all, the rural culture persisted in almost undiminished strength and to this day is related to the 20th-century culture of New Delhi, Djakarta or Bangkok much as it was to the Moghul court, to the Sultans of Java or to the royal administration of the Thai Kingdom.

Because it has for long been partially adapted to a rich and modernizing sector, it is the more difficult to change. No one would suppose that the culture of the Baluba in the Congo, or of the Barotse Kingdom, or of the Nilo-Hamitic pastoralists can be carried right through to a modernized economy; yet the Hindu system, caste and all, is alive and politically powerful in 1969 alongside the steelworks and the great commercial cities of India, and must be allowed for in the development plans of Delhi. The recognition of a new start is far stronger in Africa, though there may well be selected elements of the old indigenous culture which could be valuably included in the new amalgam. There is little in African systems so deeply embedded, so resistant to innovation as the caste system or the landlord-peasant relationship of India or the *adat* of Muslim Indonesia.[1]

Indeed, the possibility of selective development of indigenous African institutions—the Council of Elders, the tribal societies, the tenure of land by usufruct rather than freehold—gives a fruitful field for experiment and adaptation which is not circumscribed by the deep entrenchment of particular cultural patterns covering half a continent and scores of millions.

This said, the African peasant economies have much in common with the Asian. The same emphasis on survival and security; the same unwillingness to stand out and incur the jealousy of a conservative community; the same fragmentation and land-pressure in fertile areas, with the same results; the same difficulty in making major technical changes when the whole cultural pattern, in employment and earnings and women's work and religious sanction, has been built around the older practices.

But the political and social pattern in the villages is, on the whole, a less complex one in its modern form. Neither landlords nor moneylenders normally play the central part which they do in Asia. Prestige and power are more simply split between the power centres of the old (often fast-dying) system and the influence of the educated, modernizing leadership. As between the traditional Chief or Council or lineage on the one hand and the government official or the teacher with Secondary education or the young politician with the backing of the nationalist party on the other, the African tribesman is increasingly sure that the future lies with the latter group. Education, simply and by itself, will yield to him far

[1] Nearly untranslatable, but roughly 'customary law and social rules'.

greater social mobility than to his Asian counterpart; religion impinges less on his economic life (though magic is still very powerful), and in many areas it is easy for him to move into an easygoing and socially unstructured Christianity if he wishes. Obviously, there are great local differences in many remote areas of Africa where the full range of tribal custom and belief has scarcely been breached.

To stress the absence of caste and the growing tendency to back the modernizing movement is not to suggest that African societies have no internal structure—far from it—or that there are not real choices to be met if a man is ambitious. All traditional African societies have a prestige system, some an elaborate scale of ranks, and some of these are hereditary, in that only members of royal or chiefly lineages can attain them. There are bound to be strains and jealousy between the old leadership and the new. Dr. Kingsley Garbett[1] has described in detail just such a struggle in Rhodesia. Within a highly traditional society a man, not in line for chiefly position, acquired an independent standing first by forming an independent Church. Then, when cattle were introduced to the District, he seized the opportunity and became a successful cash farmer, with a growing following. He began to break with kinship rules by selling, rather than giving, his surplus produce to his kin, because the fiction that they would return it next year when he might be in need had become unreal. He made an ally of the Government and, against violent opposition from the Chief, got first a road built, then a Council established, and finally a Mission school. By the end of this phase he was certainly the biggest man in the community. The traditional leaders had been defeated; the village split emotionally and even spatially. But it had been a bitter fight, and needed a tough and bold character to sustain it.

There are close parallels here with Bailey's description of the advance of the trading frontier in Orissa, the rise of middle castes who profit from it, the relative weakening of the older dominants, and the way in which external support from government is harnessed to out-manœuvre traditional opposition.

The distribution of influence and effective administrative leadership at the lowest level in Africa is thus still confused.

[1] G. Kingsley Garbett, 'Prestige, Status and Power in a Modern Valley Korekore Chiefdom, Rhodesia', in *Africa* (Vol. XXXVII, No. 3, July 1967).

There may well be at least four directions to which the peasant may look for guidance or authority. In some areas the traditional tribal leadership, Chief or Council, may still be powerful, and certainly the lineage and community pattern will not be one to flout unnecessarily. But there will be at least three other points of power—the 'local authority', the government official, and the national party.

To give but one example of the continuing force of tribal feeling, and tribal sanctions, it is only necessary to look at the disposal of land. One essential element in modernizing agricultural structure has been, in East Africa, the programme of consolidating scattered strips into a single holding with free and negotiable title. But there have been modern instances where a Kikuyu has attempted to sell his own plot of 'Kikuyu' land and has been forcibly prevented by his lineage or community. Tribal customary rules and family obligations still form a strong limitation on the individualism which modernizing systems are apt to assume.

In the last years of the colonial system rural Local Government in ex-British countries of Africa was a focus of democratic development and an arena where the ambitious African could gain prestige and influence. The main leaders of an African District Council, obviously modelled on the Rural District Council of the English system, were responsible for administering considerable local revenues and could command a fair amount of patronage and of respect; at a higher level County Councils and Municipal Councils had correspondingly greater responsibilities and prestige. The British administration was hoping to build up a tradition of elected Local Government which would gradually take over the full load of administrative duties and thus enable the system of Provincial and District Commissioners, like the State in Marxist theory, to fade away. We shall come back to this whole issue of the shape of local administration and its relation to the democratic process in Chapters VIII and IX.

But in terms of democratic representation and dynamic initiative the British model did not carry much meaning to the post-Independence African societies. In this sense it is not parallel to the Panchayat system in India but to the Indian District Boards and Town Boards. The *raison d'être* of modern Panchayats was essentially mobilization for development among the rural masses—not the necessary but prosaic task of seeing to road repairs, drainage, the regulation of markets and the employment of school janitors with which Boards or Councils in both India and Africa were so much concerned. A much nearer parallel to the Village Panchayat would be the Village Development Committees established in Tanzania. These were essentially inspired by the national political party (T.A.N.U.) and it was the young and enthusiastic party members who felt it their business to make them work. In some degree the older Local Government system was devalued, though in most countries it continued its administrative work. It had in any case been somewhat discredited, first in West Africa and then in East, through inefficiency and corruption, with a constant tendency to overspend and go bankrupt.

The African use of the single party to mobilize peasant effort in the villages is in contrast with the Asian system, though there are parallels in the two left-wing countries of South-East Asia—Burma and Indonesia—before the military takeovers there. Certainly in India, Congress and other All-India parties were concerned with vote-catching in the rural arena; but the party branches and agents were in no sense development agencies: they were concerned with the narrowly political task of seeking and keeping power. In its palmy days the local Congress Party would virtually monopolize patronage and advancement. But it never subjected the peasantry to the violent ideological discipline and exclusiveness which the C.P.P. in Ghana or K.A.N.U. in Kenya exerted in their prime.

There has thus been in Africa some tendency to polarize modern leadership in the rural areas, the older and more substantial citizens often going into the Local Government system while the younger and more enthusiastic would more naturally go for the party cadres. Since the local party is connected directly with the national party leadership—with the most powerful Cabinet Ministers—it has glamour and potential power. The District and County Councils, in contrast, have a defined jurisdiction and are—or should be—sobered by real administrative and financial responsibilities—they cannot so easily give the generalized inspirational leadership which is the party-member's natural style.

After the first enthusiasm of Independence in Africa, when the Nationalist party was supreme, there came, in various degrees and at different dates in different countries, a good deal of disillusion at the local level with the local manifestations of party activity. Young men with little standing in the sober country communities became Branch Secretaries and were arrogant to the older community leaders; harebrained schemes wasted public money; a certain amount of violence and political blackmail spread abroad—villages in bad odour with the party got no services; party Youth Leagues became obstreperous and even violent and were often known to be the henchmen of an ambitious politician. Villagers, whose political enthusiasm is fairly quickly overtaken by the practical needs of a hard life, began to find that the District Commissioner, trained for his job and controlling a technical staff, might be more efficient and less arbitrary than the party machine; and even where the District Commissioner's job was politicized and held by a party-member, his civil service staff still tried to maintain a level of ordinary and necessary administrative standards. A great deal of useful help could come from the District Veterinary or Agricultural or Education staff, quite outside the party system. In countries where a military takeover has taken place, this reversion to straight paternal administration, provided it is reasonably efficient, has almost certainly been welcome to people scandalized by political corruption and tired of young men's arrogance and inefficiency. Tanzania is perhaps the only country in Tropical Africa in which the full effort at mobilization through the party has been kept in vigour, yet with a real concern for effectiveness in the practical administration; and it is significant that, after first politicizing the Regional and Area Commissioner's posts, the President has started to send out civil servants from Dar-es-Salaam to fill some of them.

Thus for the African small farmer in a developing District the situation is easier and simpler than for his Indian brother. He is not caught in a caste system; he will usually not have either a landlord or a moneylender to fear or appease; if he is lucky, his scattered landholding will have been consolidated. The ruling traditional hierarchy of his tribal community will not in general have vested interests which tend to keep him in any form of subjection. He has three institutional relationships to watch: first, he will be unwise to get in bad odour with his lineage and tribal system, which is still powerful in customary and domestic ways. Second, he will be unwise to cross swords with the dominant party. It should not be difficult for him to avoid both these hazards, though he may grudge his party subscriptions. Third, he has a relationship with the officials of government. He may be harried by them if he is a bad farmer or will not repay credits. But if he is a progressive and is anxious to improve his income, he will probably find that the agencies of central government have their uses. Subsidies, advice and credit will come through them or through the Co-operative; and there is every chance that he will get as much help as any larger farmer, and as much say in Co-operative affairs. There is not, in fact, such a dominant social and economic class system sitting on top of him as there is in most of Asia. Moreover, he will find increasingly in his community men of some education and some prosperity who are themselves modernizers: the head master, a successful farmer, a member of the District Council who may give elements of leadership. The analysis of sponsors of privately financed Secondary schools in Kenya (Harambee Schools) shows a mixture of traditional leaders (for their prestige), young officials in the District (for their education and contact with government agencies), and prosperous farmers (for their money and competence); and this is not a bad mixture.

Thus in some ways at least the African peasant is a freer man than the Indian. It is easier for him to follow modernizing leadership without the risk of direct and even brutal punishment by the traditional regime. He has perhaps an easier access to government help and fewer intermediaries. But if he is more free in these ways, he usually lacks the free institution of the Panchayat to express his views and to learn the disciplines of self-rule. In this sense, India, with over a quarter of a million elected village Panchayats, has taken a heroic step.

PART II
AGRICULTURAL DEVELOPMENT

CHAPTER IV

GENERAL STRATEGIES

In the last twenty years an immense amount has been written about agricultural development in Asia, Africa and Latin America. Yet there is a fairly widespread feeling that this mass of description and analysis is not yet well organized; there is not a widely applicable theory of the stages of agricultural growth related to the general state of economy and society. 'Where is the knowledge we have lost in information?'[1]

Most of the reasons are obvious. The subject itself is huge and complicated; case-studies in one discipline, such as economics, may be weak in another, such as politics. Even the excellent collections of expert articles on special topics, although they do deal with comparative development, almost invariably contain different assumptions about both the objectives of development and about the state of society to which the principles apply.

The purpose of this chapter is to state some of these alternative objectives, and the strategies for achieving them, which may be relevant to different stages and conditions.

There is a second reason for introducing these larger issues at this stage. Although the last part of this book deals with social, economic and political aspects, they cannot be simply tacked on to a section on agricultural improvement which leaves them out of account. The farmer lives in society like a fish in water, and feels its influence as a whole. Separate analysis of the elements of this medium—oxygen, hydrogen and salts, or politics, economics and administration—does not tell us enough about its composite quality—its feel, buoyancy, density. Even technical change is affected by the medium as a whole, and these effects cannot be added in as an after-thought.

It is impossible to speak of what should be done without some definition of the object of doing it; and objectives imply values. Values are inescapably a part of the total environment. In the first

[1] T. S. Eliot, Choruses from *The Rock* (London, Faber and Faber).

place, there is a question of external approval—in the modern world even wars and tyrannies cannot be easily launched except in the name of peace and democracy. But, secondly, values can easily become concealed factors in arguments about efficiency. Democracy is a collection of values, some of which reflect absolute beliefs about human dignity; but some rest upon beliefs that equality, participation and widely spread responsibility are not only 'good' in themselves but in the long run the most *efficient* method of social progress. In our present context, if the mobilization of unused human energy and intelligence is indeed the main untapped resource for peasant societies, it is easy to suggest that some form of democratic policy is unavoidable. But a value-judgement may be influencing the argument on efficiency. At least it is better to have this risk out in the open. As far as possible, the argument for efficiency should stand on its own feet. But this detachment is very partial: in the last analysis, every paragraph implies a faith.

2

The strategy of rural development is, of course, a part of the total strategy by which the political aims of a society are to be achieved, within the limitations of its physical potential and its economic relationship with the outside world.

The most difficult balance to strike is that between social and political aims on the one hand and economic ambitions and opportunities on the other. One very relevant political aim may be the attainment of some social justice, both as between rich and poor and as between rural and urban living. Another, already mentioned, may be a wish to reject the competitive, individualist ideology upon which much of Western growth was based. Such aims may lead to rejection of plantation systems in favour of a small-holder society: the tension between these two is strikingly evident in the Federal Land Development Authority schemes of Malaysia, in which a mass of small-holders are given eventual ownership rights in a series of huge rubber and palm-oil plantations. Political ideals may lead to an insistence on Co-operative production and marketing to prevent the growth of inequalities under private enterprise. They may lead to a policy based on the slower process of education and improvement of small farmers as against the quicker results which some believe might come from supporting the larger, better educated, more enterprising owners as a leading sector.

But these political aims are far less free and sovereign than they may first appear to be. For the whole form of society is deeply conditioned by physical, economic and demographic factors. Greek City States probably appeared because the country is so brutally divided by mountain ranges. Plantations in Malaya probably appear because, in a belt running a few degrees from the Equator round the world, a tree-crop economy is usually the easiest to develop, and because modern technology (especially for palm-oil) has exacting technical requirements: the F.L.D.A. system, or the 'outgrower' system for tea in Kenya, are social and political modifications of an ecological theme. Current economic necessities in particular societies may lead to a concentration on export crops, on food grains, on clearance of unused lands, on mining (almost invariably a capitalist rather than a co-operative activity). Policy on land tenure or farm size depends upon population densities, population growth-rates, land potential. The prematurity of the population explosion in terms of employment-opportunity in unindustrialized economies will have profound political as well as economic implications. In social and cultural terms, the stage of modernization of attitudes, religious convictions, education, health, the position of women will all condition the types of approach to economic advance which can be used.

In this chapter the main concentration is on these ecological and economic conditioning factors, though with an eye open for political and other implications which are developed in Part III. In particular, ecology, population density, marketing and employment are considered here as some determinants of rural development policy.

Agricultural policies are often described in terms of various general objectives. We may leave aside a few of them—defence requirements, the civic value of a 'sturdy peasantry', or the aesthetic value of a well-tended rural landscape. Perhaps the three most important objectives stated have been the improvement of total food supplies and, qualitatively, of nutrition; a substantial rise in farmers' incomes, largely by the development of a full market economy; a growth and diversification of employment. Although closely related, strong emphasis on one or another of these objectives tends to result in somewhat different policies. Can they be better related to each other and to ecological and population factors?

We may look first at the food and nutrition objective. Policymakers have approached some peasant societies as essentially a collection of local subsistence economies, with a small market sector. They have been concerned to raise production and consumption of food in each separate area, so that the cultivator and his family will either produce more food for family consumption or, where natural conditions and a market allow, will sell a cash-crop for part of his consumption.

Early administrators in India and more recently in Africa have in general followed this rough line of thinking. It was natural for them to do so. The semi-autonomy of District Administration emphasized the local horizon, and in any case the market sector of the rural economy was so often largely in the hands of plantation companies, Export Boards, or businessmen that the administrator found himself chiefly concerned, for development purposes, with the traditional economy dominated by subsistence attitudes. In face of drought and famine it was not to market forces that he looked for help, but first to government for relief measures and next to proposals for improving local food output, for water control, or for planting famine-reserve crops, such as cassava in Africa. Rather less account was taken of catastrophes caused by market failure for the growers of cash-crops; perhaps the administrators shared the peasant's belief that a farmer's first duty is to feed himself. The peasants themselves certainly often held this point of view in the early stages of economic growth and have tended to keep most of their land under food-crops despite the loss of income incurred by planting them on land where much more profitable crops could have been grown. About 95% of land in west Bengal is devoted to crops consumed within the State, and about 70% of all cultivated land in India is devoted to food crops. De Wilde[1] observes that the Kenya Extension Service does not seem to have been aware of this economic loss. But in fact it is the Kenya African farmers who naturally cling to subsistence most strongly; some of them, when first settled on ex-European commercial farms, insisted upon this insurance, even

[1] John C. de Wilde *et al.*, *Experiences with Agricultural Development in Tropical Africa* (Baltimore, John Hopkins Press for I.B.R.D., 1967).

uprooting high-quality pyrethrum to grow maize on land unsuited to it.

Poor communications to the villages—a main reason for the slow spread of specialization and internal trade—also led the administrator to think in terms of local self-sufficiency, with a cash-crop as an 'extra' by which taxes, school fees, and a small supply of consumer goods could be covered. Even in the 1960s, most of the settlement schemes in East Africa were officially planned on the basis of subsistence *plus* a cash income of £x— no doubt this gave rise to de Wilde's comment.

A variant of this first policy formulation is still concerned with food supplies, but with a greater emphasis on quality and nutrition. Population growth, and the widespread debilitation of peasant societies by some degree of malnutrition,[1] naturally provoke this concern. It will lead, at least for a temporary phase, to concentration of policy on the production of staple food crops and, probably later, on the addition of proteins and other important deficient elements.[2] This formulation may, however, differ from the 'improved local subsistence' policy quite considerably, in allowing for market forces to distribute food, and therefore for more local specialization in production.

It is interesting that both these food-centred policies are played down by Mellor:

Currently neither a crisis of famine nor of radical secular change in the relationship between agricultural and non-agricultural prices faces low-income countries. The problem of agricultural development is thus not one of meeting food crises but one of contributing to growth in income, so that people may live better.[3]

This quotation illustrates the difference in assumptions very sharply. In the light of the food crisis in both India and Pakistan in 1966–7, it is odd that it should have been written.

[1] *Pace* Dr. Colin Clark, and without insisting on specific minima in calories or other factors, the evidence of malnutrition in Asia, Africa and Latin America is incontrovertible.
[2] See, for example, V. K. R. V. Rao, 'India's Long-Term Food Problem' (Matthai Memorial Lecture, Kerala University, 1966). Dr. Rao suggests that the food-grain problem will dominate the Indian Fourth Plan (then dated to 1971) and that the nutritional target would only become attainable by about 1975–6.
[3] Mellor, op. cit.

Mellor's concentration on maximizing farm incomes illustrates the second, essentially modern, emphasis on the market economy and higher farm incomes as the principal target. In the long run rapid economic growth and rural prosperity must indeed come by a movement to commercial agriculture aimed at the market and controlled by market forces. One man will plant rice and sell it, simply because this is the best cash return from his land, in his climate, at the going market price. Another will grow pyrethrum for exactly the same reason. A third will grow grapes. Specialization, internal and external trade, the most profitable use of each tract of land having regard to its potential, communications, demand and price, will be the guiding factors, and argument about agricultural development will use the criteria of the modern market economy.

The third objective and concern is of growing importance—the problem of providing productive employment, whether in the wage-sector or the self-employed farming sector, for the mounting populations. To those who have this concern chiefly in mind, agricultural development will be seen, first and foremost, as a means of creating additional livelihoods within the rural areas (where the mass of population will long continue to be found), with collateral benefits of creating purchasing power, harnessing idle energies, and developing natural resources.

Clearly there is good reason in each of these three approaches, for each is emphasizing a real aspect of need. But a chosen emphasis is always liable to undervalue the arguments which arise from a different starting point, and each of these three strategies is apt to find a different outcome in terms of action. To treat the problem as one of improving local subsistence may result in neglecting the long-term need for specialization and a market economy; for to stress famine is likely to encourage the use of high-grade land for low-value food-grains, and to stress nutrition may result in a quite uneconomic type of local diversification. To emphasize the market mechanism tends to play down the risks both of famine and of unemployment. To stress employment risks favouring inefficient as well as efficient labour-intensive projects, and will possibly delay structural changes in farm size and in the use of machinery.

We can perhaps get a little nearer to finding the balance or sequence of strategy by looking first at the most extreme case—

famine. Any humane government must regard recurrent famine as a more urgent challenge than a low standard of living or unemployment. It is legitimate to regard a rare threat of famine —once in fifteen or twenty years—as a temporary emergency, to be met by emergency action. But there are large areas in India where the threat is not rare but regularly recurrent: the monsoon is known to fail quite seriously[1] and regularly in most States about once in five years; in Gujarat, Madras, Rajasthan, Kashmir and Rayalaseema approximately once in every three years. These are areas in which a high proportion of population have no alternative means of livelihood if the land fails them. More severe drought (50% deficiency) means that large numbers will be on public relief, and some will be dying. The scale of this problem is important. A small area—say 20,000 population—which is famine-prone can probably be dealt with by local investment, or at worst by moving population. But the State of Bihar[2] alone has a population of over 70,000,000 mainly dependent on agriculture.

It is clearly intolerable that even a tenth of this huge mass of people should be thrown into debt or public relief every four or five years. Reliance on market arrangements, by which areas of secure rainfall or irrigation should produce surpluses to feed the famine-risk States, is inadequate by itself. It is not only that it is hard to arrange—for in four years out of five Bihar will feed itself and the 'surplus' States will have to find other markets.[3] The real difficulty is that the small farmers of Bihar have no other means of earning and no savings, and therefore cannot buy the surplus from other areas in drought years.

Variations in supply on such a scale are inevitably hard to manage. A vital first step is to damp down the sheer range of the oscillation, and there are various ways of doing this. The first is a far greater and more urgent investment in irrigation and water

[1] Deficiency of 25% or more of 'normal' rainfall. See S. R. Sen, 'Growth and Instability in Indian Agriculture', in *Indian Society of Agricultural Statistics* (Waltair, January 1967).

[2] Bihar has, statistically, a 25% or higher deficiency once in five years. In 1966 the failure was over 50%.

[3] Sen, op. cit., points out that it is not the areas of secure irrigation or rainfall which produce instability, nor the areas of extremely and regularly variable and insufficient rainfall. It is the area 'where both production and instability are high which is the main culprit for the large fluctuations that occur in the national production of food-grains'.

conservation, so that a larger area is secure. The second is to develop alternative occupations not dependent on rainfall: both these measures will need some years to take effect. The third is to increase productivity in good years so as to permit storage and a satisfactory savings scheme for the farmers who contribute the reserve to stock. Finally, for the slowly-shrinking proportion of farmers who remain wholly dependent on the monsoon, large-scale emergency employment on useful public works—likely to be roads and irrigation—would both enable at least some farmers to buy food from wages and also provide a useful capital improvement. The point of this argument is to demonstrate that it is not enough to plan for a total, national output of food adequate to feed the total population, relying on a market economy to distribute it from surplus to deficit areas. There are millions of people in Asia and Africa, both farmers and landless labourers, who are not in a market economy, or only in it provided that rain falls; they are not at present able to purchase food for cash in drought years even if it is available. In this sense the battle against recurrent famine hangs upon creating locally secure subsistence or secure employment or insurance; the market system is not a full answer, and charitable relief on this scale every four or five years is not an acceptable policy.

Considerably different arguments relate to areas where populations are living near the margin of subsistence, and probably on inadequate diet, but are seldom faced by total catastrophe. These may be areas of secure rainfall but poor soil (such as much of the Zambian plateau), areas remote from markets and communications, areas where agricultural methods are poor and farming capital non-existent. There are such zones all over Asia and Africa. Here again it may be decades before a market economy can take over; the urgent need is an upgrading of the subsistence economy such as that which colonial administrators were anxious to achieve. Ultimately, no doubt, these areas will either be found to have an undisclosed potential or will gradually lose population to points of growth and urbanization elsewhere. Meanwhile, a purely market-oriented policy may not help them.

It is in the areas of high and secure potential that the development of a vigorous market economy is likely to be the guiding strategy. Such areas are likely to be already densely populated. They are naturally liable to Malthusian overcrowding and fragmentation of holdings, unless a cash economy, a wider range of employment and a growth of towns are developed quite quickly. These high-potential areas can be divided into two groups: one in which potential has long been developed and holdings are already very small indeed; the other where new potential—such as new irrigation—has only come very recently.

In the first case, change will be exceedingly difficult. The first step is likely to be even further intensification of agriculture by double- or treble-cropping and higher investments; this is happening in Bengal and may happen in, say, the Central Province of Kenya. But, as we have seen, this will only put off the evil hour for a short time, unless intensification is accompanied urgently by structural change, urbanization, and family limitation. Fortunately, when plots are very small (two acres or below), less family labour is needed and fewer family mouths can be fed; and this gives some support to the family-planning arguments. There is also likely to be an intense demand for education, so that children for whom no land is available can find non-farm jobs; and if education requires fees, this will also point to family limitation and to an eager search for marketable cash-crops.

In the second type of high-potential area—that which has only recently been developed—the sequences will differ with circumstances. Where new potential, such as irrigation or new crops or markets, comes to an already settled area, earnings will shoot up and land prices will rise even faster. It will be difficult for outsiders or poor men to get any land at all, both because of its price and because more capital inputs will be needed to farm it successfully.[1] This will stem the natural inflow of farmers from less favoured areas; in parts of Mysore, for example, population densities on dry land are sometimes higher than on the high-priced, high-yield irrigated land. In such an area there may develop a considerable patch of first-class commercial farming on reasonable acreages; and provided that the purchasing power generated is spent on *local* services (contracting, construction, processing, consumer goods and urbanization), some inflow of labour from outside will find non-farm employment. If the money is syphoned away by absentee owners or companies to distant cities, this effect will be largely lost. As middle-class farming families develop, with middle-

[1] Such an area is the Central Province of Kenya, or Mandya District (Mysore) or some parts of the Chao Phya basin near Bangkok.

class consumption ambitions, family limitation is again hopeful.[1]

In the special case of major new settlement schemes on previously unoccupied land—the Sudan Gezira or the Canal Colonies of the Punjab and Sind—holdings are often initially fairly large, and big families may be an economic asset at first. Whether a true market economy begins to develop quickly depends partly on tradition and partly on policy. In the Punjab provision was made for local towns in the original plan, and some larger land holdings were offered (prematurely, as it turned out) to create a class of yeoman farmers. Differentiation was intended, the settlers had a tradition of towns and commerce, and a fairly varied economy developed. In the Sudan, however, there was a uniform plot size and a long persistence of detailed and almost puritanical control of social and economic variegation (technical control was and is essential). This, combined with the dominance of Khartoum,[2] has probably inhibited local commercial and economic enterprise. The endless miles of forty-acre cotton farms bespeak a society temporarily (though quite happily) frozen in its tracks, though rather greater diversification is now beginning.

The lesson of these two settlement schemes would seem to be that, from the start, new settlements should be aimed at a market economy, using to the utmost the rare opportunity to select optimum size in consolidated, freehold plots; to design roads and services with future differentiation in mind, and to have in the plan the siting of processing or other industries. Unfortunately, in a vast number of small schemes these lessons have not been learned. A carry-over of the 'improved subsistence' philosophy, anxiety to relieve population pressure by maximum density settlement, narrowly agricultural rather than social thinking, have resulted in creating rather isolated and 100% farming settlements, with a strictly regulated crop rotation, in small, uniform plots, with a bare hall as a 'Community Centre', a Co-operative store full of boringly utilitarian stock, and a target income of less than £100 per family per year. Many of the settlements in Tanzania in the early 1960s fell into this trap. In fact, the advantages have

[1] It is interesting that social surveys undertaken by the Gandhigram Centre (Madras State) showed that family limitation was accepted first in the wealthiest and in the poorest families—the one from ambition, the other from the fear of starvation. This confirms the analysis above.
[2] When the proposed tarmac road from Khartoum is complete, this dominance may grow still stronger.

been wasted in creating another patch of semi-subsistence economy without the familiarity, tradition and social cohesion, the comforting familiarity of the shady tree or the old temple, which make such a life more tolerable and human in unreformed old villages. Above all, it has failed to make a new breakthrough into a fully commercial farming system.

Thus the example of these three major types of area—one where good production alternates with serious famine, one of regular but very poor subsistence, and one of high potential but in danger of overcrowding, suggests how the strategic emphasis must differ in different circumstances. Certainly the final aim is the full market economy, with the subsistence element reduced to the small quantity of fresh milk or vegetables which the modern commercial farmer may keep back for family consumption. Only this market economy, with a high degree of specialization and heavy investment, would really bring agriculture to the level of wealth it has attained in developed countries. But this is not to say much more than that the general's strategy is to win the war: there are battles to be fought on the way, and they require more precise, varied and flexible planning.

These arguments reinforce an emphasis on local ecology, both physical and human; on stages and on timing, in much the same way as in the old argument between agriculture and industry as priority targets. In each case, the full market economy and a high degree of industrialization are the final objectives. But just as a traveller in a strange country, who knows that his destination is ahead and to the left, will be worried if the road bends to the right and inclined to desert it for a tempting side-lane, so the road to the market economy and industrialization will sometimes first bend away towards improved subsistence and rural development. It is vital for the policy-maker to realize what stage of his journey he has reached.

3

The 'market system' has been used so far in general terms. But the nature of this system needs a closer look. It must be clear from the foregoing paragraphs that the degree to which market forces have penetrated any area, and the scale upon which they operate will be crucial factors in almost every question of agricultural development. In areas of poor subsistence—and usually of poor education and modern contacts—there is a long way to go before forces and private ambition and enterprise can produce major market results. It may well be necessary to introduce very limited cash-cropping within a subsistence-oriented system in order to take the first step ahead; and in these cases the market itself may have to be organized from outside by a company or officially, because (by definition) it has not grown organically in the local farming community. In contrast, in the high-potential area which is already intensively farmed, specialization in a market sense is likely to be urgently needed, and on the fullest possible scale, if the Malthusian trap is to be avoided. Between these two extremes lie many intermediate stages, each with its own possibility of advance.

The differences in degree between a narrow, local market, such as was created in African tribal systems by sale or barter of small surpluses or specialities, a nation-wide market, and the world market, need some emphasis. In special commodities world trade makes an impact even on primitive village economies. But the sale of spices, or even of the large volumes of cotton or rubber or palm-oil or coffee, all of which may come from small village plots, does not of itself bring the economy of a peasant area into an organic market system. The producers of cotton or coffee remain subsistence producers as well, living in a traditional society which may be 80% agricultural, in which the variety of occupations, skills, services and market exchange may be minimal.[1] They may sell almost nothing to each other or to the neighbouring district fifteen miles away. In East Africa this is certainly the case. In West Africa a market in terms of sales of consumer goods at village level is more developed, and some growers of cash-crops actually buy most of their food—almost 70% of it among some cocoa-farming groups.[2] Even India, with all its commerce and industry, is far from being so specialized that food production can be concentrated in the best-suited areas and among the most efficient growers.

In fact, markets are quite exceptionally patchy and uneven in

[1] They are, in this respect, specialized parts of some distant metropolitan economy in the developed world. Hans Singer remarks: 'Could it be that the productive facilities for export from under-developed countries never became part of their internal economic structure except in a purely geographical sense?' (In *International Development: Growth and Change*.)

[2] 68% according to Galetti, Baldwin and Dina, *Nigerian Cocoa Farmers* (London, Oxford University Press, 1956).

most developing countries. International trade can enter the village before a national market is developed. National markets can exist in some products but not in others. The market system becomes organic in an agricultural district and effective in diversifying employment and the growth of towns only when most farmers are farming for maximum cash income, not for 'subsistence *plus* cash'.

It may be remarked—and it looks a little surprising at first—that in the early stages of growth the export market is likely to be easier to develop, in terms of market opportunity, than the domestic. Where 80% of the population are rural, living in semi-isolated micro-economies *socially designed to be self-sufficient*, they have little to sell to each other, except across ecological boundaries (forest to savannah) which were indeed originally import-export boundaries between small groups. The most hopeful customer is someone with a wholly different pattern of consumption—the foreigner. The trouble is that, once past the demand for curios, the modern foreigner may have exacting demands as to quality;[1] and this requires some discipline and standards among producers. It was because colonial enterprise provided both a market for unmarketable local produce and the necessary disciplines that many undeveloped areas and products (such as West African palm-oil, sugar in many areas, bananas) were brought into an international market economy.

This pressure on discipline and skill can be illustrated from the banana export from Fiji to New Zealand. Bananas are grown in small patches of three or four acres, by peasant co-operatives, in narrow valleys between steep hills. They require regular spraying against leaf-streak, and at some seasons almost daily dusting against moth. They must be picked, collected by lorry, crated, carried over mountain roads to the port, and must reach the ship's hold within forty hours of picking.[2] This is putting a high strain on discipline and organization among quite unsophisticated farmers.

Nevertheless, where the market is the really critical factor, it may well be easier to develop these export disciplines than to create a worth-while local market by persuading local producers to specialize and sell to each other. Internal division of labour will

[1] Not necessarily the highest quality, but consistent and even quality, at whatever level.
[2] Facts from the Waidina Valley banana scheme, Viti Levu, Fiji.

come later, in an urbanizing and industrializing period; the process may have to be started by an export trade to quite distant destinations, beyond the boundaries of an economy stuck at a low level of self-sufficiency. The implications for farmer training, to reach export standards in the early stages of commercialization, are obvious.

4

The relation of the production system to general development policy, and particularly to problems of unemployment, needs some special thought. The introduction of market forces and specialization is not simply equivalent to encouragement of the largest and most active private entrepreneurs and the introduction of modern techniques and machinery. As we have seen, with reference to Indonesia, the policy of 'backing winners'—encouraging the wealthy and better educated farmers—really involves, in peasant societies, a policy of 'the devil take the hindmost'; there are too many of the hindmost in peasant economies for this to be acceptable. Bruce Johnston,[1] in a brilliant paper on Japanese experience of agricultural and general economic advance, has made the same point:

In essence, the contrast between the Japanese and Mexican approach to agricultural development lies in the fact that the increase in farm output and productivity in Japan resulted from the widespread introduction of improved techniques by the great majority of the nation's farmers, whereas in Mexico a major part of the impressive increases in agricultural output in the post-war period have been the result of extremely large increases in production by a very small number of large-scale highly commercial farm operators. . . . It should not be overlooked that the bulk of the nation's farmers have been largely bypassed by recent progress, and the Mexican economy is now sharply divided between a relatively affluent sector engaged either in modern industry or in the commercial subsector of agriculture, and a large backwater still eking out an existence in semi-subsistence agriculture.

Despite this evidence from Japan and Mexico, with its emphasis on social dangers, the argument for backing 'the most enterprising'

[1] Bruce F. Johnston, *Agriculture and Economic Development: The Relevance of Japanese Experience* (Stanford University, Food Research Institute Studies, Vol. VI, No. 3).

farmers is widely accepted. There are, for example, areas and crops, such as wheat in West Pakistan, which lend themselves particularly well to large-scale cultivation by mechanization. There are areas where the number of enterprising men is so small, in the early stages of advance, that to use them for demonstration purposes may be the only way to make any impact at all. Moreover, there is widespread evidence, both in Africa and in Asia, that a count of the most progressive farmers in a district will show a high percentage of men with better education, and particularly men who have been out of the village into the big world, even for a short time, and thus lost some of their parochial conservatism. Besides, it is said, much time and effort has been devoted in the past to broad-front advance and usually with singularly little success; time is too short and effort too costly not to choose the most likely points of growth and exploit them.

These arguments need careful scrutiny. It is not only that there may be technical (as against political) reasons for favouring large- or small-scale farming. It is also important, that 'most enterprising' and 'bigger, wealthier, more powerful' should be distinguished. Conditions can very easily arise in which a few individuals who have some wealth or power can sail ahead into a 20th-century farming business leaving most of their neighbours stuck in the rut of subsistence. These conditions include oppressive tenancy systems; caste, corruption, manipulation of a narrowly-spread political influence; uneven impact of education; artificial exchange rates which make the import of machinery too cheap and easy; the necessary pull and contacts to get maximum benefit from Government subsidies (fertilizer, plant-protection, cheap credit) intended for poor men. In a word, these are largely social or political advantages which do not necessarily promote maximum economic growth for the *whole* economy. It is not merely energy or intelligence but social privilege—to put it more neutrally, environmental factors—which have made these men enterprising. For there is also evidence that quite humble small farmers, with equal energy and intelligence, can become 'enterprising' if their environment is altered a little by Extension action to enable them to show it. Security of tenure, cheap credit and technical advice will go a long way to making this change; a demonstration on a small man's plot may well carry more conviction among other small men; even technical factors, such as larger acreages for wheat or paddy cropping can be and have been overcome by Co-operatives or Farmers Associations who agree in small groups to cultivate in common and share a tractor for this purpose. In pursuit of the broad-front argument it is not necessary to slide into the total egalitarianism of President Nyerere's Arusha policy, which condemns any enterprise which enables a man to make profits by employing even a little wage-labour. It is simply a question of spreading the opportunity to be enterprising, whether to individuals or groups, as widely as possible.

Indeed it is far from clear that the policy of backing existing large farmers, in an effort to gain economies of scale and the advantages of mechanization, and as a means of harnessing the energies and ambitions of entrepreneurs as a dynamic of progress, is to the longer term advantage of the national economy in peasant societies, quite apart from the waste of potential enterprise among smaller men, and the social cleavage it may cause.

There are strong economic arguments for a more equal distribution of incomes. Dr. Balogh has written:

In most parts of Latin America, and certainly in the smaller countries such as Peru, economic development has reached a point where industrialization . . . can proceed no further unless a mass market can be created for it. And a mass market can only be created for it by enfranchising economically, politically, morally and intellectually the disfranchized. A more equal distribution of incomes in this case is good not only for moral reasons but also for purely economic reasons. Now a more equal distribution of incomes in under-developed countries . . . can only be brought about by a revolutionary change in agriculture.[1]

Thomas F. Carroll[2] has made the same point (quoting Kaldor, Prebisch, Myrdal and Malenbaum) that 'the present state of gross inequality in incomes is a serious obstacle to accelerated economic growth'. He goes on to say:

What seems to matter most for growth dynamics is the capability of reform to insure the widest possible diffusion of opportunities in line with the distribution of potential talent. To the extent that land reforms

---

[1] T. Balogh, 'Land Tenure, Education and Development in Latin America', in *Problems and Strategies of Educational Planning—Lessons from Latin America* (Paris, UNESCO-IIEP, 1965).

[2] T. F. Carroll, 'Comment' on P. M. Raup's 'Land Reform and Agricultural Development' in Southworth and Johnston, op. cit., pp. 318, 320.

... are imbedded in more general social revolutions, these broader, indirect, catalytic effects are far more significant in the long run than short run productivity considerations.

In a great many situations, productivity per acre will be higher on small, intensive holdings than on large mechanized ones; and, as we shall see in Chapter V, with a large surplus of cheap labour, this matters more than production per man. 'Economies of scale' are really a correlative of more capital-intensive methods, full utilization of plant, economy in management overheads—there is not much economy in having a 5,000-acre farm worked by the hoe.

But these are not the most important disadvantages. They lie in creating a system which is inimical to the growth of small-scale industry situated in rural areas which would provide diversification and non-farm employment where the mass of population is to be found. Johnston points out the great importance of this small-scale industry in Japanese growth and its relation to employment. After noting that 'as late as 1956 nearly half of the manufacturing labour force in Japan was working in small enterprises of less than thirty employees', he goes on:

This dual pattern of industrial development, which made it possible to expand non-farm employment at such a rapid rate, was facilitated by several factors in the Japanese pattern of development. Many of the traditional products manufactured by the small-scale labour-intensive industries remained in strong demand; and many of the new farm implements that were widely used, such as a rotary cultivator-weeder that was pushed by hand, improved plows, and the foot-pedal thresher, were readily manufactured by such enterprises. Organizational arrangements, such as sub-contracting between large-scale enterprises and small factories or household workshops, were a major factor in making it possible for the latter to ... expand as efficient and viable firms utilizing techniques appropriate to the factor proportions obtaining in Japan. The spread of transport facilities and the availability of electric power in rural areas were also of great importance in facilitating this type of development.

As a more modern illustration of this process, Johnston quotes most appositely the mushroom development of small firms and workshops making small pumps and diesel engines for small tubewell equipment in West Pakistan (it is remarkably developed in Daska and in the growing industrial centre of Sialkot). He adds:

The small-scale, rural-based industries were not only important in providing increased non-farm employment but also made available essential farm inputs at much lower capital costs and smaller foreign exchange content than would have been the case if major reliance had been placed, as was originally contemplated, on large-scale public tubewell projects utilizing larger and more sophisticated pumps and motors.

Thus:

The nature of the strategy pursued for developing the agricultural sector will have a strong influence on the success of efforts to encourage a dual pattern of industrial development. With the increasing commercialization of agriculture . . . a developing country's farm sector will make increasing use of purchased inputs. To the extent that this demand is directed towards relatively simple and inexpensive implements which are within the technical capabilities of small-scale, decentralized industries, the growing market for farm requisites can provide a strong stimulus to industrial expansion. A more capital-intensive agricultural expansion path not only requires scarce capital and foreign exchange . . . but also means that the growing commercialization of agriculture does not lead to the sort of dynamic interaction between agricultural expansion and development of rural-based industries that can contribute to more rapid growth of non-farm employment as well as more rapid growth of national product.

I have quoted Johnston's paper at length because it emphasizes so heavily several factors which are vital to the central theses of this book. He is unwaveringly supporting the commercialization of agriculture and the growth of non-farm employment by industrialization. But he is supporting a type of both agricultural and industrial advance which is consonant with the real factors available, i.e. a surplus of labour and a shortage of foreign exchange. He is emphasizing private industrial enterprise, but on a small scale. He stresses also accelerating factors—transport and widespread electric power—which are compatible with this scale. He believes that this broad thrust can contribute to more rapid growth of national product, and he has the historical case of Japanese development to support the argument.

In comparing the problem of peasant societies with the record of European growth it was pointed out in Chapter I that peasant societies have no room for major territorial expansion; no technical advantage over competitors; a much higher rate of population growth; and a less differentiated economy, with around 80% of population in the agricultural sector. Thus it is hopeless to expect that their small centralized modern sector can, by its own expansion, draw a large proportion of agricultural people into paid employment at any speed which would be acceptable. There is no real analogy with the European past; and the labour-saving capital-intensive methods of the European present are even less applicable. It is therefore necessary to make a direct attack on the rural economy itself, to use the potential of human labour and skill and the under-developed potential of land.

5

At this point it is necessary to state more precisely the size and the time-scale of needed structural change from farm to non-farm employment. To take some examples from East Africa, Norbye has calculated that it will take at least forty-five years to bring half of the total labour force of Kenya into non-farm employment, assuming very optimistic rates of growth of Gross National Product and of urbanization. Gormeley estimates that the rural population of Uganda will continue to increase in absolute numbers for at least another fifty-four years. The basic problem is that the ratio of increase in wage-paid employment to increase in G.N.P. is low, while the growth of population and labour force is so high in peasant societies. Harbison gives a number of calculations for this ratio in both developed and developing countries, and suggests that, on highly optimistic assumptions, a rate of 1% employment growth to 2·5% growth in G.N.P. is the best that can be hoped for. Thus, to get a 3% growth in employment (to keep up with the population growth) would imply a 7·5% growth in G.N.P.[1]

Johnston[2] has worked out tables, on varying assumptions, for the rates at which the structure of farm to non-farm employment can change over time. Some of his conclusions are that, where a country starts with 80% of the labour force in agriculture, 'if the total labour force is increasing at 2% per annum and the non-farm labour force at 3%, at the end of *half a century*[3] the farm labour force would still be increasing at 1·5% annually and would

[1] See individual papers presented by O. D. K. Norbye, P. H. Gormeley and F. Harbison to the Conference on Education, Employment and Rural Development, Nairobi (East African Publishing House, 1966).
[2] Johnston, op. cit.   [3] My italics.

account for 68% of the total labour force'. At these rates—at present optimistic, since population growth is often not 2% but 3% and non-farm employment seldom growing at 3%— Johnston points out that it would take 100 years to get 50% of the labour force in non-farm employment and 125 years before the farm labour force began to decline in sheer numbers. He remarks that it is implausible to consider that these rates would in fact continue for 100 years—but it is only implausible because famine would intervene long before. As to maximum achieved rates of growth in non-farm employment in rapidly developing countries, Johnston found that only Mexico (with 4% between 1950 and 1960) and Taiwan have exceeded the rate of 3·7% achieved in Japan between 1955 and 1964, associated with a G.N.P. growth of 10% per annum and 'an incredibly high rate of investment'. He adds that a similar rate of growth of non-farm employment was achieved in Japan in 1883–7 and 1893–7, with a rate of growth of G.N.P. less than a third as high. This is surely extremely significant, in that it shows non-farm employment growing very rapidly *without* huge national investment during the period of small-scale, broad thrust development of the rural economy and of workshop industry; it also puts a question-mark against any rigid law of correspondence between growth rates of G.N.P. and of non-farm employment.

To bring these figures into human terms, one may look at a special problem which is of much concern in Tropical Africa— the shortage of paid employment for the young people who complete seven years of Primary education—a group who feel particularly frustrated if no employment outside unreformed hoe-farming is available to them. Out of 150,000 such school-leavers in Kenya in 1965, paid employment or further education was available for a maximum of less than 50,000. In Tanzania there were about 20,000 jobs per annum for a new annual entry into the labour force of over 200,000, of whom 45,000 were such school-leavers; Harbison[1] has estimated, for Nigeria, 200,000[2] school-leavers and 50,000 wage-paid jobs. Even an economy as small as Fiji is producing 10,000 school-leavers annually and only about 800 wage-paid jobs. These are annual figures. Over five years Nigeria

[1] Harbison, op. cit.
[2] After deducting 70,000 entering Secondary schools and 50,000 girls not seeking employment.

would accumulate 1,000,000 school-leavers for whom no wage-paid employment would be available.

The size of the unemployment problem in global terms has already been quoted in Chapter I, based on I.L.O. calculations.[1] The figures for India alone are probably more meaningful and perhaps even more daunting. Between 1951–61 the *agricultural* labour force increased from about 98 million to about 131 million; and the proportion of agricultural to total labour force was unchanged at about 70%. The estimated increase in labour force 1961–76 is no less than 70 million.[2]

These figures show decisively how long the process of structural change must be on present trends, and how enormous the proportion of farm population in most of Asia and in Tropical Africa is bound to be for the next several decades. The rate of change can be increased in two ways: first, by reducing population growth—a fall from 3% to 2% would be a possible fifteen-year target, $1\frac{1}{2}$% is almost unreasonably ambitious; this is a very long-term policy; second, by increasing the rate of growth of non-farm employment. The fact that rates of around 4% have been achieved in the past in Japan, Taiwan and Mexico is encouraging; but even this high rate should not be taken as the limit of possibility; indeed, if it were, the outlook would still be bleak.

There are two possible ways in which the proportion of non-farm employment may be increased. The first—which looks like cheating!—is to question the statistics. Statistics of employment in very small units are notoriously very hard to gather accurately. Organized factories and workshops employing even only five people can be fairly easily traced. But employment by ones and twos, and self-employment on non-farm jobs are exceedingly difficult. A recent statistical survey in Kenya[3] has revealed a volume of self-employment in rural areas, outside direct farming, which will add more than 30% to the previous official statistics of regular employment (and, incidentally, a very substantial monetary turnover). The Labour Force Survey carried out by

[1] I.L.O., Geneva, Paper MCYW 1967/2. It follows that unemployment is heavily concentrated in the younger age groups: Jamaica, 39% of all unemployed between 15 and 19 years old; Guyana 44% between 14 and 19; Malaysia over 30% between 15 and 19.
[2] Tarlok Singh, 'Agricultural Policy and Rural Economic Progress' (All-India Agricultural Economics Conference, 1962).
[3] Ministry of Economic Planning, Statistical Section, Nairobi.

Robert Ray in Tanzania[1] revealed over 600,000 people drawing off-farm incomes from miscellaneous employment, against the official total figure of about 350,000 'employed'. And indeed it is just the miscellaneous, and often casual employment, which is likely to grow most quickly in an economy where farmers' purchasing power is growing fast and where services and distribution in large units have not yet become organized. Although this employment is in the rural sector, it is relieving the land itself from providing a direct living to all those wage-earners or self-employed tailors who would otherwise be trying to cultivate; and it is increasing the farmers' market for food.

The second method is therefore a direct attempt to raise average farm incomes even faster than the rates attained in Japan or Mexico, and thus to raise the employment which their spending will create. The extraordinary advances in plant-breeding and agronomy in the last few years do make this technically possible, though organizationally formidable.

Although structural change towards non-farm employment is of high importance—and in the long run critical—it is necessary to keep separate the growth of non-farm employment from that of *total* employment in the agricultural area. For in the short run, in many situations, intensification of agriculture can give a substantial rise in farm employment too. We know that, within existing sizes of holdings, there is still a big margin for increased productivity by increased labour inputs. Japan uses 'of the order of four times as much labour per acre of rice land as in typical rice-producing areas of India, or more than twice as much per acre cropped after allowing for the extent of double-cropping'.[2] The high yields per acre ensure that this does not imply lower incomes per worker and the high labour use exists despite Japan's larger use of mechanization. 'Japan gets higher yields per man and 3 to 4 times as much output per acre (in wheat and rice) as India.'[3] The size of holding in large areas of Asia and Africa could still be

[1] Ministry of Economic Affairs and Development Planning, Tanzania, in *Labour Force Survey of Tanzania* (Ford Foundation, January 1966).

[2] John W. Mellor in Hans W. Singer (ed.), *International Development 1966* (New York, 1967).

[3] Dale W. Jorgensen, 'Subsistence Agriculture and Economic Growth', in Clifton R. Wharton (ed.), *Economic Development in Subsistence and Peasant Agriculture* (New York, 1966). I have not entered the technical-economic argument concerning the cases where 'the marginal product of additional labour in agriculture is zero'. Certainly sometimes it is not zero but highly rewarding.

reduced, provided that farming methods are of the highest quality. Japan has an average holding of 0·8 hectare against the Indian average of 2·2 hectares, and much less farmland per worker. Obviously, the Malthusian squeeze would intervene if size is still further reduced, but there is still a wide margin in some areas.

It is also necessary to remember that in many areas in Africa, and some in Asia, there are, despite the overall unemployment figures, quite serious local shortages of labour in peasant farming. In Africa, more land could be cultivated if the farming family could find and afford to employ paid labour to extend their holding.[1] This shortage appears to be a little mysterious. It is probably caused by two factors, one economic and one social. To extend the farm involves a capital element—wages to labour for clearance before a crop is sown, possibly fencing or drainage or stock; and most poor farmers have no spare capital. Without capital, and where uncleared land is fairly easily available, each family will cultivate as much as the current family can manage by hand, and newly-married couples will clear a new patch, perhaps gradually extending it over time. Thus most of the labour is 'employed'—though often for only part of the year—and there is little spare labour, and little cash to pay wages.

Secondly, the family and prestige system tends to keep young men either overcrowding their own family land or starting a new plot, or seeking work in towns, rather than working for wages for a neighbouring family of equal status. In India, where landless labour is fairly plentiful, in many areas, and new land is very scarce, the problem is not so common; where shortage exists it is mainly due to unduly low wage-rates and the proximity of a town. Low wages in turn reflect low productivity per acre. If this is so, higher productivity would both attract and absorb more labour at a higher rate.

Finally, a more productive and prosperous agriculture would not only use more labour, but more labour external to the family. One of the first effects of rising standards is to release the wife from some agricultural work, not only because men handle oxen or tractors where before, in Africa, the wife handled the hoe, but for reasons of prestige; in many parts of Asia, for the wife not to

---

[1] See Rowena Lawson, 'Innovation and Growth in Traditional Agriculture of the Lower Volta', in *Journal of Development Studies* (Vol. IV, No. 1); it was the man with most wives and children who could take up the largest acreages.

work in the fields is a clear mark of social standing. This is also true of some Muslim countries in Africa, for instance of the Sudan. Also, rising educational provision keeps more children for more years in school and therefore off the labour market. This means that more unemployed men from outside the family are given a wage-earning livelihood. Although seldom mentioned, this withdrawal of family labour, on the scale of all the millions of hours worked by women and children at present, will probably contribute greatly to reducing male unemployment, in addition to the social benefit to wife and children. But it can only happen if productivity is steeply increased.

The outcome of this argument can be put in quite simple propositions. First, too high an emphasis on using the play of market forces on the larger and more sophisticated farmers may have dangerously destructive effects on the smaller peasantry and tenantry, adding to the numbers of landless unemployed. Second, in the early stages a simple but modern technology of farm production on a broad front will be both more economical (including economy in foreign exchange) and more conducive to the growth of small rural industries and, of course, of employment within them. Third, structural change is bound to be slow; but rising farm incomes create a worth-while volume of unregistered non-farm employment, and if this were included in statistics, the rate of sectoral change might look a good deal more encouraging. Fourth, for the time being, with 70–80% of population in the rural economy, employment of the huge annual entry into the workforce (whether educated or not) must be mainly within the rural sector, including self-employed both on- and off-farm; and finally, peasant agriculture, by intensifying and modernizing methods, can in fact absorb a considerable volume of additional labour *on* the farm without lowering *per capita* incomes,[1] with higher production per acre and ultimately with great social benefit to women and children.

6

At the beginning of this chapter some hints were given of the type of relationship which exists between political aims, physical

---

[1] Peasant agriculture is an extremely labour-intensive industry with a ratio of increasing employment to increasing output of as much as 1:1·5.

circumstances and economic possibilities, with a brief note on the way in which value arguments and efficiency arguments may become confused. This was illustrated by taking three possible and slightly different objectives for agricultural development—better food and nutrition, higher farm incomes through a market economy, the creation of employment—with some hint of the policy implications of each. These were in turn tested against three different types of area, in terms of land potential, securing of water supply and population density. We have also looked more closely at the nature of the present market economy, with the rather curious footnote that the external market may be easier to develop in the early stages of growth than the internal one. We have also examined the argument for a broad-front approach rather than a narrow spearhead through large farmers, not in terms of political values but in terms of local industrialization and commercialization. This has led to a closer quantitative look at the bleak arithmetic of structural change in employment (from the farm to the non-farm sector) in conditions of rapid population growth and from the starting point of a 70–80% farm economy.

It is worth adding that the slow, uphill movement from the 80% farm–20% non-farm position, characterized by surplus of labour in the rural sector, low wages and labour-intensive methods, is eventually matched, once the 50–50% point is passed, by a rapid downhill movement in which the urban-industrial percentage grows increasingly fast, in a period characterized by shortage of agricultural labour, high wages, and rapid mechanization. This stage is beautifully illustrated by the current position in Japan,[1] and by the early stages of a similar acceleration in Taiwan.[2] It was reached very early by Great Britain, and later, but with a huge acceleration, in the U.S.A. in the last generation. The 50–50% point is thus a vitally important watershed in economic and social policy. It will clearly be of great importance that policies which have succeeded brilliantly in countries which have passed it should not be adopted by those which have still far to go to

[1] T. Mukumoto, Farm Mechanization Institute, Saitama, Japan, and A. Hosokawa, University of Tokyo, 'Changes and Mechanization in Agriculture in Japan', Case Study for the International Seminar on Change in Agriculture (Reading University, September 1968).

[2] T. H. Shen, 'The Joint Commission on Rural Reconstruction, Taiwan', Case Study, International Seminar on Change in Agriculture (Reading University, September 1968).

reach it. The example of Japan in the 1880s may be invaluable to many developing countries: her example in the 1960s is extremely dangerous.

This chapter has concentrated on certain economic and environmental criteria—land potential, density of population, markets, reliability of rainfall, size of farm, employment. It has emphasized how much purely ideological aims may be affected by these objective factors. But it has largely omitted considerations of social structure and attitudes which form the basis of the theory of stages outlined in Chapter I. It will be a great deal more satisfactory to add in these ingredients when we have looked, concretely and in detail, at some of the actual ways in which change and development take place at the farm level, and at the institutions and methods of approach which are needed there.

CHAPTER V

TECHNICAL FACTORS

The development of industrial technology in 19th-century Europe was built upon a foundation of skills and technical self-confidence accumulated over several centuries of slowly-growing manufactures. It was these skills which were needed to *make* the machines; to transform wagon-loads of iron-ore into the shining, intricate, exact forms which make a smooth-running engine. Most of us today, outside the engineering industry, are apt to think of skills as the skills needed to operate equipment, forgetting the designers and makers. But in fact this distinction between designing and using marks a crucial division in industrial societies. It roughly segregates the scientists, thinkers, designers, technicians, decision-makers and order-givers from the majority who operate machines without much share in planning or ultimate control.[1] It made possible both the success and the scale of industry, multiplying the effect of designing and managerial skill through the employment of a huge operative labour force.

It is in contrast to agriculture that this fact stands out so sharply. For, at least until the last two decades, it was never possible in agriculture to separate the planning, technical, directive and accounting functions from the actual operation of a farm. Decisions on cropping pattern, fertilization, tools and equipment, borrowing and investment, labour-use, all fall on the farmer himself. He has had to be a man of all trades in an increasingly complex world.

It is largely for these reasons that it looked so much easier to transfer industry to developing countries than to build up a modern agriculture. Purely operative skills in industry can be quickly taught. Provided that the machines are imported and the management at first borrowed from outside, a labour force to run

[1] One might almost say that in England this split takes place in the classrooms where the 11-plus examinations are, or used to be, held. See chapter on Education.

them will not be hard to find and train, whether in Africa or Asia. Even automation, with its huge output and comparatively small direct requirement of highly specialized skills in use, has been suggested as a means of accelerating growth in developing countries. Industry, moreover, in its artificial environment of closed, ventilated and lighted buildings, can operate round the year, immune from drought and flood; at least the production side is not subject to the wild fluctuations which bedevil agricultural planning.

This contrast between management in industry and in agriculture has been well put in the report of a distinguished interdisciplinary Symposium, sponsored by U.S.A.I.D. and held at Endicott House (Massachusetts Institute of Technology):

Farm decision makers are widely scattered geographically, they vary enormously in economic status and potential, they cover a wide political spectrum, they are subject even within one country to a considerable variety of institutional connections, and they exhibit a widely varying pattern of attitudes and motivations. By contrast, managerial control in industry and social overhead facilities are highly concentrated, and the development of a reasonably effective industrial labor force is infinitely simpler and more manageable than the building of a modern community of farmers. The characteristic agricultural need for unusually complex and extensive organizational and administrative arrangements poses an acute dilemma for societies whose scarcest resource is often organizational and administrative talent.[1]

In fact, a number of economic arguments prevented a large-scale transfer of industry to developing countries, not least the lack of a domestic market for mass production among the potential mass consumers—poor farmers. In Africa particularly, what little industry was created in colonial times relied both on imported machinery and imported management. The fact that both the making of machinery and the management were in the hands of the metropolitan society and its envoys appeared to reduce the receiving colony to an operator society—in Arnold Toynbee's phrase, an external proletariat. Yet, as we can see, this was not originally the result of ill-will or a plan to perpetuate supremacy,[2] but arose

[1] Max F. Millikan and David Hapgood, *No Easy Harvest* (Boston, Little, Brown and Company, 1967).
[2] Except in a few cases where industry was deliberately stopped, e.g. by Lancashire in Bengal.

naturally from the technical facts of the colonial situation itself. How far this situation will change in future will concern us in Chapter XI as we look at the longer-term economic future of peasant societies. In Asia, particularly in the Indian sub-continent and among the overseas Chinese, commercial and managerial skills were more developed, and more purely domestic industry sprang up. But in both continents industrial growth was fairly quickly checked by the lack of markets, and particularly the lack of purchasing power in a predominantly farming society. The modernization of agricultural production and management became essential. This was a problem which could not be solved by borrowing, and was in any case far more extensive and difficult to attack.

It had been achieved—though not completely—in the developed countries over a long historical sequence of changes. It was done by separation from communal to individual holdings—though not necessarily to freehold units; by adding complexity to crops and rotations; by the use of organic fertilizer—dung, bones, oil cake, guano; by bringing in mechanical power and the design and maintenance services from the industrial sector; by scientific plant genetics; and, almost last of all, by the elaboration of chemical fertilization and control, which has made possible a far higher flexibility in rotations and crop-planning, even to constant repetition of a single crop. The English historian would recognize in these stages the agricultural revolutions of the 15th and 16th centuries; next, enclosure and four-course rotation; next, the vast growth of organic fertilization in the 19th century; finally, the tractor, plant genetics and chemicals leading to a highly industrialized agriculture since 1919.[1] It is only in the very last stage that some management specialization has become possible, partly by the service which industry gives to farmers in supply and maintenance, partly by borrowing from industry concepts such as cost-accounting or work-study. Agriculture, in its heavy capital structure, business management and use of factory techniques, begins to look more and more like industry.

That such a transition will have to take place in Africa and

[1] See, for the organic fertilizer story particularly, F. M. L. Thompson, 'The Second Agricultural Revolution', in *Economic History Review*, 2nd Series (Vol. XXI, No. 1, April 1968). Thompson mentions that it is really the third revolution—the first two being the cash economy (16th century) and enclosure (17th—18th centuries).

Asia is certain; that it will follow the same order is, as we shall see, far from certain. The sequence of change reflects particular historical, geographical and social accidents—the order in which the exact sequences came to maturity, the nature of temperate agriculture and local social patterns which may never be repeated.

If we look at the attitudes to peasant farming which characterize the Colonial Powers during their period of dominance, it will not be hard to see why both Africa and Asia virtually failed even to start this agricultural revolution. Asia seemed to Britain, France and Holland a highly valuable and rich domain. India in the 18th century was already far advanced in towns and craft skills. British development effort, when it came in the 19th century, was primarily in engineering—to build the railways, to bridge and dam the rivers, to create within this vast addition of territory the industrial background which was being built in the British age of railways, canals, docks and bridges. While the Administration concerned itself with law and order and a framework within which the peasantry could live in peace and without gross oppression, the engineer revelled in the creative opportunity; the two met mainly where famine threatened, for flood control and for communications to move stocks of food. Communications and irrigation, on the Indus, on the Ganges, on the Krishna or the Cauvery Rivers, were their great memorials. The peasant farmer made what use of them he could. In Ceylon, Malaya, Indo-China and Indonesia plantation was more dominant[1]—again a concern which had little relevance to the standards and development of peasant agriculture. In the Philippines the landlords of the Catholic Spanish regime were succeeded by the businessmen of America; neither cared for the small tenant. The sheer size of the peasant mass, the gap in language and feeling of community between rulers and ruled, the tiny numbers of colonial staff, made any notion of wholesale rural advance unthinkable at that time.

African colonial rule has a rather different atmosphere. Tropical Africa was not seen as a rich inheritance, save in certain highly specialized ways, chiefly for mineral extraction and palm-oil. The British motives were a strange mixture of missionary zeal, trade interests (in West Africa particularly), mining enterprise, vaguely prestigious and vaguely strategic foreign policy, slowed

[1] Partly, as we have seen, for ecological reasons.

down by a considerable governmental reluctance to undertake a costly and perhaps unfruitful burden. Perhaps the Belgian conquest of the Congo came to have the strongest economic motive as its enormous mineral wealth was revealed; next in importance come the mining developments spreading from South Africa to the Copperbelt, the palm-oil and cocoa trade, and the notion of white agricultural settlement in Kenya and French North Africa. None of this concerned the small peasant farmer save for the West African trade. Indeed—and this is quite unlike the Indian story—all the Europeans in Africa felt that Africans had very far to go. They were not likely to contribute to economic advance for untold generations; they would have to be administered, Christianized, perhaps even welfared—in a large degree, their government and welfare would have to be paid for by European enterprise. The mining enterprises were European to the hilt; the Boer farmers, the white farmers in Kenya, Algeria, Rhodesia, and the giant plantations were of European provenance; economic 'apartheid' was built into European colonization of Africa, at least on the economic front, far more widely than in South Africa alone.

Even engineering works were much less stressed in Africa. The Belgians developed river transport on the Congo and a mining railway; the British built a farming railway in East Africa, a mining railway to the Copperbelt, a trade railway in Nigeria. But the Niger was untouched; the Jinja Dam on Lake Victoria was not built until the 1950s, nor the Kariba Dam on the Zambesi. Only in the Sudan and Egypt was the Nile tackled, in the interests of farming, with something like the energy and vision shown in India. Perhaps it was felt that the Africans were not ready to respond to such huge investments as the Indians had been. Certainly, the international mobilization of capital aid for indigenous mass development had not yet got under way.

Thus it is no wonder that the detailed problems of African or Asian peasant farming were so neglected. This is not to forget the efforts of individual administrators and enthusiasts, the concern of the Administration when famines threatened, or the considerable achievement in slowing down the widespread destruction of potential by overgrazing in the open hills and plains and by 'slash and burn' in the forests. But, save for Indian irrigation, the development of peasant agriculture was not the main focus of European effort. It was very late in Africa, mainly since the second World War, that detailed study and the beginnings of effective planning were brought to bear upon African or Asian farming.

It was not (as we now realize) that there was no basis of skill and experience among the farmers. Granted the conditions, the equipment available and the lack of any outside supply or support, few Westerners would have liked to tackle the problem of making a livelihood, which was somehow solved year after year by native farmers. If there was any resource of skill upon which to build development in Africa comparable to the skills upon which European industry had been built in earlier centuries, it was in farming, not in industry. The experience of European plantations was useful on the technical side, but only rarely did it apply to food-crops—research on those was pathetically weak, whether in West Africa or Malaya, even in 1960. Rarely did it apply to animal husbandry either. Above all, there was little understanding of the total management problem which the subsistence farmer faced. Almost all the technical problems, the structural and institutional problems, and the administrative problems remained to be solved.

It is to these three main subjects that this and the following two chapters are devoted. The task is to achieve in the right order—not necessarily the European order—the same essentials which have proved necessary in the past to move to industrialized commercial farming. The first step is unquestionably a deeper understanding of the real predicament of the peasant farmer. Thereafter, it may not be necessary to tackle land tenure first—possibly the very latest European achievement in plant genetics and chemical stimulants and protection will come first, and mechanization, which preceded it in Europe, will come later. Two things are certain: farming will become more complex, and external support in farm management will be essential; for the problem of the unsupported all-purpose manager-operator has to be faced. Second, the industrial supply base for modern agriculture, in chemicals, machines, equipment and service, will have to be developed. The technical progress of agriculture is not an isolated affair which can go ahead while industry stagnates. It is one which will stimulate and test the whole economy in a way which the most industrially ambitious government would wish.

Finally, it may be encouraging to remember that it is only

quite recently—in many countries since 1945—that concentrated thought and scientific experience have been devoted to peasant agriculture on a nationwide scale. It is not that effort had failed; except in India, it had barely gone beyond the pilot stage or scattered experiments by individual enthusiasts. It is with this thought in mind that we can turn to look first at the detailed ways in which change is taking place at farm level.

2

It is quite easy to make a list of all the things needed for agricultural advance. They include better land preparation; better seeds of better varieties; better methods of cultivation; better implements; more fertilizers; better balanced rotations; better plant-protection; better animals and integration of animal husbandry into the farm economy; controlled water supply; better transport, roads and bridges; cheap fuel and power; double or treble cropping; better storage facilities. There is also the vitally important list of institutional factors—land tenure and size of farms; credit; Co-operatives; marketing arrangements; research and Extension (including farmer education)—these are considered in the following chapters. It is easy to see and to say that *all* these factors must eventually be looked after if agriculture in peasant communities is to reach the highest standards. It is also tempting to pick on one or two of the factors and argue a case that these have a super-priority—some advisers are for fertilizer, some for water, some for roads, some for good and guaranteed prices to the producer. A more sophisticated idea is 'the package deal', which is the basis of the Ford Foundation programme in India— though the package is largely limited to high-yielding varieties, fertilizer, water, plant-protection, credit and an improved Extension Service.

This attempt to establish priorities is natural. It springs from the fear that to attempt everything at once is impracticable, both in terms of organization and in terms of finance. Planning (sacred word) is a matter of priorities. But even the exponents of the 'package' must have a lurking apprehension lest, because the package is incomplete, one of the absent factors might prove a deadly obstacle to success. Suppose that splendid crops are produced but cannot be moved for lack of roads or lorries? Suppose that there is a surplus and prices collapse? Suppose that there is no foreign exchange for tractor-fuel or steel for irrigation pumps? These fears are realistic, for precisely these things do happen, and often. For the total revolution of agricultural production hangs on nothing smaller than the total functioning of the whole economy as far as agricultural inputs and equipment, prices, foreign exchange, power, water supply, roads and transport are concerned.

If everything is a prerequisite for success, the process will never start. We are therefore quite naturally driven towards Albert Hirschman's[1] philosophy, that listing prerequisites for general economic development is a mistaken approach; if this is true in general terms, it is also true of the more limited—though still large—agricultural sector of the economy.

The kernel of Hirschman's view is that growth is essentially a process of linked stages, in which one step so alters the situation that a second step becomes both desirable and possible; and the second step points to and facilitates a third. Yet here and there it suddenly seems to go wrong. For example, Hirschman goes on to say: 'The investments of one period will call forth complementary investments in the next period with a will and logic of their own.' Alas, this is exactly what has *not* happened on many occasions in developing countries: very large and expensive installations have been put up and have remained islanded—obelisks of modern technology towering over the unaltered bush.[2]

It is vital to examine just why this statement of Hirschman rings false for developing countries, though it rings true of the process of development as it was seen in Europe and America. The answer is to be found in distinctions between 'growth' and what may be called 'construction'. Western economies grew from one step to another much as Hirschman suggests, because each step grew out

[1] Hirschman, op. cit. It was this problem of multiple, simultaneous prerequisites for agricultural growth which formed the subject of the Endicott House Conference (above, page 108).

[2] I had in mind a remarkable statement of Leontiev, quoted by Sir A. Cairncross, in *Factors in Economic Development* (London, George Allen and Unwin, 1962):

'An industrially backward country may take the dramatic short-cut of building a few large up-to-date automated plants. Towering up in the primitive economy like copses of tall trees on a grassy plain, they would propagate a new economic order.'

Vast modern plants certainly exist in very backward areas and the visual-picture is splendid. But they do not propagate a new economic order.

of the one *before*—as well as giving rise to the one after. This in turn was because there was no other more developed economic system in the surrounding world from which something could be borrowed which was discontinuous with the situation 'before', and sprang from different antecedents. This is only to spell out what is obvious in extreme cases—that to throw a steel works into a subsistence economy does not call out complementary investment by any will or logic of its own.[1]

Thus, in face of the huge list of things required to change peasant agriculture, neither the choice of one or two superpriorities, nor an incomplete 'package', nor the introduction of some large discontinuous change in the hope of 'spread' effects, is a complete alternative to the impossible task of doing everything at once.

Nevertheless, the central government must do something: and the basic answer is indeed on Hirschman's lines—that one step shows the ways to the next—with the proviso that each must be genuinely linked to the one before. There will be differences as to the right initial step between different countries and between different zones of the same country, and this has implications for the process of Planning which will be considered later. First, we must look more closely at this process of sequential growth as distinguished from the attempt to construct a wholly new economy—the attempt to jump from stage 1 to stage 10 without the growth linkages between them.

3

Each step in agricultural change is indeed a good deal more complex than it first appears. Consider fertilizer: at first sight it would seem a simple business to encourage and enable farmers to put some fertilizer on a crop they are already growing; surely this is not surrounded by a host of complications and consequences? Yet indeed it is. There are, of course, technical problems. The crop may grow too lush but weak-stemmed and lodge before harvest; a good deal of research, based on local soils and climate, will be needed before the right amounts and mixtures are found;

---

[1] I developed this argument a little more in *The Best of Both Worlds?*. See also the reasons given by Gunnar Myrdal in *Asian Drama* (London, Allen Lane, 1968) for the lack of spread effects from colonial investments.

possibly a new variety which is more tolerant of fertilizer may be needed; Mexican wheat and Philippine rice, both with this characteristic, started an agricultural revolution in the Punjab and in the paddy lands of Asia. Again, more fertilizer is likely to mean more weed too, unless the standard of cultivation is improved, and this in turn may mean more labour or the improvement of implements. René Dumont, in noting this, adds: 'The handplough must be perfected and ploughs drawn by animals brought into general use[1] before fertilizers are introduced. They became widespread in Europe only after centuries of good farming and decades of rapid agricultural progress.'[2]

But let us assume that this knowledge is available—agricultural effort did not start yesterday. There are still large implications. The peasant will at first need credit to buy fertilizer, and a crop failure due to drought will leave him with a cash debt and no means of repayment.[3] If his crops are much larger, storage will be needed.

If indeed the farmer uses a new variety, it may well have a different taste; it may be rice which is too sticky or not sticky enough, or wheat which is too soft to make good *chapattis*. Except in famine times, the consumer also has a say.[4]

Again, it looks simple enough to persuade farmers to sow certain crops three weeks earlier than is their custom, because this may have disproportionate effects on yield—René Dumont[5] constantly emphasizes this for cotton in West Africa, and it appears to apply strongly to jute in East Pakistan, and no doubt to many other crops. But the ground may be so hard that the hoe or the ox-plough cannot break it until the first rains start, and this may be too late. A new plough, or a tractor, or irrigation is needed. This is not the only difficulty: to sow early means to have the land clear of the previous crop and labour available for

[1] Very far from general in Africa, though achieved in most of Asia.
[2] René Dumont, *False Start in Africa* (London, André Deutsch, 1966). Of course, one reason why they were late in introduction was that modern chemical fertilizers were not invented.
[3] Unless he gets it from the landlord, repaying a share of the crop; and in this case a poor crop does not load him with a money debt; hence the security of the landlord system.
[4] During the last war, when shipping to carry cereals to Arabia was short, rice-eating peoples there were allocated wheat, and considerable numbers died rather than eat it.
[5] Dumont, op. cit.

cultivation; in double-crop systems, if the harvesting and winnowing is a slow hand-process, there may not be time to sow the second crop at its best moment; in single season systems the farmer may be so busy planting his food crop when the rains come that he has no time to plant cotton until too late.

Thus just these two simple issues—fertilizer and early sowing—have taken us far afield—into research on new varieties, disease control, consumer preferences, new tools, labour constraints, storage, marketing. They start to emphasize the step-by-step way in which one successful change may start another, raising a new problem but perhaps also creating the will and the means to solve it. They also underline the great importance of local and perhaps temporary conditions. Dumont gives some interesting examples of their step-by-step improvement, in which the added product at each stage, and the improved condition of the farm, makes the next stage worth while and possible to finance.[1]

The whole question of integrating animal husbandry into the economics of the individual farm illustrates with equal force the complexities, and also the gradual approach which may be necessary. In highly developed Western agriculture the ox gave way to the horse long ago, and the horse to the tractor within the last generation. The effectiveness of tractors makes them a standing temptation for developers; but notoriously they are often highly uneconomic when introduced to much of peasant farming at its present stage. It is not only that animal traction or even hand cultivation may be cheaper: it is that animals have other functions in a peasant economy—they give milk, dung, transport to market, power for threshing, eventually hides and horn and bonemeal. There is a long process of separating out the functions of traction, of manuring, and of milk and meat production before the mechanized mixed farm makes its appearance. The farm manager for Mymensingh University farm, East Pakistan, instructed to mechanize, found that he still could not work the farm effectively without twenty-two oxen.

Naturally, there is a great temptation to jump the steps from hand-cultivation to tractor, because it seems uneconomic to have both forms of capital—animals and machines—when

[1] Dumont, op. cit. The example I have in mind is the gradual transformation of scrubland through a sequence of fencing, grazing, mowing of pasture, ploughing and planting of improved meadowland.

farming capital is so short: it was even suggested to us in an Indian agricultural university (by an American) that electrification of main ploughing and harvesting operations might be the 'dramatic short-cut'. Indeed, animals are a heavy burden to peasant agriculture as well as a necessity. There are long periods in the year when they are not working much but have to be fed and tended; on very small acreages the allocation of even a small plot to grow fodder means a serious sacrifice of food-crop land; in consequence, in poor areas, the cattle are half-starved, produce little milk and are too weak to draw an iron plough. However, the co-existence of both cattle and tractors characterizes some of the richest mixed farming in the world, once each is given its proper function; ironically, the tractor carries food to the cattle. But the process of separation of function is critical.

The conditions in which the tractor can become a total substitute for animals involve many related changes—another means of threshing which does not need oxen; different organization of transport to market; if possible, elimination of dung for fuel and plaster;[1] quite probably, land consolidation or at least a co-operative crop pattern, so that the tractor can cross farm boundaries freely; new design of the tractor or tiller or thresher itself; and, above all, a basis of already thriving farm economy, so that the capital expenditure is commensurate with an already higher cash earning from the farm. Detailed study of the economics of tractors in peasant farming at Comilla (East Pakistan)[2] shows conclusively what stringent conditions are needed before it is economic; and similar results have come from studies in Africa.

Again, the introduction of new (and often exogenous) crops or crop varieties has implications as to the whole level of research and organization available in any country at the time. New crops will demand additional care and skill from the farmer; but this has in fact proved the least of the problems—African farmers, properly taught, have learned to grow the highest quality of tea or coffee, with quite exacting cultural requirements, in a very short time. The organization of supplies to the farmer which are beyond his control may be more difficult. Bureaucratic control of the issue

---

[1] If the tractor is used for traction, and high quality animals for meat and milk, there will still be dung: but it is better used as fertilizer than as plaster or fuel!

[2] Anwaruzzaman Khan, *Introduction of Tractors in a Subsistence Farm Economy* (Academy for Rural Development, Comilla, E. Pakistan, 1962).

of fertilizer or credit; poor organization of the distribution of irrigation water in canal systems, or bad maintenance or power failure in pumping systems may completely wreck the farmers' efforts to grow a more demanding crop. The seed or the credit to buy it is late, so the crop is sown late; the fertilizer for a hybrid maize seed-farm lies unwatered on the ground, because the pump has failed, and the result is a failure of simultaneous flowering of the two parent strains;[1] the Agricultural Department does the first spraying in good time but omits the second—these failures may cost the farmer dear if he has already committed capital to the venture.

Plant-protection, usually associated with a new crop, itself demands perhaps an even higher general level of effort. A variety which is resistant in the experimental station, in field trials, and even for the first year or two of farm use may suddenly go down to a new strain of disease, and these new strains are constantly developing—indeed, it was said in England in 1967 that we had temporarily not a single commercial wheat resistant to rust.[2] There is thus a constant battle being waged, in which the research scientists are endeavouring to keep one jump ahead of the disease. To integrate this scientific work with farm practice implies much scientific efficiency (a large financial investment in itself), extremely rapid and effective transference of research results to plant-breeders and seed-farms, and an alert farming population able to read the journals and alter practices continually to keep up with the moving battle of research versus disease.

This recital of difficulties, apparently without solutions, is in danger of becoming irritating, and perhaps ridiculous. For progress *has* been made, not merely in the last few years but centuries ago. Half the economic crops of Africa were introduced from other continents and long before the colonial period in some cases—maize and cassava from the New World, to instance only two absolutely staple elements of African subsistence, without mentioning the more recent introduction of temperate crops and cattle

[1] Observed near Vijayawada, Andhra Pradesh, India, due to failure of the power supply.
[2] Some suggest that adaptation of disease organisms is developed in experimental stations, where the disease organism can learn to adapt among the great variety of crops grown in proximity in experimental plots—just as disease organisms are accumulated in hospitals.

breeds in the highlands of Kenya or the introduction of rubber to Malaya and West Africa. How was all this achieved, in a new environment and ecology, new variants of soil, bacteria, virus, fungi, insects and climate, and largely before the invention of many modern chemical controls?

Often at great cost, and over substantial periods of time; locally at first, and often painfully—Lord Delamere is said to have lost £80,000 of private money in introducing wheat production in the Kenya Highlands; the control of tsetse fly in Africa has still not been effectively achieved, despite huge expenditure on research and futile holocausts of game.

In fact the sense of hopelessness in face of so many possibilities of mischance or mistake is due to direct comparison of the situation as it now is in many countries and the final situation as it could be, omitting the steps between; and it is the central argument of this chapter that attempts to make this jump by radical innovation are bound to meet with disappointments in their early stages. The more gradual sequence of mounting improvements is in fact an extremely hopeful one, and can be illustrated again and again. It is the pressure of time which breeds impatience; yet the step-by-step process, by any wider standard, is not in fact so slow. Ten years is not a long time if each year shows progress; and ten years has shown almost unbelievable progress in some places.[1]

There is, in fact, a considerable acceleration compared to historical processes, simply because the final result to which the process is tending is known. The very existence of developed science and of historical analysis is one of the great accelerating influences upon which the thesis of this book depends. But acceleration is not total telescoping. It may take only two or three years to move from one stage to another—a move which took thirty years in Europe; it is the attempt to go from A to Z directly which fails.

There are many favourable sequences. The introduction of line as against broadcast sowing, as an improvement in itself, prepares the way for both mechanical cultivation and for an accurate spacing of plants. The skill developed in contour-ploughing, introduced as a measure of soil conservation, prefaces the skill needed to lead irrigation water over long distances with only a few inches of fall. The introduction of sugarcane may give a cattle-food which

[1] For example, the Central Province of Kenya between 1957 and 1967; in Taiwan, Mexico, several States of India, etc.

does not require or reduces a separate allocation of land for fodder-crops. The mere building of a country road can have multiple effects—a crop can reach a factory or market; the Extension Officer can get around more quickly; men can get to work further afield; crops can be collected to central storage instead of being eaten by rats (most peasant farms are too small to carry farm buildings); traders can reach the village, both to buy crops and to offer for sale consumer goods which are one of the incentives to cash-crop production. Indeed, if there were to be super-priorities, roads might be very high among them.

But it is not only these physical factors which are involved. Each step is changing the farmer's attitude, essentially from the subsistence-survival principle to the idea of farming at least partly for a cash income, and, finally, to the idea of farming as a business run on business lines. Selling a small surplus off the farm is only the beginning of this process, and both in Africa and Asia it has long been customary, at least as barter. What is often new is to make the main basis of the farm a cash-crop, with a gradual dwindling of the food-crop, until finally food is being purchased for cash. Each step gives a little added self-confidence, and, ideally, each step should go some way to paying for the next. The building up of farm capital is a fairly slow process, and although good credit systems should help it, government cannot possibly afford to carry the whole load; it would be inflationary to pump out credit far in advance of the stepped increases in productivity. De Wilde[1] gives a good example of progressive investment by farmers in the Elgeyo–Marakwet area of Kenya. They first made some money from potatoes, used it to establish pyrethrum, and then used the pyrethrum profits to go into high-grade cattle raising.

While the farmer is gaining management skills and confidence, there is some time available to train and deploy a better Extension Service, to build up the research activity which will be increasingly needed, and to strengthen and simplify the supply and distributive system for fertilizer, seed and chemical sprays. West Pakistan particularly was recently struggling with this problem, handled by the Agricultural Development Corporation, because the new programme of high-yielding varieties, with their seed, fertilizer, water and power demand, had dashed ahead of fertilizer supply and administrative training.

[1] De Wilde, op. cit.

Again, the institutional systems—co-operatives both for marketing and credit, farmer-training, technical services and maintenance—need a little time to mature and to select from many competing methods and doctrines. Tenurial reform and Land Consolidation inevitably take their time and are, indeed, far more likely to proceed quickly if the farmers are already mentally on the move towards a more commercialized agriculture through earlier steps of advance. In some cases co-operation in production can be achieved without the legal consolidation process; for example, in some rice-growing schemes in Dacca District (East Pakistan) as many as sixty separate holdings of rice-land down a long curving valley were being tractor-cultivated as a unit and irrigated by pump: this scheme rested upon a system of voluntary farmer-co-operation stimulated by a vigorous Extension Officer. Exactly the same was being done in Kerala, sometimes over blocks as big as 2,000 acres. Group farming of cotton appears to have grown up almost spontaneously (though no doubt with help from Extension Officers) in some parts of Central Nyanza (Kenya). In the Buret area of Kenya (Kipsigis tribe), 'the whole process of enclosure had taken place through *ad hoc* judgments in the Courts without a single legal enactment or any direct enforcement of policy by the Administration.'[1]

In many cases, in Africa as well as Asia, a single technical factor—for example, a pump which is only economic if it serves several smallholdings—is the basis of co-operation which may only later turn into a Co-operative proper with far more varied functions, including credit, agricultural supplies, and marketing. The point of co-operative action, and the disciplines it involves, are far more easily grasped by the farmer in relation to such a single and obvious technical requirement than if a government official, out of the blue, urges the establishment of a formal Co-operative, and then produces the pages of paper about its constitution and rules which the farmer will not easily understand and may well be too cautious to sign. Once again, because we know the final stage, we are tempted to insist upon it, before the steps which make it palpably desirable and necessary have been experienced.

Thus the complexity of cause and effect in social affairs is just as much a reason for optimism as it is for discouragement—

[1] J. W. Pilgrim, 'Land Ownership in the Kipsigis Reserve' (E.A.I.S.R. Conference, 1959).

indeed, much more so. Discouragement arises by looking at the desired final effect and realizing how many coincident factors would be needed to achieve it—that is, reading backwards from the objective to the starting point. Optimism springs from looking at the same process forwards, and realizing that even a single small change is polyvalent, demanding and often facilitating related adaptations in several fields; these adaptations in turn open new opportunities, also polyvalent. Once the trend is set, it is possible to see all things (or at least many things!) working together for good. A situation where several factors are interdependent and mutually supporting is usually described as a vicious circle in the context of developing countries; but just the same kind of interdependence can cause one change to set off a chain of favourable results.

It is also encouraging to remember, once a change for the better starts, what a massive force pushes it forward, a force which the government does not have to supply because it is within individual ambition. The first real break in the vicious stability of poverty and dependence not only opens new vistas but often closes the way back. Once a man is committed to farming for cash, he will not easily go back to farming for subsistence; perhaps he cannot. Both ambition and fear will push him forwards to new adjustments and even to increasing risks. Structural change in the farm and changes in the habits of family consumption quickly become almost irreversible, save under really dire conditions.

4

To start this process of change by small steps involves a close knowledge of exact local conditions. There may be fairly similar conditions over a wide geographical area with homogeneous farming conditions and social strucure. There is great (but imperfect) homogeneity in the Gangetic plain of India or in the Savannah belt of West Africa, covering in one instance several large Indian States and in the second large tracts of several African nations. But similarities of this kind are more rare in reality than the generalizations of the geographers suggest, partly from variation in human organization—Bihar differs from the Western Uttar Pradesh—and partly from particular variations in soil, climate, topography, proximity to roads and markets, and many other factors. For this reason, great national 'drives' for the introduction of fertilizer, or feeder roads, or Co-operatives quickly fade except in those particular patches where they happen to give the exact stimulus which will start a chain reaction. Even within a single Indian District—which will mean at least 1,000,000 people in perhaps 2,000 square miles or more—there may well be sharp differences in need and response. It follows that a very high degree of discretion should be given to those who know an area intimately in deciding where to break into the circle of the rural economy with most effect. Ultimately, this means that Plans have to be the sum of a very large series of local plans,[1] often wholly different in emphasis: in one area water and fertilizer may be the first answer; in another, feeder roads and guaranteed prices; in a third, land consolidation and credit. Save for areas quite exceptionally uniform in a multitude of factors, it is impossible to establish a single set of priorities which will cover all cases. As we shall see later, this is a most unwelcome doctrine at the level of central government and in Planning organizations. Welcome or not, it happens to be true.

5

But this concentration on organic growth, on multiple small changes gradually evolving to new structural forms—this is surely a vegetable's view of the world? The mind goes back to the heroic scale and vision which can characterize human effort. To stand by the Pont du Gard in Provence and conceive of the immense achievement of Roman aqueducts or of the Roman irrigation of North Africa; to walk by the lakes and canals engineered around the temples of Angkor Wat in the Cambodian forest; to drive through the rich irrigations between the five rivers of the Punjab, the greatest irrigation scheme in the world in its day, or to fly over the chequered cultivation of the Sudan Gezira, won from the desert in our own lifetime—this surely sets the scale and reach of human endeavour which should be in our minds in facing the challenge of development of a continent?

These towering achievements do indeed need courage—the kind of courage which leads a man to see the natural world waiting to be tamed and shaped into the service of man; courage

[1] Suitably reconciled with overall financial and other constraints.

to destroy whole valleys and move their populations; vision to see a richer, wealthier life when the surgical shock of the bulldozers and dynamite is forgotten and the new landscape emerges. But another kind of vision is also needed—the detailed vision of how small human lives will be lived in this new landscape. It is one of the remarkable features of the modern world that these two attitudes, so rarely combined in any individual, are at last beginning to be married at the Planning level. The volumes written for the Volta River project, the even wider and more detailed work of the United States Reclamation Bureau on the preparation of the Mekong project are uniquely modern.

It is not our business here to comment on these gigantic ventures. From the small farmers' point of view they could be regarded almost as part of the natural environment—the sun's heat or monsoon rains—under which organic life must find its way. Nationally and internationally, their costs and the comparative benefits which might have come by spending the resources in other ways are largely beyond definitive calculation; there are too many legitimate variables and different assumptions, each combination of which would give a different answer. Perhaps we should indeed take the farmers' view and regard them as an upheaval of the natural order from which international agencies, acting as Olympians rather than as economists, foresee benefit for the race of men below for centuries to come. Let us hope that these Olympians are wise.[1]

But in any case, when the cataclysm is over, the problem comes back to human size. For on these new millions of acres small farmers must live and work the land. The problem of agricultural advance is not solved by these convulsions; at best it is made easier to approach. There is a freer choice of policy on new settlements, as to size of holdings, crop-patterns and much else; and there is, presumably, a higher potential from the investment.

[1] I am, of course, aware that modern economic-mathematical methods can usefully put at least an order of magnitude to the costs and benefits and the alternatives in time and method. But at the present rate of technological and social change the state of the world in 1990 is a vision or a guess. The danger of the mathematics is that it has a spurious look of accurate forecasting (and is therefore more difficult to abandon) when in fact it is only presenting clearer alternatives for a choice which must still be made. 'Only Gods know the future, only prophets foretell it, only fools predict it.' Some at least of the qualities of all-seeing Zeus are needed by the Olympian planners, and such qualities are not included in the Economics syllabus.

Yet even these advantages, bought at a high price, have their dangers. For the design of settlement will usually be forced to abandon the step-by-step path of growth and introduce, at a single leap, a whole cluster of changes. Mellor quotes a long passage from Dr. Richard Bradfield which so well describes this that it is worth quoting in full:

Under the heading 'Irrigation adds More than Water', Bradfield says: 'Both farmers and government planners often fail to realize that when you supply plenty of water to a soil-crop complex, you do more than merely add water; you change the effectiveness of every other factor in the system, and consequently, need to develop a new system of management. The varieties of crops grown before irrigation had probably been selected for generations for drought resistance. The farmers wanted a variety which would produce some food to feed his family even during a very dry year. The relatively rare years in which there was plenty of rain did not greatly concern him. He got a little 'bonus' during such years. But the drought resistant variety is seldom capable of making maximum use of the improved water supply. A new variety which will give the highest yields under the new moisture regime is needed. New cultural practices are also needed. With plenty of water the plant population can be increased. The rate of fertilization and possibly even the ratio of nutrients in the fertilizer will have to be changed. The weed problems will be different. New crop rotations which will use the land more efficiently become possible with a dependable water supply. This will call for changes in the traditional marketing system. The amount of water used will have to be properly regulated. Too much or too little will reduce net returns. Salinity may become a problem sometimes for the farmer, sometimes for his neighbors. This list of changes is incomplete but is sufficient to show that when you make abundant irrigation water available to a community, customs developed for generations must be changed. If maximum use is to be made with a minimum of costly mistakes, an experimental farm should be set up in the area, to work out the changes in soil and crop management needed five to ten years before the irrigation water is to become generally available.'[1]

Alas, it is seldom that the full range of changes is foreseen, and even more rare to find that farmers have been warned in good time and trained to meet them. In the huge resettlement of Ghana farmers, flooded out by the Volta River dam, an elaborate agricultural scheme was drawn up officially for the resettled families.

[1] Mellor, op. cit. The quotation is from Richard Bradfield, Presidential Address, Seventh International Congress of Soil Science, Madison, Wisconsin (1960).

Each farmer would have twelve acres and grow six crops (maize, cowpeas, groundnuts, tobacco, sweet potatoes and legume hay). Strips of each crop would run across several holdings, on the model of the Belgian *paysannat* experiments in the Congo, so that common mechanized cultivation and pest-control could be employed. Crops were to be sold co-operatively. The crop scheme made a very bad start. In the words of Dr. Lawson,[1] among the reasons for failure were, 'the farmers had no previous experience of the co-operative system'; there was 'inadequate publicity and extension service. Farmers had an almost complete lack of knowledge of the scheme or of the new system of agriculture which they were being told to adopt. They were, from the start, mostly reluctant participants'; and, finally, 'the reluctance of the farmers to change to a cash-crop economy and give up their partly subsistence agriculture which provides them with the security of adequate household food supplies. Farmers were not accustomed to managing incomes received entirely in cash.'

It may well seem strange that mistakes of this magnitude could still be made in the 1960s in schemes to which such volumes of pre-planning had been devoted. Yet the same happened in many of the (now curtailed) Tanzanian settlement schemes. Recently (1967) in visiting North-East Thailand, we saw the resettlement area for farmers flooded out by an expensive dam and irrigation scheme. They had had short warning; were moved on to dry land not commanded by the dam; were inadequately compensated for their lost houses, and they hated the government accordingly. Yet this was a scheme intended to show the government's concern for these farmers of the north-east. Strangely enough, some of them partly restored their position by becoming fishermen on the new lake—a coincidence with the Volta scheme just mentioned, where 'The only marked success has been among the fishermen; these have greatly increased their income from the prolific supplies of fish in the lake.'[2]

Certainly, things could be—and sometimes have been—better managed. But the constant difficulties and even failures of these 'clean sheet' schemes of multiple simultaneous change—and

---

[1] Rowena Lawson, 'The Volta Resettlement Scheme', in *African Affairs*, (Vol. 67, No. 267, April 1968). (Summarized from a paper to the African Studies Association seminar, School of Oriental and African Studies, September 1967.)
[2] Ibid.

examples by the dozen could be quoted from all over the world—are not wholly due to inexperienced or faulty planning. Certainly there is plenty of that; but the main trouble, even where much thought has been given, lies in the sheer degree of change suddenly imposed on a peasant community at a single blow.[1]

There are three main conclusions to be drawn from the experience of large schemes of rural 'transformation'. First, they are almost always very expensive, both in cash and in the use of administrative manpower, in the short run. If they absorb a high proportion of the available resources for the agricultural budget over several years, this can have a very bad effect on progress elsewhere.[2] For countries in a hurry, short-run gains, yielding additional income for reinvestment, are of high importance.

Second, they are socially extremely difficult. The quotation from Dr. Bradfield underlines the multiple adjustments needed when only one factor—water supply—is changed; and the whole burden of this chapter emphasizes not only the inter-relatedness of small changes but, even more, the *sequence*—that one change, successfully negotiated, opens the door to a second and a third. There are indeed occasions where radical change pays, often because the new situation makes irrelevant some of the traditional social restraints on progress—for example, where young settlers escape from the conservatism of fathers and elders; where a few volunteers pioneer successfully and attract others to their success; among refugees who are forced to adapt or perish; among people already somewhat acclimatized to change and cash economy, who carry their adaptability with them. At present these are special cases, not the rule.

Third, these large schemes seldom cover more than a small proportion of the national farming population, or even of those for whom improvement is urgently necessary. The problem of improvement within already settled areas remains the central one.

[1] Government enthusiasm may even add gratuitous difficulties. For example, in the Lomaivuna banana scheme in Fiji, the houses were deliberately scattered, to prevent or discourage the men from indulging in their best-loved social custom—long evenings spent together over the bowl of *Yaqona* (kava).

[2] In 1964–5 it appeared from Development Estimates in Uganda that over 40% of the current development budget for the country was devoted to schemes of tractorized Group Farming (not unlike the Volta scheme). See also Hal Mettrick, *Aid in Uganda—Agriculture* (London, Overseas Development Institute, 1967).

6

This caution about radical, large-scale transformation may seem discouraging, because the existing pattern of agriculture has been so difficult to alter in any dramatic way. But discouragement would be misplaced. There is increasing evidence that the potential of many existing areas is far higher than had been supposed, granted investment which is justifiable even by short-run considerations; that farmers will respond to new opportunities rightly presented; and that modern biological, chemical and mechanical technology has great gifts to give in the immediate future, even to the existing structure of peasant farming, and over very wide areas. Once again, the period over which intense modern thinking and adequate resources have been devoted to rural development is very short; the successes, here and there, have indeed been dramatic. Even overall figures of agricultural advance, running to 4% per annum, or even higher in many countries in recent years, are remarkable, and better than many now-developed countries have achieved in their growth period. They are not, indeed, high enough, because of the appalling rate of population growth: but it is this population factor which has prompted discouragement where there is really reason for great hope. It is indeed a general theme of this book that the whole approach to agricultural advance should be far more imaginative and ambitious, both for general reasons which I have already sketched and in particular areas. Small increases in productivity and earnings are not only inadequate to the times; they are ineffective in spreading change by demonstration, and in accumulating capital; and their timidity is often unnecessary. Let us look more closely at both potential and achievement.

In tropical areas the availability and the control of water is the outstanding technical factor: without water in the right place, in the right quantity, and at the right time, all agricultural choices are second best. In Asia a good deal has been done about this. Yet even in India and Pakistan, where most has been done on the largest scale, the unused potential is still enormous. The total irrigable area of India could be as much as 150 million acres out of the 300 million acres cultivated. At present the irrigated area is approximately 70 million (40 million from wells, tanks and minor sources, and 30 million from major schemes). It has risen from 50 million since 1950. Of the present irrigated area only about 30% is carrying more than one crop; the intensive agricultural programme is covering only 32½ million acres (1967)—a tenth of the cultivable area and less than half of the irrigated area. In East Pakistan, with its network of rivers and its enormous annual floods, only 30% of the cultivated area carries winter crops, mainly for lack of water. U.S.A.I.D.[1] reckon that there are 11 million acres which could be watered by lowlift pumps—4 million for winter rice (*boro*) and 7 million for other crops. The Third 5-Year Plan provides for only 750,000 acres of this to be used.

Although there are still several major schemes in the pipeline (for example, the new Tungabhadra River scheme in Northern Mysore, and the huge Rajasthan canal), a great deal of this potential in India lies in better use of surface and groundwater by small pumps and wells. The enormous increases of tubewells in the Pakistan Punjab, and Sind, and in the Gangetic plain of India is well known: about 8½ million acre-feet were added to supplies in the Pakistan Punjab in the last few years. This is very far from the end of that story. In Bihar, notoriously famine-prone, only 0·8 million acres were irrigated in 1950, 1·88 million acres in 1966, out of 21 million net crop-acres. The eventual plan is to irrigate nearly half the cultivated area. But there are many other areas in India where wells and pumps could contribute enormously —for example, even in the Deccan. Over large areas boring to 130 feet would supply assured water to small acreages; already the luckier farmers are getting water in quantity for several acres of irrigation at between 30 and 70 feet. A grid of such wells, controlled in numbers to prevent over-use of the groundwater supply, would make a major (not a marginal) contribution to farming incomes. It is almost normal for a successful well to pay for itself in increased output over three years. The difference in earnings as against a drought-resistant traditional crop grown with rain (and failing in bad drought years) and a high-yielding variety grown with assured irrigation is a difference between about Rs. 350 per acre and Rs. 1,000 or more on a single crop. If double-cropping is added, the differential is nearly doubled. For fancy crops, such as grapes in Andhra and Mysore, the cost of establishment, with well water, is about Rs. 30,000 per acre; the annual net profit is Rs. 10,000 to Rs. 15,000 per acre. Irrigation makes a poor man into a

[1] U.S.A.I.D., *Agriculture in Pakistan* (1966).

rich man—as one official remarked in Hyderabad, 'the spread of irrigation equals the spread of political power'.

There is one particular advantage in pump irrigation, in certain circumstances, as against the shallow flood irrigation in 'tanks' which is traditional in, for example, Madras and Mysore States, or for that matter in North-East Thailand. Evaporation is much lower—to spread shallow water under a tropical sun is a recipe for evaporation. Cultivable area flooded is far less. Supplies from below ground are likely to last quite well in a year of drought when surface 'tanks' are empty or only half-filled. There are immense social-administrative advantages. The well is where the farmer wants it—on his own land, under his own control. The perennial difficulties of distribution of canal irrigation through field channels and the administrative staff needed to solve them are avoided. Finally, the need for power for pumps has been a tremendous stimulant to rural electrification and a means of paying for it. Where electricity has come there is not only light in the villages but power for a host of small processing and even manufacturing purposes.

If we add together the acreages in India which are irrigated but not double-cropped and the acreages which could be covered by groundwater alone (bearing in mind the fact that with assured water high-yielding crops with fertilizer can be grown, whereas without it neither the variety nor half as much fertilizer can be used), this together mounts up to a potential which, even with current population growth, could make India an agricultural exporter within a decade or less. The same is true in Pakistan. The same will one day be true of the whole Mekong Basin.

In Tropical Africa nothing like the attention to water supply and control has been given, except in the Sudan. In the dry fringes of the Sahara and on the low-lying coastal belt of East Africa there are certainly problems. Yet in East Africa the water-potential of the Rufigi Basin in Tanzania is only starting to be tackled; very considerable quantities of water run to waste in Kenya during the rains; in Zambia the Kafue River is only now to be harnessed; there is still potential on the Niger. Although the vision of bringing dry land or desert into cultivation is the most beguiling, it is probably in the well-watered lands of Africa that the potential for improvement is bigger and certainly cheaper. Targets have too often been set at improving a single rain-fed crop, rather than at double- or treble-cropping. Income targets for individual farmers are set too low—a target net income of £10 per acre plus subsistence for a family on ten acres of good land would make an Indian laugh:[1] even £30 per acre would be very low in terms of modern yields which are being achieved widely by small farmers. The best cash-crops in Africa—coffee or tobacco, for example—can yield £70–120 per acre gross cash; and while these can only be grown in some areas, and possibly to a quota, hybrid maize and sorghum, cotton well grown, fruits, dairying, horticulture, beef cattle well managed, have great and unrealized potential. It is not so much lack of potential but lack of adequate ambition, intensity and investment (roads, water development, high-yielding varieties, short-term credit) which is holding down some parts of Africa to *per caput* incomes of £20 or £30 which should be rising to £60 or £100 in the favoured areas. Water conservation, control and utilization have a great deal to do with this.

Much has already been said of the new high-yielding crops which modern plant geneticists are providing so fast. But not all the benefit is for irrigated, highly fertilized production. A 90-day variety, with good drought-resistance, may vastly improve prospects in rain-fed areas liable to fluctuations in annual rainfall, giving a yield where a 130-day crop would fail completely. A castor-bean, developed in Hyderabad,[2] with a 125-day period, compared to 175 days for the older type, can enter a rotation which the older one could not. Fodder-crops are still capable of major improvement; cattle-feed from wastes is still poorly developed; as growers get higher yields per acre for main food-crops, so the chance to use less land for them and some for fodder becomes greater even on the three-acre or four-acre farm. At present considerable efforts on the animal breeding side, including Artificial Insemination Centres, are being largely wasted because the animal gets too little food to develop its genetic capacity. Even in a University cattle centre (Kerala) 10,000 gallon cows were giving 6,000–7,000 gallons for lack of proper feeding.

There is still surprising potential in improved agronomy. Long-established traditions are being challenged. Dr. Bradfield, for example, has questioned not only the value of 'puddling' paddy fields but the orthodox Japanese method of transplanting paddy as

---

[1] This is an actual proposal in East Africa not a flight of fancy.
[2] Produced as a chance mutation under radiation.

against broadcast sowing.[1] Even the belief, hallowed by tradition all over Asia, that a paddy field should be flooded and kept flooded is yielding to the knowledge—acquired long ago but not applied—that higher yields can be got with much less water, if it is controlled and timed correctly. In 1968 we heard a Divisional Commissioner in Mysore record that he had authorized the planting of a second crop (in 1967) despite the fact that water in the Krishnarajasagar reservoir could not suffice to flood the fields. The water was rationed to less than two-thirds of normal use: the crop was heavier.

Finally, despite the valid criticism of hasty and over-heavy mechanization, the use of power still holds a great reserve of possible progress. Human muscle on sun-baked or half-water-logged land will never create a high standard of living. The economic conditions, the conditions of tenure, the nature of soils, the design of equipment, will all need careful watching. But it does not need Olympian foresight to foretell that in twenty years the use of mechanical power on peasant land, especially perhaps in Asia, will have increased by several hundred per cent. It is strange to find in Africa the hesitant and often critical approach to animal power. The use of oxen is indeed growing, though very slowly, in Tropical Africa—sometime ago there were said to be over 10,000 plough oxen in the Eastern Province of Zambia.[2] There are special difficulties of tsetse fly and other endemic disease problems; but the ox has proved its value for some thousands of years in very varied conditions; perhaps there is some insularity in even so big a continent as Africa that it should be so coolly welcomed?

Still barely over the horizon, and as yet in Asia only, there are the first signs of an even more radical development. The monsoon is a bad master in India: it is preceded by killing heat in the plains, and monsoon work is carried out in high temperatures and humidities which are hard on man and beast. But the winter climate in Central and North India, Pakistan, the Philippines and for a shorter period in Thailand, is reliable and bracing. There is no danger of devastating floods. The sun is there, and the land is

[1] Richard Bradfield, 'Towards More and Better Food for the Filipino People and More Income for the Farmers', *Agricultural Development Council Paper* (December 1966). (Reprinted from Address to the Philippine Society of Agricultural Engineers, Manila, May 1966.)

[2] See George Kay, 'Agricultural Production in the Eastern Province of Zambia', in *Journal of Administration Overseas* (Vol. 5, No. 2, April 1966).

there: all that is needed is a reliable water supply. In East Pakistan there is already talk of making the winter food-crop the main crop, by lift-irrigation and water control. In the Philippines Dr. Bradfield[1] is convinced, and by trial, that the winter dry season is the ideal season for crop growth, if water is supplied. The poor area of North-East Thailand will have increasing irrigation in the winter season; there are large areas of Western Pakistan, and many parts of India, where the winter rains are doubtful, but the tube-wells still run.

The whole concept of an agriculture treating the winter *plus* irrigation as a major cropping season, with certainty of water and far better conditions of work; of treating the monsoon as the annual replenishment of rivers and groundwater, and good for a crop in lucky years—this looks forward to a time when the environment is really mastered, and when the insecurities of drought and flood become gradually marginal and not central to the peasant's security. It would mean adjustments—the pleasant season of marriages and visits would be curtailed; work would continue for more of the year and more mechanical aid would be needed to harvest quickly and to re-sow in good time. But the possible gain is enormous, both psychological and economic. Where it is possible, agriculture would at last begin to share some of the certainty of control which has long been the privilege of industry.

7

All this tempting potential will only become actual if it can be fitted both into the national economic capacity and translated into real profits on the individual farm. The larger national economic issues are considered in Chapter XI; it remains to look very briefly at a few of the implications at farm level.

The new farming is certainly more complex: so was the four-course rotation in England. It involves the farmer in a longer, more closely integrated pattern of farm management and one which runs over a period of two or usually more years. Double- or even treble-cropping involves rotations and an ingenious fitting of one crop period to water supply and to the preceding and following crops—the farmer can no longer follow the yearly repeated routines. Rotations and farm management in peasant agriculture

[1] *Agricultural Development Council Paper* (December 1966), op. cit.

have quite suddenly become a widespread and urgent concern. It is not that tradition did not include rotation: 'slash and burn' farming in Africa was geared to high fertility in the first year after burning, followed by a slow decline and an adjustment of crops until the time came to abandon the plot and burn again on a new one.[1] But now new crops, with new time periods, are coming in, and new combinations are necessary. The Deccan grape-grower can grow a vegetable crop after the first heavy water duty on the vines drops away. One small Government demonstration farm in Thailand[2] was showing an amazing variety of integrated and intensive cultivation—a paddy field, with a rattoon[3] crop of paddy growing in the irrigation ditch; egg plant on the top of the bunds; pigs, fed with the small crabs which infest the irrigation channels; mushrooms grown in a rice-straw compost pile; bananas on the boundary, and small intensive areas of Chinese cabbage and legume crops. On the larger scale rotations and variety need not be so complex, but they require new thought and knowledge.

In the narrow pursuit of food-grains in high-yielding varieties, the question of rotation in India has lagged somewhat behind: farmers cheerfully proposed to grow an apparently endless succession of hybrid maize on the same field. It is here that the Extension Service will have to play a far more active role. As an example of the work load, over 225,000 'farm plans' were prepared (partly for working plans, but also as the basis of credit applications) in the Tanjore District of Madras in 1967; the area covered was over 1,400,000 acres.[4] No doubt these plans were simple, indeed almost certainly over-simple. Possibly some would not have met with the approval of an economist or agronomist. But the great advance is that the peasant is learning to think of farm planning in a more conscious and purposeful way. His own farming skill and knowledge of his land, yard by yard, will soon enable him to plan better than most of his advisers. Africa too, in certain parts, has entered the farm planning epoch. Land consolidation, which is now an immense programme in Kenya

---

[1] See especially *The African Husbandmen* for examples mainly from Central Africa. The same is true wherever shifting cultivation is still practised.

[2] Agricultural Economics Department, Ministry of Agriculture, at the Chainat Dam.

[3] Where the plant sprouts again after the first harvesting and gives a second yield.

[4] *The Intensive Agricultural Development Programme in Thanjavur* (Madras Government, 1968).

particularly, is normally accompanied by a farm plan for the new consolidated holding; and most of the million acres (and more) of European land resettled by African smallholders has had a plan for each settler.

Professional economists would often criticize these plans, sometimes severely. No doubt both in India and Africa the subsistence emphasis has often led to excessive attention to staple foods, the export emphasis to traditional staple exports: one can see paddy grown where it should not be in India and food neglected in Malaya because rubber dominates. The answer lies in a greater output and a greater use of agricultural economists who can take an active part, with the Extension Service, in making rotations economically as well as agriculturally sound.

It is not that such micro-economic work has not been done: India is particularly rich in it and conducted a series of massive Farm Management surveys. It is that in the past the work has been too centralized and largely out of touch with the executive agencies of Extension. The situation is changing. Visits (1967-8) to Agricultural Universities or Colleges in Pakistan, India, Thailand, and earlier to Malaysia, and the Philippines have left a personal impression of extremely lively teams of young economists much more in touch with local field conditions and with government agencies. The same is true in some parts of Tropical Africa, where this work has accelerated notably in the last five years.

This work will be of high value both to the government Extension Services and to the Planning Departments, in bringing far more realism to the concept of the farm as a small business run by an often harassed man. It will certainly modify the over-simple assumptions about labour use, the costs and returns to purchased inputs, the constraints of time and equipment on sowing or harvest. The feed-back to government policy on such subjects as fertilizer prices in relation to yields of the new crops will be particularly useful.[1] It was widely stated in India (1968) that the

---

[1] Purchase of 1 kg. of ammonium sulphate costs 1 kg. of polished rice in Japan as against 5 kg. in Thailand. The net profit from application of nitrogen was ten times as high in the U.S.A. as in India (Mellor, op. cit.) There is no doubt that these relationships help to explain the enormous discrepancy in fertilizer use. Figures of total application of N, P and K in kgs. per hectare are given as Japan: 246; Holland: 204; U.K.: 53; India: 1·5. Margaret Haswell, *Economics of Development in Village India* (London, Routledge and Kegan Paul, 1967).

constant price-rise in farm inputs combined with vigorous government efforts to reduce food-grain prices was already beginning to endanger technical progress; the export levy on rice in Thailand is certainly distorting the farming pattern there; in contrast, prices well above the world level for maize in Kenya (1967–8) are both giving the farmers unrealistic margins and preventing the possibility of export of what is now a large surplus in good years.

Again, the possibility of substituting electric pumps for bullock-power in raising water depends very obviously on the unit cost of electricity, and Miss Haswell[1] has shown how accurately these varying costs are reflected in practice in different areas.

It is not necessary to continue these economic examples which, when stated, are painfully obvious. The remarkable fact is that they have been so recently stated, or at least so seldom observed in the actual practice of agricultural administration and in Planning overseas. Only a few years ago discussion raged on the issue whether African subsistence farmers were, in any full sense, 'economic men'. In the context of the full (Stage I) traditional system, this discussion had some point—although the most frequent conclusion was that even very simple people were more 'economic' than had often been assumed. In discussion of developing farm practice (Stage II), such discussion is not necessary: farmers have repeatedly proved as good or better economists than those who advise them—and not unnaturally: their life depends on it.

8

This chapter opened with a sketch of the stages through which agriculture passed in Europe and the peculiar difficulties of the small unit of management as methods become more complex and industrial. It suggests that the same changes towards added complexity and flexibility will have to be achieved by modern peasant economies, but by no means necessarily in the same order —an order at least partly decreed by historical factors, such as the

[1] Haswell, op. cit. There is no end to these examples. Two from Tanjore, with somewhat opposite implications, might be quoted. The cost of aerial crop-spraying there works out at about Rs. 10 per acre; knapsack spraying at Rs. 3 per acre. In contrast, tractor-ploughing in many local conditions in the same District is costed at Rs. 18 per acre as against Rs. 20 for bullock-ploughing. Enthusiasm either for or against 'modern methods' is meaningless in general terms.

comparative development of different branches of knowledge. When the actual process of change is put under the microscope, a maze of inter-relationships is revealed, which poses a seemingly impossible challenge to the innovator if all must be completed together. The answer to this is to avoid the unreal difficulties which this reading backwards is apt to create. The Darwinian evolutionary process, producing far more complex and fine systems, proceeded from simplicity by a constant sequence of viable[1] modifications, each of which opened possibilities of new adjustments *which were closed before*. The social process follows the same principle, though it can be both accelerated and controlled by conscious effort rather than chance mutation. It is, however, just the difficulty of achieving multiple *simultaneous* changes, instead of a chain reaction, which is apt to bedevil the major 'transformation' of agriculture which is implicit in many of the large-scale revolutions through investment and settlement which have been attempted.

Subject to these reservations, the technical potential for development is far higher than it was once fashionable to believe. If I have emphasized water control more heavily than any other factor, it is basically because sunlight, water, and nutrients are the three fundamental plant requirements. Sunlight is given, nutrients can be supplied if necessary from a bag—but cannot be used without water. The rest of the necessities—the usual list of seed, credit, transport, market—are indeed necessities; but the final *level* of success depends upon the production process. There is great potential in improved genetics, in revised agronomy, in mechanization, all of which have been briefly mentioned. But the final target is control of the environment, and here we can see on the far horizon the possibility of a critical strategic gain—twelve-month control of water.

The technical attention to agriculture has far outrun the detailed economic attention which has been given to the peasant farm, not as a sociological abstraction but as a one-man business. As this modern study progresses, we can hope to see far greater adaptation and realism in major policy towards the small farm and its needs. But neither technique nor economic policy will overcome the farmer's need for help as operator-manager. This implies organizations and institutions directly designed for his support.

[1] And unviable ones, with the penalty of death.

CHAPTER VI

STRUCTURE, TENURE, INSTITUTIONS

'The evolution of a different art of living and working together'—these are the simple words with which Herbert Frankel[1] sums up the process of development. They are not only shorter but contain more of the essential truth than an attempt to define and distinguish systematically the structure and institutions of society and the ways in which they facilitate or hinder development. Institutions are the channels through which social (including political) action flows. But the formal description of these institutions seldom describes very usefully the real nature of the action. The established art or style of how things get done in a society—for example, how appointments get made—may be through patronage or the loyalties of the extended family, clan or tribe; and this may continue to be the case even though there are formal institutions—such as a Public Service Commission—through which things appear to be done. We are concerned in this chapter with the existing structure of the agricultural economy, as seen in the size and shape of holdings; and with the institutions—such as forms of landownership, tenancy, private enterprise, Co-operatives—through which its business is done. But we are always concerned with the realities behind the formal institutions, the actual art of working together which has been achieved and the ways in which it may persist or change.

Earlier chapters have already laid much of the foundation for a modern approach to this subject. There are four points of special emphasis. The first is the need for new institutions which will give to the self-isolated village community a reliable and growing contact with the outside world—the market, technical knowledge, social and political support. The second is the concept of Stages—Stage I when society and its institutions and attitudes are primarily

[1] S. H. Frankel, *The Economic Impact on Under-developed Societies* (Oxford, Basil Blackwell, 1953).

traditional; Stage II, the transition, with the beginnings of modernizing institutions and techniques, but with continued reliance on much of the traditional framework; Stage III, the open market economy and the open political society with the institutions which they need. The coexistence of all three stages (or certainly of the first two) within a single country involves a careful adjustment of the effort to create new institutions locally, and will help to explain many of those cases which have much confused agricultural policy, where precisely the same institution succeeds in one place and fails in another, or fails in 1955 and succeeds in 1965 in the very same district.

Thirdly, we have also seen, in Chapter III, that the power situation at village and higher levels profoundly affects the growth of modernizing institutions. In this chapter we are bound to be concerned with the power of the individual landlord over tenants and the collective power of landowners in the political society; with the emergence of alternative types of power and leadership—through newly successful modern farmers, through group or co-operative action, and through the development of political forces in the rural economy which balance or overturn the traditional power-structure. New institutions, if they are not merely camouflage for the old system, will need either new leaders or a change of ways among the old ones; such changes are not too common, unless a change of interest runs with them.

Finally, technical change itself will certainly facilitate and may even require institutional change. Traditional society and its agricultural practices evolved over centuries into a total response to environment—it can be described as a marvellous system of security or as a vicious circle. Because it is a whole, it is very difficult to break into the closed circle of relationships simply by an institution which does not change the dominant technical environment round which the old system was built. It will be seen as an attempt to arrange unchanged old things in a new way. But a new high-yielding crop, new irrigation, settlement on new land, even a new market and a road to it may force society to recognize a new situation for which new social arrangements are both needed and possible. It is this functional relationship between a new technical opportunity and a new institution which can be critical. The attempt to install Co-operatives or Panchayats or Development Committees without first creating a new economic opening is heavily handicapped from the start. Society may pretend to use it, but it will only be dressing its old ways in new and ill-fitting clothes. We have seen in Chapter II that even an apparently rigid traditional society is capable of absorbing change; but it will only do so for good reason, to meet real changes in its needs and opportunities.

The possibilities and methods of technical advance differ greatly by local area and by timing, as we have seen. This will be just as true of attempts to change the structure of agricultural holdings and the organization and institutions which can be developed in support.

2 SIZE OF HOLDING

For once it is possible to state decisively that the fragmentation of a farmer's holding in several discontinuous plots is a deadly enemy of modernization. Land consolidation, however it is done, is essential sooner or later, and the considerable expense of achieving it must be faced. It can have additional benefits if it is associated with small-scale farm-planning: for the technical personnel necessary for consolidation can also be used for a second purpose—to give technical help in crops and methods. Equally, the practice in many parts of India and Pakistan by which tenants are constantly allocated different fields for cultivation is damaging. Shifting cultivation in traditional form, whether in Asia or Africa, though it may be the best solution in the given conditions of fertility and skills, implies that the conditions must be changed by investment and research or the area eventually abandoned for subsistence agriculture.

The question of the size of undivided, individually-worked holdings raises far more complex issues. The arguments on this issue are constantly masked by confusion as to aims—is the aim to maximize output per acre or output per man, the number of livelihoods which a square mile can provide or average income per head? Here quite clearly two major factors are variables—the type of agriculture which is possible on a certain stretch of land (intensive or extensive), and the density of population which that area is forced, for the time being, to sustain. These factors are in practice closely interrelated.

Because this is a complex problem, it will be easiest to illustrate it from a simple table, making firm assumptions about the type of land and the density of population. Let us assume, therefore, a stretch of agricultural land of good potential, and see the type of results which might be expected by farming it in various units. The area assumed is 600 acres (c. 1 square mile). The population is 1,000 people in 180 families.

Table 2

Alternative Uses of Land by Size of Holding

	No. of owners and holding	Gross output per acre (£)	Total gross output (£)	Labour*	Output per man (including family) (£)	Net** Reward to family (£)
A.	6 × 100 acres	30	18,000	30 plus 6 family	500	W / 6
B.	20 × 30 acres	35	21,000	40 plus 30 family	300	X / 20
C.	50 × 12 acres	40	24,000	50 plus 75 family	224	Y / 50
D.	150 × 4 acres	45	27,000	225 family	133	Z / 150

* Assuming A farmers each use 5 paid workers, B use 2, C use 1 and D none, and that B, C and D use 1½ equivalent adults of family labour averaged through the year, while A only works himself as manager.

** The family livelihoods provided are respectively in A 36 = 20% of all families; in B 50 = 28%; in C 100 = 55%; in D 150 = 83½%.

A further basic assumption of this Table is that more labour-intensive farming secures higher yields per acre, whatever its costs. This is in line with world averages, where, for example, the American yields of cereals per acre are lower than the British, which are in turn lower than the Dutch or Japanese. It is also borne out by the Farm Management Studies conducted by the

Government of India.[1] The question of investment per acre is, of course, especially relevant in developed countries; it is not analysed in this Table, but it is assumed that investment is higher in the large, mechanized farm; that it drops fairly abruptly on the thirty-acre farms and falls to a minimum on the four-acre holdings.

The table, however schematic, brings out certain relationships which are vital to the argument. First, it is assumed that total gross production rises with intensity of labour. This implies that we are considering an area in which small-holdings are modernized as far as possible; and this is in line with the general argument which is concerned with the *desirable* pattern of land-holding during this stage of modernization rather than with pure description of the present situation.

Next, production per man employed (including the owner or tenant) drops as holdings get smaller. There is a rapid drop from the 100-acre farm to the thirty-acre level—thereafter a more gradual fall. This fall would, of course, be partly balanced by the larger amount of capital employed on the larger farms.

It is when we look at the total social and economic effect of these patterns that the real significance emerges. It is assumed that this stretch of land (almost one square mile) is densely populated, say at 1,000 to the square mile, that is, about 180 families with an average of six members. The big farms would give a direct livelihood to only 20% of families. The twelve-acre farms would cover 55% of families, and the four-acre farms over 80%.

We cannot calculate what the net return per farming family would be without making unreal assumptions about such things as fixed and recurrent costs, rent, interest on capital. But since the total net return for the same total area is divided by 6 among the big farmers and by 150 among the small ones, the differential must be very large—perhaps £1,000 to the big men as a reward for capital and management; perhaps £100 to the small men as a reward for capital, management and their own and family labour.

Since there are only 180 families, it is obvious that there is no need to consider two-acre holdings—there would not be enough owners to go round.[2]

---

[1] See, for details, Morton Paglin, *American Economic Review* (Vol. LV, No. 4, September 1965).

[2] But in Comilla District population density is about 2,000 per square mile and average farm holding 1·7 acres.

Production per man, which is of course far highest in the big farm, is seen to be extremely misleading as a target in the circumstances of peasant societies. It is in any case a meaningless concept except when accompanied by a figure for production per £1 of capital employed—an automatic machine illustrates this. But it is meaningless in another, less technical sense—for in a given area *it neglects all the men in the area who are unemployed*, and whose production is zero. If there were indeed 180 heads of household in this square mile (of whom only 36 were employed on the big farms), and if no other occupation but agriculture were available, production per man *for the area* would be £18,000 ÷ 180 = £100. While, of course, there are some other occupations, on the average they would not cover more than 20% of householders, another 36 men, leaving 108 heads of family unemployed.

This is quite obviously a ridiculous result. An area with six big farms could only have such a population if about 60% of householders were employed in a town.

I have put in this *reductio ad absurdum* simply to drive home the point that the talk about larger units of production, or economies of scale, or raising productivity per man is all highly deceptive in large peasant areas of the world where alternative employment outside agriculture is available only to a small proportion of a dense population. In the densities which actually exist, and in the employment situation as it actually exists, smallholdings in these areas are inevitable for many years ahead. Only where we are dealing with an area of far lower density does any question of large, mechanized farming arise. At 300 population to the square mile (about 50 heads of family) and 20% non-farm employment, the large farms become at least a possibility. Most of the dry areas of tropical Africa fall far below this density; but their potential is often equally low.

This situation is only what is to be expected from history. The richer areas have attracted more dense settlement and have been subdivided into small-holdings; the dry or poorer areas have necessitated larger holdings for the merest subsistence, and therefore less dense population.[1] The point of increasing production per man is to increase it *on the existing size of holding* and *with*

---

[1] Except in very special and temporary cases where land is unobtainable in the rich area and population increases rapidly in the dry area near by—the case of some areas in Mysore has already been quoted.

the existing labour force, not to achieve an essentially false statistic by introducing more capital-intensive agriculture in larger holdings with less labour, which will show a higher output per man actually employed but will neglect the existence of massive unemployment. The point of introducing extra capital where there is high population pressure on land is either to enable the same number of men to produce more in a given time or to increase the marginal return to extra labour.

Part of the reason why this basic economic argument is constantly neglected is the deeply engrained belief of those who live in a developed economy that it must *always* be better to use a machine rather than a man, or indeed an ox. At labour costs of £60 per man per annum and a huge army of under-employed, this is simply not generally true;[1] it can only be made to seem true by costing only the isolated operation and pushing the consequent unemployment into a limbo of inconvenient facts which someone else must face.

A different and more valid argument as to size of holding relates to certain capital inputs which require a minimum area for economic operation. An obvious example is the pump or tubewell. The prejudice in favour of size at first favoured the larger pump units, notably in the earlier programmes for Pakistan. It has now been conclusively demonstrated, both on paper and on the ground, that much smaller units can be more economic in many areas (especially in East Pakistan).[2] Nevertheless, common use of a pump or well will still often be necessary where holdings are in the range of two to fifteen acres for normal basic crops, and it is here that co-operative common use can come into play without changing the unit of tenure. Water supply differs from the large tractor in that it can be made available simultaneously to many users; not until there is a better range of very small tractors or tillers will they become economic for small individual users; there are severe (but not total) limitations on contract services. It has at last been realized that the creation of better small tools and minor mechanical aids, economic for the smallholder, is a more sensible

[1] One model farm, worked by Japanese farmers in India with a high level of mechanization, was not showing any higher net profit than similar farms worked by Indians with ox-ploughs.
[2] See particularly Ghulam Mohammed, 'Development of Irrigated Agriculture in East Pakistan', in *The Pakistan Development Review* (Vol. VI, No. 3, Autumn 1966).

approach to productivity under small-holding conditions than an attempt to enlarge holdings to suit machinery designed for the larger farms of temperate, developed countries.[1]

It is only when the non-farm sector passes the 50% level that larger holdings and larger machinery become useful, as labour shortage begins to show itself in the farm areas. An argument on a somewhat different plane concerns managerial capacity and enterprise. It is said, and with some point, that the kind of man who can really develop a fifty-acre farm will be so responsive to technical advice and innovation, so much more willing and able to take risks and experiment, that an agricultural revolution must foster such men and provide opportunity for them. Although in theory twenty small-holders should achieve a higher output per acre, in practice they will be so security-conscious, so daunted by the risks of experiment, that innovation will not take place, or will take place far more slowly.

There is clearly an element of truth in this argument, especially in the early stages of modernization. But there are dozens of major examples where an improvement, once demonstrated successfully on the small scale, has run through whole communities of small-holders like a forest fire. Particularly has this been true of the introduction of a successful cash-crop, for example, African-grown coffee in East Africa. Certainly, demonstration is needed; quite possibly some insurance is needed even more. To give but one example of insurance, a highly successful scheme for replacing wheat production on sandy soils in Rajasthan by a rotation of wheat, maize and burseem, associated with cattle and poultry, was largely made possible by the provision of a small buffer stock of wheat in reserve, to protect the farmers against famine if the experiment did badly in the early years. The result was not only higher earnings but a progressive increase in land fertility which increased wheat yields as well.[2]

Thus the argument from managerial skill in support of a general argument for larger holdings is certainly unproven, since a

[1] However, there is some evidence from India that although the 'early adopters' are usually the men on larger farms, the yield per acre is higher on the smaller units.

[2] I am indebted to Mr. Tristram Beresford for this example. In Mexico a Church organization had similar success by guaranteeing a farmer his normal net income if he adopted practices which, if successful, would in fact raise it by 100% or more.

widespread increase of skill has quite frequently been generated among small-holders in the right conditions.

A reverse procedure, of actually *reducing* units of tenure, has, of course, been followed in some countries, both in the redistribution of old European farms in East Africa, and on a very wide scale in India and Pakistan by legislation prescribing maximum holdings, the surplus land being allocated to what are, in effect, lease-holders of Crown land, but with virtually freehold rights provided their payments are maintained. The experience in most of Kenya seems certain to result in higher total production except in certain areas where land suited only to extensive farming has been split into uneconomic units, and except for a serious (though possibly temporary) recession in some of the high quality livestock farming. In the Indian sub-continent, despite extremely widespread evasion of the Land Reform laws, fairly considerable acreages have passed into tenants' hands. With many local exceptions the effect has been to increase productivity, not only because the new holders are more enterprising now that they have secure tenure, but also because landlords have themselves decided to make their reduced holdings more productive, either by returning to manage them or by appointing managers with a development policy.

In effect, climate, soil, agricultural potential and social institutions have, through history, produced certain densities of population and average sizes of holding. In extreme cases of overcrowding, and during the continuance of high population growth there will of course be a case for extension of the cultivated area (where possible) and for deliberate creation of non-farm employment in order to relieve pressure, to prevent holdings from becoming even smaller, and to avoid the deterioration of the land itself which excessive pressure can cause. There will also be a case, where the size of holdings impedes technical advance, such as by irrigation, for forms of group-farming or co-operation. But in general the chief effort must be to increase production and incomes on existing small-holdings as the most direct route both to the relief of poverty and malnutrition and to the creation of non-farm employment generated by rising farm incomes. There may even be a case, under population pressure, for subdividing large units of land which is in itself capable of intensive production. In the less crowded areas, not only in Africa but also in India and

Pakistan, there is still room for striking increases in productivity and intensity of farming as expenditure on water and feeder roads and on research into crop and animal husbandry begins to make a deeper impact. These areas may make an increasing contribution to employment.

These technical, ecological, population and employment factors mainly point to a moderately varied pattern of size of holding, containing at least some units of larger size, even in fairly dense settlement, in order to gain any possible advantage from greater enterprise and to try out technical innovations, although it is not impossible to achieve these ends by Co-operative action in favourable social circumstances.[1] We must now turn to the social problems of ownership and tenure, which so largely influence the existing pattern as it is, and attempt to see what changes are politically feasible, and with what costs and benefits.

3 TENURE AND LAND REFORM

Forms of tenure present a more difficult issue, especially in Asia. It is true that in Africa tribal and traditional forms in some areas —particularly the most backward—do inhibit agricultural advance, especially by dispersal of plots. But they are beginning to yield fast in some countries to Land Consolidation, followed by freehold title to the consolidated farm. In general, tribal custom is a far less formidable obstacle than an established landlord-cum-moneylending system such as is traditional in much of Asia; it yields more easily to the evident benefits of modernization and it does not carry high level political support at the centre, which a landlord class can usually exert. Save for certain densely crowded patches—in Eastern Nigeria, round Lake Victoria, on the fertile slopes of Mount Kenya, Kilimanjaro or Elgon—shortage of resources in Africa has been not so much a shortage of sheer acreage but of tools, power, knowledge, infra-structure, water control and effective agricultural research to make use of available land resources or to develop them by investment; constraints have not been in the exploitation of landlords but in the poverty of

---

[1] The argument is, of course, greatly foreshortened for the purposes of this book. But it agrees with the main conclusions of the admirable and well documented discussion by K. L. Bachman and R. P. Christensen in Southworth and Johnston, op. cit.

capital and technique in face of soils and environment which, on average, are poorer and more hostile in Tropical Africa than in monsoon Asia.

In the present situation it is necessary to face squarely the fact that the very small cultivator, whether owner or tenant, whether in Africa or Asia, cannot radically improve his farming and his income without a great deal of help, whether direct to the individual or through Co-operatives, or by both means. In much of Asia the landlord/moneylender system in fact provided help, by the provision of some credit and some services and inputs, against a payment of 50% or more of the staple crop (not usually of subsidiary crops or earnings) according to the amount of help provided. There have been many and sometimes gross abuses of this system. It is criticized not merely on grounds of oppression, both financial and personal, but on grounds of lack of development. It is certainly possible to substitute Co-operatives or some form of bureaucratic help, an Extension Service, a Marketing Board, a plantation or processing company, a public Corporation, either alone or in combination: it is not possible to achieve major progress by abolishing the landlord—or indeed the customary tenure system of tribal areas in Africa or elsewhere—without a more efficient substitute.

There are three main approaches to the reform of a landlord system. The first is the Communist. There are certainly many who believe that a total political revolution is necessary, to sweep away the entrenched landlord power, before peasant agriculture can be emancipated and developed. If we leave aside what may well be the chief objection—the disorganization and bitterness of the process of revolution—there still remains the problem of effectiveness in development terms. For, after the clean sweep, agriculture must still be organized; and the nature of the substituted method, which puzzles non-Communist countries, has also puzzled Communists. That these problems have not been well solved in Russia may be significant, but it is not critical to this argument. The main point is that the destruction of landlords is only a part of the task; the larger part is in providing an effective alternative.

The second approach is by major Land Reform without total revolution. It may take the form of a total reallocation of land to cultivators, with some form of compensation to the old owners; of legal restriction of size of holding, with a distribution of land above the limit to cultivators; or simply of tenancy reform, designed to give the tenant total security if he pays a legally controlled rent.

The third method is vigorous and progressive taxation of land, which puts a heavy pressure on the larger proprietors to develop or quit.

All these non-Communist variations are subject to one major condition, and all have certain dangers. The condition is an effective political will for reform. How this will is generated and sustained becomes a critical issue; for a typical landlord society is naturally dominated by landlords, both centrally and locally. One means lies in the development of a strong industrial and commercial sector which can balance the landed interest in central government. Another is a political 'revolution', not always violent, leading to a reforming dictatorship or near-equivalent—there are many examples in Asia and Africa (Egypt, Pakistan, Iran). It has been the revolution of the Independence struggle, or its sequel, with its socialist aims, its need for mass mobilization, and its emphasis on development, which has resulted quite frequently in a reform of this type. In India it has been a combination of Gandhi at the peasant level, Nehru socialism at the intellectual level, and development philosophy at the Planning and administrative level, with some help from the modern sector, which resulted in the Land Reform programme. Both in Japan and in Taiwan, where Land Reform has been outstandingly successful, acute development needs (in Taiwan combined with a military dictatorship and American aid) have given the necessary power and follow-through. In the Philippines, where the political will was largely lacking, three Reforms, radical on paper, have had little effect in practice.

Political will at the centre may not be enough. Even a highly efficient Administration may not be able to give reality to the reforms at village level, where quite junior officials are faced by the determination and resourcefulness of a dominant landlord class and by the fear and insecurity of an illiterate and unorganized peasantry, fearful of losing the security of a bad system without cast-iron assurance of protection if they oppose it. There are many ways in which a big man can ruin a tenant who claims his rights too strongly.

It is here especially that the dangers of radical reform show. If the central legislation is full of loopholes which the landed interest has secured, not only will evasion be widespread or even almost universal: the processes of evasion are apt to work against the very group of small-holders which Reform was meant to help. In India and Pakistan, maximum holding laws are evaded by multiple registration of title within the family, and by claiming huge exemption under provisions excluding land in personal cultivation or orchard lands. But in this process tenants may suffer. In Maharashtra, after Land Reform, it is said that 1·7 million acres were repossessed by owners, depriving 101,000 tenants out of 150,000[1] of their tenancies; no doubt many tenants were re-engaged, but as labourers. Very small owners, and landless peasants who had relied in the past on leasing an acre or two from big owners, found it impossible. New settlers on land sequestered by the Act find that an overstrained or inefficient government is not able to give them even the vital small services of credit, supplies, protection which the landlord gave, however high his price;[2] for the landlord is a patron, a source of credit, a market, perhaps also a source of support in law-suits, and even a local police force for the small man. Land Reform is not simply a change in land tenure. It can sweep away a whole system of social relationships and social security, bad as it may be: something must be put in its place.

Clearly, even these partial, evaded reforms have a development effect. Some land from large estates is made available to the landless and worked more intensively; landlords work their own diminished land harder; absenteeism is reduced; new methods and even new capital come into agriculture, provided that reform coincides with a high demand and price for food supplies. It is not the medium-sized or large farmer who really suffers, but the smallest holders and the landless who need to rent, the dependants paid for services by a few bags of grain from the big man's fields. Only a small proportion benefit from new tenancies on sequestered land. Moreover, the administration is demoralized and even corrupted in some degree. It is hard to expect the small official to resist all the pressures—bribery, false witness, falsification of records, intimidation—which the local landlord can exert; it is

[1] Ram Joshi in Myron Weiner (ed.), *State Politics in India* (New Jersey, Princeton University Press, 1968).
[2] The Lower Indus Survey found that grantees of sequestered land had great difficulty, for lack of landlord services, including, for example, protection from wild animals. Some slipped back into a quasi-tenant relationship quite thankfully.

demoralizing to be administering legislation which is notoriously evaded with impunity.

These dangers suggest that if Land Reform cannot be made fully effective it may do more harm than good, at least in social terms. To be totally effective means political will and political power at the District level and below, so that central legislation is supported there. In democratic states there is machinery to evoke this—the Indian Panchayats are the largest example. Whether this machinery in fact works in support of the small men or the big is a question for later discussion: it is a critical issue for the success of Land Reform.

It is therefore the more necessary, in some circumstances, to look at less radical methods of achieving at least some results; and these circumstances will probably be in those societies where the tenant is still deeply held in dependent and traditional attitudes and where the political system at village level is not an effective guarantee of small men's rights. Taxation needs political will at the centre and effective administration locally; but it does not interfere so directly with social relationships. It will certainly exert a development pressure, and has arguments both from economics and from social justice behind it. It is a good deal easier for the small man to give a vote to a national party which supports it than to enforce newly granted tenant rights against a patron.

It may well be that a more modest programme of stiff taxation, combined with a programme of maximum holdings, which hits only the biggest and least justifiable estates, will be the best interim solution for many countries. First, it recognizes, for what it is worth, the development effort of the middle-sized entrepreneurial farmer—the dangers of this as a *general* policy have already been emphasized. In some countries this effect is already considerable. Hla Myint states that in India:

The most remarkable development has been the rise of commercial and even capitalist agriculture, with individual holdings ranging from 10 to 50 acres, employing wage-labour instead of family labour and using improved methods of cultivation and an increasing amount of capital. This type of farming now takes up about 65% of the total area under cultivation.[1]

---

[1] Myint, op. cit. The 8th Round of the All-India Social Survey found that 71% of all holdings were of less than 5 acres, but covered only 15½% of the total acreage.

This surprisingly high figure is enough to emphasize the importance of this middle sector. It is hardly necessary to repeat that there is the other side of this picture—the 35% of land held by small owners and tenants, and the growing group of landless. This commercial farming provides both a demonstration effect and a tax base; and the tax base should provide funds for services and aid to smaller men so that they can in fact benefit from the demonstration.

It is not in India alone that this middle-class farming is growing. The new high-yielding varieties, government subsidies on fertilizer and credit, new irrigation, have made commercial agriculture highly profitable in some places. In the Chao Phya delta in Thailand rich men are investing in land (and with deplorable tenancy conditions) because there is a killing to be made from these new opportunities. In Ankole (Uganda) a new ranching scheme is really only accessible to men with considerable initial capital. In Kenya highly paid civil servants and others are investing in high potential land wherever they can find it.[1] (President Nyerere has forbidden this in Tanzania.) Over a long period of time the Ghana cocoa industry was built up under a peculiar entrepreneur-tenancy system which has made many rich men.

In realistic terms, there are clearly some considerable benefits from this development. It springs from a basic fact that, in certain circumstances and with new techniques, agriculture can at present be highly profitable. The demonstration effect is not simply in new techniques; it is in this very rehabilitation of agriculture in prestige and profitability terms—a rehabilitation often vainly wished for by those who deplore the non-agricultural content of Primary education, which reflects a wish to escape to the towns, and the low social esteem of farmers.

It is also a reminder of the essential services which a modernizing 'landlord' can supply and which small cultivators must somehow obtain. Confirmation of this appeared recently, in a somewhat unexpected way, in the description of a scheme operated by a District Council in Lesotho for providing a tractor and threshing service to a tract of country cultivated by small, traditional farmers. After severe difficulties and failures, the following system at last brought success:[2]

---

[1] In Kenya these new landowners have been nicknamed 'Delameres'.
[2] Sandra Wallman, 'The Farmech Scheme—Basutoland (Lesotho)', in *African Affairs* (Vol. 67, No. 267, April 1968).

Farmech then arranged to share-crop with the tenants. . . . Farmech brought to the transaction seed and tractor power, the landholder brought his field and his labour in the hoeing and harvesting. The harvest whatever its size, would be divided equally between Farmech and the landholder. Farmech thus provided the landholder with credit, and shared with him the risk of loss. Because it increased the yield of the fields it serviced, the value of the project was demonstrated and local opposition virtually dissolved in the first season.

'Farmech' in fact became a landlord, though probably giving a far more limited service than a good landlord in India, who gives much more than this for his 50% of the crop.

There are three conditions which should be applied to the large commercial farmers. First, progressive taxation. Second, a very careful assessment of the effects on employment: profitable farming may create considerable indirect employment, to offset against the probable reduction in tenants or direct labour, but mainly if the profits are locally spent or invested and spent on services and consumer goods rather than gold ornaments. Third, the provision of opportunity to the vastly greater number of smaller farmers, so that they at least have a chance to share in the new techniques and profits. We thus return again to the organization for a substitute service, and to this issue the remainder of this chapter and most of Chapter VII are devoted.

4 CO-OPERATION

There is a huge literature on Co-operatives, to which it is unnecessary to add as far as general principles and methods are concerned. But the very contrast between their success in some circumstances and failure in others does suggest that their applicability in different stages of peasant society is still not fully understood.

Experience both in Africa and Asia suggests certain limited circumstances in which Co-operatives are highly likely to succeed. The first, on the productive side, is simply as a means of sharing an expensive facility—for example, a tubewell or a threshing machine. In this case, the purpose is clear and understood; the benefit is obvious, and the organization and overheads required can be of the simplest. There is great scope for this limited co-operative action in irrigation, transport, artificial insemination, storage, refrigeration, common use of threshing or decorticating or dairy machinery. Indeed, many such co-operative arrangements exist without the formal structure of a Co-operative, and it can be a serious mistake to insist on the forms and rules and paperwork of the formal Co-operative, at least until a growing organization makes them necessary.

A second case of fairly easy success lies in the relation between the growers of a cash-crop and a local processing factory—sugar, tea and many types of milling and canning are examples. Here again organization can be of the simplest, and both object and method are easily understood and clearly beneficial. A commercially run plant with clear arrangements with the growers may work just as well as a Co-operative.

In the realm of marketing, the most obvious case of success is where there is a single funnel through which products must pass, and this is most often true of export crops. Coffee, tea, cotton are examples in Africa; in many cases the crop never enters commercial trade channels until the point of export, moving from Primary Society through a Union to a Marketing Board. Where there is a single buyer, it is extremely easy to issue crop credits, deducted when the crop is delivered. Once marketing Co-operatives go outside this simple system, and particularly in the marketing of crops for internal consumption, where private traders are competing with them, there are great dangers of failure. The merchant, with a stub of pencil and the back of an envelope, knowing prices and market conditions by heart, is quicker, less burdened by overheads, more aggressive and more economical than the average Co-operative Secretary, who must show his accounts to his members, and who is burdened by instructions and resolutions, by the need for written records and public defence of his actions.

Yet another case for successful co-operative action is found where producers have an urgent need to combine against suspected exploitation. Buyers have many means of coercing peasant sellers —not merely by false weighing scales but by keeping the seller waiting expensively in town until he is forced to accept a lower price or cart his unsold produce back to the farm. It was an argument of this type, against the private cotton ginners, which started the successful Mwanza (Tanzania) cotton Co-operatives, now handling a gross turnover of over £20 million per annum from a peasant-grown crop.

These examples, based on simple technical advantage, a single market channel, or an urgent desire to combine against abuses, point by contrast to the likelihood of failure in other cases—cases where the Co-operative is in strong competition with merchants; cases where it is pressed or forced upon a peasant community without their invitation;[1] cases where the Co-operative is a government organization rather than a self-governing co-operant group;[2] cases where a Co-operative, initially successful on a simple scale, has grown over-ambitious in multipurpose activity, ending up as an Extension Service, a manufacturer, a Credit Bank, and a transport undertaking. In at least some of these functions a commercial firm is far more likely to work economically than the semi-trained staff of a voluntary organization. The examples point also to the danger of attempting a pure credit co-operative, where loans are not secured by automatic deduction from crop-purchase; where the conditions for credit are far less flexible than those of the moneylender, even if the rates of interest are lower; and where the margin is so small that the Co-operative accumulates funds extremely slowly.

All these difficulties have been evident in Asia and some in Africa. Indian and Pakistani Co-operatives, tightly attached to government departments, have often found themselves outbidden by merchants on the internal market; unable to lend for social expenditures (such as marriages) which give the moneylender half his business and are vital to peasant society at a certain stage; clumsy and burdened by committees and regulations; hampered by faction in commiteee rule; entering fields in which commercial management is more skilled. In Africa, where Co-operatives for export crops through monopoly channels have succeeded widely (though not invariably), the attempt to handle internal maize-marketing, to start consumer co-operatives in competition with the village store, to buy produce in competition with the market 'mammies' of West Africa, to run transport in competition with the one-man contractor, have very frequently come to grief.

It is useless to belabour the principle of co-operation with these failures, or with the cases of defaulting treasurers and corrupt

---

[1] It has been quite common in India and Pakistan to give Co-operatives a monopoly of fertilizer distribution, thus forcing growers to join.

[2] In some Kenya settlement schemes, settlers are automatically registered as Co-operative members when they enter their plot.

secretaries which constantly occur—in a corrupt society corruption will use any channel which comes to hand, and Co-operatives are no more (though no less) condemned by this than any other social institution. In the circumstances of small-holding peasant agriculture, the principle of co-operant action is in many instances the only escape from the closed circle of poverty. The point is to use it for clearcut, understood and fairly narrow purposes; to use extreme caution in extending it beyond them; above all to refrain from erecting Co-operation as an ideological cure-all for the inevitable difficulties of a distributive system operating on the narrowest of margins in a poor society and dealing with the gross fluctuations in output and demand which characterize agriculture, where production is at the mercy of the seasons and demand is fickle.

It is this ideological use of Co-operatives which has probably done most damage. 'Founded by farmers in the interests of farmers' is a Co-operative motto which is common in England. Government sponsored Co-operatives, used to exclude the growth of middlemen or capitalism, are usually not founded by farmers, nor do they always seem to be in the interests of farmers.[1] The whole morale and dynamic of Co-operation is thereby lost; Co-operatives are treated as another branch of bureaucracy, the secretaryship is just another job with opportunity for gains on the side, the Executive Committee is the usual clique of village bosses. This is not a new way of living and working together.

The fundamental value and function of Co-operatives, as an alternative to landlordism, is not to revolutionize the entire commercial system of an economy. Its organization and staffing is seldom good enough for any such ambitious task. Its value, in our context, is the far simpler one of organizing the *first* flow of production and marketing, because this flow is originating from tiny units, from producers with the slimmest resources, with no insurance, with no wide view of the market, with little or no capital, from ignorant and powerless people who need to combine for protection and for access to capital which is beyond their single means. Once this flow from 300 four-acre farms is collected together, is there any reason why its further handling in the market should be any different from the handling of produce from

[1] As a recent example, the Co-operatives in parts of Tanzania were offering 25*s.* a bag for maize which could be sold for 40*s.* to merchants.

a single 1,200-acre farm? Indeed, there are many occasions when the very success of co-operative ventures may be the reason to discontinue or limit the Co-operative. For by raising incomes, and knowledge, and capital reserves, this starting mechanism may have brought producers to the point where they can get better service through commercial channels. While small amounts of fertilizer or pesticides are used, the Co-operative or Extension Service may have to distribute them. Once the demand is trebled and quadrupled, the big fertilizer and chemical firms will quickly find an interest. Recently, in Thailand, an American Company[1] has had a very considerable success in combining sale of inputs and sale of produce in the corn market.

In India and Pakistan the semi-political troubles of Co-operatives loom larger. Thorner[2] quotes instance after instance where a single dominant family have captured the chairmanship of the Panchayat, the Co-operative, the processing factory and the political branch. Holding so many different threads of influence, they are virtually unassailable. Even where this is true, there is balance to be weighed. Not all the powerful are persistently wicked; quite a few, from mere self-interest, are energetic and efficient. Nor is power nearly so automatically self-perpetuating in modern India as it used to be. The political situation is much more fluid; high caste and economic power are not necessarily correlative, and village Panchayats in at least some areas have a growing self-confidence. Some of the younger educated men are taking over power from older village leaders, are using new elements to support their rise, and are committed to development. Even if their motives are self-interested and their methods sometimes questionable, a good innovation is taking place, and some of the benefit rubs off on the poorer citizens. This more encouraging situation is not yet typical; but society must use the sources of energy and leadership which it has, for want of better.

It is in this context that the work of Comilla Rural Academy (East Pakistan), under the leadership of Akhtar Hamid Khan, has made such a deep impression on those who have seen it. In an area of small-holdings, with nearly 2,000 population to the square mile, the Academy, in close collaboration with the District Admin-

[1] The California Company.
[2] Daniel Thorner, *Agricultural Co-operation in India* (Bombay, Asia Publishing House, 1964).

istration, has fostered the growth of a series of Co-operatives focused in a Union at the *Thana*[1] headquarters. The service given by the Union is simple—by 1967 a rice-mill, storage and marketing of rice; a cold-store for seed potatoes; a dairy unit; classes for women; a small tractor service; regular training and information on agricultural methods by the Academy and the Extension Service in complete collaboration; research on local farm economics at the Academy. There are a number of associated non-agricultural Co-operatives, such as those for pottery-makers, rickshaw-pullers, and brick-makers.

There are four vital principles which guide this work. First, frequent meetings of *all* members of the village Co-operative, designed to ensure that management does not fall into the hands of the usual small committee of magnates—the model is an extreme Athenian face-to-face democracy. Second, the choice of leadership. Each Primary has not only a Chairman, who may well be a magnate, but also a manager, and the latter is a youngish energetic farmer, who is paid a very small sum for his services, with an incentive element for successful results, and is available on the spot in the village to assist all members. In fact, because the magnate is often too busy and has other interests, the manager often plays a dominant role. Third, regular training. The managers come into the Academy once a week for training, and this is kept up over long periods. Fourth, concern not only for farmers but for the whole family and the whole community: the women's programme, started with some difficulty in a Muslim society observing *purdah*, has been particularly energetic;[2] and the peripheral Co-operatives, such as the brick factory and the rickshaw group, recognize the importance of non-farm occupations and earnings. There is little danger of a split between increasingly prosperous farmers and the more dependent groups of craftsmen and services.

One might add two other factors of great use—the small-scale locally-based research on social and economic conditions carried out by a young graduate teaching staff in the Academy; and the common training courses for members of different departments—Agriculture, Community Development, Revenue Service and

[1] 'Thana' = originally a police division. Population about 100,000 to 150,000, in 10–15 square miles, very closely approximating the Indian 'Block'.

[2] And has incidentally modified the *purdah* rules a great deal.

others—which help to ensure that all agencies in direct contact with the life of the *Thana* are co-ordinated.

From the records of shares and savings in the Co-operative headquarters, it is possible to issue credit to any member within forty-eight hours of the application. Recovery of loans is effected by deduction at the time of crop-purchase. Considerable savings accounts are being accumulated.

There are two points of special administrative interest. First, the Primary Co-operatives at Comilla are based on small villages where 100% face-to-face management by all members is possible. In contrast a good deal of impressive progress has been made in Mymensingh District (also East Pakistan), based on the local Basic Democracy unit, that is a group of roughly ten villages. It can be argued in favour of the Mymensingh system that the village is too small a community, rent by too intimate factions and jealousies; that the group of villages lessens this danger, and that the use of the Basic Democracy unit marries the political with the economic, strengthening the new political system by giving it practical tasks. It can be argued on behalf of the Comilla system that the Basic Democracy Union falls between two stools—neither small enough for immediacy of personal participation of villagers, nor big enough to command adequate resources, which at Comilla are supplied from the *Thana*.

Second, the focus of education and economic services at *Thana* level at Comilla—that is within about seven to eight miles of the most distant part of the area—is certainly more effective than a focus at the more remote District; India is also delegating to the 'Block' level, though perhaps not enough.

It may seem extravagant in a book of this wide range and generality to devote pages to a single small scheme. But Comilla is being used as a pilot scheme from which far more widespread development can be started in East Pakistan. And it is from the detailed thinking about the dynamics of life and organization at this very lowest level that some real insight and progress can be made. It is a main thesis of this book that policy must arise from the most local of local analysis. Most of the factors upon which the success of local structural change depend emerge from this single study—leadership, management, training, research, practical and accessible economic services, co-ordination of government advice. Although it is always dangerous to generalize from an experiment which owes so much to the personality of its originator, the Comilla experiment does appear to have thrown up principles and methods which could be applied over a great range of densely settled peasant economies, without requiring a genius to run each unit; it is the first step which counts.

5 CREDIT

The need for credit is apt to be over-generalized. De Wilde[1] has most usefully pointed out that much of the development in Tropical Africa has been carried out with surprisingly little or even no official credit. He estimates that not much more than £1·1 million of official credit was issued between 1948 and 1964 to African agriculture in Kenya for an increase of production of over £10 million; and that in Nyeri District most coffee planting was self-financed. Although credit was needed for the tubewell revolution in West Pakistan, relatively little came through official channels: family borrowing among middle-level farmers accounted for most of it.[2] Obviously, the best source of capital is from the surplus of successful farming, and it is far less likely to be wasted; people handle their own profits with economy and care. Moreover, successful people become credit-worthy people quite quickly, and commercial suppliers are happy to give them credit without elaborate government schemes. De Wilde points out that official credit may be most necessary when a successful farmer is moving on to a more expensive investment which is beyond his current means, and that it is probably the easiest form of credit to give and the most successful.

Far more difficult is the use of credit to hasten the breakthrough from partially subsistence to mainly cash farming. Credit for seed and fertilizer between sowing and harvest, given by the first purchaser of the crop, is widely established in peasant countries, and has been for centuries in some of them. It can be, as usually in Asia, from landlord to tenant. Where this relationship does not

[1] de Wilde, op. cit.
[2] The All-India Credit survey (Reserve Bank of India, Bombay, 1955) and surveys carried out in the Lower Indus Basin, confirm the very high proportion of credit (over 80%) which came from friends, family and other non-official sources. The sample survey of credit sources (Central Statistical Office, Pakistan 2nd Plan) gave an even higher proportion—92·5% in West Pakistan. Surveys in East Africa show the same type of result.

exist, as in so much of Tropical Africa, it is likely to have to come through a Co-operative or through a firm, such as the Tobacco Company which finances out-growers during the crop season, or through a crop Marketing Board. But trouble arises where the creditor does not buy the crop; and it might be said that in the very early stages of development from subsistence the rule that the creditor should buy the crop is vital. There are too many needs in peasant life which may be felt as more urgent than debt-repayment, once the peasant has the full cash payment for his harvest in his hand.

For this reason, securing of debt on land at the small peasant level is usually either ineffective or dangerous. There are too many reasons why repayment may be impossible. If the moneylender is the creditor, default may mean the loss of land or freedom; if the government, or Co-operative, is the creditor, it will either shirk taking possession of the land (which makes the security ineffective) or incur so much ill-will as to endanger its whole relationship with farmers. It was alarming to hear African Extension Officers recommending land consolidation 'because then you will have a title to land and can borrow on its security'. The *taccavi* system in India—loans granted by the District Administration on the security of land—has indeed worked fairly well. But it is based on a great deal of detailed knowledge of the farmer's credit-worthiness and the high reputation and efficiency of the Indian Administrative Service. In most States it has mainly been used to tide over emergencies (drought or typhoon) and in such cases very little recovery is in fact expected; it is essentially relief.

The second difficulty comes in areas where agriculture cannot be protected, by irrigation or otherwise, against the hazards of drought or other natural catastrophe. Here again, the building up of insurance and protection, even if it is not complete, may have to come before any widespread development of credit systems. Natural hazards are bound to mean loss, and there is no reason why the creditor should not share at least some of the loss with the cultivator, if he knows the risk and charges for it. Moneylenders may do this at 'exorbitant' rates; official institutions, lending at socially acceptable rates, will lose a great deal of money.

A third difficulty arises where the cultivator has too little land to support himself in food *and* grow a cash-crop. It is suggested sometimes that in these circumstances some agency should give him a subsistence credit until the cash-crop matures. The extreme cases of this system are apt to be in settlement schemes with a slow-maturing cash-crop. In Malaya the major schemes based on rubber with a subsidiary crop of fruit involved subsistence payments to the settler (in some degree against work done in initial clearance, planting and weeding; but to a large degree for subsistence, against future repayment) which may have to be continued for at least three or four years (when his subsidiary crop may come into bearing), while he is waiting the six or seven years for the young rubber to come to tapping age. The West Nigeria settlements were also involved in long subsistence payments, accumulating a debt of £2,000 or more which the young settler is supposed to pay off from eventual profits. This sum is so big as to be simply beyond the imagination of most young African farmers. Some of the Tanzanian pilot settlements also burdened the settler with £600 or more of debts for clearance, services, subsistence and other charges. Such schemes need extremely careful design and management (which has in fact been given in Malaysia); and probably require large-scale units which can carry quite a large administrative and supervisory overhead. On the small scale they can be very expensive and inflationary, and frequently end up in writing off very large sums of money. Moreover, the attempt to recover costs breeds hostility between the Settlement Board or Authority and the tenants, with many evil consequences, especially where the Extension Service is used as a debt collector.

The real criticisms of some of these schemes are two. First, in many cases they are an awkward compromise between a plantation and a settlement: the settlement element arises from promises of land to the landless or overcrowded. The Malayan schemes in many cases were simply opening up new forest areas to rubber, which could most naturally have been done by major companies. The Muhuroni Sugar Scheme in Kenya is equally a sugar plantation in fact, but notionally divided into small-holdings, on which the 'tenant' can be absentee and contract to have his weeding done by the overall management.

Second, some schemes have attempted a complete jump from subsistence to pure cash farming, with credit for subsistence bridging the gap between the two. This is a false use of credit, and another example of telescoping: for the farmer needs to move gradually, and not in one bound from growing his food to growing pure cash-crops. The experience of the Shell experiment at Borgo a Mozzano would show how important the *sequence* of steps is to the final commercial economy.

There remains the awkward issue of credit for social expenditure. The plain fact is that it should not be given as such. A formal advance of capital is supposed to be against an expectation of profit from its investment. There is no financial return on an expensive marriage, at least in the short run. This is the attitude of official organizations, and this is why the poor Indian peasant will go to the moneylender rather than to the bank or the Co-operative when he wants cash for this purpose. The moneylender will lend precisely because the capital is *not* likely to be repaid; high and compound interest can be squeezed out for years, ending perhaps in a foreclosure on two valuable acres. No doubt peasants will continue to mortgage their future for many more years in this way. The only contribution which formal credit can make to this gloomy prospect is by meeting the farmer's other, agricultural needs, in the hope that this will rapidly improve his cash income and enable him to finance his social costs out of profit. The answer lies in savings. Savings clubs of various descriptions, analogous to the Funeral Clubs of 19th-century England or the West African *esusu*[1] societies and their counterparts in Asia provide a temporary improvement. Successful Co-operatives can run a savings scheme by encouraging the farmer, when his crop is sold at harvest, to put some of the receipts to a savings account. One local Rajah in Orissa ran a highly successful savings scheme on his own initiative, by selling tokens for very small amounts.

In the nature of things, small credits to a mass of small farmers in often inaccessible sites are expensive; some subsidy to the administrative costs may well be needed, with a rate of interest which can seldom fall below 9% and may well be 12%. When amounts are small (£20–£50) and duration short (the growing season), the interest rate is not too important to the farmer, and it is in any case lower than the moneylender's rate. Supervised credit, given partly in kind, secured against crop proceeds, should present few difficulties. Crop failure from natural catastrophes (drought, flood) can be dealt with by conversion of the loan to a

[1] A system by which all members pay a regular contribution and each member in turn takes out the whole fund when a major need for cash arises.

two- or three-year repayment period, as is frequently done in India.

The long-term transition which development should bring is to a situation where the farmer can buy his smaller inputs from the local store, on normal commercial credit; his stock or equipment on longer credit terms; his capital improvements by borrowing against assets from the bank. In passing, this does not imply the necessity of a 'capitalist' system—store, tractor-factory, bank can be Co-operative or State-owned if ideology so prefers. In making the interim arrangement which a traditional or transitional society needs, this longer objective must be held in mind. By so doing, there is less likelihood either of prematurely attempting the final form or of freezing transitional arrangements as though they were final.

6 MARKETING

In those parts of peasant economies which are most traditional and nearest to pure subsistence, the market for food-crops is not a major factor. If food prices are high, this may be seen as a disadvantage by those who need to supplement subsistence by even small purchases;[1] share-croppers are protected by payment in kind, and not much concerned if their share of the amount of grain could be priced high or low in monetary terms. But very large sections of peasant cultivation are now involved in world commodity trade, in the rather partial sense outlined in Chapter IV, and the prices for groundnuts, palm fruit, coffee or cotton offered by the buying agent are important to them. They are not much concerned with the destination of their produce, whether it is to travel fifty miles or 5,000 to the point of consumption. They are primarily concerned with the market in a concrete physical sense —the place where buyers and sellers meet—or in the personal sense—the company buying-agent or merchant or Co-operative in direct contact with them.

In the next stages of modernization the physical market place seems to play a major part, but it is mainly handling the small change of agricultural life—the exchange of subsidiary specialities (a few cabbages, some beans, spices, fruit, eggs—often crops

[1] See Darling, op. cit. The poorest farmers said, 'What are prices to us? We have to fill our bellies'.

grown by women for pin money) against minor groceries, utensils, trinkets, cloth. The staple crop may be handled either by sharecropping or (particularly with export crops) by special buyers, often buying at the farm gate. In very general terms, modernization and development will tend to increase the importance of these bulk buying arrangements and decrease that of the market place for food which itself becomes more specialized—the vegetables come from horticulturalists, the food is packaged; on the other hand, the range of non-agricultural goods in the market is wider and more sophisticated, purchased by the cash from the main crop, not from the few cabbages. In some cases—for example, in West Africa (Kumasi in Ghana or Onitsha in Nigeria), these second-stage markets may become enormous. But this represents a certain freezing of the development process, as well as a vast congestion of transport. The modern merchant with a telephone, dealing in even more specialized articles of modern trade, buys through intermediaries for scattered customers. Agricultural products go off to special destinations—the grain to a mill, the vegetables crated for a distant town, the milk to a processing plant. The 'market' becomes a consumer's shopping and service centre in a modern town.

Thus in some degree the requirements and institutions needed for marketing change as the process of specialization grows. In the early stages the first necessity of marketing is a physical market which the seller can reach quickly and cheaply with produce, and a very local buying agent for major crops. In physical terms this mainly requires feeder roads and better transport. The second necessity is storage, to even out prices between harvest gluts and later shortages. The third necessity if the market is to grow in size and specialization, is information and a skilled intermediary between local production and the wider pattern of demand. Because this third step is the most controversial and difficult, it has attracted most attention; it will be considered below. But in the early stages of agricultural growth and diversification the physical factors of access and storage are crucial. Margaret Haswell[1] has pointed out that in South India eleven kilometres is the maximum limit for ox-drawn transport to a market, and quotes the relationship between the price of grain to the producer and the distance from the market:

[1] *Economics of Development in Village India.*

Village	Paddy Price Index (Highest = 100)
Dusi	100
Eruvellipet	90
Palakkurichi	75
Gangaikondan	64
Vadamalaipuram	34

The market distance from Dusi is seven kilometres on good roads; from Palakkurichi, twelve kilometres on rough roads; from Vadamalaipuram, over sixteen kilometres on rough roads. Detailed studies, for example by the British Road Research Laboratory in Sabah,[1] and in various other areas, including the 'Friendship Highway' in Thailand by the Brookings Institution,[2] have shown how direct is the relationship between highway investment and the growth of cash-crop agriculture, although the road will normally be a necessary rather than a sufficient condition for this growth.

The fact that cheap and pest-proof storage of food-crops has in many parts of the world defeated efforts at solution can only indicate inadequate input of scientific effort. Considering the range of construction and container materials and the range of chemical controls, this problem cannot be insoluble. One of the biggest scandals in India is the loss of grain from government go-downs, which is even more serious than losses after harvest on the farm—if your bin contains the family's food supply you will guard it carefully.[3] Storage and transport together are of high importance, especially where climatic factors have the greatest influence on output. De Wilde remarks of Africa: 'Since surpluses and deficiencies largely depend on climatic factors, they seldom coincide in point of time',[4]—a fact which makes for wide fluctuations in cash prices and confirms the farmer in his preference for growing food rather than cash-crops. In these circumstances the market is marginal and highly unstable. Storage and better roads help both

---

[1] R. S. P. Bonney, *Relationship between Road Building and Economic and Social Development in Sabah* (Ministry of Transport, Road Research Laboratory, 1964).

[2] G. W. Wilson, B. K. Bergman, L. V. Hirsch and M. S. Klein, *The Impact of Highway Investment on Development* (Brookings Institution, Washington, 1966).

[3] There are heavy losses on the farm before harvest, from field rats.

[4] de Wilde, op. cit.

to even out fluctuations and to spread the market over wider climatic and production zones. For surpluses and deficiencies, in rain-fed agriculture and with poor roads, do often coincide in point of time, but they may be fifty miles apart.

Let us turn now from physical to institutional factors. The unique and central problem of peasant economies does not lie in developing a wholly original system of trade and marketing, once produce has reached a certain bulk in a centre with good communications. Its uniqueness lies in the small size of the original producing unit, bad communications and the lack of diversification of product and demand. The other peculiarities of agricultural produce in *any* economy lie in its perishability, the long cycle of production leading to inflexibility of supply, and its dependence on climatic factors. These other factors may require major manipulation of the market at national level, by systems of guaranteed price, or subsidy, with which the developed world is familiar, and for which blueprints of all types are available. It is, at the present time, the first link in the marketing chain which is critical in peasant societies, and it is for this reason that road access, storage and co-operative representation of small growers have been emphasized here.

Once farm produce has reached a major local market, a most complicated process of distributing it follows. With increased specialization, some will be sold back to other local farm producers; some will be sold on to a major urban market; some may go into an export channel; some may go to a processing factory; some may be held against anticipated improvement in price. Provided that the first seller of produce from very small units is representing the grower's interests—some form of Co-operative—and provided that this seller can compete effectively with the merchant buying direct from these small units, it is difficult to believe that any bureaucratic or institutionalized marketing system which a developing country is likely to be able to administer will be more effective than the private merchant in the further stages of marketing, except possibly in handling a major export crop.

India and Pakistan and West Africa are fortunate to have a massive corps of skilful indigenous traders. East and (to a lesser degree) Central Africa have benefited greatly from immigrant traders who have performed the intermediary and wholesaleing function. The whole of South-East Asia has benefited from the overseas Chinese traders,[1] though some countries have spent much effort in trying to expel them: Burma had both Indians and Chinese merchants who played a vital part in specialized trades; but in many spheres, and especially in the buying of the vital rice crop, they have been displaced and Army officers put in their place. For any country in Africa or Asia to neglect this resource of commercial skill in pursuit of a bureaucratic distributive system for ideological or racial reasons could well set back the progress of agricultural modernization for years. Marketing Boards can be efficient; but their innate tendency is to raise their overheads to levels too near to those of developed countries, and out of scale with the value of the crop and the poverty of the growers, and also to set aside large sums for price stabilization or for investment outside agriculture.[2] The result is a margin of as much as 50% between payment to growers and the market price, with extremely discouraging effects on production.

In the first two stages of market development we have emphasized roads and storage, bulking of produce from weak individual growers, probably by Co-operative means, and a commercial distributive system to handle the next stage of the marketing process, with exceptions, particularly in export crops, where a central marketing board, properly controlled, or a major company may do as well or better. We have also recognized the peculiar conditions affecting agricultural crops (climatic fluctuations, inflexibility of supply) in any economy, which may require national action for insurance or stabilization. It remains to consider how this system can go forward to a third stage, involving a much higher degree of specialization in both production and distribution.

On the grower's side this involves higher specialization in the crop grown, far closer attention to market requirements, and an endeavour, either through Co-operation or by commercial partnership, to add more value to the crop by processing, or packaging. Some of the success of the Casa del Mezzogiorno in the development of South Italy lay in bottling wine or olives rather than selling the year's produce of vineyard or olive grove in bulk. The

---

[1] See Matooka, op. cit. 'The commercialization of rice production on the mainland of S.E. Asia and of cash-crops in the islands could not have been accomplished without the activities of the overseas Chinese.'

[2] See particularly the writings of Peter Bauer for West African Marketing Boards, and Cyril Ehrlich, David Walker and Walter Elkan for East Africa.

little bottle of olives on the supermarket shelf represents a fantastic price per olive compared with the price a bulk purchaser will give. The grower selling for this type of market has to observe far more stringent standards of size, ripeness, constancy of supply, superficial appearance—Australians only get really beautiful apples when an export consignment has to be sold domestically. It is said that Kenya recently lost a major contract for tomato-canning because the Company needed a standard product and a constant flow which a mass of smallholders could not meet.

Thus one requisite for expanding the market still further is not a problem of institutions but of agricultural standards. But there remains the search for a skilled intermediary, who identifies the possible market and turns to agriculture for supply. It is no discourtesy to officials to suggest that they are seldom skilled at this art; their training and experience is not directed to it. To find new markets requires both a high degree of imagination and a great practical business skill. How does a man with a single lorry in a small Perthshire town build up a fleet of heavy road transporters carrying fish from the landing stage in Aberdeen to Florence and Rome?[1] Not many officials, or even economists, would have envisaged this venture, and fewer still would have carried it through successfully.

A good number of developing countries have real difficulty in finding and developing such skills. Manpower surveys seldom take much account of them; educational planning usually does not allow for them. They are usually caught from the atmosphere of a trading economy rather than taught in schools. Not only is their origin thus somewhat mysterious to the official mind but—worse still—their existence is often mildly or violently resented: trade and marketing have always been the Achilles heel of socialist planning. It is, I think, for this reason that so many developing countries are apt to reach a platform after quite a satisfactory and rapid rise from traditional to transitional production and marketing arrangements. A few substantial export crops (for which a world market is long established) are adequately handled; small-scale markets for subsidiary production are developed and become saturated; a few processing companies—sugar mills, tea factories, tobacco factories—get established, and then there is a halt. The

[1] An example from one of the 'Down Your Way' programmes of the B.B.C. (September 1968).

rise of the cotton, coffee and sugar industries in Uganda illustrates this: there was an enormous social and economic change between 1910 and 1939, with the still existing record for cotton production in 1938; but the next thirty years from 1939 to 1969 seem to show a loss of momentum.

The next stage will demand a peculiar combination of much increased skill in the growers and imaginative enterprise in marketing—the transition from selling in an Onitsha-type market to selling processed and packaged goods, with a high value added, to modern consumer markets. If it is hard to know how to create these marketing skills, at least they need not be discouraged and persecuted.

CHAPTER VII

CONTACT WITH THE FARMER

The choice of agency for making effective and helpful contact with the farmer clearly depends directly on his situation and attitudes, and many of the criteria used in the previous three chapters will apply. There are in fact more tools to hand than is always remembered. Apart from a government Extension Service and Co-operatives, which are most commonly discussed, there is the possible role of an Agricultural Development Corporation; of private merchants and suppliers; of elected Committees of various kinds (Panchayats, Local Government Councils, Farmers' Associations); of Party cells and activists; of the whole District Administration regarded as a development agency. There is also a great range of methods for contact and training. The purpose of this chapter is not to describe some preferred tool or ideal method, but to discuss which combination is likely to be suited to different situations—situations affecting not only the farmer but the government itself, which will be limited by its resources of finance and manpower and by commitment to political ideals and methods.

Certainly the Extension Service is the obvious focus for discussion, because it is a necessary tool in almost every situation. But this statement is far from implying that it can or should be the spearhead in all situations, and it says nothing about the many forms which Extension can take. It is naturally tempting to fix upon the almost universal weakness of this Service in developing countries as the prime cause of delay in agricultural progress. Over huge areas it is indeed too thin on the ground, poorly equipped, meanly financed, and sometimes badly trained. It is easy to point out that one junior officer, with a bicycle which he must buy himself, sketchily trained, supposed to cover 1,500 or 2,000 farmers spread over thirty to fifty square miles,[1] is not going to make

---

[1] For example, density of population: 300 to sq. mile = 50 families of 6 members = 40 farming and 10 non-farming families per sq. mile = 2,000 farming families to 50 sq. miles.

much impact. This situation is readily compared with that in developed countries, where one better trained Extension Officer with his own transport deals with only 500 or even 250 literate farmers, with the support of an active private sector, and a vigorous trade Press. Perhaps more relevantly, it can be compared, within developing countries, to the deployment of a far heavier Extension force on particular schemes in which the Government is deeply interested—1 Officer to 250 farmers in the Sudan Gezira, or even 1 Graduate Officer to as few as 100 settlers in some experimental settlement scheme.[1] If this strength is needed in areas carefully chosen for development, often with considerable pre-investment and careful farm-planning, it could plausibly be argued that a 1:2,000 ratio over the country as a whole is so thin as to be totally ineffective. In that case, the very considerable funds needed to maintain and administer it would be largely wasted.

The argument is particularly tempting because the means to remedy those 'weaknesses' are straightforward. More training, a bigger output of Extension staff, better equipment and transport, more active research related to real field problems and effectively transmitted—all these are simple recommendations, and indeed they have considerable validity. For unquestionably agricultural development did not get its fair share of finance and attention in the early years of Independence, when industrialization was the favourite child.

Nevertheless, if the argument is pursued to its conclusion, the result is daunting. The financial cost of creating a 1:500 well-trained Service with good equipment and transport for an 80% rural economy is relatively enormous. India has trained at least 70,000 Village Level Workers, who are normally High School graduates; it would be necessary to train as many again to reach such a target. At the higher level, if there are to be 2 Extension Officers, who are college graduates, to each 'Block', more than 10,000 would be needed, giving a proportion of 1 to about 5,000 farmers; at present there is only 1 college graduate to each ordinary 'Block', 2 per 'Block' in the more intensive areas, and 4 in the most intensive. There is one jeep available to the 'Block', mainly used by the Block Development Officer. In East Africa, taking all levels of field staff together, there is about 1 officer to 1,500 farmers. The comparison with developed countries is

[1] E.g. the wheat-growing scheme at Upper Kitete, Tanzania.

misplaced—they can afford such a Service just because both agriculture and industry are already developed, because the agricultural sector is relatively much smaller, holdings fewer and larger,[1] and because such countries are not poor but rich. 'Weakness' is not simply negligence: it is mainly poverty.

Further, to suggest that agriculture can only be got on the move by applying a large force of government officers spread all over the land is to neglect a great deal of intelligence and enterprise within the farming community itself and also within the commercial sector which serves it. Plantation companies carry their own Extension Service on the profits of their crop: it is simply a management expense. The Tea and Tobacco Companies and Corporations in East Africa provide an Extension Service to thousands of small-holder growers. Some successful Co-operatives do the same. In these cases it costs the government nothing, and the farmer a very small fraction of the price for his crop. Even the better landlords in India and Pakistan cover much of the ground of Extension—provision of fertilizer, better seed varieties, possibly some mechanical services—as well as many of the functions of a credit agency and a marketing system. They may charge far too heavily for it, but at least there is no burden on public funds. If every landlord in India were to be shot at dawn, it is tempting to ask whether government could replace their functions by a salaried Extension Service at the same cost to the community. The same question could be posed by abolishing the private merchants, the cotton-ginners, and the sugar-cane processors and replacing them by a marketing bureaucracy: would the grower get more, or less, for his crops, and would the total community, urban as well as rural, be richer or poorer in consequence? These costs are not always counted.

In fact, such questions are unanswerable in a general form: the answers depend on circumstance. Those favouring Extension and Co-operatives are very apt to be based on exceptionally good public systems replacing exceptionally bad private systems. Certainly, a single Extension Officer in the Shell experiment at Borgo a Mozzano more than paid for his salary in increased production and increased government revenue resulting from it—but this was a handpicked graduate operating continuously in a small area of

[1] Imagine an extension service in England if 70% of holdings were of less than five acres—the Indian situation.

considerable potential and within reach of sophisticated markets, and the cost of the graduate's original training was not included in the calculations. Certainly, some coffee or cotton Co-operatives in East Africa have done better than the private systems—or lack of system—which preceded them. But when government attempts to repeat these successes on a full national scale, with the full costs of additional training institutions and the *average* performance of the personnel which can be attracted into agricultural work at fairly low salaries and in fairly primitive and isolated living conditions, the reckoning is apt to become less favourable. On the other side of the argument, those who favour market forces and private enterprise have been apt to assume a market system and a code of practice among merchants which may exist in developed countries but does not in many peasant societies.

2

It is clearly more profitable to turn away from these generalities and look more carefully at a few of the specific situations in which Extension must work, starting with some differences between backward and progressive areas. It is certainly helpful to distinguish two roles of Extension—as the spearhead of government effort to initiate change, and as a service to a farming community which is already on the move. Each of these two roles may be needed in different parts of a single country. It is fairly clear that the spearhead function is dominant in areas where little or no modernization has taken place and where purchasing power is low. There will be little attraction here for private commercial enterprise, and there will be few farmers who need a high grade of technical advice and service. If government does not enter the arena there will be no effective agency of change. To be effective, the Extension Service will need quite a large number of simply trained staff, to follow up advice, probably to arrange for supply of necessary inputs in sub-commercial quantities, to help and advise in the early stages of new institutions. If it is really intended to develop the area, several arms of Government will be involved to cover production, credit, marketing, tools and new investment.

But a further distinction between backward areas is needed here, between those backward areas where potential is good but progress is held back by poor methods and inadequate institutions, and those where major new investment is a prerequisite for any real progress. In the latter a great deal of Extension effort and public funds can be wasted in making trivial improvements without any real solution to problems of production and marketing. Unless and until the investment is made, the Extension staff are helpless and discouraged. This does not mean that such areas are to be abandoned to their fate in perpetuity. Normal welfare services of Health and Education will continue, and a skeleton agricultural staff can be available for advice. Time itself and accident—discovery of a mineral resource,[1] the siting of a trunk road, a new market—may alter the situation and disclose a means of advance. Meanwhile, the temptation to retain an ineffective and discouraged Extension Service must be resisted: the money and staff are needed elsewhere.

In the relatively backward areas which have some existing potential there is an awkward problem of the enforcement of necessary rules—measures to prevent erosion or to control diseases of cattle or crops. Enforcement is absolutely necessary and requires authority, which is not likely to be found among the culprits themselves. Yet this enforcement obviously conflicts with the conception of the Extension Service as the farmer's friend. It is quite true that enforcement unaccompanied by practical help has bedevilled government relations with farmers. But the attempt to devise an alternative service (for instance through a University), which performs only the welcome tasks, has even worse results, in demoralizing the government staff and endangering the whole relationship between government and farmers, which is bound to be critical in just these backward regions. It has to be recognized that good farming requires discipline—discipline which will be even more necessary at later stages when high production depends on the regularity of spraying, water-control, grading, inoculation. The Extension Service is performing an essential training task in its enforcement work. Those who come late to advise and comment, especially in Africa, constantly underestimate the long years of persevering effort which had been needed to develop these elementary disciplines.

The same impatience with the apparently slow performance and meagre results of the Ministry of Agriculture and its Extension

---

[1] For example, the reported discovery of a rich diamond mine in Botswana, or the existing mines in Tanzania. By providing employment and a local market for produce such centres can transform the local agriculture.

staff is at the root of other attempts to find a substitute, by creating special Development Corporations, or bringing in other Ministries. There is, indeed, room for the Development Corporation in certain set schemes where major capital investment is involved and a type of managerial and financial expertise is needed which is alien to government departments. It may also serve a purpose, in the absence of a strong commercial and industrial sector, in mobilizing technical equipment and inputs. But as an alternative to Extension work in the field the results are, once again, to devalue the prestige and weaken the morale of the central Ministry of Agriculture—a situation very evident in Pakistan. The intervention of additional Ministries is even less excusable and more disruptive. In Thailand no fewer than four Ministries, including eight Departments[1] *outside* the Ministry of Agriculture, take a hand in organizing farmers groups, Co-operatives and Extension work (Agriculture, Interior, National Development, Prime Minister's Office). After such a period of confusion it will finally appear that the Ministry of Agriculture has the technical knowledge, most of the trained staff, and most of the field stations, and a demoralized Ministry has to be rehabilitated. It is especially unfortunate that such attempts to dodge the problem of creating an efficient Ministry of Agriculture and a suitable Extension Service have come in some countries just at a moment when the new high-yielding varieties, new investment in irrigation and a new general priority to agriculture could have given new and much needed prestige to the Extension Service in the eyes of farmers.

In contrast, in areas of active innovation, the Extension requirements are wholly different. Technical service rather than primary farming education is needed, and technical service of sophisticated quality, including the advice of economists and farm planners. This implies higher qualifications and close research support. It is dangerous to assume that the example of the best farmers will simply 'rub off' on to their less skilled neighbours. Farmers with less knowledge, or capital, will attempt to grow new varieties without following the full cultural pattern, with results not only

[1] Departments included Office of Accelerated Rural Development (Prime Minister's Office); Community Development Department, Public Welfare Department and Lands Department (Ministry of Interior); Royal Irrigation Department, Land Development Department, Land Co-operatives Department, Co-operative Credit and Trading Department (Ministry of National Development).

bad for themselves but causing adulteration of seed, the spread of disease, spoiling of the market by uneven quality, and even disillusion with potentially valuable new techniques which have failed through misuse. The stakes have in fact been raised for the whole community, and both advice and control will be necessary. Thus a saving in low-level personnel may be more than offset by the need for more highly trained and highly paid staff.

3

We may now turn from distinctions between Extension in different circumstances to a look at the contribution which can come from within the community itself. Among the various policies which seek to find and use local leadership are those concentrating on 'progressive farmers', or 'master-farmers'; policies based on groups or clubs of farmers; policies using *animateurs* chosen by the village community as contact-men and given training by government;[1] policies channelled primarily or even exclusively through Co-operatives; policies using Development Committees, Panchayats, or Basic Democracy groups, with a junior Extension Officer as a servant/executive rather than as a leader or adviser; policies using local cells of a governing political Party.

It is extremely dangerous to attempt to arrange the virtues and applicability of these variants by using a few criteria, not merely because circumstances differ so widely—primarily in social background and tradition, but also by factors such as population density, pastoral or agricultural conditions—but because any kind of orthodoxy is so liable to unthinking general application and in consequence to mistakes.

Yet, despite this risk, experience does suggest a few principles, of which perhaps the most reliable are in negative form. At least some orthodoxies can be destroyed. One false god has already been named—making the formation of a Co-operative virtually a condition of agricultural help; unco-operative Co-operatives, forced on a village, seldom work well or last long. Another may well be the attempt to institutionalize the 'progressive farmer', whether as a

[1] Mainly in the Franco-phone areas of Africa originally, but also elsewhere under different names. The Comilla system of village Co-operative 'managers' is not far away.

channel of communication or (still worse) as an agent of propaganda and persuasion. The mere fact that a farmer is progressive is of great importance: neighbours will silently note his growing prosperity; some will ask his advice; some will buy his better seed or hire his tractor. Such a man is already recognized as one type of 'leader' in many villages, if he has other qualities which elicit respect; in the remarkable development of market-gardening at Aranjuez (Trinidad) the most successful gardeners are quite clearly in such a position.[1] But the moment he is seen to be the special favourite and the acknowledged tool of a government service, not only will jealousy sharpen but his influence may well decline. This is partly because others do not feel that they could do as well (since they have not special government backing) and partly because his advice may now seem no longer objective and village-allied but propagandist and government-allied. Naturally, progressive farmers will come more often to demonstrations and training courses; will use the Extension Officers more; will help to form a Co-operative. Thus they will be a channel in any case: to make them an institution will not add to their value and risks destroying it.

It is here that a neglected issue comes to the front—how far can Government conceal or camouflage the fact that it is pressing farmers and villagers to do certain things by using a village member, even if duly elected, as their agent, in the pretence that Government is only 'responding' to 'demands' from the people? The wish for camouflage springs from the knowledge that villagers in most peasant societies look upon Government with at least some scepticism and often with extreme, traditional suspicion. Bailey,[2] from experience in Orissa, has argued with some force not only that 'outsiders' (government officials, 'men who come in bush shirts on a bicycle or in a jeep, never on foot') are regarded as exploitable; further and more importantly, that it is virtually impossible for villagers to become internal agents of the outsiders without losing the confidence of the village. They may be useful and necessary as brokers, but they will be suspect. His conclusion is that what counts with the village is not propaganda or persuasion

[1] A. A. MacMillan, *Aranjuez: Agricultural Development in a Suburban Setting*, Proceedings of the Second West Indian Agricultural Economics Conference, Trinidad (University of the West Indies, 1967).
[2] 'The Peasant View of the Bad Life'.

but 'operational success'—some additional irrigation water, a new variety which succeeds, remission of rent or defeat of a greedy landlord. There is a clear implication from this argument (though Bailey does not state it) that since camouflage deceives no one except perhaps the government itself, what the government wants to do it had better do openly, and had better take care to do well.

Rather different issues arise where the help of the community is expected to be given, not through individual 'progressives' but through a committee, elected by universal suffrage and allegedly representing the combined will of the community (as in India), or, as a variant, through a local group of a national *parti unique* through which the national will is expressed (as in much of Africa). In the case of the Indian Panchayat, in so far as it can be regarded, after two or more elections, as genuinely expressing the will of the majority of the village, and in some degree in opposition to 'government', it can be argued that villagers will identify with it rather than regard it as a camouflaged arm of government; and this may be true even if it is led by the traditional village magnates. The Basic Democracies of Pakistan, in so far as they are seen as a mechanism of support for the military regime, are more suspect on this count.

The party cell or branch at village level cannot so easily be identified with the general will of the village. It is in itself more of the nature of a faction, often of the younger members, and just because 'the Party is the Government and the Government is the Party',[1] it is rightly regarded by the ordinary villager as an arm of government, distinguishable from the Administration but identified with 'outside' pressures. Moreover, as de Wilde[2] points out, it is particularly prone to act as the local agent for national campaigns and 'drives'—for adult literacy or youth service or tree-planting or Co-operatives—drives originating from the central government and often hopelessly out of step with real local needs.

Thus it does not seem likely that in areas other than those of higher political development—of which more later—the use of voluntary or elected or political agencies in development will be a full or effective *alternative* to a strong Extension Service, though it may be a most valuable addition. Certainly the Panchayat, the

---

[1] A slogan of the C.P.P. in Ghana.
[2] de Wilde, op. cit.

secretary or 'manager' of a Co-operative, the chairman of the Young Farmers or Progressive Farmers' Club, or the leader of a party-organized Development Committee, will be useful contacts for the Extension Officer. The Panchayat may take a good deal of responsibility for social betterment, relieving the Community Development Department; but it is not designed to deal with technical agricultural matters by itself. The Extension Service has to serve, and to be seen to serve, all groups in the village, small farmers as well as big, faction B as well as faction A. It has to find more than one point of entry and of continuing contact, and to avoid being 'captured'. Above all, it has to have real and successful answers to local operational problems.

But as local committees grow in competence and maturity, and as they recruit a new generation of progressive farmers into their ranks, the most junior Extension staff will no longer be in a position to advise them or indeed the leading farmers. At this point these junior ranks would be better employed as the servants of Farmers' associations, or Co-operatives, or Development Committees (whatever may be their local name). It will remain important that the technical guidance should continue to be given to these Committees and Associations from the better qualified and more senior staff of the Extension Service.

4

These somewhat negative conclusions have not gone far to solve the initial difficulty—the problem of financing an Extension Service large enough and good enough to be effective. Indeed, the implications are that a strong force is needed both in backward areas of good potential and in areas where rapid progress has started. It will be a different type of service—in the backward area a spearhead with plenty of junior staff, in the advanced area a highly qualified technical service. The Stage II areas of transition probably put the heaviest demands of all on the Service, requiring both numbers and quality.

We can, however, see a few points where economy is possible. First, in backward areas of poor potential, the Service can be at skeleton strength, at least until a sound investment for development can be identified and carried out.

The second possible economy lies in concentration of training.

There seems little doubt that the Farmers' Training Centres in East Africa, or the 'Rural Academy' as at Comilla or Peshawar, associated with services of Co-operation, storage, processing, or mechanical maintenance, with a strong interdisciplinary staff and adequate mobility for field visits, make a larger impact on agricultural practice over a fairly wide area than would the same or even more staff operating there but dispersed by ones and twos. More services can be given economically, more ideas are generated, the focus of effort can be shifted more easily from one group of villages to another, support from higher echelons (such as an Agricultural College or University) can be more effectivelo deployed. There is a stronger contact with the market, a more convincing show of strength and prestige, less loneliness and more reward for the individual officers. Moreover, concentration of personnel from various separate departmental services—Extension, Credit, Co-operatives, Community Development—makes common training and a team approach to the village infinitely easier. In areas of dense population and good potential the economic base should be sound enough to support a sizeable team and services at 'Block' level. In sparsely settled areas, and in backward areas, this concentration of farmer training is not usually possible.

Thirdly, more finance for the Service has to be found from its chief beneficiaries, the farmers. There are several possible lines of action. The first, already hinted at, is to transfer the control and cost of the most junior staff to the institutions of the rural community itself, if they are sufficiently mature. For many cash-crops quite small crop cesses at the first stage of marketing can finance junior staff, once their value is recognized. For the more general food-crops, a small addition to Land Revenue assessment, or equivalent tax allocated to the local employing body, could be used.

Next, at least in India and Pakistan, there is a strong case for higher land taxation. Miss Haswell[1] has demonstrated that the larger landlords are pocketing far too high a proportion of taxable capacity—sometimes as much as 66% of the surplus between production and the subsistence needs of tenants and labour. Increased taxation might well force the landlord to choose between more active development and sale of land; and it would help to finance the Extension Service. It should not be difficult to make this taxation progressive, so that it falls where it is intended—on

---

[1] Haswell, op. cit.

the larger and less developed holdings—and to prevent it from being passed on to tenants.

As Sir Arthur Lewis has constantly pointed out, the general issue of raising the finance for major agricultural development can only be solved, in political terms, by making the direct burden of taxation mainly locally raised and locally administered:

> Farmers resent paying taxes for which they may get no return. However, if the services are provided by local authorities under their control, to whom the taxes are paid, the farmers can see what they are getting for their money, and are more willing to give voluntary labour as well as pay more taxes to meet their own needs. Decentralization thus raises taxable capacity. The thesis popularized by western sociologists and political scientists that economic development requires highly centralized government is a dangerous myth.[1]

Next, it may well be best to encourage private enterprise or a public Corporation closely linked to the Ministry of Agriculture to take responsibility for certain limited areas where a single high-value crop is dominant, particularly where it is associated with a processing plant—tea, sugar, tobacco, rubber and other tree crops are typical examples; the Gezira cotton scheme is probably the largest of all. This need not necessarily imply plantation methods with direct labour; outgrower or tenancy systems are perfectly practicable. But the cost of Extension should be borne on the crop as a management expense, thus relieving the central Treasury and also ensuring a small measure—it must be small—of local taxation on the grower.

When all these possible measures of economy are put together, there will be at least some saving of central recurrent revenue. Nevertheless, Extension will still need more money: if agriculture is indeed a priority, it deserves to get it.

5

One more special topic must be briefly mentioned—the role of the University in Extension. There is no doubt about the training role. The specialist advice in a score of fields must come from University-trained men; and the University has a great opportunity to run refresher courses and inter-departmental courses for

[1] Sir Arthur Lewis, in Southworth and Johnston, op. cit.

co-ordinating local policies. The role of research is equally essential, though there will be argument, which can only be settled in local circumstances, whether the University should take over or merely support the existing government research and testing stations. In either case the University specialist should be at the elbow of the field Extension worker.

The more difficult issue arises largely through the influence of American thinking, which has inclined so strongly towards America's own practice of giving the University responsibility for executive Extension work in the field and in direct contact with the farmer.

Certainly in India this allocation of responsibility to the new Agricultural Universities, with their strong Land Grant College flavour, has caused much confusion and heart-burning. In the early stages the University has often taken over a limited part of its area for experiment and training with direct Extension work. Full of energy and ideas, anxious to prove the thesis that the University can do the job far better than the old government Extension Service, the University moves in with more staff per 1,000 farmers than the government could afford in the general service, better qualified staff, and staff supported by transport and other facilities which, again, would be too costly on a national scale. Moreover, it is part of the philosophy that the University Extension worker should be the farmer's friend, and only his friend: not for them the unpopular task of law-enforcement; not for them even the administrative chores of constant meetings with parallel or superior staff, the statistical records which government needs, the monthly reports and routine inspections. In consequence, they may achieve a few spectacular local successes—'more in six months than the government has done in six years', as one American Extension advisor remarked to us.

Naturally, there have been severe tensions, and some hard things said by Directors of Agriculture and by the regular government staff. They have right on their side. Nothing could be more destructive of morale for the regular Extension Service than to have this subsidized competition creaming off the more attractive parts of the job, and particularly now, when at last the new high-yielding crops have given Extension something really worth while to give to the farmer. Nothing could be more disruptive of a co-ordinated approach of many government services than to have a rogue element, separately administered, carrying out its own policies in the very centre of the stage. Moreover, the University is not even answerable for what it does: if there is a catastrophic crop failure, it will be the Minister of Agriculture who answers in the State Parliament, and the Government Director of Agriculture who will be blamed—not the Vice-Chancellor of the University.

For many historical reasons, both in Asia and Africa, the effort of agricultural development has been channelled through government. This was partly because government has authority, and in the early stages authority was (and is) needed; partly because government controlled a wide range of necessary services —irrigation, engineering, road construction, Co-operative Development, Education, Community Development and others; partly because government controlled finance; partly because government had the co-ordinating mechanism in the District to see that all these worked together. To compare this situation with that of 20th-century America is to see at a glance how totally different the situations are. If ever there was a thoughtless transfer of inapplicable experience from one civilization to another, this is one.

Despite this muddled thinking on Field Extension, the Universities have done much good. New approaches, new finance, new enthusiasm, higher qualifications and expertise have been injected into the agricultural campaign. The whole potential for change has been given a new power. In many areas the Agricultural Faculty has set up a local programme of field research, usually led by a senior staff member and including young post-graduates and sometimes undergraduates, which involves detailed study of an individual village and its farms and giving some help to the farmers (Kasetsart, Khon-Khaen and Chiengmai Universities in Thailand, many in India and Pakistan, some in Tropical Africa). This not only adds greatly to realism in University work but accumulates far more detailed knowledge of farm economics. In Thailand the Economics section of the Ministry of Agriculture has teams of two or three men in eight different provinces doing both research and demonstration. This type of experimental work is of great value, if Ministry and University are closely co-ordinated. When the administration and responsibility for general Field Extension have been reviewed and clarified, the prospects for University help are good.

6

This chapter has not covered a great number of interesting and important issues concerned with Extension—training, methods, the support of programmes by radio, film, and Farmers' Bulletin, the problem of illiteracy, and much else. They are omitted because many excellent books and reports have covered them very fully. Nor has it covered the question of co-ordinating the various departments and agencies which come in contact with farmers; this is not only of high importance but relevant to our subject, and it is dealt with in Chapter VIII as part of the general problem of administration.

The disturbing fact is that, despite all the thought and wisdom which have appeared in the reports, Extension has not had the widespread and general success in provoking rapid growth and change which has been expected of it. It is for this reason that this chapter has concentrated on a rather different approach, in considering in more detail the type of area and potential to which effort is to be applied, the stage of modernization in attitudes and economy, the resources of government in both manpower and finance, the nature and maturity of community and political organization, and the relation between these elements of a single equation.

The essential quality of this argument lies in its stress upon a moving, developing situation. At one extreme, Government is forced to initiate, teach, control and quite often compel. It is paternalist and in direct contact with the farmer and the village, because modernizing local institutions are still weak. At the other extreme lies a society far more capable of progressive self-government, aided by a growing private enterprise, financially stronger from its greater productivity and needing from government high-quality technical service, a good administrative and fiscal framework, and research. In developed countries farmers are not ruled by District Commissioners, nor are they constantly admonished by Extension Officers on how to do their job; credit is given by farm suppliers or banks, and commercial firms seek eagerly an opportunity to contract. Farmers buy supplies from shops and dealers, and keep up to date with markets and techniques by reading the journals.

It is towards this kind of society that development is aimed.

There is a long road to travel from traditional peasant agriculture to this developed state, and the stages cannot be simply jumped, though they can be shortened. It is a movement away from a wholly administered system, in which the State must provide motive power, control, supplies, credit and a market, to a self-powered system, using all the facilities of the market, to which the State and the Universities provide technical service and an economic framework within which agriculture can get on with its job in reasonable security. The stages in this transition are all-important: to each of them, in their particular social and ecological and political context, Extension policy must adapt itself.

If there is one point which stands out from the whole argument it is that, despite all means of economy, considerably more financial resources are needed for effective contact with the farmer. This fact has been demonstrated in the field many times; an outstanding example is the agricultural revolution in Kenya's Central Province which would never have taken place without a very heavy expenditure on 'close administration'—far heavier than any capital inputs into the area. It has been the persistent inability or unwillingness of aid agencies to accept that aid to administration is a true investment of capital, with a large financial pay-off, which has helped to delay recognition of this fact.

PART III
THE GROWING SOCIETY

CHAPTER VIII

ADMINISTRATION

There is a rough natural history of the development of administration, reflecting the growth of societies in economic complexity and civic consciousness, and the range of services which government is expected to provide. There are variants in this evolution, adapted to the pressures of environment; but it is possible to pick out certain sequences of growth which are common to many countries and periods.

For considerable parts of Africa we should really start with the transition from a mass of smallish tribes and peoples to centralized national governments. There are also plenty of places in Asia where purely tribal situations continue. There are major groups of tribes in the hills of Burma and in Thailand, Cambodia and Vietnam; relics of primitive people in the mountain spine of Malaya; tribal cultures in Sabah and Sarawak and in parts of Indonesia and the Philippines, and large patches of tribal people all along the Himalayas and in enclaves in India and Pakistan.

But for our purpose it is enough to start from a point when some *imperium* stretching over wide areas has been established (usually in the past by military conquest). We are dealing with central governments of considerable States, even if the consciousness of nationality is sometimes feeble and patchy and even if they have dissidents or special tribal areas. We are also dealing with extended rural administration rather than with city government; the development of the Greek City-State is largely a different story.

We may first look very roughly and selectively at some of the chief phases in the administration of countries which have reached a stage of empire (such as the Moghul Empire) or of feudal monarchy.[1] In the early imperial stage local rural society is governed,

[1] 'Feudal' is not used here in any exact European sense; it is a shorthand for a system in which the monarch presides over a society in which provincial life is ordered by a hierarchy culminating locally in some major overlord, who is in turn obligated to the monarch.

in an all-purpose way, by a mixture of its own tradition of customary rules and by a few major impositions from above. The feudal lord (or governor, or general) and the tax collector are the two main agents of local rule. The concern of the centre is threefold. The first and often the most anxious, is to guard against revolt by a provincial governor or (worse still) by a combination of them. As late as 1920 in Thailand the governors of provinces were forbidden to meet each other, except under the eye of the King in Bangkok: the sentence for such a meeting outside Bangkok was death. Where the provincial governors were military there was always a danger that they might march their army on the capital: Roman Consuls were forbidden to cross the Rubicon with their legions. Some of the Kingdoms of Africa—for example, the Ashanti—were equally nervous of their generals.

The second concern is to raise taxes and troops. The third is to prevent a peasants' revolt—though this would at first concern the province more than the centre. The government taxed, enforced peace, and punished; it did not provide services to the nation. From the peasant's point of view the three external dangers were the tax-gatherer, the levy of troops, and forced labour for prestigeful or strategic works. Since social or economic services from the centre were negligible, there was no need for 'county' or 'district' organization; the village or tribal group was the main unit; the overlord or landlord was the next: the whole system was designed to work automatically, with each tier regulated by the next higher one.

Such a system could last a long time. In cases where it settled down the next long stage which is particularly relevant is marked by two main changes. A civil service is created at the centre (as, for example, in the Chinese Empire). Gradually this service gains power, regularizes central administration and comes to dominate the local governors—a Secretariat is appearing. Secondly, Law becomes more important. It may be the King's Law, or the Muslim Law, or the British or French Law brought into colonial territories. In some degree, Law also weakens the local hierarchy of feudalism, landlords, princelings, rajahs, emirs. In conjunction with the secretariat, it begins to make government into uniform, national government under the Law rather than feudal government under the local lord. In some respects and in some areas, the British occupation in British India marks this change. The District governor is not only the Revenue Collector but also the District Magistrate; and the magistracy[1] becomes an immensely important part of his function. A civil service and a magistracy begin to take over from royal or military government. The relation of the Law to executive government takes many twists and turns. In some ways it is the enforcing arm, as the Justices of the Peace came to be in England. But in many ways it is also a freedom to the local citizens, because it can override local oppressors, and because, even in the hands of an executive—say, the District Commissioner— it is a restraint on his own arbitrary decisions. Subject peoples have known how to turn the Law against even the hand which wields it.

Some colonized areas went through this phase, though at different dates. India certainly passed through it; even in the Princely States the concepts of a civil service and of a rule of law were gradually imposed. Indirect rule (for example, in Nigeria or the Malay States, or the Sultanate of Jogjakarta in Indonesia) recognized a traditional local sovereignty and a customary law. But all the time a professional civil service and Western Law were creeping in.

In the rural areas such a post-feudal type of government still gives few or no services. It is concerned that the customary pattern of agricultural life should continue. To prevent unrest and maintain stability it may insist upon regularization or improvement of landlord-tenant rights; it may register and regularize boundaries and tenures and settle disputes concerning them.

Towns create a rather different problem. Life in them is more complex: services (lighting, fire-control, elementary sanitation, markets, roads, policing, water supply) come to need some form of public action which is scarcely needed in the village or is provided by customary means. Moreover, the feudal hierarchy, based on land and military service, is not a handy means of urban government. It is natural, therefore, that it is in towns that some form of licensed or chartered self-government should first arise. Towns also, because the town-dweller is outside the feudal-agricultural system, and because contact is wider, more free, more varied and sophisticated, provide an obvious starting point for

[1] It is interesting that J. S. Mill habitually refers (from a background of Roman studies) to the ruler as the magistrate.

self-government; some form of elected municipality usually precedes any form of rural self-government above village or clan level.

The third stage in the development of administration (we are now concerned with the last two centuries in Europe) is marked by a great increase in the services or regulation which government begins to give, because the state of the nation seems to require it. It requires it because forces arising within the community (not the government) have suddenly burst out in a wild gallop of production and change, generating wealth, poverty, startling achievements and gross abuses which the government neither engineered nor even foresaw. There is therefore a great increase in the bureaucracy. Two changes take place in its nature. The very small governing elite, such as the Secretariat in India, is now too small. Departments or Boards and their Directors begin to proliferate— for Education, Local Government, Health and Sanitation, Prisons, Roads and Railways, Poor Relief, the regulation of wages and industrial practice. A veritable army of intermediate officials and government or quasi-government clerks begin to appear. At the lowest level they are under-paid they are petty officers who can oppress the simple citizen, because the Regulations are behind them; they are open to bribery because the postal, or railway, or taxation, or Poor Law clerk has a power to deny the simple citizen what he wants and needs, and can hide behind the Regulations unless the 'dash'[1] is forthcoming. A little later, and higher up, tension begins to grow in colonial administration between the 'heaven-born' Secretariat and the technical Departments. Men of specialized training, in Health or an exact science (even in Agriculture!), are beginning to appear and question the high administrator with his training in Latin and Greek. Government becomes more subdivided, larger, more specialized, more rigid. The probability of corruption involves a multiplication of checks and counter-checks, authorizations and counter-signatures, forms and legalities.

It was at this late stage in Europe that large-scale 'Local Government' covering rural areas became essential (County

---

[1] I have used 'dash', normally used of West Africa, because it carries the connotation of a customary gift from petitioner to chief or patron, without the essentially European and morally condemning connotation of 'bribe'. As countries become Europeanized, 'dash' becomes 'bribe'.

Councils came in Britain only in 1888), simply to devolve the detailed functions and to spread out petty officialdom from the capital city into local administration, whatever its structure might be. By this time feudal and customary systems based on land have broken down in the industrial countries: bureaucratic government, central and local, has supplanted them.

In the fourth stage, with the growth of industry, the size and complexity of economic institutions in Europe is growing apace. Giant institutions grow up, evolving wholly new techniques for their internal administration; a growing range of services is provided by them on a scale which at one time only government itself could have attempted. The control of these new entities complicates the task of government; but they also offer to it new models of management and an alternative to the use of a bureaucracy for getting things done. For by this time the problem of devolution without total loss of control is becoming a major concern.

Contemporary trends in developed societies take this process far further. Economic life, now increasingly international in organization, has built up an immensely powerful force of its own, almost beyond the control of national governments. Administration, highly professionalized, is concerned to regulate, arbitrate and cushion the shock of change, to resolve the tensions of social inequality, to provide new institutional channels through which new forms of relationship can flow, occasionally to launch into immense economic ventures with techniques borrowed from the private corporations. Local administration is fully organized in a comprehensive network at three or four levels, mimicking the shape of central government, more and more bureaucratic and less felt as self-government. The citizen is the subject, obtaining his carefully regulated and uniform services. More than a century ago de Tocqueville foresaw, as it were in a bad dream, the regulatory pressure of the modern Welfare government:

> Above this race of men stands an immense and tutelary power, which takes upon itself alone to secure their gratification, and to watch over their fate. That power is absolute, minute, regular, provident and mild. ... It covers the surface of society with a network of small complicated rules, minute and uniform, through which the most original minds and the most energetic characters cannot penetrate. The will of man is not shattered but softened, bent and guided: men are seldom forced by

it to act but they are constantly restrained from acting; such a power does not destroy but it prevents existence; it does not tyrannize, but it compresses, enervates, extinguishes and stupifies a people, till each nation is reduced to be nothing better than a flock of timid and industrious animals, of which the government is the shepherd.[1]

This is not exactly an accurate forecast—nightmares do not provide them; but it is interesting as a view from 1840 of the destinies of a full Welfare State. It is important for our purpose to remember that the 'network of small complicated rules' (and therefore the mass of clerks to administer them) arises from the attempt to regulate and reform a society which had virtually broken loose during its development process.

2

We have traced a sequence of growing complexity in administration, from the King/Emperor with feudal lords, generals or provincial governors to a huge and detailed bureaucracy, working through representative institutions at three or even four levels. It is this last, modern, stage which exercises great pressure of example on developing countries. Their problem can be summarized in two general statements. First, in the late colonial period and at Independence the modern example was thrust on their attention (and sometimes partly installed by the departing Colonial Power) at very different stages of their real social development. Some were in a tribal stage; some feudal; India an empire; some wholly rural, some half-commercialized. Their governments have had to face simultaneously almost all the problems of administrative development which the developed countries tackled one by one over centuries. The pressure of the 20th-century environment, the entirely different political atmosphere in which, say, feudal problems have to be tackled, tempts or forces developing countries to apply far more difficult and complex solutions to problems dealt with more simply in earlier ages.

Second, they are assuming the burden of complex regulation before the main process of economic development has taken place —a process which both necessitated regulation and gave the finance and manpower to achieve it.

[1] de Tocqueville, *Democracy in America* (London, Oxford University Press, World's Classics Edition, 1946). First published 1840.

The result is a crisis in administration which is affecting almost every developing country; it is also a crisis in politics, as the next chapter will show.

Take first an example which has its parallel in the very earliest stages of imperial or feudal growth—provincial disaffection. In Africa, with its very recent State boundaries, the ancient problem of rebellious provinces or submerged 'nations' is clearly still to solve—Southern Nigeria is one example among many. It cannot with approval be solved by executing the provincial governor, though the old method of force is being used, amidst world-wide protest, by military intervention in Biafra. One key difference is that early empires did not have to deal with representative institutions in their provinces; the provincial lord or governor was a King's man and almost total authority was delegated to him: the means of ensuring his loyalty were often very subtle.[1] But if he failed, he was executed (unless he became King) and replaced by another. The trouble between Delhi and the Nagas, between Buganda and the Uganda Government, the tension between Luo and Kikuyu in Kenya is not so easily dealt with. Today it is very hard for a nervous central government to allow delegation; yet delegation is critical for rural development.

Next, there is the process of replacing the traditional hierarchy, which in effect managed local affairs without much burden on the central government. It has to be replaced for various reasons. First, because it may often rest on some form of quasi-feudal land ownership, which is felt to be incompatible not only with development but with the modern democratic objection to property or noble birth as a source of total power. Second, because a developing government needs agents fully responsive to its detailed policies. Third, because development, reaching right down to the farmer, needs technical programmes and personnel which the old system cannot give. This displacement—the curbing of the Nigerian Sultanate and Emirate, the removal of the Indian Princes, or of the Kabaka of Buganda, or the abolition of the Indian *zamindars* —will present political problems. Even if they are solved, a substitute must be created. It will be a bureaucracy, with an admixture

---

[1] The means by which the Kabakas of Buganda managed their provincial representation, and comparable arrangements in other African Kingdoms, would illustrate this. See, for example, Audrey I. Richards (ed.), *East African Chiefs* (London, Faber and Faber, 1960).

of political or representative influence varying in different countries.

In India the small, elite bureaucracy was first created by the British. It was composed of carefully chosen men, from a highly selective education, held together by the overwhelming morale and tradition of a service isolated from its home society. In time, as the services of government grew more numerous, and particularly as the twin factors of immensely detailed land revenue collection and of Law expanded, a great army of minor officials was built up both at headquarters and locally—the *patwaris* and the local police in the villages, the clerks and ushers and sergeants of the multitudinous Courts, and finally the lower staffs of the growing Departments. In 'British India' this was direct administration; in the Princely States it was a pressure on the ruler—not always at all successful—to adopt and conform. Much the same policy was followed in Africa,[1] with the same delayed and imperfect implementation where indirect rule was dealing with more powerful and widespread Kingdoms than a local Chiefdom.[2]

When the new independent governments took over, they were faced with creating their own system, either in the old image or in a new one. To create an elite civil service at the top they used the University as a training ground, often drawing from a specially favoured school (Katsina College in the Nigerian North, or Achimota in Ghana, and comparable colleges in India and Pakistan).[3] To achieve the traditions of detachment and objectivity which they sought was, of course, harder: for the entrants could not but still be conscious of their local origins and loyalties and of the pressure from within their own society and kin, which the colonial staff had never had to face. In Asia, and particularly in India and Pakistan, where localization took place much longer before Independence, the traditions were often fully passed on, even re-emphasized. In Africa, the training had less time and more difficulty; yet on the whole the production of a top bureaucratic cadre has been remarkably widely achieved.

But the problem of the lower ranks has not been solved, any more than it was by the colonial administration, or by the 19th-

[1] In Africa, however, the same detailed land-mapping and recording was never carried so far—a lack which is badly felt today.

[2] The administration of Northern Nigeria has been cynically, but not altogether falsely, described as 'an autocracy ineffectively supervised by the British'.

[3] In Thailand the earliest University (Chulalongkorn) grew from a school for Royal servants.

century governments of Europe. In a society as poor as most developing countries, so held in kinship ties, where the humble and perhaps illiterate citizen is helpless in face of even the junior clerk, who can cheat him so easily with written papers and simple lies, the problem of impersonal honesty and conscientious work is almost insoluble. The citizen does not pay heavily in salaries for his officials; he makes it up in small cash payments, or, where he can, through the obligations of kinship between petitioner and clerk. Indeed, kinship runs to higher levels—a crowd of very humble people will often be found outside the office of the Minister whether in Lagos or Lahore: they are not only constituents but often kinsmen too. Bureaucracy has not yet altogether shut off access to the top: the Malay rulers continue to give audience to humble subjects as part of the tradition of their rule. But these are exceptions; the mass of small officials, too numerous to supervise, too poor to refrain from small abuses, remains a problem and a burden.

This poor quality of the lower ranks is a constant anxiety to governments in developing countries. They wish to use government agencies for large programmes, and they wish above all to win the confidence and collaboration of the farmer-citizen. Both objects can be defeated by failure at the ground level. Better discipline, often advocated, is extremely hard to enforce where kinship and patronage is so strong.[1]

But there is also a different kind of problem, which affects senior administration too. Politics and patronage may run right through the administrative system. In Thailand or in the Philippines, and certainly in many African States, an ambitious Minister will have his clientele, often within the civil service. Despite the Public Service Commission, he will contrive to gather them round him in important posts, sometimes robbing weaker Ministries of their ablest staff; and in return he will expect support for his policies. We are seeing, in fact, how the older style of social engineering pervades, dominates and exploits the new-fangled

[1] In one developing country very recently the principal and the whole Governing Body of a school had to threaten resignation before discipline applied to a pupil with kinship ties to the Minister could be enforced. Another difficulty, especially in India, is the appeal to the Courts: an employee suspended for misconduct can drag a State Government through such wearisome and expensive litigation that the very attempt to maintain standards may not seem worth while.

tool of bureaucratic structure to maintain and even enlarge its influence. These are, of course, troubles which Europe experienced in earlier days, as the diaries of Pepys, a civil servant in the Admiralty, have shown. The trouble is that in developing countries it has been necessary to create a very large bureaucracy before the kinship, tribal or patronage system of older origin is even half forgotten, and before the educational system is equal to the task.

One result of these difficulties is a gross over-load on the top elite, made far worse by the pressures of modern development effort, both national and international. Month by month, almost week by week, donors and international agencies are suggesting projects, sending experts, requiring information, meetings, facilities, tours and demonstrations which the local administration must somehow handle. The few top men are overwhelmed by a triple burden—to serve their Ministers in the constant series of political crises to which new governments are prone; to deal with international contacts and visitors; and, somehow, to direct and keep moving the routine tasks of a Department which will have a programme far larger than its staff can manage. Delays, mistakes, and ill-considered projects are not merely a reflection of poor supporting staff in the middle layers: they reflect a government machine grossly overloaded with its own programme and the additions which well-meaning donors press upon it. In Africa the young top administrators are carrying a much bigger load than their expatriate predecessors, with less consistent direction from above, far less support from below, and less experience. To say that they have managed remarkably well—as they have—is beside the point: the need is to improve their situation.

There are four main methods of doing so: to increase the staff; to delegate to local government; to decentralize the work of the administration itself; to create special agencies for special tasks.

There is a real need, in development administration in Africa to strengthen the top staff selectively. It is useless to add more clerks. The Universities in Africa are now producing an adequate flow in most countries, excluding the very small ones such as Malawi, the ex-High Commission countries in the South, and some of the small States in French West Africa. Key Ministries—Agriculture, Treasury, Planning, Education—need them, and need a first-rate Staff College to help with training. The trouble is likely to be a shortage of recurrent revenue to pay them. Recently, more possibilities of obtaining this have begun to open. In Agriculture particularly there is at least talk of a possibility of grant and loan finance from donors to cover, say over five years, a vigorous increase in the Extension Service provided that the proposal is married to a credible scheme for rapid agricultural advance which will be revenue-generating within the period. The World Bank and some bilateral donors are now more open-minded on this subject. Such an expansion involves needs for additional training, both at University level, and perhaps especially, for Field Officers; for equipment, maintenance and repair facilities, storage, transport and mass communication equipment. This is a field too much neglected by donors; recurrent revenue spent in this way is a form of investment, and probably far more productive than the same sum spent on machinery. Technical assistance and aid to local salaries in 'project' form is also possible in other subjects—Planning and Education are examples.

The second cure, the possibility of off-loading central government work on to elected Local Authorities, is much less hopeful in Africa, as a means of helping the central administration. It has other theoretical virtues, in political training and the mobilization of local interest. But, for the countries really short of good staff, it may make matters worse. For County or District Councils or Boards would need good and quite numerous staff, depleting the centre still further, and their administration would load the centre much more than a straight-line chain of command through trained Provincial and District Commissioners. Moreover, if the historical analogy is useful, in many countries in Africa it is too early to do this. The range of services necessarily concentrated at County level is not really great, because life is still so often lived at village and sub-District level.[1] Neither political nor economic nor educational advance is as yet great enough to man such Councils with men of quality, integrity and wide experience. Ghana and Nigeria could do it; in East and Central Africa it is far more doubtful. In

[1] In fact, there are differences from place to place. In some the village is effectively the largest traditional unit for most purposes; in others, a rather larger chiefdom; in some areas even greater spheres of traditional administration. In Tanzania before Independence there were half a dozen different shapes to local government—Chiefs as Sole Authority, Chiefs in Council, part-nominated bodies and wholly elected bodies. Such inconsistency was certainly intelligent; but it looks untidy.

limited fields, such as Primary education and some other subjects, a good deal can be done by this means everywhere; in major responsibilities probably not yet.

It was a desire to politicize local administration which led many African governments to create political representative local government, not the desire to off-load administrative burdens. On the whole it usually made matters worse. Among country people to whom politics is new, the violent activities, promises and counter-promises of politicians can quickly create an acute sense of insecurity and anxiety, in contrast to the limited certainties which a paternal administration provided. Moreover, planning from the centre is made more difficult. For these and other reasons some governments (Kenya, Zambia) have tended to go back to a renewed emphasis on Provincial and District administration.

The third possibility, administrative delegation, is certainly more hopeful. At the sub-District ('Division' in some African countries), at District and at Provincial level more executive power could no doubt be given, and with great benefit to flexibility in local policy. Some reinforcement of staff would be necessary, but at a level which would not involve such strain on the centre—the District and Provincial Commissioners are already in post and are usually men of some experience and quality. Delegation through the administrative machine does at first appear to raise fewer problems.

The trouble in a delegated administrative system lies in the length of the chain of command, the multiplicity of those chains where Departmental rather than all-purpose administration has got a grip, and in the quality of poorly educated and badly paid staff at the lowest level of all. It is these small men who come into direct contact with the village and the farmer. They cannot be given discretions, are usually badly supervised, often operate with written instructions which are out of relation with what it is possible or sensible to do in their local circumstance. They are often seen as emissaries of 'government' enforcing mysterious and even senseless regulations, who must be bribed or evaded in order that the ordinary needs of village life can be met—at best a particularly tiresome form of local taxation, at worst a petty tyranny. We have come full-circle to the complexity of the task matched against the resources to meet it. In rural areas of Europe, at a comparable epoch of development, not a quarter of the task was attempted.

Moreover, there is a host of reasons why all forms of delegation and decentralization are difficult. One has already been mentioned—the fear of regional disloyalties. A second lies in shortages—of foreign exchange, development capital, equipment and much else. The central Plan, laboriously checked to ensure consistency between sectors and priorities for scarce resources, is hard to keep in trim if major elements are handled by local discretions. This argument is dangerous—there are cases where a small sum spent locally might be far more effective per £1 than the large expenditure conceived centrally; such smaller projects are often defeated because they are 'not in the Plan'. But the prestige of Ministers, the fact that senior civil servants feel bound to 'think big' and know better than provincial subordinates who 'submit' plans to them, all tend to produce a Plan which is in large units, which looks to some distant end-result[1] rather than to initiating a process of change, and which strains resources to the limit. Planning can easily become a dangerous enemy of growth.

A third difficulty lies in the centripetal attraction of the centre. The best brains, 'the best people', are concentrated in the capital city, and this centralization feeds upon itself, attracting the best of each new crop of young men to it. Career-opportunity, intellectual company, social life, all pull against the prospect of work in a distant province obeying misguided instructions which stream down from the (ignorant) Headquarters.

A fourth method of relieving administrative pressure on the civil service as such is to transfer functions from government to a statutory 'Corporation'; it allegedly has the virtues of more direct and businesslike management and of being free from political pressures. This is an attempt to adopt methods which came in the very last stage of development in the West,[2] and which have proved difficult to manage. The method probably has its best results in an industrial context. But in agriculture it is beset by grave difficulties, and it is particularly unlikely to succeed, except for pure plantation work, or for certain background functions of finance and technical or commercial supplies. For one thing, it needs personnel, and if good men are in short supply it

[1] Cf. Singer, op. cit.: 'Your plan must be based on your present resources. It is a wrong approach to ask yourself first what you need . . . ; if you do that, you will inevitably arrive at a Plan which is beyond your present resources.'

[2] In 1969 Britain is just in the process of converting the Post Office from a government Department into a Postal Corporation.

will simply rob government itself. Next, the very absence of civil service control gives opportunities for financial cheating or undesirable patronage in countries where this problem is still acute. Finally, business organization was not devised for, or experienced in, the initiation of change among thousands of small peasant farmers. It is unlikely to make even as good a job of this as the government Extension Service, and in any case will probably steal their staff. The Agricultural Development Corporation in Pakistan, already mentioned, which virtually superseded the Extension Service in certain zones and certain services, illustrates this well.

Shortage of trained manpower is, of course, particularly acute in Africa; in Asia shortage of staff, except in a few countries, has not been so great a problem. But the need to delegate and the difficulty in doing it is just as great. In some areas, as we shall see in the next chapter, the time is more ripe for delegation to elected bodies; but there are still relatively few where the continued supervision and, if necessary, the veto of the administration are no longer needed.

3

We have seen some of the causes for a crisis in administration described in negative terms as a series of unsolved problems. Indeed, the problem of accelerating growth is far harder (as has long been recognized) in this area of human relationships than in the area of technical change. Yet something has been learned from experience and can be applied, even in this difficult field. The task is to find a style of administration fitted to unique circumstances, and it is possible to make at least some suggestions, in the field of central development administration, in the field of co-ordination, and in the field of participation. But the hardest issue of all, and for our purpose the most critical, is that of delegation.

First, it is worth emphasizing once more the critical importance of delegation for agricultural development. It is not only that effective agricultural policy must be essentially local policy, to fit as closely as possible the physical factors, the population density, the stage of modernization and attitudes reached locally. It is also that most really fruitful experiments, often capable of wider application, naturally emerge from local initiative—naturally, because they depend on the sensitive appreciation of local problems which only comes from immersion in them. These successes may spring from the local administrator—the District Commissioner who really set Kilimanjaro coffee growing on its successful career; from private enterprise—the Punjabi farmers who grasped the possibilities of tubewells and have installed 30,000 in five years; from a teacher and a leader—Akhtar Hamid Khan at Comilla; from a Mission—the Youth Settlement at Nyakashaka in Uganda under C.M.S. leadership; from a single farmer who finds the new path to success; from a Co-operative system, such as that which raised cotton production in Mwanza District (Tanzania) from 50,000 to 250,000 bales in less than a decade. In each case there is a release of potential which assumes dimensions quite disproportionate to its cost. Money is short in the Districts; there is little danger of wastefully expensive schemes; and it is this very capacity to make £1 turn to £10 (rather than £1 million to £2 million, if it is not lost) which is vital to growth.

In this crisis of peasant societies, where every scrap of local knowledge and initiative is needed, the task of finding and supporting every hopeful sign of growth is critical. There are things being well done in one group of villages which are unknown thirty miles away, because a different officer is in charge or the mountain intervenes. To find, support, link and expand these initiatives involves giving to the local area a degree of trust, a delegation of both financial and policy-making power which is still appallingly difficult to extract from the centre. In India the case is incontrovertible: a single District will have more than a million inhabitants, which is more than have some member States of the United Nations; a State will have 30 millions—more than the whole East African Community of Kenya, Tanzania and Uganda, more than Canada or Australia. England had only 5 millions in the 17th century, yet power was widely dispersed, to her immense advantage. Delegation is not a modern invention: it happened in States far less developed than those of modern Africa; it is centralization which is modern and, in the circumstances of peasant countries, disastrous.

Perhaps the first step towards a solution is to make central administration itself more creative and flexible. In both Africa and Asia the problem of creative development administration (as contrasted with administrative control of a development which has emerged from the community itself) demands changes both in the shape and in the tone of administrative practice. The watertight Departmental divisions, the rigidity of establishments and postings and grading systems—all derived from the colonial model of developed countries—are a serious handicap for a developing function. Almost all development projects are inter-departmental —in most agricultural schemes, roads, schools, disease control, credit, buildings, water engineers will be needed not merely agronomists from the Ministry of Agriculture. The easy ability to form project teams, to second staff to them, to create special temporary grades for the purpose, and to dissolve the whole organization again when its job is completed—all this has long been practised in large-scale industry. It is certainly hard if not impossible to create under the traditional Establishment system of Government. Some break with this tradition is needed.

Secondly, the strong technical and professional element in modern development demands a new relationship between the Provincial and District Administration and the officers of the technical Departments at their level. Paradoxically, it must give the Administration a wider span of co-ordinating responsibility and yet less detailed authority. In India and Pakistan the history-based prestige of the Indian Administrative Service or of the Civil Service of Pakistan, as against the status of Agricultural or Educational or Co-operative officers and Departments, is strong enough to co-ordinate. Indeed, in a sense it is too strong and can become extremely dangerous where amateurs are overriding professionals on their own ground; the morale and initiative of the technical men is constantly damped down by the superior attitude of the 'heaven-born' Administration. The idea that responsibility must be matched by detailed authority is over-simple in modern conditions.

Here again there is a lesson to be found in modern industry. The same problem of general co-ordination of expert services has long been studied there. Is the Works Manager in authority over the Works Chemist or Works Engineer, or does each refer to the General Manager, Chief Chemist, Chief Engineer respectively when there is disagreement? It was a political scientist, Mary Parker Follett,[1] who most cogently analysed this issue, pointing

---

[1] See the collection of writings by Mary Parker Follett in *Dynamic Administration* edited by Metcalf and Urwick (Bath, Management Publications Trust Ltd., 1941).

out that, in a modern technological society, it was insoluble in terms of authority. Co-ordination there must be, and not by the 'snakes-and-ladders' system of constant reference upwards and instructions downwards along parallel lines. Technical expertise there must be; it is too advanced and too important to be over-ridden by amateurs. It is the job of the co-ordinator, whether Works Manager or District Commissioner, to elicit truth rather than exercise authority, by drawing out from each expert the expert grounds of his objection or suggestion; he acts as a chairman, not as an authority figure. This is most evident in the management of a scientific organization: the truth may be found by the most junior scientist, and it is useless for authority to over-ride it. There is also a 'truth' in agricultural situations, and it may be the most junior officer, in closest contact with the farmer, who tells it. The concept of the paramountcy of the facts, expertly assessed, and the replacement of 'authority' by chairmanship has long been familiar in industrial administration. It is strange that the more sophisticated thinking in industry on these issues of the chain of command has scarcely been considered in political science, from which it originated.

Granted a central administration better shaped for development and a system of co-ordination at lower levels intelligently led, there remains one further essential—some system for the expression of needs and suggestions by the administered. Because this, in practice, becomes a political subject, it is considered in the next chapter. But here it is enough to say that this direct participation and first-hand expression of needs is *not* met by establishing County Councils or any 'representative' institution which moves at all far away from face-to-face relationship with the individual villager. There may be a place for representative 'Local Government' in rural areas, although, as we have seen, it was a latecomer in Western development, long after the local representative systems for municipal services. But the history and literature of Local Government is not in the style and atmosphere of development, and it carries quite different overtones from 'participation'.

4

At this point it may be best to describe straightforwardly a single system of rural administration and development which is probably the most complete and logical solution to the three main issues—delegation, co-ordination and the involvement of local effort in both a political and a development sense—to wit, the Indian system.[1]

It is essentially a system of two parallel lines, one administrative, one democratic, closely linked at four points—village, Block, District and State; for the moment the Union Government in Delhi can be neglected. For convenience, Table I is repeated here.

The administrative line, running downwards, starts at the State Secretariat and Development Commissioner, with other Departments (Agriculture, Co-operatives, Works, Irrigation, Community Development) alongside. At District level the Collector (now seen as a Deputy Development Commissioner in addition to his other roles) is the acknowledged co-ordinator; but there are senior District representatives of other Departments alongside him. There is nothing new in this, and in Africa the concept of the Provincial and District Teams corresponds to it. In one State (Andhra Pradesh) the Collector is built up even more, by delegating to him the full powers of the State Directors of Agriculture, Co-operatives and so forth, the existing Directors being up-graded into the Secretariat in advisory and policy roles. In most States the D.C. is given additional staff to match his development responsibilities, and in some an additional Revenue officer to lighten that part of his load.

Below the District there are two lines. The old Revenue and legal Service runs down next to *Tehsil* (or *Taluka*),[1] with a Sub-divisional Officer (and magistrates), who has his spiritual home at District H.Q. and the Tehsildar, who is concentrated on Revenue and lives in the Tehsil: this line ends up at village-level with the '*Patwari*', the village revenue-clerk.

The other line runs to the Block, which may or may not correspond exactly to the Tehsil. The Block is a development organization, in charge of the Block Development Officer, a regular civil servant seconded from one of several possible Departments—Revenue, Agriculture, Education are common sources. He is directly responsible to the D.C. for all operations, although he is

---

[1] Among many sources, including our own field-work in India and Pakistan in 1967 and 1968, I am particularly indebted to the large and thorough volume by Dr. Sugan Chand Jain, *Community Development and Panchayati Raj in India* (Bombay, Allied Publishers, 1967).

[2] 'Tehsil' and 'Taluka' are interchangeable words: Tehsil is used mainly in North India, Taluka in South.

Table 1 (repeated)
Agricultural Administration in Indian States

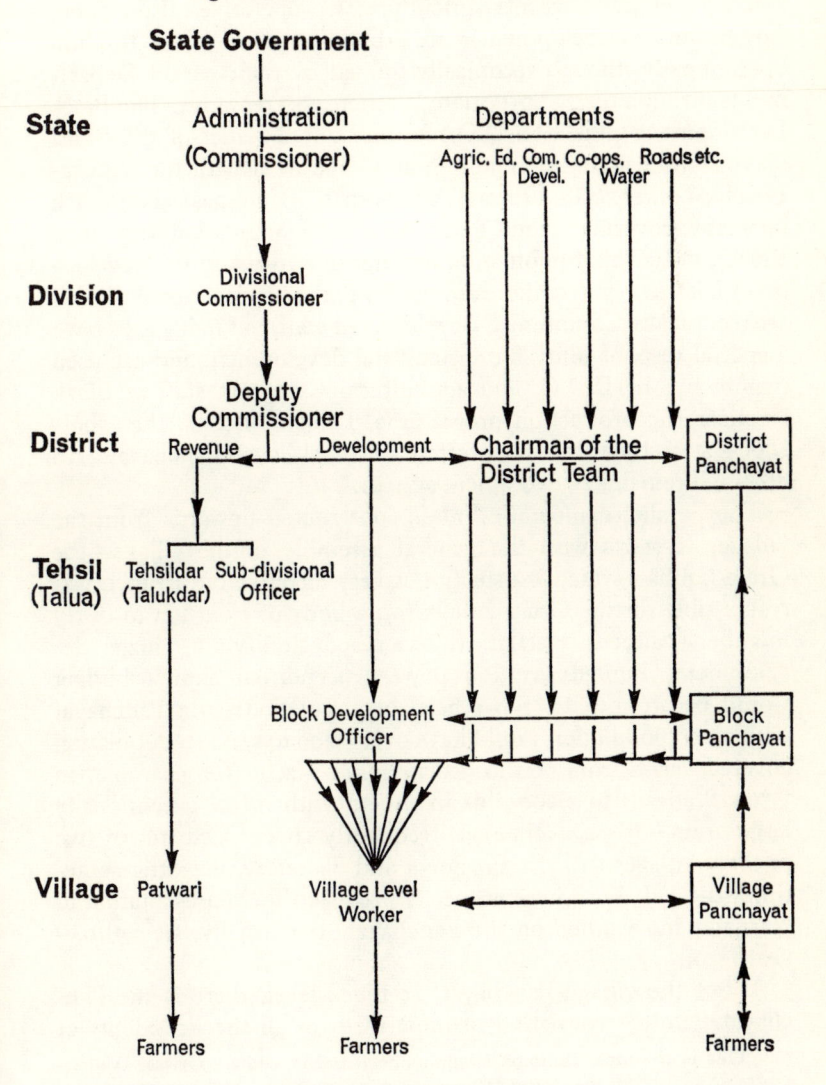

State	State Government → Administration (Commissioner)	Departments: Agric., Ed. Com. Devel., Co-ops. Water, Roads etc.			
Division	Divisional Commissioner				
District	Deputy Commissioner — Revenue / Development	Chairman of the District Team	District Panchayat		
Tehsil (Talua)	Tehsildar (Talukdar), Sub-divisional Officer				
		Block Development Officer	Block Panchayat		
Village	Patwari	Village Level Worker	Village Panchayat		
	Farmers	Farmers	Farmers		

on the strength of the Panchayati Raj or Community Development Department for Establishment purposes. The vital novelty in this position is that the Block level officials of other Departments (such as those of Agriculture, Co-operatives, Education, Community Development) are directly responsible to him operationally, though technically guided by their parent Departments through their appropriate District representative. The Block Development Officer (B.D.O.) is undisputed leader of the Block team. This second line ends up at village level with the Village-Level Worker (Gramsewak, or woman Grammasewika) each normally covering about 6,000 to 10,000 population (ten to a Block), or half that population in Intensive Agricultural Development Districts, where there are twenty to the Block. These V.L.W.s are technically Community Development staff, but today they have a special responsibility for agricultural development and are used mainly by the B.D.O. and agricultural Extension staff at Block level for the production programme. In some States, the whole Block staff has been transferred to Block-level Panchayats; in others, it remains a government system.

The parallel democratic line is constructed upwards from the village. It starts with the general assembly of the village—the Gram Sabha—which is usually not very effective but in theory is responsible for the Gram Panchayat, a body of from ten to thirty members, directly elected. It has responsibility for village development, limited taxation powers (a normal annual budget would be around Rs. 2 per head of population: so a Panchayat with 2,000 population would have over £200 to spend). Population covered varies from 700 to 900 in some States (for example, in Uttar Pradesh) to 2,000-plus in others with a few exceptionally large units (Orissa, Kerala). It frequently covers a cluster of two or three villages. It has a President and Secretary, the latter sometimes the V.L.W. There is special provision for representation of Harijans and women on the Panchayat. It normally has a three-year term.

Above the village Panchayat, at Block level, there is the Panchayat Samiti,[1] consisting in most cases of all the Presidents of

[1] This is the most common single name (Andhra, Bihar, Orissa, Maharashtra, Punjab), but the reader may come across Anchalik Panchayat or Panshad (Assam and Bengal), Janpada Panchayat (M.P.), Kshetra Samiti (U.P.), Panchayat Union Council (Madras), Taluka Panshad (Gujarat), or Taluk Board (Mysore).

Village Panchayats plus some additional nominated members, including the Members of State Legislative Assemblies (M.L.A.s) and some others.[1] This Block Panchayat has considerably larger financial and administrative resources[2] and duties; it is serviced by the B.D.O. and his Extension staff from all relevant Departments.

At District level is the highest level of the Panchayat system —the Zilla Parishad. There are large differences in both method of election and function of this District council. In Gujarat, Maharasthra, Punjab and Uttar Pradesh it is directly elected, and in these four plus Andhra it has executive functions. In most other States it is indirectly constituted, consisting of the Chairmen of the Block Panchayats, with some additions (M.L.A.s, M.P.s). In Orissa it has been recently abolished. Where election is indirect, the Zilla Parishad is normally consultative (except in Andhra). Where it is executive, it has taken over almost all the functions of the older District Boards, which were the Local Goverment organizations covering the normal range of services, corresponding fairly closely to a County Council.

By 1963 over 200,000 Village Panchayats had been established in India, covering 95% of rural population (there is no formal system in Kerala, Jammu and Kashmir). Today it can be regarded as virtually the universal system in India.

Only some special features of interest can be mentioned here. First the variations between States point to different degrees of boldness or caution in handing over power from the Administration to democratic systems, in two main respects. Some States— indeed most—give very great emphasis to the Block Panchayat, but restrict the District level Panchayat to advisory functions, no doubt because the Block council is primarily a collection of village Presidents, close to the ground, elected on village franchise. In contrast, a District Council, directly elected from a population of possibly 1,500,000, must inevitably be a Party-political system. Secondly, some States virtually hand over the Village and Block level staff to Panchayat control (Maharasthra actually hands over the District staff as well), whereas others keep a firm grip on the administrative staff. There is almost every shade of difference

---

[1] In Mysore the Block Panchayat is *directly* elected, and there are modifications in some other States, e.g. Madhya Pradesh and Punjab.
[2] Up to about Rs. 10 per head of population, i.e. Rs. 1 million or more.

between transferring almost complete responsibility to the Panchayats and treating them almost wholly as consultative.

Administratively, the system boldly resolves the difficulty that a central government must be divided into Departments, whereas a village, and the process of development itself, are indivisible wholes. The solution is to put the point of reunification of government services at the Block, which is the lowest point which commands adequate resources and staff, and to make this co-ordination decisive by the outright decision to give the Block Development Officer operational command over all services at his level and below. In the areas of intensive development the Block is further strengthened by doubling the number of V.L.W.s and quadrupling the number of agricultural Extension staff at Block level. Andhra has gone further in focusing the system a second time at the District level, making the D.C. and the Chairman of the Zilla Parishad into a two-man 'Development Board' with virtually complete policy control of the District.

This concentration of authority in the Block Development Officer is, of course, a dangerous decision, giving great additional power to the generalist administrators[1] and breaking the direct chain of command from the Director of Agriculture through District Agricultural Officer to the agricultural Field Officers at Block and Village level. It thus conflicts with the industrial thinking just quoted in emphasizing authority rather than chairmanship in the co-ordinator.[2] It is natural, at the present stage, that the bolder decision is taken in India, though it has its penalties. There were indeed many complaints from some Departments about this, and particularly about the 'Revenue Service mentality' of the District Administration in some areas.

Politically, there are many points of extreme interest, most of which must be put in their fuller context in the next chapter. Here it is enough to point to the hesitations between direct and indirect election; the decision—taken only after great argument—that M.L.A.s should sit on Block Panchayats, thus introducing a party-political element even where the original village elections

---

[1] It is sometimes emphasized even further by giving to the *revenue* arm of the administration powers of supervision over the *development* Blocks, e.g. the Divisional Revenue Officer may be called upon to inspect and report on the working of a number of Blocks.

[2] In practice, most small industrial firms do the same; it is only the most sophisticated which clearly distinguish authority from chairmanship.

were, at least nominally, not on party lines; and the decision in some States to combine in a single District Council both development functions and routine Local Government functions.

Inevitably, with two parallel jurisdictions, and in a transitional phase, there are bound to be confusions and clashes. In the effort to define responsibilities, documents will have on different pages 'The Panchayat Samiti[1] will be responsible for development in its area', and 'The Block Development Officer is charged with the co-ordination of development services in his area'; 'The B.D.O. is operationally responsible to the D.C.', and 'The B.D.O. is responsible for executing the decisions of the Panchayat Samiti'. In practice, a really strong Panchayat will largely direct the B.D.O. and a really weak Panchayat will be prodded and pushed into giving at least approval to the plans which the B.D.O. and his staff are in fact initiating and administering. But despite these natural difficulties, the strategic intention is clear. It has been admirably summed up by a most distinguished Indian, Tarlok Singh, when Deputy Chairman of the Planning Commission:

To secure the development of the rural economy, the entire machinery of district administration had to be strengthened and identified with the welfare of the people. This involved steps in three directions—firstly, provision of technical skills through a network of extension services; secondly, a co-ordinated approach to the village community and the problems of the peasant; and, thirdly, building up institutions by means of which the people could largely undertake development through their own initiative and participation. These steps led to the emergence of Community Development and the National Extension Service and, in due course, to the establishment of democratic Panchayati Raj institutions at the district and Block levels in addition to the Panchayats in the villages.[2]

5

It may seem unbalanced to devote so much space to one country's arrangements. It would be possible to describe the Pakistan system of Basic Democrats, elected from each village to form a Union Council covering about ten villages, and thereafter by indirect election and nomination to form a pyramid to State

[1] At Block level. The quotations are actual examples.
[2] Tarlok Singh, op. cit.

level—a system more dangerously political than India's and perhaps less firmly rooted in a real social unit, such as a single village or closely connected cluster. It would be possible to describe the system of Village Development Committees in Tanzania, and the balance between TANU Party influence, elected local government influence and the administrative chain of command. It would be interesting to compare the balance between administration, political activity and County Councils in Kenya, or (when it appears) the new constitution for Ghana. But the value of the Indian example is that it covers almost every question which can be raised on these topics; that it has been evolved over twenty years of independent government, by trial and error, by many large States adopting their own variations, with specific application to rural development in a huge and poor peasant economy, by some of the more sophisticated thinkers in the world. It provides a large number of practical case-studies of the effects of a dozen different administrative and political experiments in local development; and it has been carried through in a resolutely democratic country with elections on universal suffrage from the smallest village council to the Parliament of 500,000,000 people in Delhi.

It remains to ask how far the system as it stands could be adopted outside India, or outside Asia. Certainly there are some factors in it which are not repeated in all countries. First, a very strong administrative system; second, a supply of University and High School graduates which in India is ample for the purpose (though patchy in quality), for example, the Agricultural Extension Officers in the Blocks are normally all young men with a Degree in Agriculture; third, a considerable experience of Local Government and public commitment to the democratic process and an acceptance of this process by officials.[1] There are, indeed, many countries in Africa and some in Asia which could not match any of these three requirements at present. There are some which could match the first two (administrative quality and manpower) but not the third.

For countries which cannot match the experience of India in

[1] It could be said that many Indians have a rather cynical smile about democracy, and it is true that, in social terms, there are extremely strong feudal, authoritarian and plutocratic forces in India and much social inequality. Yet India is proud of maintaining, at least at elections, an open democratic system which continues to work, however erratically, and to mediate social change.

local representative institutions and in the control of them by administrative means, it is the higher layers of the Panchayat system which it would be most dangerous to copy. Once these become the undisputed arena for party politics—whether of one party or two or several—both the development effort and the relation with central Planning is apt to be submerged. If local representatives see themselves as politicians whose business is to win power and patronage or to retain it against all comers, chaos in local affairs is very near. It has been proved at the State level in India on many occasions, in Bengal and in Uttar Pradesh, to take only two examples in 1968; in many such cases—as in Kerala earlier—the central Administration has had to take over. That it has not happened so dramatically within the Panchayat system at District and lower levels is due partly to the intense focus on development in the new Panchayat regime, to the considerable powers and immense prestige of the Collectors and their staff, and to the more direct participation of farmers at the lower levels, whose interests are more practical than narrowly party-biased.

6

The opening of this chapter sketched in the roughest outline some stages of development in past societies, as they moved from the simplest imperial or feudal government to modern industrial development—a transition to growing diversity of energies in the community and growing complexity of control and services in the government. The problem of developing countries lies in their attempt to *create* both the dynamic energy and the detailed supervision and range of services in one bound, before the gradual build-up of education and initiative in the community. They thus attempt to foreshorten the painful process of creating a reliable and effective bureaucracy. These difficulties can be expressed in many ways. There is the attempt to build a modern, impartial, merit-based bureaucracy before older styles of social action (kinship, patronage) have lost their hold. There is the attempt to create representative government in very backward rural areas, in a type of society which was ruled in the past by very simple authoritarian means—the Law, the magistrates, the landowner. There is the attempt to supply out of poverty a range of personal and social services which have only been supplied historically out of wealth. There is the attempt to avoid the abuses of past industrial growth by regulation; but industry and commerce in many peasant countries are not the runaway horse of the European 19th century—they have scarcely learned to trot. Finally, there is the attempt to achieve all this before the level of literacy has reached even 50%.

The three main methods open to developing countries to stimulate and accelerate the processes of growth are by administrative action at the farmer's level; by political action to mobilize local energies; and by encouragement of any entrepreneurial initiatives, whether in industry or agriculture, which may be arising within the community. The last method may be self-denied by strongly socialist countries from an objection to capitalism and a fear—not ill-founded—of accentuating social inequality.

The difficulties of administrative action, involving a large bureaucracy, have been illustrated already. For essential services, such as agricultural Extension, there is no evading them. Training, discipline, the gradual whittling down of tribal, kinship, patronage and corrupt influences by action from the very highest leadership of the country is one means of control. The other is a rigid economy in inessential services, cutting out some of the more sophisticated social and industrial services, so that essential government officers can be better paid and at least a little less subject to pressures. There are possibilities of reshaping central administrative methods into a more dynamic shape, of clarifying procedures for co-ordination, and of further delegation to the best of the provincial and district administrators; in this field the experience of industry would be useful.

The possibility of mobilizing local energies by methods just described as 'political' shows more obvious hope. It has been a true instinct in Africa, and a sound evolution in India, to lay great stress on this. Participation in development *is* possible in peasant societies at the village level, and especially by the farmers. It can indeed be channelled through local, face-to-face representative committees, whether in Panchayats, in Co-operatives, in the direct 'Athenian' democracy of the Comilla system, in Village Development Committees, Farmers' Associations and the like. Although such work must be described, in a broad sense, as political—it is certainly not bureaucratic, and in one-Party States it is likely to be animated by Party members—it is not *sui generis* with types of large-scale representative Local Government, such as County Councils, which are partly a manœuvre for delegation of bureaucratic services and partly designed to train for self-government rather than for development as such. That party politics should enter both the 'participation' and the 'Local Government' arena is inevitable, but there is much more hope that their good effects will be felt and their bad effects minimized in the lowest tier, where village people know their interests and control them directly.

In sophisticated countries such as India it may well be possible to carry up the participatory system to larger units—even to District—and fuse it with Local Government, though some States have shown great caution in this and some have refused. In many African countries, where traditions of Local Government are much shorter,[1] these representative institutions with wide areas have had a very chequered career—they are apt to overspend their funds, whether honestly or not, and collapse, besieged by angry teachers demanding unpaid salaries; indeed, this has happened often enough in India too. It may well be better to recognize that the Administration is better able to handle the limited services which are necessary at these levels and to build larger Local Government units only slowly.

To build an administrative service which is competent, honest, imbued with a spirit of service, and willing to listen to local people; and to provide means by which local communities can make their voice heard and combine in local action—these are the first two tasks. They are still far from completed in a great number of countries in the world. To achieve them requires a balance between the reality of political power in any given society, the ideal of regular and impartial administration, and the value of dynamic popular participation. It is now necessary to look at political power more squarely.

[1] India had District Boards in the 19th century.

CHAPTER IX

POLITICS

Politics, at its ephemeral level, concerns the rivalries of power; at its deep, secular level it concerns the order of society. The deep political problem for developing countries is the search for an order; the ephemeral, but critical, problem is to prevent the rivalries of power from ruining the nation.

Order is not any particular political system. It lies in a framework of related values, widely accepted in a society within which the individual life is to be led. Acceptance is never total: the order is modified through time both by its own imperfections, by great environmental changes and even by the lonely and often heroic rebellion of individual minds against these imperfections.

In the reality of daily life the order answers for the mass of people the huge question of their place and tasks and possibilities in life. Even in the harshest circumstances, their aim will be to live as 'well' as possible within it. In addition to the natural hopes of a fair share of good times as well as bad, 'well' also carries a social and moral tone and, at its core, a religious one. The great religions have supplied a basis for the order and the patience to support it; none of them have promised easy times. Within it certain real pieties can grow up, extending from the central religious core to the order itself and even to the common ways and common tools of life. No one who has met simple people living within such an order can fail to notice the contrast of their acceptance with the anxiety of our own disordered life.

Naturally, it is the religious writers who have gone furthest to define this sense of order. Perhaps it is best to quote one, certainly lonely and heroic, who speaks, not from the past with all its differences, but from the violence of our times—Simone Weil.[1] The order should involve equality:

Equality consists in a recognition, at once public, general, effective and genuinely expressed in institutions and customs, that the same amount

[1] Simone Weil, *The Need for Roots* (London, Routledge & Kegan Paul, 1952).

of respect and consideration is due to every human being, because this respect is owed to a human being as such, and is not a matter of degree.

But this (a definition of the 'human dignity' now so passionately reaffirmed by colonized countries) is compatible also with 'hierarchism':

Hierarchism ... is composed of a certain veneration, a certain devotion towards superiors, considered not as individuals, nor in relation to the powers they exercise, but as symbols. What they symbolize is that realm situated high above all men, whose expression in this world is made up of the obligations owed by each man to his fellow men. A veritable hierarchy presupposes a consciousness on the part of superiors of this symbolic function and a realization that it forms the only legitimate object of devotion among their subordinates. The effect of true hierarchism is to bring each one to fit himself morally into the place he occupies.[1]

Not only in Europe in earlier centuries but wherever in the world a settled peasant society grew up, some order reigned. The great world religions symbolize it and testify to it. And indeed, within animist societies an order, though of a very different type, has been evolved and has been guarded just as jealously, as the sole protection against the wild and against the mystery.

There is a striking parallel with the statements of Simone Weil in those from the African anthropologists:

These sacred symbols [myths, dogmas, ritual beliefs and activities], which reflect the social system endow it with mystical values, which evoke an acceptance of the social order which goes far beyond the obedience exacted by the secular sanctions of force. The social system is, as it were, removed to a mystical plane, where it figures as a system of sacred values beyond criticism or revision.

Or, again:

An African ruler is not to his people merely a person who can enforce his will on them. He is ... the symbol of their unity and exclusiveness and the embodiment of their essential values. He is more than a secular ruler; in that capacity the European government can to a great extent replace him. His credentials are mystical and from antiquity. [1]

[1] Meyer Fortes and E. E. Evans Pritchard (eds.), *African Political Systems* (London, Oxford University Press for International African Institute, 1961).

This balance of equality and human dignity on the one hand and of some hierarchical system on the other is at the root of the basic political differences which exist between countries in the developing world today. It is not merely a question of academic philosophy. The philosophy of, say, President Nyerere on the one hand and of the Northern Nigerian or the Malay hierarchy on the other has the most direct effects on development policy and practice—on the authority of administration, on the attitudes to private enterprise, on the acceptability of forms of government. In some at least of the developing countries an old hierarchy still commanded very considerable respect and acceptance when Independence came. In some, an extreme form of democracy was brought in without a slow transition but as a sudden revolution.

2

In the colonized countries, above whatever local order had existed, a widespread peace was gradually imposed by the invading Powers—in the East for about a century, in Africa for barely half that time. The wars which had rolled over the Indian peasantry for as long as recorded history at last came to an end. The tribal battles of Africa were suppressed. Many simple people, both in Asia and Africa, acknowledged the white man's peace and, for this at least, blessed him. But Empires which provide this outer framework of security may do little to change the ancient order at the level of village life; nor can they, of their very nature, create a national order among subjects.[1] At Independence the emerging nations found their old order unchanged at the deep level and certainly unsuited to new tasks. If they looked to the developed countries for a new model, they found in the white man's world energy, certainly, but neither internal nor external peace. The energy at least they needed; symbolized as democracy it had been part of the Independence struggle. Today in countries once supposedly quiescent—the resignation of the East, the African relaxed and laughing between bouts of violence—the most violent political energies in the world are breaking out, from Indonesia to Cuba—the politics of a secular, disordered, democratic world.

National politics came to these new societies in widely varying ways. In Asia the transition was not always abrupt. Perhaps

[1] Cf. Fortes, op. cit. The Europeans could replace government, but not the whole order.

continuity was greatest in India, Malaya, and uncolonized Thailand. Gandhi's great movement, which did indeed touch the life of the masses, was in some senses an appeal to the old Indian order (or its myth), threatened by foreign ways and indeed by those Indians—industrialists, financiers, intellectuals—who were following foreign models. It did much to reinforce the Hindu order, and also to reform it by the great attempt to renounce the worst elements of caste. Certainly, Nehru's vision of India (secular, socialist, industrialized) was a new and disruptive element; but it was a vision from Delhi, high above the village life and barely intelligible to it. Moreover, the strong administration of the old British Empire still ran on in Indian hands, and the Hindu order of the village ran on beneath its shadow. In Malaya, the traditional Muslim order, somewhat softened and modernized, seems to have taken over. Thailand had no violent break— Buddhism and monarchy continued. In the Philippines, an American commercialized democracy was superimposed on a Catholic colonial system—the revolution from below was crushed forty years earlier with Aguinaldo. It was otherwise in Indonesia, Indo-China, Burma, where the fiery forces of the democratic revolution were let loose at once.

In Tropical Africa, however, it is this fiery element which has almost universally prevailed. Only in a very few places (Ethiopia? the Fulani Empire? the Kingdom of Buganda?) was there an established order which stood a chance of surviving into Independence. Most African States were in fact sections cut from the tapestry of tribal life which blanketed the continent, a zone of neighbouring tribes held together only by the common administration of a colonial government. Almost to a man, their new leaders came preaching democracy and socialism, the ideas which, seeing themselves as revolutionaries, they had borrowed from the revolution in the West.

That these ideas were largely irrelevant to the real social texture of their countries, and, except in the most naïve and verbal form, unintelligible to the great mass of African people, was bound to cause trouble. At the start of Independence in most African countries there was a breathing space, given by the continuance of the administrative system which provided a firm platform from which political speeches could issue and indeed on which rivals could fight each other for power without great effect on the society below them. But where, as in the Congo, administration was suddenly and almost totally withdrawn, chaos and warfare were bound to follow. It is even possible to see Katanga supported by the Belgian interest indeed, but also by many solid Africans, trying to hold back from the edge of the fiery cauldron which Lumumba and the left-wing democrats had created.

In fact, in the African nations between 1950 and 1960, there was only a small band of potential leaders who had the chance to see beyond the immediate environment, intellectual as well as physical. It was the Universities of the West which gave this opportunity. These men were not described by the colonial administration as a handful of agitators simply because they taught revolt against the colonial power: it was also because they were fired by ideas borrowed from a different world and a different history; ideas which did not seem to fit the simple necessities of rural improvement and local administration in which the District Officers were—often enthusiastically—engaged.

Thus it is possible to divide the new politics into two main groups. In most of Africa a radical democracy triumphed; there is at least the attempt to make a single, violent transition from a tribal order to universal suffrage, often through the medium of a single 'party' system.[1] This mode of action, often supplanted by a military coup, applies also to some countries of Asia, notably Burma, Indonesia and North Vietnam. In the second group— India, Pakistan, mainland Malaya, Thailand—and in Africa perhaps Northern Nigeria and Ethiopia—a pre-existing order is the object of slow democratization. In the broadest possible terms, the first group is in search of a new order which has not yet been found; the second is in danger from the continuance of an old order, if it cannot adjust enough to democratic criticism, both within and outside its borders. We may now attempt to see, in more detail, the problems of each group, taking Africa first, and India, as a sample of the order in Asia, second.

3

During the anti-colonial struggle the African leaders had to mobilize a show of support from the villages and tribal areas—

[1] 'Party' in quotation marks because a 'party' originally implies one of two or more contestants. With this note of caution, the quotation marks will be dropped.

to get support from the disappointed or unemployed in the few large towns was easy. It was then that there emerged a strange kind of politics between the leaders and the villagers in which, on both sides, the outward form did not correspond with the inner realities. Before Independence the divergence was not quite so great: for the leaders preached that colonialism was the root of all evil and must go; and their listeners could be persuaded to believe it too. But when the external enemy was gone, the game of politics had still to be played, but mainly with local counters. To the village listeners the political theory was largely meaningless; but clearly there were gains to be made, local and even personal interests to be forwarded, by selling votes to the politicians who needed them. The defeat of an unpopular Chief, the favourable settlement of a tribal land dispute, the opportunity of salaried official jobs, a new road to the village or the lifting of an irksome restriction on hunting or cutting forest could be the bargain for support.

On the politicians' side, the formal party theory was perhaps equally unreal, for use chiefly in the external politics of the developing world.[1] For most of them the aim would be to amass a following, to be and to stay on the winning side in the rivalries at the top. Thus for the individual politician, with many rivals eager to replace him and perhaps only the slowly dwindling memory of his part in the Independence struggle to justify his place at the top, the support of his home tribe or community was vital, and on his side, he was quite prepared to meet the bargaining villagers halfway. There have been many who played politics simply as a tough game of power. These are the ephemeral politics of bargaining and power, with all their dangers.

But at the point of truth, on the lonely pinnacle at the top, there have been and still are some men of high ideals—a Nyerere or a Kaunda—to whom the vision of a fresh start, a new, co-operative and just order, is intensely real. They have a hard task, because the human tools they have to use may break in their hand, because the peasant masses may seem perversely materialist, because the economic environment remains stubbornly poor. There are others—Kenyatta or Mboya in Kenya—who are more empirical, working their way forward through compromise, whether with

[1] Cf. Srinivas, op. cit.: 'Agreeing to progressive resolutions satisfies our consciences and assures us of our worldly prospects, while at the same time our sense of facts assures us that nothing will be done.'

foreign capital or tribal interests, or between the conflicting pulls of Pan-African policy on one side and valued Western helpers on the other. They may indeed retain the vision but yet see how long and winding the road must be. They look more tolerantly on the signs of change within their own society, provided that they are signs of growth. Yet for neither of these types of thoughtful African leadership is the desired goal or the practical means of reaching it clearly seen. Their borrowing of democratic theory from the developed world is not particularly serviceable in their own; and the endeavour to pick up and use for modern purposes the values and institutions of the older African world suffers from a fatal defect: these values and forms were the product of the old environment, designed for subsistence and security, not for rapid economic growth. 'Ujamaa' in Tanzania has already been quoted as the clearest of examples.

In fact, there is reason to think that the next step could be surprising. For both social texture and individual attitudes are beginning to change fast in some parts of rural Africa, wherever the process of modernization through an agricultural programme shows signs of success. The slogans of the Independence era begin to lose their freshness, for many of the original political objectives of the revolution have been achieved. Except in southern Africa, freedom and a seat in the United Nations have been won. Neo-colonialism from the original colonial Powers can scarcely be credited; indeed, these Powers are so absorbed with their own problems that the danger is not of too much Western interest in Africa but of too little. Insensibly, the focus of concern moves from the external world of ideological politics to the internal, and especially to poverty. High on the list for action is the transformation of the rural economy from 'subsistence' to commercial farming, from the traditional to the cash economy.

This is not an empty form of words. Wherever progress is being made, farmers are persuaded to earn more, to grow cash-crops and buy food, to count their success in cash per acre, to change customary tenure to freehold title, to borrow, to employ non-family labour, to invest and sell. And because they do not live in an economy but in a society, this is a movement from the traditional to the cash society. There will be a tendency to slough off the obligations of the traditional order, together with some of the needs and fears which long ago created them; a move towards greater individualism. This is, of course, quite compatible with a co-operative society, at least in such services as marketing. But the member of a 'Co-operative' is wholly different from the member of an extended family. The co-operator is acting, not simply as a member of a total community but in an institution in which only one of his roles is relevant—the role of an individual producer of grain or cotton. There may well be confusion to start with; perhaps the Co-operative will consist of a single kinship group, or perhaps the Secretary will favour his own lineage; but eventually the logic of the situation will show through. Appeals to the old tradition and institutions will have a limited life. They may make a bridge to new institutions by the outward similarity of their form; but the content is wholly different.[1] As the farmer sees new opportunities of prosperity, he will see also the need for new institutions through which to pursue his ends. Even the Hindu, Muslim or Buddhist order in Asia is now beginning to crack and splinter under the pressures of development and its new values.

In the long run, it is an obligation of politics to be relevant. In a word, the politics of the Independence struggle are largely irrelevant to the problems of economic development of the peasant community in Africa. As new interests and attitudes begin to emerge in the villages, they will have to be reflected in the political arenas. It may well be that, for a time, there will be semi-Utopian local societies—perhaps in Tanzania—just as there were in the earliest Puritan colonies of America and just as there were Soviets of sailors or workers to captain ships and manage factories in the first days of the Russian Revolution. But whether the purity of the new ideal harks backwards to a golden age or forwards to a new world, in fact it is in danger of limiting the complexity and specialization in social growth. Not even in the short run of ten years can an African village which is making speedy economic growth remain purely a community of co-operant and equal farmers; for some will become processors and some transporters and some labourers and some craftsmen and some clerks. If society is not differentiating, it is not growing; as it differentiates, it becomes less like the traditional society of the past. The virtues

[1] The common use of old traditions of communal labour is an obvious example; in the past, men worked like this on limited occasions, because there was no alternative. Now, the government could do it, or the cash system could do it, by paying wage-labour.

of the past need not be lost completely: there can be care for the poor and restraint on the rich; but the institutions through which this is achieved, and both the moral and emotional tone, will be new. This is not a cynical dismissal of the ideals of many of the best in Africa; nor is it the ridiculous assertion that only through individualist capitalism or full-blooded Communism is any economic progress possible. It is simply to say that the new order of society in peasant countries which avoids both extremes will be subtle and complex, and its shape is not yet to be seen.

In South and South-East Asia the same dilemma has been true, although in a more advanced form. The countries which made a radical sweep at Independence—Burma, Indonesia—have yet to find a way forward which excludes the Communist solution and yet preserves some of their ideals. But in Malaya, Singapore, Thailand, India, Pakistan, where commercialization is advanced and accelerating, it is the opposite issue which is posed—the way to avoid the inequalities and oppressions which marked economic progress in the West and for which so high a price is being paid there today. It is with this frame of reference that we can look briefly at the actual relevance and effects of political life near the level of the farming economy. Because commercialization is more advanced in India and Pakistan, their problems, already more visible, may be the most revealing.

4

Indian politics are changing fast, in two ways which are connected: how close this connection is would need a great deal of detailed research. At the State and All-India level the decline in Congress strength, twenty years after Independence, was always probable; it is only surprising that it lasted so long. In the politics of patronage, the certain winner has at first a huge advantage, since supporters expect a return for their votes;[1] for at least fifteen years Congress had this pull. But new issues arise, the regime of patronage creates its own opposition of the unpatronized. Moreover, as the States have become more powerful, patronage from a State government,

---

[1] See, for example, a remark made about the Chief Minister of Mysore, quoted by Srinivas, op. cit.: 'Shri Hanumanthayya wants to rule strictly and impartially, but he must realize that the electors don't want it. They want him to confer favours on the people who have elected him. We want returns for what we have done.'

even if it is in conflict with the majority at Delhi, may bring big rewards, even though the State's share of central government favour may seem to be imperilled. At the State level local issues may become those which really divide the political vote. The Americans would understand best how a Federal Party can so adjust its policies, State by State, to be sure of at least substantial backing everywhere; and Congress, with its total spectrum of interests, less tied to principle than the more polarized parties which challenge it, might even yet contrive to straddle the All-India scene. How well it will learn this trick the next Election will show.

But—and this is the second change—new interests are beginning to appear, for which perhaps none of the major parties have fully allowed. Rural society is splitting not into two main groups—the big landlords and the poor—but into three. The prosperous medium farmer is the new appearance—the man with from ten to fifty irrigated acres; the man who has really grasped what the new agricultural programme can do for him. As he appears and multiplies, the whole group from which he comes begins to split. Some—the smaller owners and secure tenants, will strive to follow him; some will go down and join the landless and the labourers, forced out by rising rents, by modernized methods, by the gradual breakdown of customary arrangements or cash farming replacing subsistence over a slowly growing area. Numerically, this bottom group is already large and may grow faster. It could make room for a Peasants' Party which would attack not only the landlords but possibly the 'kulaks' too. Where and how this split will come is still uncertain; for an alternative combination, in some States, would be for both the small tenants and the 'kulaks' to press for tenancy reform, to strengthen their position against the big landowners, the merchants, the moneylenders, the caste dominance in local politics. A new pattern of politics is on the horizon.

It is within the Panchayat system that this issue will be crystallized, for here is an organization unquestionably in touch with the realities of village life. In a State of 30 million inhabitants there may well be 10,000 Presidents of Village Panchayats,[1] each directly elected, and each also sitting on the powerful Block Panchayat, through which the main development effort of the Administration is being poured. Who these men will be, and how they will vote,

[1] 80% rural population is 24,000,000; 2,400 average population per Panchayat.

will depend very much on the tenure system of their Districts and on the success of the agricultural programme. As one example, a low food price meant little to customary subsistence tenants or craftsmen whose pay was a share of rice or wheat at harvest; perhaps it meant little to the landlord who was comfortable enough. But to the landless, to the progressive cash-farmer, to the landlord investing in expensive modernization it will mean a great deal. Security of tenure will mean a great deal. Marketing through Co-operatives may range merchants on one side and perhaps the small and middle farmers and the Administration on the other. Round the bare meeting-rooms of Panchayats at Village and Block will be ranged, not so often now the leadership of a customary society but a group of men with precise and often divergent economic interests for which they will seek political support. The more powerful the Panchayat system becomes, the more State (and, by inference, Federal) parties will need to capture it. These are, and will increasingly become, the politics of rural development.

In Pakistan both regional and local differences will weigh perhaps even more clearly and heavily. In West Pakistan it has not, on the whole, been the biggest of the landowners who have been responsible for the leap forward in production. It has been the middle farmers of the Punjab. They, and with them the growing agricultural industries of Daska and Sialkot, will be a new and powerful political force. In East Pakistan with its commercial atmosphere, smaller holdings, dense and sophisticated population, the political pattern may well be dominated by a middle class, but of a very different nature. Whether the Basic Democracy system will in fact provide the forum where the new politics of development is fought out depends on how long it lasts and whether it could survive an eclipse of the President who founded it. But by bringing a real political life close to the village it has unquestionably started a political process which will, if necessary, find other channels of expression; it will not die away.

5

What part can the Administration play in this situation? In theory, the answer is simple: it will do what the politicians instruct it to do. In practice, it is not so straightforward. In New Delhi the

Administration, with the Planning Commission and the host of special institutions concerned with economic and social policy, is certainly powerful in forming opinion. With the backing of Nehru, and because Congress has represented too wide a range of interests to impose a narrow policy on the administrators, the Administration has done much to keep India on a steady course of social reform and agrarian development, with a tinge of State Socialism in its political colour. In the States, where more dogmatic Parties may come to power, where it is less easy for the civil service to dodge or deflect direct orders from a political government determined to have its way, the room for manœuvre is much smaller. Indeed, in some States a Collector who too often crosses the path of a powerful State legislator could find himself posted to a distant and uncomfortable new District; a Block Development Officer who does the same with the Chairman of the Panchayat Samiti could suffer the same fate, and perhaps more easily, because his office does not embody so much of the prestige of the Administration as the Collector's does.[1] But in most States the Collector is still a Great Power, even in face of a District Panchayat. It is not altogether unrealistic to suppose that, at least in some degree, the Administration, under a landowner government, can still play its traditional role of 'Protector of the Poor'. This was equally true in Pakistan under Ayub Khan's regime.

The Administration plays a large part in the preparation of policy and in shaping the tool for executive action. What is put up to Cabinet, and the form in which it comes, plays a large part in what issues with the stamp of political approval. And from that moment onwards there are in fact huge discretions within the administrative system as to the form and the tone of what is done. The vast apparatus of Panchayati Raj and the Block system owes its existence largely to thoughtful administrators: the fact that a system so finely balanced, as between the official and the elected instruments, can work at all, and has achieved so much, is a tribute to their skill.

All that has been said of patronage, of the power of political bosses in the Districts and Blocks and even in the village, is true. Perhaps this power will assert itself yet more strongly through

---

[1] See particularly Hugh Gray, 'Andhra Pradesh' in Weiner (ed.), *State Politics in India*, for a revealing statement by a Block Development Officer on this situation.

these local instruments which are now to its hand; perhaps Panchayati Raj will indeed prove to have given to the existing magnates a strong injection of statutory and political authority over and above their economic grip on village life. Certainly, unless some form of Agrarian or Peasants' Party arises to check this, it is a possibility in some States which cannot be excluded. But the possible emergence of a new political force in the farming interest, the idealism of some honoured political leaders, and the commitment of some of the Administration itself to 'the protection of the poor' will certainly modify and may go far to counterbalance this danger. The equation 'politicians instruct: civil servants obey' is far too simple to describe a society as complex, as able, and as well supplied with men of force and integrity, both in politics and in administration, as India is today. In so far as Delhi is pushed above the battle by the strengthening of State political and financial power, it will also be able to play, perhaps increasingly, the role of statesmanship rather than of political manœuvre. Politics may move in favour of the big men or of the smaller progressive farmers. On the outcome of this issue the direction and nature of agricultural policy will greatly depend.

6

Much writing on development simply *assumes* a political system within which development is possible. But, unless politics can provide a framework within which development can take place without constant uncertainty and even violence, all other aspects of development policy fall to the ground. It is useless to think only of stable, skilled, paternal administration of rural development; it must have a political base. And even administration backed by local participation is not enough. In many countries, particularly in Asia, changes in the local power structure are needed before administration, even with local committees or associations, can develop local potential—and changes in local power mean political change.

What is required of a political system to enable rural development to go forward? First, the political will to create a development situation—we have seen this particularly in relation to land tenure. Second, provision for the expression of local needs. Third, a method of establishing and supporting or changing a central government, and a method which does not, of its very nature, result in the constant disruption and distortion of the local development effort.

As to political will, the situation in most of Tropical Africa is not really difficult. Without an established landlord and merchant domination of the rural community, there is no obstructive power which needs to be broken. The old chiefly power has been undermined; the last obstacle, and that weakening year by year, may be some still solid tribal culture, often among pastoral groups such as the Masai or Samburu in Kenya, which is impervious to modernization. This is increasingly a marginal problem, and probably solved by administrative and technical policies rather than by politics. This brings out an implication of key importance—that in Africa it is the process of establishing and supporting a national government for which party politics is primarily needed, and not for local purposes. The process of turning customary tenure into some form of individual tenure can be done administratively with the aid of local participation.

But in Asia, political will to break those parts of a land tenure system and of local power structures which inhibit development is a necessity for progress. It can only be generated by a politics which goes to the mass of farmers and enables them to exert political power, by votes and with protection from reprisals. It is this requirement—that party political action (not merely participation) is needed at local level—which raises so many difficulties. The chief of these difficulties is that the offer of representative local institutions will be seized and monopolized by the existing magnates who have means to bribe or terrify the village voter; that to let politics into the local arena may result in constant faction and disruption; and that the very process used for national elections every few years may politicize and disorganize local development, even if party political representation and responsibility is not institutionalized there. We can deal with these difficulties in order.

In India we have seen already that universal suffrage in the village Panchayat system is tending to break up the unquestioned control of the old dominants. It is an uneven process and a slow one but it is in train. The danger lies more in the second difficulty, the side-effects of party politics. But in some other countries in Asia the first hurdle has not been surmounted. In much of West

Pakistan the big landowners are still unchallengeable; in the Philippines no real break in a thoroughly bad tenancy system has been achieved; in Thailand, the Establishment, often immensely rich, is still protected by a non-elected government, and the proportion of tenancy in the central plain of the Chao Phya River is high—though it is low in the poorer areas of the Korat Plateau in the Northeast. India remains the critical experiment in using universal suffrage at local level to effect political change.

The value of an elective system to Panchayats has been shown— it offers a way for suppressed but potentially progressive forces to break through, and it forces the traditional leadership to take at least enough notice of popular demand to retain their seats. Its danger is in exchanging the dominance of landlords for the dominance of party bosses and a thoroughly corrupt party machine. The issue is well illustrated by the controversy between those who favour indirect election from the Village Panchayat to the Block and from the Block to the District, and those who favour direct election to the Block Panchayat (for instance, Mysore) or the District (for example, Maharashtra). Indirect election carries village Presidents to the Block and Block Chairmen (usually village Presidents) to the District: it thus emphasizes the first face-to-face election to the Village Panchayat. Direct election, on the other hand, is more clearly party-political; in its favour it is said that timid electors may fear to vote against a magnate in the village but are more free to follow their own will in voting for a District representative, who will not (with rare exceptions) be their landlord, patron or employer. The same argument is used for higher elections: 'landless labourers may hesitate to oppose their employer for control over local government but need not fear sanctions by supporting opposing candidates for more remote Assembly or Parliamentary seats'.[1] Moreover, industrial and other interests are represented at higher levels and tend to modify the landlord influence.

Against it opponents urge that at least Village Presidents are close to the ground and genuinely concerned with local problems whereas the political candidates in direct elections at District or even Block may be simply ambitious politicians. It is clear that the resolution of this argument depends on the freedom of the village elections. If, *de facto*, the old power-holders get through, direct

[1] Weiner, *State Politics in India*.

elections to the higher tiers may be helpful in bringing in new forces; if new progressive forces are emerging at village level, it is better to carry them up to more powerful positions.

This may seem a very local and detailed argument. But it is vitally important, not only in India and Asia generally but also in Africa. For it illustrates sharply the distinction between participation—ground-level expression of real, local development needs in units small enough for the expression to be relevant and concrete—and party politics, which express more general, vague support of a political philosophy, a sectional interest (not necessarily economic—it may be religious, or linguistic, or ethnic), or simply the expectation of patronage from backing a winner.[1] In detailed local terms, participation is more likely to aid development but where, as in India, political will at the centre is needed to change conditions (of tenure and so forth), party politics may be essential even at the local level.

The danger of politicizing local affairs is, of course, faction. This word has a peculiarly Indian connotation at present because of the admirable recent work of political scientists there.[2] But it is much quoted by Thucydides as the bane of Greek political life and the destroyer of cities; it dominated the Renaissance scene in Italy, and has appeared in strength wherever political activity is wholly aimed at winning power and patronage for one group or another, rather than with differences of economic or social policies and the broad interests of large groups of the population. Faction is relatively harmless in aristocratic States; whether one group or another gains power and its perquisites, major policy for the nation may be unchanged and even seen with long vision and experienced judgement: much of English 18th- and 19th-century government had large elements of purely aristocratic factionalism. But when factional success depends upon a democratic system—on humouring voters—then racial prejudice, religious intolerance, linguistic bigotry, caste affiliations, and many other human frailties, however horrifyingly irrelevant to the needs of development, will become the currency of vote-catching.

Faction is equally operative in Africa, although it tends to have

---

[1] Cf. the observation of Srinivas on the expectations of Mysore voters to get advantages, not impartiality, from the candidate they support (p. 226).

[2] For example, that of Paul Brass in Uttar Pradesh, and the Myron Weiner studies (both quoted *supra*).

other names—often tribalism. But because a politician seeks support in his tribal homeland, it does not necessarily mean that he is tribalist at heart; it may simply be the means to reach a personal ambition of power and influence and to gather the most obvious and easy support for his faction. As Brass has observed, the successful politician is one who can gather in additional support (outside caste in India, outside tribe in Africa) without losing his basic block of tribal or caste votes. Faction split Western Nigeria and led to the fall of Awolowo and the later Enaharo plot and trial. Faction in 1967 and 1968 has blackened the name of State politics in India, as the rival groups fight it out with kidnapping and fisticuffs in Bengal and elsewhere.[1]

Obviously, there is a period of acute danger in the early years of a democratic system when it is installed before the older pattern of patronage has weakened, when it has to appeal to a semi-literate and dependent electorate, and at a time when major divisions of social and economic interest have not yet crystallized in the community to form a basis for arguments on policy rather than on faction. There is, therefore, the more reason to exclude party politics from the arena of local development and participation as far as is institutionally possible, except in those countries where a change in political will at the centre is a precondition for local development. Clearly, some form of political representation is needed to form a central government; it is by no means so obvious that it is also needed to conduct local administration in the circumstances of many developing countries today. We are here faced with the third difficulty—the means of preventing a system, intended for electing central Assemblies and Parliaments, from bedevilling the management of local development.

If things are as bad as this, why have not India and many other States fallen into total chaos? There is a clear answer to this. First, some of them did virtually collapse (Pakistan is one; there are several in Africa): they were in a sense rescued by a military or semi-military dictatorship, or the chaos was anticipated by the achievement of total power by a single party (such as TANU in

---

[1] In one State Assembly (February 1968) one factional group thwarted by the inaccessibility of their enemy in the Chamber (he was sitting on a raised dais), dashed out into the streets, secured a stepladder, and, returning, triumphantly stormed his citadel and prevented the passing of the Estimates.

Tanzania, UNIP in Zambia), which creates a totally different kind of political activity. The tendency to move to monolithic government in developing countries, either a dictatorship or a one-party system, is too widespread to be coincidence. It represents a failure of multi-party politics to work in these circumstances. Monolithic government enables the administration to get on with the development job. The continued steadiness of administration has played the key role, not only in Africa but in India itself, where democratic politics, in a more mature society, have just managed to maintain a workable structure.

Nevertheless, some means of constituting a central government has to exist. It is easy to pick holes in democracy: 'Democracy is a very bad system of government; the trouble is that all the others are even worse.'[1] To create an entirely new system of government by any means except the use of suffrage is exceedingly difficult. The main variants in this century have been the Bolshevik party system, Fascism, and the one-party systems common in Tropical Africa. If we leave Fascism on one side, the main point of interest lies in the differences between the Communist and the African one-party solution. They are clear. The Communist system is based upon a small, highly indoctrinated, highly centralized, Jesuitical party nucleus, with branches spread through society which effectively control local activity on lines strictly laid down. It is a bureaucracy as well as a government. Most of the African parties, on the other hand, are mass parties which anyone can join without apprenticeship or training; they are intended to mobilize enthusiasm, and to act as channels of communication between people and government. Although in many cases there is in Africa a highly generalized party philosophy, often elaborated by a leader in sophisticated language and form (Senghor, Sekou Touré, Nyerere), it represents an attitude and aspiration rather than the strict directives through which the Communists retain control. Thus, unlike the Bolshevik Party, the African parties may be good for mobilization and participation, but are not equipped to administer.

They may, however, be well designed to *form* a government which will use a professional administration as its executive. From the village party-committee through higher levels it may be possible to maintain a process which is both fairly representative of

[1] Attributed to the late Sir Winston Churchill.

local needs and opinions and also a selecting and winnowing process through which the eventual M.P.s will appear. Nyerere's experiment of giving local people an extra chance, through un-rigged universal suffrage, of approving or disapproving the local party's choice of candidates is an additional refinement, which has worked well once. Whether it would work as well again depends upon the degree of rigging which local candidates may achieve, now that they know the procedure better.

The conclusion seems to be emerging that a one-party system may be a reasonably satisfactory method of forming a central government in Africa, basically because, in present conditions, a two (or more) party system will produce conflicts which are not concerned with alternative policies—the mass of African society is not sufficiently diversified, or organized into interest-groups, or perhaps sufficiently educated to make policy a criterion. The conflicts will be factional or tribal or based on personal rivalries of politicians; and such conflict is not helpful to society.

Secondly, there is no reason to suppose that the one-party system should imply the establishment of representative Local Government. The same difficulties and the failures which beset earlier experiments of this kind, in India as well as in Africa, are likely to be repeated. In the early stages of Independence it was natural for the central government to wish to have close political surveillance of the District Administration. Tanzania, Zambia, Ghana, Eastern Nigeria, to name only four, had political Commissioners to see that the civil service administrators caught the new atmosphere and the new aims of the Independence movement and the party leadership. The party needed control; it had to fight rivals at the political level, and it needed to 'de-colonialize' the Administration, especially where a considerable number of expatriates were still in the District service. This modification is quite different from establishing an all-purpose elected, political council to do the job of District administration. The appointed political Commissioners will be senior leaders, in close touch with the central (Party) government and more likely to follow its policies than a locally elected Council; and they will be served by a professional administration, paid by the central government, supported by central Ministries, rather than by servants of a County Council. Indeed, as Independence grows older and more self-confident, there has been in some African countries a tendency to rebuild the prestige and authority of the Administration (now wholly Africanized) in the provinces and to reduce somewhat the influence of the local politician.

It may well seem that a country which has an elected central government, some degree of choice in local candidates and a wide opportunity for participation at local levels has enough political activity for the time being; as sophistication, development and experience grow, the institutions for participation may also grow into full organs of self-government. For some countries this growth has still far to go.

Thus for the Indian-type situation, where the Administration is certainly good enough to provide stimulation and service to farmers, we are left with the problem of amending systems of tenure and of emancipating a new group of progressive farmers. It seems more probable that this can be achieved from a combination of Union and State party-political pressure than by giving additional political power to local elected bodies which so largely will consist of those who have most to lose. In Africa, in contrast, the Administration still needs maximum support, both centrally and locally. Possibly the one-party system can do two essential jobs—to stimulate and lead local participation at a strictly local level, and to form, in effect, the constituency from which a central government is drawn by a winnowing process. It is highly unlikely that it can also play any effective administrative role as well.

7

Finally, we return to the question of an order in society. In much of Asia a traditional order exists and has a religious core to support it; but in its political aspect it needs modification. Perhaps nowhere is this more true than in Thailand, where growing levels of education will necessarily increase criticism of a highly unrepresentative regime, and where the hostile propaganda of the Left has been openly flouted by the American alliance and by direct military intervention in the Vietnam war. Where, as in Burma, the old order has been overturned, the military successors are faced with the dilemma of becoming a permanent 'temporary' government or of risking a politicization which may be hard to control—the same is true, though in somewhat different conditions, in Pakistan.

In Tropical Africa it might be said that no large-scale and effective order exists, save perhaps in the highly Islamicized areas on the West Coast. Even the old order of large and sophisticated peoples—the 5,000,000 Nigerian Yoruba, for example—is not genuinely adapted to a modern economy. The many forms of animism do not provide a universal religious core, or a common doctrine, or a basis upon which science is easily built: Christianity, though widespread, does not really dominate either institutions (such as marriage) or ideals; Islam, perhaps the easiest to adopt in terms of simple observance, goes deep only among a few. In political ideology neither capitalism, nor a socialism recognizable by its Western originators, nor Communism is wholly accepted. The tendency to look backwards into African social history for a characteristic 'African' order, even to invent dreams and visions based upon it, comes up against the fact that the real African order, as it has been lived for centuries, is one adapted to harsh subsistence circumstances, a great poverty of technique, and an isolated world.

There is little choice to be had from the West, which is convulsed with the effort either to find a new humanistic order which is credible and disciplined or to demythologize and renew the Christian tradition from which its civilization rose. From the Communist East, the rigidity of Bolshevik discipline, whether Russian or Chinese, is not attractive to newly liberated countries with so many open choices before them—possibly the more inventive compromises of Yugoslavia or, if they survive, Czechoslovakia, may seem more attractive. In terms of agricultural development the Bolshevik solution has had a bad history, particularly from its habit of enforcing universally wrong judgements taken at a distant centre. The African utopian solutions, where backward-looking, have the opposite disadvantage—a tendency to Puritanism which, in their case, is apt to freeze development in its tracks. Nevertheless, they are capable of modification, and they do contain the essential moral and spiritual elements from which an order could eventually emerge. Western countries, burdened by their immense bureaucracy, imprisoned to some degree by their own materialism, would be well to look on such new experiments in developing countries with a sympathetic eye. It is surely through politics that an order will emerge; but it will have to come through a true political philosophy. Until that comes, the unprincipled politics of faction, tribalism, patronage, personality is a dangerous animal which will need tight control. A political scientist remarked recently that: 'Politicians are not concerned with economic development: they are concerned with political power.' Of ephemeral politics that may well be true; but unless they are governed by a deeper, secular political vision, the prospects for development are poor indeed.

CHAPTER X

EDUCATION

In the context of rural development it is especially the task of education, aided by technical progress, to open a way out from the enclosed society of the village into a wider world both by helping to create new attitudes and by improving skills. This chapter deals mainly with settled peoples with some modern contact. It does not apply so closely to hill tribes, many mobile pastoral societies, or to those in a pre-development stage. Warlike hillmen and pastoralists are enclosed in a different way—by their own unsubdued self-confidence which does not wish interference (or education) and may greet it with a spear or a home-made rifle. There are such both in Asia and Africa. They are a special problem, beyond the range of this book.

Behind Mud Walls was a happy choice of title for the Wisers' book,[1] a metaphor for the circle of suspicion and fear which surrounds the villagers' life. The Wisers paraphrase their attitude as follows:

We do not trust the outside world and we are suspicious of one another. Our lives are oppressed by mean fears. We fear the rent collector, we fear the police watchman, we fear everyone who looks as though he might claim some authority over us; we fear our creditors, we fear our patrons; we fear too much rain, we fear locusts; we fear thieves, we fear the evil spirits which threaten our children and our animals; and we fear the strength of our neighbor.

These are groups of whom 70% or more are normally illiterate,[2] and who feel a tremendous suspicion of the outsider. 'Everyone who comes to us or to whom we go thinks of what he can get from us—be it money, or grain, or personal glory.'[3] Because the villager is ignorant, he fears to be credulous with outsiders (he

---

[1] Above, Chapter II.
[2] India 74%, East Pakistan 78·5%, West Pakistan 85·5%, most of Tropical Africa between 75% and 85%.
[3] W. H. and C. Wiser, op. cit.

may believe tall stories from fellow villagers) because he believes their aim is to cheat. These outsiders are probably literate 'educated'. Listen to a Southern Italian schoolmaster: 'Study and education has helped some people to succeed ... with their education they are able to exploit ignorance. They are able to cheat more dexterously.'[1] This well-founded fear of cheating by those who are better educated has a great political importance: it is one root of race prejudice, against the slicker Indian in Africa, Chinese in Malaysia or Burma, European in many places. It can bring support to dictatorships—as Banfield[2] points out, some peasants value 'strong government' (even Fascism) because it lays down rigid prices, rigid pay for fixed hours—in fact, it reduces cheating. But, above all, as Brewster points out so well, this fear imprisons the villager in a world too small and limited for economic growth. Until he can learn not to try to cheat and exploit the outsider (because he fears to be cheated), he can never join and work with the outside institutions which he needs for marketing, for technical help, for support even against the powers which control him within the village itself. Even in industry, the Indian or African family firm has frequently set a limit to development at the limit of family employees: an outside partner or manager is not trusted.

There is another fear, of a change even in the details of the traditional order. For how is the villager to know that it is indeed a detail, that it will not spread, like a pulled thread in a cloth which runs down half its length? The known order is his bulwark, as well as his prison, and in one sense the threat to any item of it threatens collapse of the whole. It is this fear which is at the base of much exaggerated traditionalism, whether of Hindu or Muslim, of Mau Mau in Kenya, of millennial movements, wherever they may appear.

The suspicion described by the Wisers is more typical of Asian societies long exposed to the power of landlords and patrons and the exactions of Government. Africa, before the colonial period, was more threatened by the direct brutality of slavers or war-parties from neighbouring tribes. The colonial governments which succeeded and suppressed this have been more remote

---

[1] E. C. Banfield, *The Moral Basis of Backward Society* (Glencoe, Ill., Free Press, 1958); also quoted by John M. Brewster in Southworth and Johnston, op. cit.
[2] Ibid.

and more paternalist, less feared and suspected. Independent African Governments should have an easier task in establishing more open and friendly relationships at village level.

The antithesis of fear is trust. Who is to be trusted? There was sometimes one special case in colonial territories—the white administrator: secure, well paid, neutral in a foreign quarrel, he was not usually in the cheating game. But in the normal run, there are two qualities which may earn trust: to be poor and to be learned—learned not in the monkey-world of cheating and competition, which is the world of the literate and half-educated, but as a guardian of Truth and of consolation. To be rich is suspect—how did the *patwari* get his silk waistcoat except by cheating? To be poor and learned is to be a monk, a Brother, a priest—in a lesser degree, a village schoolmaster. It was the proudest claim of the mediaeval monastic orders, or of the Buddhist priesthood, that they fulfilled this duty; it is still the claim of the poor priest and of the poor missionary today. And perhaps the bitterest complaint of the villager is when this trust is betrayed. Piers Plowman, whose description of the poor would fit many an Asian village, flayed the greedy friars:

Friars? All the four orders	I found them there
Preaching to the people	and glosing the Gospel
For their own profit . . .	
Money and their preaching	soon meet one another
God's love has turned trader . . .	

In many Buddhist countries the same bitter complaint arises—in Thailand there is a whole repertoire of scandalous jokes about the monks—yet a continued reverence and service is paid to them: the same applies to the Hindu Brahmin.

Reverence is continued because, in many ways, the villager also longs for education. First, because the learned are thought to have eternal Truths which are needed and worshipped through the myths—the Ramayana, the great African creation myths, the Christian myths too. Perhaps this truth is seen mainly as consolation—a way of accepting the hardship and narrow limitation of village life by reference to some divine order which decreed it.

It is also refreshment, because the myths, and the dances or songs or ceremonial are beautiful and distract from the daily grind:

But the Gods, taking pity on mankind, laid down the succession of recurring feasts to restore them from their fatigue and gave them the Muses, and Apollo their leader, and Dionysus as the companions of their Feasts, so that, nourishing themselves in festive companionship with the Gods, they should again stand upright and erect.[1]

It is because the myth has so many values that betrayal is so heinous.

Second, in a far less profound sense, education is sought because it is Power—partly the power not to be cheated, partly the power to escape out of agricultural poverty. Third, because to the young it is the possibility to explore, and to the old it is the insurance against being excluded from the vitality and the companionship of the community as it becomes more literate. To see the delight of an old man or woman, perhaps over 70, who is given a 'literacy certificate' by some bright young Community Development worker is to realize what this means.

Modern education in developing countries, particularly at the Primary level, must learn to be worthy of this reverence and desire for education, and to use it honestly. The schoolteacher will be poor: he can also earn trust if he can convey at once the best of the local religious tradition and a glimpse of those later truths of science and of reality in the modern world which will enable both parents and children to avoid regressive attitudes and to look with more confidence on the world outside the walls, a world which they desperately need to enter.

On the positive side, there is at least one part of education which the farmer has already, despite illiteracy. Within the means at his disposal, he has the skill of managing his land and crops, handed down with small amendments from father to son through many generations. As with many traditional skills, it will take an agricultural economist quite some research to put on paper all the possible choices and constraints of his farm management and to plot an optimum from them; it is often the course which the farmer (granted his values and preferences) has chosen. In this field the farmer has some confidence and great interest. A technique is more honest than a person; over the years it cannot lie; it is under command and can be put to the test. Here the teacher, whether in

---

[1] This passage, translated from Plato, is quoted as the theme of Joseph Pieper's book *Leisure the Basis of Culture* (London, Faber and Faber, 1953), which is well worth pondering in this connection.

school or farmer-training centre, has an easy gift to give. It is not so much a question of improving the farmer's skill: it is a question of putting better means—tools, seeds, chemicals, water, power—at his disposal.

These paragraphs have sketched perhaps the very first tasks of education in helping the villager to walk out more confidently into a wider world, emphasizing the trust which education must win, the continued support which is needed from some system of values and observances, the need for technical help in improving the means of livelihood. Before looking at the modern educational problem in developing countries, it will be useful to sketch, almost diagrammatically, the sequences of educational development in the West, because this history explains in significant ways why the educational systems transferred from the West to Asia and Africa over the last century took on a form which did not always put these first tasks first.

2

In early mediaeval Europe, education at simple levels gave to the child the Christian order, even before literacy. And it was through religious education that a very few found 'social mobility'—they became clerks, they might become the advisers of Kings, from Thomas à Becket to Cardinal Wolsey.

Two other forms of education also came very early. The first is the sophistication in the ways of the world that foreign trade and merchanting gave—the escape outside the village of members of a trading economy. The other, far more important, is education in craft technology, given from father to son, master to apprentice, outside the schools altogether. As Professor Blackett has pointed out, Europe developed a high technology long before Science was available to describe and develop it—from the Gothic cathedrals, built without benefit of engineering textbooks, to the beautiful refinement of agricultural tools, and later to most of the early techniques of the industrial revolution. Science, although fast developing in the early 17th century, did not catch up with technology until the late 18th and early 19th centuries. 'Technical education' only became possible in formal academic institutions when there was Science to explain coherently the technology which had grown by a purely practical path.

The last two main branches of education—modern Arts and Science—developed quite late. Humane education, of which Theology was the first queen, was gradually secularized, particularly after the Renaissance brought into Europe the full knowledge of Greek philosophy and Roman administration. From the religious core, political science, economics, sociology and the other Arts subjects broke away into a secular modern form. These were the subjects introduced into overseas universities. Similarly, a whole range of physical sciences, in proper academic form, became part of the Secondary and University syllabus.

Here, then, were five main types of knowledge—socialization of the child in the moral and religious order, *plus* literacy; knowledge of the outside commercial world; the technology of everyday life; academic Arts education; formal Science. Socialization through Christianity was in fact in conflict with the dominant African or Asian order, and has been only locally and partially effective. The next two elements—worldly knowledge and rural technology, both learned in Europe outside the school system—were almost totally lacking in Africa. It was the last two types of education, the Grammar school approach to the Arts and to Science, which dominated the educational systems established overseas. The small amount of craft technology, taught in Trade Schools, was almost wholly concerned with the tiny 'modern sector'—building in brick and concrete, plumbing, painting, mechanical and electrical fitting, and similar skills which were wholly irrelevant to 70-90% of the population, who lived in mud or wooden or bamboo houses, with no plumbing or painting, no mechanical objects, no electricity supply—people earning a livelihood from the land with very poor equipment but with very considerable experience and skill. Science and Arts both pointed towards a University; technical education towards an urban-industrial environment; literacy to a clerical job. Almost nothing pointed to the life of three-quarters of the population living on the land.

The fact that religious socialization has been imperfectly modernized, the lack of widespread facilities to improve rural technology, and (in Africa particularly) the lack of commercial sophistication gained by contact with a mercantile world—these are perhaps the most significant omissions in the education transferred from the West.

3

Most developing countries have faced the same educational choices and problems at Independence, though at markedly different stages. In the more backward countries there is, in the early stage, an emergency period, in which the acute shortage is of higher education, to produce manpower in replacement of expatriates in government and to provide for the expansion of the economy which all countries plan to achieve. There is a perennial shortage of financial resources. Inevitably, the first choice is to devote them to expanding Secondary and University education. This is the era of 'High-level Manpower Planning'.

The second stage is mainly marked by three issues. 'Unemployment', concealed by partial self-employment on the farm, is revealed as such because those who have had schooling, even at Primary level in Africa, begin to leave the farm and search for wage-paid jobs. The rural economy becomes a huge dam holding underemployed manpower, which may at any moment be breached and flood into shanty towns. Next, the pressure for more and more education begins to grow. Even in the village parents realize that the old order is changing, too late for their own life, but not too late for their children if they can learn the new tricks. Third, there may be growing concern at the widening gap between the educated few in wage-employment and the rural, uneducated mass: perhaps particular concern at the extraordinary privilege of graduates in new, expensive Universities.

At this point choices seem very difficult. What is the good of further expanding Primary schooling if there are no jobs for the pupils? Yet political societies must listen to political pressure, and pressure for more schools is mounting in the villages. A good deal will depend on the stock position at this stage. If high-level manpower is felt to be short (as in Tanzania, Zambia and many more countries in Africa), the emphasis will continue on the upper strata, with just enough attention to the lower to keep down protest. Quite often, at this stage, privately financed schools will grow up fast, to meet insistent demand. If the stock of college graduates is beginning to overshoot employment needs, the tendency will be to switch from the humanities, where the surplus normally starts, to technical education at both Secondary and higher levels.

The third stage, in many countries the present one, is precipitated by the growing menace of unemployment and a realization that the rural sector, by far the largest, is lagging and holding back the whole economy; and that only within it is there room to provide a livelihood (not necessarily wage employment) for the fast-growing population. Attention switches back to Primary education and literacy, and to arguments about the economic need for an educated farming population.

In some countries by this stage, higher education may already have got out of hand. In parts of India and in the Philippines, frr more college graduates are being produced than the economy can absorb at levels which could justify the expense of training them; and, inevitably, standards have dropped, colleges are overcrowded and badly equipped, examinations are the be-all and end-all. In developed stages of this sequence (Kerala, Bengal) a college degree has become almost wholly a status symbol still eagerly sought. Education may also be a profitable industry for private entrepreneurs, who raise money for a college, appoint themselves and their relatives as Principal and Staff, and even get government grants for their endeavours. Education becomes a spiralling industry, unrelated to economic need. The era of 'college-educated unemployables' (a self-description in Bengal) has started, and is very hard to end. It applies, eventually, to engineers as well as Arts students—there are many thousands of unemployed engineering graduates in South India and the Philippines already.

Kerala[1] is an outstanding example of this situation. With by far the highest literacy in India and rich resources, it has a *per caput* income 15% lower than the all-India average. This poverty, of course, reflects the population density but, *nota bene*, poverty has not been modified by high educational output; education by itself does not create economic growth. High population density and unemployed graduates are liable to be found together—Bengal, Iboland and Western Nigeria are other examples—presumably from intense pressure to find non-agricultural employment. But this is not a simple correlation: both Burma and

---

[1] See especially K. J. Charles and P. G. K. Panika, *Education and Economic Development—A case study of Kerala* (Development Digest, Vol. VI, No. 1, January 1968). The total literacy figure is 47% against 25% for all India: women's literacy is 38·9%, against 12·9% for all India.

Thailand have gone through a period of excess University output, although densities are far lower and actual output relatively small. Concentration on a single capital city and very poor development in the rural areas, both agricultural and industrial, can have the same effect. It leads to the absurd situation that University graduates emigrate from predominantly illiterate countries to the West; and that a Degree or Diploma becomes a form of purely social prestige expenditure on a par with expensive weddings and funerals. Countries which are still expanding higher education without much regard for real (rather than hoped-for) employment opportunity, and particularly those which have reduced the levels of University entrance in order to catch up more quickly, might well take a warning from this.

The reasons for this situation have been partly stated here and are familiar. As Sir Arthur Lewis has remarked, the highest rewards in society go to those professions where specialization comes latest in the educational system. Those who turn aside into technical or vocational training after Primary or Secondary education seldom catch up with those who continue a general education into the University. In consequence, it has been especially hard, in developing countries, to build up a good technical/vocational system. Technical institutes and agricultural training colleges turn themselves into Universities at the first opportunity, because only so can they attract able students. It has now been necessary in many countries to put the umbrella of University status over these post-Secondary institutions, with the risk that the University will in fact become a vocational training institution or, alternatively, that the technical institution will spurn its function of producing technicians (always desperately needed) in order to run less applied Degree courses. Examples are legion. The technical college in Nairobi became a University College; the agricultural college at Morogoro (Tanzania) is to become a Faculty; the technical college at Enugu acquired University status, as did the college at Kumasi; the training college at Zaria is merged with Ahmadu Bello University; the University of the South Pacific in Fiji will take under its wing a number of vocational institutes.

For all these reasons a common pattern is found in both Africa and Asia. There is a large Primary system of poor quality, yet seldom covering the full age group and with a heavy fall-out;

from 20% to 40% adult literacy; an academic Secondary system oriented to rapidly expanding Universities; and extremely poor post-Secondary vocational training. Moreover, as educational output begins to expand faster than employment-opportunity, the formal qualifications for entry to vocational training are raised. In some ways, the African situation in the middle 1950s gave more hope to the villager than it does today. For the boy who completed his Primary school course could train as a policeman, field assistant in agriculture, Primary teacher, hospital assistant, and much else. Today, entry requires a grammar education to School Certificate or Matriculation, and as the best Secondary schools are usually in or near towns, the urban boys have the advantage. Thus even the short ladders for the Primary leaver have been knocked away. In almost every country technical education for the rural

Table 3*

India: Enrolment at Different Educational Levels: (000s)

		1950–1	1960–1	1965–6 (est.)
1.	Classes I–V	19,154	34,994	51,500
2.	Classes VI–VIII	3,330	6,705	11,000
3.	Classes IX and above	1,220	2,960	5,240
4.	Vocational and Technical schools	117	278	440
5.	Universities, Arts, Science, Commerce	302	732	1,100
6.	Engineering and Technology (Degree level)	4·1	11·4	28·0
7.	Engineering and Technology (Diploma level)	5·9	25·8	52·0
8.	Medical Colleges	2·5	5·8	11·5
9.	Agricultural Colleges	1·1	5·6	8·0
10.	Teacher Training (Secondary schools)	5·8	19·5	26·0
11.	Teacher Training (Primary schools)	70	123	160
	Totals	24,212	45,861	69,566

* V. K. R. V. Rao, 'Educational Output in Relation to Employment Opportunities, with Special Reference to India', in *Manpower Aspects of Educational Planning* (Paris, UNESCO/ILRP, 1968).

economy has been particularly neglected. The Extension services have an inadequate establishment and even that is usually full of unfilled vacancies; the staff is poorly trained and of low prestige. The figures for enrolments in India give this picture quite well (see Table 3).

The Universities are producing far more students than all forms of vocational education put together. Agricultural colleges, although rising at almost the highest percentage rate of growth, start with 1,100 students in 1950 and reach 8,000 in 1965, compared to 80,000 engineers. Yet 70% of India's population is agricultural.

The details of this situation are immensely complex, and in any case it is not necessary to discuss them here. It is evident that a state of considerable confusion about fundamentals has arisen in the course of a tug-of-war between politics, prestige, manpower planning, and purely educational policy. It is for this reason that this chapter started from a few fundamentals, and to those we can return, in the hope of finding a way through the wood.

4

The distinction between education as truth (about the nature of the world and man's place in it) and as power was phrased in the opening of this chapter in terms of the religious ages. Truth, clothed in myth, was seen as fundamental or divine, justifying the order of society and consoling for its hardships. In fact, in the hands of poor priests and ignorant people, the clothing of myth perhaps concealed, in what we call superstition, all but a fragment of the inner truth it claimed to give; but it reassured and consoled none the less.

In the countries of major religions which are still vigorous, truth, because it is felt primarily as embodied in the social order, in fact corresponds to the socializing element of education. The child at home is brought up into the order, to know his duties to kinsmen and to others, the duties of his caste or class or occupation or age group, the values of society, the pattern of life which is to be assumed. Most of this comes in the home, some in the Temple or Koranic or Mission school, some, indeed, in the ordinary State Primary school of a Hindu or Christian or Muslim or Buddhist society. In Burma and Thailand it is even usual for young men to shave their hair and spend a year as a monk; in modern jargon, this is part of the socializing process.

We must ask, as a huge question too seldom even asked and certainly unanswered, how this process is to be carried on in the animist societies, scattered over Asia, but concentrated in huge tracts of Tropical Africa outside the fully Muslim countries. Tribal education of course achieved it in the context of animism and traditional culture. Christian missions played a major part in African education—and they have fought against the animist order. African State schools virtually ignore it: the school teacher knows that it exists, and was perhaps brought up in it himself; but it is not his job either to teach or to combat it. Leaders, endeavouring to form a modern nation from a collection of tribal cultures, in the main shirk interference. Tacitly, modern economic relationships are allowed, and perhaps encouraged, to override the older cultural beliefs. The well-educated, as individuals, may be really or nominally Christian; but Christianity is not the ethos of the whole society. The lack of common values and common rules of conduct is strikingly obvious in most of the new African States.

Perhaps this policy vacuum has been unavoidable. For in animist Africa and in the countries of major religions in both continents a process of redefining 'truth' is going on: it is part of the modernizing process. In the main it is a process of secularizing and specializing. The 'truth' about the social order begins to divide into the Arts subjects, as it did in Europe, drawing all the time nearer to the natural sciences, pushing religion gently, almost imperceptibly, into a private philosophy and a sequence of public festivals and ceremonials which have an emotional release, a refreshment with a nostalgic flavour. This process, which is of great importance to development, is mediated very largely by education, at all its levels and especially in its higher stages. To pull it into the open to reveal its future implications in their starkness, would certainly evoke the most violent religious and conservative reaction. Nehru, in his insistence on a secular State in India, went very near the flash-point; Pakistan gave way to the Muslim hierarchy and declared itself a Muslim State; Africa has avoided the issue altogether, or sought to revive a partly mythical 'African' order of co-operation and unity. Nkrumah ordered African libations to be poured at public festivals—perhaps the most blatant of the archaisms.

We can now look at this issue more sensibly in terms of the practical problems and policies of educational planning. To deal first with the role of education both in socialization and in redefining the nature of social truth, it becomes clear how immensely important this will be both in breaking through the village walls, and, at its higher levels, in producing an intelligent, informed, and tolerant climate of opinion among the leaders and teachers of society. If we look again at the pattern which has actually grown up, we see a huge growth of mainly 'grammar' and examination-bound education, which gives first literacy and then the qualifications for a clerk, an urban-industrial job or government service. These were the jobs that first became available through education. In consequence, the swelling demand for it, even from village level, is in fact a demand for education as a job, as power in a small way, not through the genuine sources of power (which are technical and objective social knowledge and skill) but through an ability to pass examinations and manipulate words.

The most obvious reaction—and it has a great justification—is to increase the technical content and bias of education, from Primary upwards, stressing the practical skills from small farming to complex engineering. But it has great danger in this simple form. There will be the temptation, which parents might well approve, since it is 'power' they want, to leave the realm of socialization and the teaching of a new type of social truth to the home and to the unrevised atmosphere of animist, Hindu, Buddhist, Muslim or State school. If this were done, social truth would be left embedded in a religious superstitious age, totally at variance with the modernizing economic and social process. There would be a gross divergence between ancient human attitudes and modern technical skills. On the contrary, the role of humane education at the Primary level is to see that social education is kept moving; and at the highest level to produce the economists, the social scientists, the statesmen and one section of the planners and administrators who are indeed the Teachers of a modern society, and who find increasingly that the subdivisions of their subjects are untenable in face of the wholeness of the living social order. They need, in the end, the widest of modern but humane 'interdisciplinary' education if they are to direct and co-ordinate the technological specialists who provide them with development power. This need not be a very large group: it must be in a sense an elite group of the very highest quality; for the bad teacher is worse than no teacher at all.

In those countries, fast increasing in number, which have already made provision for a limited necessary range of 'higher manpower', even if the output has not yet come, and in those where higher education, heavily overweighted on the humane side, is already producing a surplus, the implications are fairly clear. If the technical agricultural revolution is to succeed, and if the village walls are to be broken down, there must be a return to the expansion and to the qualitative improvement of Primary schools in their full capacity as socializing agents, and a great expansion of simple technical education at a low and middle level applicable to a modernizing rural economy, and available not in the city but in the rural areas. Simultaneously, at the top of the educational pyramid there is needed a new and vigorous insistence on quality or excellence in at least a small section of humane education, even if this means raising entry standards and performance in a few, or even (in small countries) one university. Somewhere in society a standard of excellence, perhaps above all on the 'Arts' side, must exist. A second-rate engineer has at least some skills to give to society; a second-rate Arts graduate has very few indeed; he is not the guardian of modern Truth but more probably part of the clever and cheating world which lives off others.

5

In practical detail, the task of both expanding and improving Primary education (the only formal education which at least 90% of an age group can hope to have in many developing countries at present) is bound to be a fairly slow one, not so much in training new teachers but in re-training the existing ones. The content which a modernizing Primary school needs to have is not a technical agricultural syllabus. The qualities which it, and lower Secondary, should aim to produce have been admirably laid out by V. L. Griffiths.[1] He concentrates first on attitudes—an enquiring mind, willing to question a tradition or superstition; a mind willing to plan ahead, rather than passively accept fate,

[1] V. L. Griffiths, *The Contribution of General Education to Agricultural Development, Primarily in Africa* (Agricultural Development Council Inc., New York, 1965).

now that Nature can be better controlled; care and accuracy in measuring and calculating—one day this will be a vital quality in using fertilizer, insecticide, in grading for the market, in farm accounts; a readiness to work hard and beyond set hours; a readiness to co-operate in new institutions; a recognition that change is continuous. Second, there are the usual skills of reading, writing and calculation, plus handiness in odd jobs at home or on the farm. Third, in terms of knowledge, some appreciation of very simple economics—values and prices—and 'an elementary insight into scientific method'.

It is this last factor which is needed so desperately. Modern Geography, not the abominable list of place-names, could explain to a child the differences in human ways of life; history, not a list of dates, could tell him why his society is what it is; simple biology, not bad smells in a laboratory, can make every plant and animal interesting—the list is endless. It may be impossible to train the lower levels of teachers to do this; but it is too early to say this before it is tried.

There is next the question of continuity. In the educationally backward countries, well over half of all children will have had either no education at all or up to four years only.

Table 4

Educational Progress of a Single Age Group—Available to enter Primary school in 1961-2 (Tanzania)*

	Number (000s)	Per cent
Did not enter school (1961–2)	117	46·8
Up to 4 years' education	81	32·4
Up to 7 years' education	45	18·0
Entering Secondary (1969)	7	2·8
	250	100·0

* G. Hunter, *Manpower, Employment and Education in the Rural Economy of Tanzania* (Paris, UNESCO/IIEP, 1965).

If we look at the total crop of six years' children in 1969 in two groups—children aged 12, 13, 14, and young people aged 15, 16, 17 assuming they entered Primary at about age 7–8 years and

Secondary at about age 14–15 years, the result is as follows (rounded):

Table 5

Educational Status of two Groups of Children in 1969 (Tanzania)

Children (*12, 13, 14*)		Young People (*15, 16, 17*)	
Never in school	350,000	Never in school	350,000
Up to 4 years	240,000	Up to 4 years	240,000
Up to 7 years (some still in school)	160,000	Up to 7 years In Secondary schools	135,000 25,000
	750,000		750,000

We thus reach a total of 1·18 million children and young people between 12 and 18 years old in Tanzania in 1969 who have had either no education, or only four years; and another 320,000 of whom 295,000 had seven years and have left school or are about to leave, and 25,000 who are still in Secondary schools. These are to become the young adults of the villages. UNESCO have just estimated that out of the total of 5,350,000 African school children 3,816,000 (71%) will be classified as adult illiterates in 1969 when they reach the age of 15. Against the 5% annual increase of enrolment in Primary schools aimed at in 1961 (Addis Ababa Conference), only 1·8% per annum has been achieved.

There seems to be an immensely strong case, as the 'higher manpower' situation improves, for carrying at least two-thirds of the children (instead of one-quarter) through the full Primary course of seven years, and, secondly, for giving at least a large proportion of the 15–17 year olds at least one day a week of continued educational contact, through young farmers' clubs, scouts, evening classes, craft classes, or whatever can be most suitably arranged, using existing buildings and calling upon every educated person in the rural community—and perhaps on University students on vacation—to take a hand in this. There are such people—Community Development staff, Agricultural and Cooperative and Health Extension staff, retired teachers, progressive farmers, and many more; mobilization for rural development means mobilizing voluntary and part-time effort, not merely paid full-time staff. If this job is not done for young people, at the height of their potential energy and idealism, they will be left to stagnate, and half the investment in their education will have been wasted.

There is a further group in the community for which far more could be done—the adult farmers themselves, and the craftsmen, and the women who support them. The Farmers' Training Centres could be expanded to cover a wider range, including simple technical courses, courses for women, courses for Co-operative Secretaries, courses for book-keeping, for driving and maintenance. One day these Centres could become rural polytechnics on a scale which it is now difficult to imagine.[1] It is more than doubtful whether the peasant farmer, at the present stage in Africa or Asia, needs formal Secondary education—it is in any case impossible to provide it. There is indeed evidence in plenty that farming innovation tends to start with the better educated, but chiefly because, in many cases, they are men who have been outside the village in some other job—perhaps even as soldiers they have seen how the bigger world works; they are less intimidated by village conformity; in a word, it is not the schooling as such which made the difference but the opportunity of wider contact which schooling gave. In some degree the Training Centre, Polytechnic, Farmers' Club, District Training Centre (Kenya), Rural Academy (Pakistan), even an enterprising V.L.W. training college which sends its students out to practical work on the farm,[2] can bring outside contact to the farmer in a more continuous and intensive way than the formal Extension service, from shortage of time and staff, can command.

To galvanize the rural economy may be cheap in capital, but it is bound to be expensive in recurrent revenue—not only in the expansion and improvement of rural teaching in the formal schools, but in the host of post-school social and training activities which are needed and which will bring the villager out from behind his walls. It can only be financed, over time, by the growing prosperity of the rural economy itself, by taxing it reasonably but courageously, and by a new attitude to Aid in donor countries

[1] At the time of writing there is a proposal in Kenya to combine in a single District Development Centre the Farmer Training College, Community Development Training College, and proposed training units for Co-operatives and Commerce. The Centre would also service Village Polytechnics.

[2] Such as Madurai District, Madras State.

which will recognize investment in Extension (salaries and local costs) as every bit as much investment as the provision of (often unsuitable) industrial plant and hardware. The schools, over the long term, will help to modernize the conceptions of Truth; what government can give to the adult farming community at the moment is not exhortation, not simply words which they will suspect (from government above all), but a new range of technique and the credit and resources to use it, which they will accept because success is demonstrable and rewarded in cash.

At higher levels of education one might well hope to see a far more practical and scientific element in Secondary schools, perhaps eventually made easier to introduce for two reasons. First, because, as literacy grows and the proportion of potential clerks mounts, other occupations will be more attractive—in the past, the academic emphasis of schooling reflected at the same time the prestige of the administrators, the shortage of literates, and the predominance of clerkly jobs in an undifferentiated economy. The second reason could be a sharp narrowing and upgrading of the purely academic—Arts—stream, leading to a narrower and more exacting entrance to Universities on the humanities side. In the cases (such as the Philippines, or Bengal or Kerala) where College education is already hugely expanded, the tactic may be to concentrate on creating a few centres of excellence.

Again, with a modernized Secondary syllabus there would be room for far more, and more practical, post-Secondary vocational training. The technical college, where boys learn industrial skills, is a familiar sight in towns. Not so the Agricultural Polytechnics, the Institutes of Rural Technology, the Gandhigrams[1] and Comillas, situated in the farming regions, teaching at post-Secondary level such subjects as survey, levelling, irrigation, mechanical maintenance, soil chemistry and fertilization, farm accounting and farm-management, Co-operative management, pest control, rural building and construction of all types, designs of storage, seed multiplication, animal genetics, nutrition, crafts and processing industries. If even one of these were established in place of every third college turning out poorly trained Arts students in some countries, the hope of economic progress might be greater.

It is a hard saying, but much of the cost of such education,

[1] The Gandhi Memorial Centre of rural training, education and research in Madurai District, Madras State.

above Primary level, will have to be paid by parents. Every single one of tens of millions of parents would like his child to have a free Primary and Secondary education; but in poor economies there is simply not enough to go round. Selection by ability may work fairly well at the highest levels, but lower down it is highly inefficient and the examinations it involves help to distort the teaching In a situation, which is increasingly common in the developing world, where parents are prepared to pay heavily for private, profit-making schools outside the government system, often of the poorest quality, it would surely be better for government itself to collect the money and provide the school.

We are concerned with education as an accelerating factor in the transition from social conditions of 1660 to those of 1970. Inevitably it needs a heavier and more expensive formal structure than was available or needed in the slow-growth societies of the West, where the process of slowly changing apprenticeship was enough to pass on old skills and modify to new ones, where there were wide contacts with the outer world, and where the human order of society also changed slowly and imprinted itself upon the child at home and in every daily contact of life, even if school was not available. For both India and Africa there is a discontinuity, a break in both skills and attitudes, too great to entrust to apprenticeship and general environment. The burden of this chapter is to suggest a great improvement of the Primary system, in modernizing human attitudes; an opportunity to develop skills far lower down the scale, through informal youth associations, through formal polytechnics, through 'evening classes' of the simplest kind; a modernization of the Secondary programme in a practical, applied direction, with a smaller but high-quality Grammar stream; and, where necessary, a radical constriction of higher humane education, to wring out the very best of quality, and to divert a higher proportion of Secondary pupils into post-Secondary applied vocational work, or into the Science streams of the University. T. S. Eliot[1] has remarked that 'the attempt to spread elite learning to a growing mass of people will be to adulterate and cheapen what you give'. This has happened wherever a mass of poor B.A.s is turned out. The old qualities of Scottish education, turning out first-rate farmers, teachers, philosophers and engineers,

[1] T. S. Eliot, *Notes Towards the Definition of Culture* (London, Faber and Faber, 1948).

are more apposite to developing countries than the mass systems of most of Europe and America.

If there is one activity in developing countries which needs to be intimately and wholly related to their tradition, to their present condition and to their future needs it is the activity of education. For the dominant element of peasant societies—the peasants themselves—this has not been achieved.

CHAPTER XI

ECONOMICS

Earlier chapters have referred to many economic issues in some particular context, and particularly to the economics of agricultural production and local marketing and employment. But it is necessary to look at the wider picture—the economic position of developing peasant societies in the whole system of world trade, and their special difficulties, which formed the opening analysis of Chapter I.

The usual starting point for such discussion would be to assess the size of the gap between developed and developing countries and the possibility and best method of narrowing it. But this is not very profitable. For, in fact, no really satisfactory yardstick exists for measuring the gap. The measure most often used, a comparison of National Income per head, is misleading. It includes, as income in developed countries, the costs of combating many disadvantages which may never arise in tropical countries—the dirt of a coal-fired production system, transport congestion, protection against severe cold, and much else; and it under-estimates, because money terms have to be used, certain real benefits which new countries have which cost very little in those terms.[1]

There is a second good reason for avoiding such estimates. They tend to fix attention on some remote goal of output or income rather than on the steps needed to advance from the present situation to a better one, and this is exactly the attitude which leads to unhistorical and premature decisions. Moreover, the enormous uncertainties of the future—political uncertainty for one, technological for another—make any attempt to forecast levels of production and consumption twenty years ahead largely speculative.

However, it is inevitable that these questions should be raised:

---

[1] A good deal has been written on this subject, unnecessary to quote in detail here. The more radical critics suggest that figures for income per head in many developing countries might even be multiplied by a factor of 3.

some glance at the horizon is necessary from time to time. It is obvious that developed countries use far more resources per head —KWH of electric power, calories or high-grade protein, public and private transport, medical care. Yet even these indicators, which are rather more convincing than money calculations, in fact suffer from many of the same detailed disadvantages. It is perhaps better not to look at such comparisons, which do not compare like with like and provoke either useless jealousy or useless gloom, but to look at the absolute level of reasonable necessities in developing countries, and the chances of improving their provision. If, decade by decade, this provision is improving fast, this is the best reason for satisfaction.

It is often said that the rich are getting richer and the poor poorer. In fact this is not true. The gap may be widening, but the poor are getting richer: Paul Hoffman recently estimated average growth in national income in all developing countries at over 4% per annum (1960–7); this may be too slow, but it is not regression. The greatest importance of the gap is not in comparisons but in the practical effects it may have in actually making local improvement easier or more difficult. Disparity in coexisting economic systems is not necessarily a bad thing, but it requires its own economic answers from both sides.

If we look for a moment at some basic elements which need improvement in developing countries, the size of their task becomes a little clearer, and perhaps a little less discouraging. Among consumer goods and services, a good food supply is of first importance followed by clean water supply, housing and domestic equipment, clothing, transport, and, as soon as possible, widely available domestic light and power. Consumer services obviously also include medical care (and equipment, drugs, buildings), education (and paper, printing, buildings), and some degree of personal insurance.

Production needs include extractive machinery and tools (agriculture, mining, fishing, forestry); factory machinery and hand tools and equipment; office plant; storage and heavy transport; communications (road, rail, air, post, radio, telephone); major water control; power. This is not an ambitious list, if the production plant is designed only to produce the essential consumer goods and services, and not (except for export) the mass of fripperies which developed countries consume.

It is clear that these groups are in ascending order of difficulty for developing countries. Food production, though critical, is largely possible from internal resources; education and health have to be paid for by higher productivity, mainly in extractive industries in the poorest countries; production plant and producer goods generally are extremely difficult—the base of heavy industry is lacking in most of Africa and many parts of Asia. Most of it, in most countries, will have to be purchased by exports.

In a vitally important sense, the situation in developing countries is absurd. They are faced by critical shortages in the minimum list, and yet they have a massive under-employment of human energy. This is not the Keynesian situation of unemployment, where both skills and productive plant were available but idle. Labour which is unskilled, except in farming, and unused or misused resources are available; the shortages are in production tools and in training. Training, in modern conditions, can be quite quickly remedied by intensive, narrowly focused effort. The shortage of production equipment—raw materials, tools, machinery, work places, power distribution—remains.

2

We thus reach a central question. How much development can be achieved by the mobilization of unused internal resources, and how much only by a system of exchange with the developed world? Until very recently the general thinking has emphasized exchange—developing countries selling tropical food and raw materials, and tourism, in exchange for producer goods and major infrastructure. There is a minor addition in the form of outright grants of Aid; but this involves a serious and deep commitment of developing countries to the exchange system by the acceptances of so-called Aid in the form of loans repayable in foreign currency. George Woods[1] estimated in 1966 that, on present trends, these interest payments would equal the annual Aid flow by 1980. The endeavour to increase foreign earnings by selling manufactures to developed countries, pressed at the UNCTAD meetings, has had little success. It is not only the mounting total of debt which causes

[1] G. Woods, 'The Development Decade in the Balance', in *Foreign Affairs* (Vol. XLIV, No. 2, 1966).

concern overseas. The fact that so much bilateral aid is tied to purchases from the donor distorts the import programme; developing countries find themselves buying very expensive goods far down on their list of priority needs, because these are the goods which the donor can supply.

These difficulties have caused some developing countries to change their attitude and to put greater emphasis on self-reliance, partly for political reasons ('*Le Camboge s'aide lui-même*'), partly from disenchantment with the way in which the exchange system has been working.

The arguments for concentrating on exchange are traditional in the West. There are the usual arguments on comparative advantage and the gains from trade; for example, the fact that, granted rain or irrigation, there is sunlight to grow tropical crops right through the year, as against the dead winter season of cold temperate zones. There is the argument that the world is irreversibly one, and that the *mise en valeur*[1] of the resources of land and population in the developing world can only be accelerated by using both the skills and capital of the developed world. It can well be argued that the gap in technology is unbridgeable—since developed technology strides further ahead every year—and that the world will inevitably be divided into the makers of machinery and the users of machinery, as indeed single societies are internally divided now.[2] It can be argued also that tourism will become of far greater significance, as the developed world seeks variety, sunlight in winter, wild Nature, opportunities of study and refreshment and perhaps even of service. Finally, it is possible that it will pay the developed world to concentrate on sophistication and buy simple manufactures from overseas—this is only an extension of the comparative advantage argument. Minerals, crops and raw materials, tourism, and possibly simple manufactures would have to pay the price of exchange.

The opposing view is that the basic economic problem of developing countries is the absurdity of simultaneous shortages of

[1] I use the French phrase not from snobbery but because 'exploitation' carries overtones in English and 'development' is vaguer. 'Development of the potential of' is a little clumsy.

[2] See Chapter I. See also a stimulating paper by Professor J. P. Nettl, 'Study in the Strategics of Political Development', in the seminar on 'The Politics of Development' (Institute of Development Studies at the University of Sussex, June 1968).

production and under-employment of human and natural resources; that the answer must lie in developing work places and tools suited to trainable skills and local markets;[1] and that the exchange system so far has not done this but rather created a small, sophisticated modern sector, leaving the mass of people and potential unharnessed. Internal mobilization is bound to mean fairly massive credit-creation; and this in turn means devaluing an over-valued currency, which makes import too easy, export too hard, and encourages capital-intensive methods at precisely the wrong moment. Credit-creation must be partly matched by saving from a prosperous agriculture. Certainly, some imports of skills and techniques will be needed, though at a minimum of critical points; tropical products and tourism will have to pay for this, and for the existing load of debt-repayment. But to allow the developed countries to fulfil their need for markets by condemning developing countries to tropical crops and tourism would mean perpetual dependence. It follows that industrialization must be achieved, largely on the basis of the domestic market and domestic skills.

Concentration on the rural sector, both for production and employment, will be right for many countries for the next decade, although, despite every effort at family limitation, it will not solve the problem of employment for already-born children and for the inevitable future growth. However, as time goes on, the internal market in developing continents could be widened by creating their own economic community, within which a gradually widening range of manufactures could be exchanged.

There is clearly no question of *either* the exchange system *or* local mobilization; it is a question of the type of exchange which will most help local mobilization. Further, there are great differences in circumstances. For the oil Sheikhdoms or for Zambia with its copper sales, or for countries heavily subsidized by America for strategic purposes (South Vietnam, Thailand, Taiwan), foreign exchange is not the key problem: for many others it is critical. We therefore need to look far more closely at what local mobilization and self-help means, and what degree and type of exchange with the outside world is implied by it.

The basic argument in this book has run roughly as follows. Higher productivity and more specialization in agriculture = higher purchasing power and more intensive labour use = a

[1] The argument of the Intermediate Technology group: see Section 5 below.

market for consumer goods, services and in-puts plus some public savings. This in turn stimulates local industry, using 'intermediate' technology, and urbanization. This in turn increases the market for agricultural produce. Exports (agriculture, minerals, tourism, wider *regional* trade and specialization) provide the foreign exchange for imports of heavy capital production goods and specialized items. Finally, in the longer run, the more purely peasant economies, now at a higher level, are integrated on a regional basis, with a few centres of heavy industry placed where the mineral resources and engineering skills are best. Three or four of the links in this argument require a closer look.

3

Food production to a satisfactory dietary level, even for the great increase of population which is inevitable, should be well within the technical capacity of the developing world. The capacity of land already in cultivation could be more than doubled over twenty-five years by better methods, better tools, double-cropping, fertilizer and increased irrigation, both from major surface dams and by the use of groundwater. An average of 3% growth per annum would be enough to do this and thus keep up with an *average* population growth of 2% per annum, with a small margin for increased consumption. If we could assume a 4% growth off existing land, plus an extra from new land brought into cultivation, the margin for improvement would be ample—indeed an increase of 60% or more in average consumption of the increased numbers. It would certainly need to be as high. As Mellor[1] points out, the rate at which demand for food increases with increasing income is very high in developing countries, and a doubling of incomes would certainly result in at least 50% extra expenditure on food,[2] including a higher proportion of more expensive items. In addition to internal consumption, export production of food and fibres could be maintained and increased (market allowing) from the existing land and labour force. In the early years of this intensification, population and employment would both increase in the

---
[1] Op. cit.
[2] More precisely, if food expenditure is normally 60% of income, and if the income elasticity of demand for food is 0·8, about 50% of the extra income will be spent on food.

agricultural areas. Later, structural change would begin to accelerate through the growing level of non-farm employment generated by higher farming incomes.

4

Increase in non-farm employment should imply quite a rapid increase in urbanization. As Etherington[1] has pointed out in East Africa, present rates of *total* increase in urbanization are not very high, even though the large city may itself grow very fast. If urban population is only 20% of total population, and grows at 6% per annum, with a total population growth of 2% per annum, the percentage of urban-rural population will change fairly markedly over twenty-five years but total rural population will still be as high.[2] With a 3% population growth, rural population would in fact be higher in absolute numbers at the end of the period. The dramatic increase in big city populations (as in the Congo in Africa) is apt to conceal the fact that the absolute rural population is growing, not shrinking, at the same time.

The growth of non-farm employment is not, of course, exactly equivalent to the growth of urbanization; much of the increased service to more prosperous farmers may well be in the village itself. But, as the Wisers[3] noted, modernization, in India at least, does tend to reduce the element of traditional craft services inside the village and to create new, perhaps semi-mechanized, services in a neighbouring town. In general terms, therefore, there will be a tendency, in agricultural conditions where payments tend to be in cash rather than in kind, for the smaller villages to become more wholly agricultural[4] and for shops and services of a rather more sophisticated nature and with a wider catchment area to

[1] D. M. Etherington, 'Projected Changes in Urban and Rural Population in Kenya with Reference to Development Policy', in J. R. Sheffield (ed.), *Education, Employment and Rural Development*, proceedings of the Kericho Conference (East Africa Publishing House, 1967).

[2] Original population 20 urban 80 rural—100
Total population 100 × 2% for 25 yrs.—160
Urban population 20 × 6% for 25 yrs.—80
Rural population after 25 yrs.—80. 50% rural/urban
At 3% population growth, total population will be 200, urban 80, rural 120, % rural/urban 60%.

[3] Op. cit.

[4] This is confirmed by the Japanese team which studied rural conditions in Gujarat and West Bengal. See Tudasche Fukatake *et al.*, op. cit.

grow up in larger villages or towns. As soon as this service becomes a full-time occupation and the family moves to town, an additional food market is created, and also employment in housing construction and urban services generally. There will be a tendency for employment to snowball faster in towns, provided that the basic local industry is flourishing (agriculture often, but mining or other industry too). The town also further stimulates the psychological break with village life: it becomes a centre of unorthodox views and untraditional behaviour, multiplies contacts and commercial opportunities in almost geometric progression, and sucks in rural population (which is highly desirable at early stages) to a point where shortages of labour in agriculture begin to be felt, rural wages rise, and it becomes economic to mechanize some agricultural operations.

The whole issue of urbanization in the unique conditions of modern developing countries requires far more research. There has been anxiety at the mushrooming of a few big cities, both in Africa and in Asia, and a good deal of attention has been paid to this. But some puzzles remain, and in particular the failure of towns to appear in zones of very high population density (1,000 to the square mile or more) and some prosperity. The traditional divisions of town growth include the defensive town in areas of local warfare; the market town; the administrative town; and the industrial town. All these are obviously affected by communications and geography—the opening to a mountain pass, the crossing of a river, and so on. But there are more detailed determinants. For example, in a time of unsurfaced roads and animal transport, towns will serve an area often limited by a radius of ten miles or so —the early English markets are an example. But if the road is tarred and lorry transport is available distances will get much bigger, and the tendency may be for fewer, but larger, towns. Again, subsistence production obviously does not encourage town growth, whereas a diversified, market-oriented farming should do so. Yet on the one hand the large towns of the Yoruba people in Nigeria ante-date the colonial period and at least 'modern' commerce, while on the other there are areas of considerable cash-cropping in Bengal or Kerala or Tanjore District of Madras, all very high-density agricultural zones, where recognizable towns, rather than dense but un-nucleated settlement, do not seem to spring up naturally. It is possible to drive thirty miles in Tanjore District through what appears to be a continuous village, with paddy fields stretching to the horizon on both sides of the road beyond the single ribbon of housing.

The size of operational farm units affects this position. A mass of small owners and tenants is clearly likely to spread itself over the countryside, as in East Bengal, or in Ibo country or Tanjore, simply for quick daily access to the land; plantations, particularly when European-founded, tend to have estate housing behind the perimeter fences, a series of labour lines rather than either a village or a town. It is not only the modernization of farming but the growth either of processing industries or of other small industrial plants, exploiting other local resources of markets, which seems to be critical in town development, simply because it concentrates a nucleus of labour which is relieved of the daily need to go to the fields.

Because of this great complexity, in which factors of geography, tenure, communications, density of settlement, commercialization of agriculture, existence of processing or other industry all play a part, it is impossible to give any general recipe for policy intervention in stimulating town growth. Certainly, the attempt to create a town where no signs of a town have appeared naturally is exceedingly rash. Such an attempt, for example, was made in Bemba country[1] (North-East Zambia), with the deliberate aim of offsetting the attractions of the Copperbelt towns by creating 'city lights' in the country. The town was to be the focus of a new progressive agricultural settlement, therefore electric power, Secondary school, and other temptations were included in the scheme. But it did not succeed. In the Volta River resettlement scheme at least one 'trading centre' was laid out by the planners; but the traders preferred to settle in shacks a short distance away, at the landing stage for a ferry.[2] There are many more examples of abortive 'planners' towns'. A great deal more research is needed to identify the critical factors which enable or prevent urbanization in densely settled rural areas.

Government have never given great encouragement to urban growth (except on their own terms of attempted urban construction). For one thing, the 'drift' to towns has been due to the

---

[1] See Report of the Rural Economic Development Working Party, Government of Northern Rhodesia (Lusaka, 1960).

[2] Personal communication from Dr. R. W. Chambers.

poverty of the rural life rather than to real employment opportunities in the town, and this has simply produced evident and deplorable urban conditions instead of concealed and unheeded under-employment on the farm. A second reason lies simply in the squalor which is apt to mark the earliest stages of town growth and the public expense of clearing it up. Towns are apt to grow as shacks around a crossroad or some other feature which tempts traders. Moreover, the first inhabitants are agricultural people, whose sanitation has been the nearest bush, and whose refuse bin the domestic pig. Such a group can quite unconsciously produce a hair-raising urban slum in a very short time. The attempt to prevent[1] this is apt to kill the town. Proper shops, with proper building lines and proper sanitation involve rents or rates which make simple trade, in its early and tender stages, wholly uneconomic. East Africa in particular has suffered from over-enthusiastic and sanitary-minded planners, whereas many West African towns (even Ibadan) have contrived to grow with indigenous building standards and without disaster. The Belgian planning of some parts of the African town in Leopoldville (Kinshasa today) was one of the more intelligent compromises between minimum standards and natural economics and preferences. Perhaps the growth of towns and town government in the American West in the 19th century would also have some lessons. If town growth is to be both vital and educative for its citizens, and not grossly expensive to public funds, self-government and self-finance, subject to intelligent but not excessive supervision, is likely to be the best compromise between the sanitarians and the economists.

5

The development of small-scale industry, with cheap work places and cheap equipment, has been greatly canvassed lately, and particularly by the Intermediate Technology group under the leadership of Dr. Schumacher. It is one of the peculiar difficulties of the present situation of developing economies that the natural growth of simple productive industry which gave diversification and wealth to Europe between 1500 and 1800 seems unnatural and hard to create today. For example, the use of wood gave to the peasantry of forested country in Europe a huge range of full-time

[1] In the old-fashioned sense of 'get in before'.

or part-time occupations, one of the last of which is the gypsy making clothes-pegs. *The Agrarian History of England and Wales* notes:

In the wooded districts of central England one peasant labourer in three, and in Hertfordshire two in three, engaged in some kind of woodcraft. Many labourers in woodland parishes possessed tools for felling, hewing, cleaving, sawing, adzing and carting timber. They must have spent their spare days, and much of the winter, making spikes, pales, poles, gates, posts, rails and laths for fencing and walling.

After detailing a whole number of other crafts—making looms, wooden bottles, taps and handles, brooms and besoms, spoons, trenchers, casks, wagons and wheels—the passage concludes:

Forest areas were the natural workshops of an agrarian civilization largely dependent on wooden tools and implements for its work; the number and variety of local crafts, often highly specialized and recondite, was legion.[1]

There were other big uses for wood (shipbuilding, housing, and furniture are obvious examples). Nor was it wood alone that provided employment. The textile industry was even more important; spinning and weaving of hemp and flax 'occupied the spare hours of nearly a third of the labouring population',[2] quite apart from the even larger woollen industry. Nailing, potting, brickmaking, charcoal-burning, cutting 'turf coal' and a score of other occupations added the vital extra shillings to the cottagers' income, and considerable extra production to the economy as a whole. Indeed, even export trade benefited: we hear of a man contracting to sell no less than 8 million billets of wood over four years, mainly to France.[3]

These crafts and the trading activity which went with them largely disappeared into factories in the 19th century, having provided a vital bridge between the peasant and the industrial ages—vital in employment and in the growth of both technical and commercial skills. It is one of the major difficulties of modern peasant societies that so much once made by hand, with wood or leather is now made with metal or plastic, involving both materials, capital and skills which many peasant societies do not possess. The temptation is either to import them or do without them.

[1] Joan Thirsk (ed.), *The Agrarian History of England and Wales*, Vol. IV, 1500–1640 (Cambridge, Cambridge University Press, 1967).
[2] Ibid.   [3] Ibid.

To find the balance between conscious archaism, 'arty' tourist knick-knacks, cottage production which is simply more expensive and less efficient than factory production and, on the other hand, usually centralized and sometimes over-capitalized modern production is exceedingly delicate. The troubles of Gandhi's '*Kadi*' industry are one example:[1] yet the handweaving of saris for weddings is still an extremely lively and useful industry in India, organized in modern co-operatives. The Wakamba woodcarvers in Kenya sell heavily, even to New York; cottage industries in the Chiengmai area of North Thailand (lacquer, silver, parasols, rice-paper, and above all Thai silk weaving) are important. The Singer sewing-machine outside the hut or Asian *duka*[2] in Africa is the commonest of sights. On the other hand, village shoemakers (for example, in Kenya) cannot compete in price and range of colour and size with the plastic shoes which the Bata Company turns out by the million by modern and intensively managed methods.

It is therefore exceptionally difficult to generalize. But in some cases the most hopeful approach is exactly the marriage of 17th century scale with 20th century technology: the use of extremely modern methods and materials to meet the need for small and cheap equipment and facilities. Food storage is one example—it is inconceivable that modern research could not turn out a cheaper, pest-proof method of storing crops than the very expensive concrete buildings which at this moment are going up all over India and Africa.[3] The Japanese range of power tools for tillage and other agricultural operations is another example; efficient ox-carts, wheelbarrows, fencing, water-lifting equipment, construction methods, new materials, all have a contribution, not only in higher productive efficiency in the hands of the user but in employment at the point of manufacture. Intensive research, local and field-based, is needed. The rural sociologist and economist should be the source of suggestion and analysis of demand and cost; they need also the technician with a flair for both simple design and extremely modern techniques to translate their suggestions into equipment, and the government to put up at least

[1] See V. M. Dandekar, 'The Role of Small-Scale Industry in the Indian Experience', in the Kericho Conference Report.
[2] Shop.
[3] A number of experiments, including a small and cheap silo, are already being tested.

pilot financing for pilot use; businessmen will move in very quickly wherever the chances of profitable sales look good.

It is perfectly possible to build up quite a range of industry without possessing a heavy industrial base. Imported steel is relatively cheap at present. What is needed is an engineering industry, at first on workshop scale, which is capable of working metal. This is available in many parts of Asia, but very scarce indeed in most of middle Africa. In East Africa the facilities of Nairobi as an engineering centre have been described as the best between Cairo and the Republic of South Africa; and they are certainly not very extensive. Zambia and Katanga have a big nucleus of industrial skills, and there are patches in West Africa, but there is still far to go. In East Africa the immigrant Asians played a critical part in building up industrial and commercial skills at the middle level. But few of them acquired citizenship, and they are now leaving in large numbers. This loss will further retard the commercialization of the local economies. Cairncross[1] has remarked that at the beginning of the industrial revolution of the 18th century, 'there can scarcely have been an industry in England which did not owe its origin to immigrants'; but the violence of nationalism was not then so strong.

In the longer view, a full development will need a base of advanced industry, spreading its effects over regions wider than the present national boundaries. In Africa potential is widely dispersed. There is one existing nucleus of varied industry in the Republic of South Africa, very considerable potential in the Copperbelt-Katanga area—a railway to Tanzania may spread its influence—and possibilities in West Africa with its large resources of power, aluminium, Nigerian oil and growing industrial skills. The Lake Victoria basin, on the other hand, including East Africa, Rwanda and the Eastern Congo, is more likely to be based on high-grade agricultural, processing and consumer industries. The current, politically-inspired attempt to spread engineering and industrial effort evenly throughout Kenya, Uganda and Tanzania is a serious set-back to any hope of developing any large-scale complex of industrial skill and interrelated industries.

In Asia there is no need to look far for major centres—India and Pakistan, Singapore, Japan, Hong Kong (if it survives) and, later, Indonesia all have the enterprise and potential.

[1] Cairncross, op. cit.

In a word, the long-term prospects of industrialization are good in Asia and at least fair in Africa. It is the next twenty-five years which will be difficult.

6

The type of economic planning and control needed to achieve the kind of programme which is likely to suit developing countries needs some special thought. Unlike most Western planning, which is financial and aggregative, or Russian planning, which tends to deal with very large blocks of production, planning in the usually mixed economies of peasant societies needs to be capable of some very large schemes *and* a mass of very small ones which cannot be left to private enterprise in many countries because the enterprise does not exist or is politically unacceptable.

This mixture of very small and very large types of development imposes special problems on planners. There is plenty of literature and international expertise on the physical and engineering side of the big scheme. The weakness has been in realistic understanding of the preparation needed to ensure that farmers can use the new water or newly opened land when it becomes available—Thailand provides one striking example of relatively huge expenditure on water control and irrigation in which the water is becoming available long before any coherent policy, based on thorough research, is ready to guide the agronomic programme, before the farmers have been educated to the new ideas, and before the necessary institutions for production and marketing have been thought out.[1] In the end, the big scheme needs as much local, detailed thinking as the small one—indeed more, because it often involves more abrupt change in traditional methods and outlook.

Planning for broad-front, local advance demands a style far different from that implied in most of the books. Polly Hill has made a significant contribution to thinking on this subject in her 'plea for indigenous economics'.[2] After pointing out that the kind of assumptions that Western economists and econometricians

[1] I have in mind the Nong Wai, Lam Pao and Lam Pung irrigation dams. In the first two irrigation water was scheduled to be available to farmers in October 1968. Certainly by January 1968 almost nothing had been done in a coherent way to prepare or train farmers for it.

[2] Polly Hill, 'A Plea for Indigenous Economics', in *Economic Development and Cultural Change* (Vol. XV, No. 1, October 1966).

usually rely on are not valid in many developing countries (for example, there may be not one 'labour force' but seventeen different labour forces in a single country, according to local cultural conditions), she points out that the usual questionnaires for research cannot really be drawn up until the socio-economic research is in fact completed 'by questioning and observing people while actually at work'. In fact, the descriptive process is incomplete, and this must precede the analysis.[1] The most realistic planners are likely to be those who fully understand the motivation and economic pattern of local society, for the simple reason that they were born into it, or because they have taken the trouble to study it, through social disciplines and in great detail.[2]

The danger of aggregative planning, when the aggregates rest on many questionable additions of like with unlike—and also on questionable statistics—has recently been stressed by many economists. Of course, the grocery list of small items of proposed development must be costed and totalled, in both financial and manpower terms, in case the bill is too big to pay. The danger is that the derived totals gain a life of their own, and the Plan becomes an aim to reach certain target magnitudes—a rise of $x\%$ in *per caput* income, or $y\%$ in crop production—rather than a series of proposals to meet local needs and opportunities with the resources available.[3] Hans Singer's remark, already quoted, that a plan must start from resources rather than needs (that is, targets), is here particularly significant. This will imply an overall financial plan but a high degree of delegation to local initiative in taking advantage of local opportunities as they arise, instead of nailing down each area to a set number of 'projects' and leaving nothing over for exploiting the quite unexpected tactical openings which will appear as the Plan period runs. The method in some Indian States (Madras for instance) by which Blocks are given a few minimum objectives, but also a range of optional targets (either centrally *or locally* suggested) from which they can make a choice, seems to go a long way in this desirable direction.

[1] One grave weakness of the present fashion for mathematical, quantifying work is that it rests on a wholly inadequate descriptive base.
[2] Such a detailed agricultural study is proposed in Bihar by a team from the Institute of Development Studies at the University of Sussex.
[3] See also Colin T. Leys, 'Notes on the Planning Process' (Institute of Development Studies Seminar on *The Politics of Development*, June 1968) at the University of Sussex.

Finally, the management of prices for agricultural products will set a difficult but vital task, as agriculture modernizes and specializes. The emphasis of planning has naturally been on production; prices have been relatively neglected. But—to take one example—if a production programme based on high-yielding crops with heavy inputs of fertilizer, or pest-control, really begins to succeed, the relation of price of product to price of inputs is going to become critical. Sudden success in food-grain outputs is bound to result in lower prices per ton to the farmer. But meanwhile there is a strong tendency to reduce fertilizer subsidies (because their aim of encouraging farmers to use fertilizer has been achieved) and to allow all input prices to rise. If these two opposite movements proceed much further, the whole economic equation which makes it profitable to farmers to adopt high-yielding crops will go wrong. The control of agricultural prices on both input and output sides, which is exceedingly difficult, is a condition of effective planning for the agricultural revolution. It was a remarkable achievement that the Indian Government was in fact able to keep prices reasonably stable when the sudden glut of the 1968 Punjab wheat harvest came on to the market. A little earlier it was largely government action in guaranteeing grain prices to the farmer which set in train the remarkable expansion of wheat production in Pakistan.

7

The argument of the chapter has concerned the type of exchange relationship which is possible and desirable between the industrialized and the developing societies in the world. It has emphasized a more direct attempt to mobilize more energetically the resources of land and labour in developing countries. This is a long-term argument, in two respects. First, it looks beyond the present moment in which a few obvious openings for introducing sophisticated technology overseas have been exploited. It looks to the moment, now arriving, when economic growth has to spread far more widely through the mass of population, at present largely excluded. Secondly, it concerns the long-term political prospect, which will be grim indeed if the mounting pressure of increased numbers in rural areas—*which is inevitable*—is not met squarely by increasing employment and earnings in those areas. There may be short-term gains for small sections of developing societies in the present policy which mimics the complexity and sophistication of industrialized countries in a tiny sector of the economy. For the long term the moral, political and economic arguments for a far broader attack coincide. In harder economic terms such an attack corresponds to the proposition that poor societies must create their capital by a good deal of human labour, because they cannot make or afford to buy more than a small share of the complex equipment of the rich, and because simple, relatively unskilled societies must start from relatively simple tasks.

The argument that mass production industry does offer unskilled repetitive work neglects three facts—that there is not yet a mass market, except for very few commodities; that heavy foreign exchange costs are involved; and that, at least in Africa, capital and interest payments will tend to be foreign, as well as much of the management personnel.

But the logic of the argument for internal mobilization still insists on a considerable element of inter-dependence and exchange. It will require import of the products of heavy industry and of many machines; major expenditure on control of the environment and particularly the control of water; the borrowing of highly specialized skills and wider experience, and the repayment of present debt. All these involve calls on foreign exchange, and in total will strain the resources of most developing countries to the utmost without adding a single inessential item.

There is no long-term reason for pessimism on this economic front. The economic world is growing faster than ever before on the demand side—in population and in the expectation of consumers. Developing countries should certainly have their share in this expansion, partly because the new techniques are learned and spread over the world in so much less time than it took to develop them. It is mainly the short-term problems which are difficult, with the exception of population growth.

Perhaps other elements of international contact should also be looked at in a rather different dimension. Tourism has been mentioned, and for some countries is of growing importance. It carries a certain unpleasant flavour, of catering for the luxuries and insensitiveness of the rich, flaunted in the face of the poor. But this is partly because only the rich have been long-distance tourists in the past, and partly also because standards are apt to be relaxed outside the critical eye of the home society. Nothing could be more unattractive than a vision of tropical countries as a playboy's paradise, and there are examples of it.

But there is a different and much less questionable kind of 'tourism', if the term can include not only the innocent enjoyment of novelty but the pursuit of interests, and of learning, and of a sense of service, and indeed of economic opportunity. 'One world' is not an idle phrase—the developing world is being brought into the field of interest and possible reality of millions of people in developed countries whose counterparts only a generation ago saw it only as garrison troops or in highly coloured pictures in a book. It is not for nothing that the Universities of Europe and America have developed, in not much more than a decade, a sudden growth of Departments studying development overseas in all its aspects. In fact, far more is known of the real life of Asia and Africa than in the times when rich countries were actually responsible for ruling them. If this has become an academic fashion, there must still be a reason for it.

Some at least of the motive lies, among the young educated groups in the West, in a real intellectual interest, in a sense of a world to be rediscovered, in a sense of sympathy, in a sense of claustrophobia within highly organized societies where the sense of superfluity and impersonality can become oppressive.[1] In some senses the same motives which took Englishmen to America, to Canada, Australia, New Zealand still operate today and, perhaps even more widely than before, in many of the richer countries.

When the suspicions of the Independence period are less vigorous, economic opportunity—employment by foreign governments and employers, or private professional work—will become both more attractive and more possible. Scientific study alone could be a major element in this. Luxury hotels on the palm-fringed beach are one way of earning foreign exchange, for a few months in the year; an institute of marine biology or of plant genetics, originally staffed by foreign scientists paid from overseas, operating for years and offering an increasing share in its work to a growing group of local scientists, is another, less socially dangerous and perhaps more profitable in the long run from its effect on development of local resources. The British Government's 'Study and

[1] Another argument for not providing tourists with a replica of the world they are escaping from, even if the cabaret girls wear grass skirts or none at all.

Serve' scheme for young graduates exactly meets this motive, and there are enough young men and women of goodwill in Europe and America to make this form of contact on a considerable scale. It will never match the flood of ordinary tourists; but the type of tourism a country attracts depends on what it offers. Mountaineering, game-viewing, natural history, the study of antiquities, and a host of other recreations, in the full sense of the word, do not carry the implications which a small section of tourism has. There is still opportunity for adventure, achievement and contrast in the developing world.

The expansion of world contact is not likely to slow down for long. At the time of writing there is a pause, even a slight withdrawal, by the developing countries to reassess their programmes and attitudes, and by the West because of internal preoccupations and a passing moment of disillusion. But it need not last long. Provided that Asia and Africa are making a genuine effort towards self-reliance, and that there is some falling-off in the smash-and-grab raids on foreign enterprise, they can increasingly make their own terms as to the type of foreign assistance which they accept. If the major world powers can resolve their present confusions in monetary policy, which results in rich countries pleading bankruptcy as a reason for cutting down aid to the poor, a better flow of both aid and investment will become possible. Purely trade and business relationships may well increase, as the fear of domination recedes in developing countries and their rate and sophistication of economic growth increases. Despite the paramount need for internal mobilization, and indeed to assist it, the exchange between developed and developing countries should start a new period of expansion, both in personnel and trade, when a fresh and more healthy basis for it has been evolved.

PART IV
CONCLUSIONS

CHAPTER XII

A NEW PATH

The formidable differences between the situation of developing countries today and that which faced the Western world in its main period of modern growth were summarized in the opening chapter. Individually, many of them have been mentioned elsewhere, notably and in great detail in Myrdal's *Asian Drama*.[1] But the full inferences have not been drawn. The developing countries, from their relative weakness, cannot and may not wish to follow the same course as the Western countries at their moment of greatest relative strength. Though many similar things will have to be done if the daily life of peasant societies is to be enriched and liberated, their path of change will be unique. It will not be exactly the same things which are done, nor in the same order, nor by the same methods, nor in the same modality. Already it is impossible to find a parallel in history for the situation of Malawi or Sabah today; for amid elements of a 14th-century, or even prehistoric, background are elements of the 20th century, both physical and psychological. Several chapters have brought out how impossible it is to recapitulate earlier paths of growth, and not only in economics—in the growth of administration (VIII) or of politics (IX) or of education (X).

It is easy to say 'a new path', but to foresee the path becomes an act of prophecy, since the precedents, such as they are, are ambiguous, or misleading, or irrelevant. Some modern techniques, which are adaptable to a social situation different from that in which they were developed, are transferable; some are not. But to this distinction between transferable and non-transferable elements of modernity another and different distinction must be added. It is a distinction between the prescriptions for progress.

The older prescription is still constantly quoted and pressed upon developing countries. But a vigorous criticism of it is growing up, not only in the Communist world but in the heartlands of

[1] Op. cit.

industrial development in Europe and America. And it is not only the old orthodoxy of the West which is followed by developing countries: they catch by infection the idea and protests of 1969. It is worth looking more closely at this critical, revolutionary movement which is running through the developed world, for it may have a close relation to the future in Africa and Asia.

Perhaps the greatest tension in the West is summed up in the words 'What shall it profit a man if he gain the whole world and lose his own soul?'. The world is worth gaining. Few would believe that the energies and intelligence of man, as expressed by Shakespeare,[1] were not meant to be used in the mastery and improvement of his wild environment. The rewards have been great indeed, and not to be denied to any society of men in the world from the poor Indians in the Andean *altiplano* to the Dyaks in the forests of Borneo. But the societies which, from time to time, have made great steps forward in such mastery and achievement have needed a powerful social organization and discipline to do so. In all ages this is at first seen as benefit. War is stopped, famine relieved, men and women can raise a family in security and hand what they have won to their children. Yet it is not long before order and discipline become stifling. Often they have been built on injustice; usually they end up in privilege. The sacrifice of values becomes too high. Revolt and (in its best sense) anarchism raise their head again.

The Russian Revolution marked the first shattering revolt against the new industrial order. It was a revolution more against injustice and privilege than against the fret of discipline and materialism. The Communist Manifesto of 1848 foresaw the destruction of old values and ideals which the industrial bourgeoisie would bring. Already 'it has put to an end all feudal, patriarchal, idyllic relations', 'has left no bond between man and man than naked self-interest, than callous cash-payment'. Already, cries the Manifesto, 'all that is solid melts into air, all that is holy is profaned, and man is at last compelled to face with sober sense his real conditions of life and his relations with his kind'. Marx foresaw this destruction with a certain savage glee; Matthew Arnold, his contemporary, saw it only with nostalgic sadness as, at

---

[1] 'What a piece of work is a man! How noble in reason! How infinite in faculty! In form, in moving, how express and admirable! In action how like an angel! In apprehension how like a god!' (*Hamlet*, Act II, Scene 2).

Dover Beach, he dreamed of the sea of faith, and could hear only 'its melancholy long withdrawing roar', as the waves drew back over the shingle.[1] But neither Marx nor Arnold, speaking of 'a new world struggling to be born', foresaw that the new and greater bureaucracy, new representative forms of local government, welfare, the huge material gains from the productive system and science would gloss over the loss of other human values for nearly a hundred years. It is only now that this loss begins to be widely felt outside a narrow intellectual circle. It is only now that we can see even the Russian Revolution as, in a sense, a betrayal, because it imposed an even stronger and more authoritarian discipline and materialism. Arnold's new world was not to be the new world of freedom but much nearer de Tocqueville's vision of democratic society: 'A flock of timid and industrious animals of which the government is the shepherd.'

It is against the bureaucracy, 'the Establishment', the callous materialism, the lack of 'participation' and (in America and Southern Africa and elsewhere) the arrogance of the dominant European over the non-white peoples of the world that the modern revolution is brewing. In the West, the County Councillors or Rural District Councillors, all very properly elected and 'representative', coalesce with their own officials in supporting their own decisions, as they drive the bulldozer through villages for a new road extension, for a factory in the bluebell wood, a pylon in the cottage garden, despite the despairing protests of their electorate.[2] Peoples with some long history and quality of their own—the Welsh, for example—curse the English civilization of Birmingham as it invades and bribes them so easily with its cash to give up their rivers to motor manufacturers and their landscape to developers. There arises a profound disbelief in politicians because they seem only to dig society more deeply into its rut, appealing to the old prejudices and slogans (whether of Right or Left), which belong to the past, and unable to comprehend the deeper restlessness against the very structure and values of society itself. The American Election of 1968, the election of the Party bosses, was a portent. There arises, in Yugoslavia, in Czechoslovakia, a revolt against the

---

[1] *Dover Beach* (1867).
[2] A French café owner in the valley of the Loire remarked, as he gazed at a large new factory glaring out of that beautiful landscape, 'progress ruins everything (le progrès abîme tout).'

rigidity and the lies of orthodox Soviet doctrine. There arises in the Universities of the West a revolt against the entrenched 'establishment', the traditions and rules which not long ago seemed the fine fruit of wisdom and experience. Above all, in industry the old resentment against a managerial system which excludes participation breaks out even more strongly in the traditional but uncreative channel—the demand for yet more money; the demand, in the French revolt of 1968, for 'participation' was the first really large-scale evidence of a more creative urge. The young generation of the 1930s in Europe reacted against the first World War and unemployment by violent, ideological remedies—Fascism, Communism and the like; the young generation of the 1960s reacts against all ideologies by a revolt in the destructive tradition of anarchists. It is a restlessness against the disciplines which have succeeded so well, and against the materialism which has gained the world but lost its own soul.

It is in respect to the old prescription for development and to this new unrest that the greatest single difference is found between most of Tropical Africa and most of Asia. Many countries in Asia—India, Pakistan, Thailand, Malaysia, the Philippines—with a landlord system and a propertied upper and middle class, have already gone far down the old road. They have much of the capitalist order already, and the problems of their politics are to conserve or to modify and transform it. Burma, Indonesia, North Vietnam are, outside China, the only revolutionaries. By contrast, in most of Tropical Africa the problem is not to modify an old order but to create a new one from the start. In this contrast, the Asian conservatives have an early lead in development—they rely upon trusted methods which have worked elsewhere. But they run the risk of losing the cup of success just as it comes to their lips: for they will encounter, much earlier in the sequences of growth, the disillusion with its ways and values bred in the West and from the Soviet bureaucracy.

Thus, if the function of progressive politics is mainly reform in Asia, it is mainly creation in Africa. It is for this reason that the tool most often chosen in Africa is the compact band of leaders in a one-party system, unified, in the best cases, by a general philosophy and using the thousands of party-cells and branches to communicate aims and to make possible participation. A strong centre and face-to-face participation in development at the humblest level is the essence of this programme. It corresponds remarkably well both with a development need and with the political mood of the late 20th century. The big hydro-electric and irrigation projects demand central finance and planning, but the working of the project is a matter of creative and educative relations with thousands of small farmers, as the water, with all its possibilities, at last comes to each man's furrow.

The old system, with its multi-party politics of economic interest-groups in a society already differentiated, finds it natural to build up tiers of organization—subdivision, District, State, Union—both politically and administratively. But for the revolutionary one-party systems the function of intermediate representative organs is less clear. Direct participation at the level of the farmer and the village is real and necessary; from that level there is quick political contact, through the Party, to the centre itself. There is little economic differentiation in 80% agricultural societies and few genuinely regional services; in consequence, there is little need for representative government, and its corollary of political faction, at these intermediate levels. There is, indeed, a need for intermediate structures of some kind between the intellectual leadership at the top and traditional attitudes and conditions at the base. But such structures are more likely to be useful if they grow through modernizing rural associations (Co-operatives, Farmers' Associations, banks, settlement committees, and the like), in which party politics would be at best irrelevant and at worst destructive.[1] It is for this reason that delegation of administrative authority, through convenient units, has seemed a better solution than decentralization to local representative government. The very best of African educated manpower—there is little enough of it—is needed for administration and research. It will not long tolerate domination and frustration by corrupt Party bosses at local level, as several military revolts have shown. Nyerere's decision to make civil servants members of TANU was not so much a politicization of bureaucracy as a bureaucratization of politics. It recognized that development needs expertise as well as political enthusiasm.

[1] P. C. Lloyd has remarked that, where the electorate is largely semi-literate, universal suffrage re-emphasizes ethnicity—the very tribalism which Africa particularly wishes to extinguish. See *The New Elites of Tropical Africa* (London, Oxford University Press for International African Institute, 1966).

It would be false to see in all, or even many, African States so simple a political theory as that outlined. One-party systems and one-party politicians can be corrupted into a hierarchy of privilege and personal enrichment just as easily as the commercial and capitalist systems of the older dispensation. But here and there, in East Africa, Zambia, perhaps in the new Ghana, a new pattern of political activity and development planning does seem to be emerging. It is a system which emphasizes participation at the point where it is real and personal, and which controls the necessary bureaucracy, not by representation which so easily loses reality, but through a pervasive Party animated by a single ideal.

To developed countries, with a far more complex social system, such ideas seem profoundly dangerous, after their experience of the Nazis and of the degeneration of Bolshevism from a dedicated party into a bureaucracy, wooden when it is not brutal. But condemnation in Europe of systems which are degenerative in European circumstances cannot be extended to condemnation in many far simpler societies, where the zest of a new idealism is needed to re-establish energy and self-reliance after colonial rule and where both administration and politics need a direct simplicity. Part of the current protest in the West springs from overcrowding and the destruction of privacy and natural beauty (which is not only valued by the middle classes, though mainly enjoyed by them in the past); and this does not apply to most of Africa or Asia. But the larger part springs from a lack of participation in industrial management and a failure of the representative idea in social and political life. In these respects some of the revolutionaries in Africa and Asia have—and quite consciously—struck a blow for human values which will find increasing sympathy and response all over the world. Simone Weil[1] remarked that we ought to wonder 'whether even the black man, the most primitive of colonized peoples, had not after all more to teach us than to learn from us' in the art of living together. Social complexity will come to Africa as development proceeds, and bring its own problem; but for the time being the task is to liberate and harness energy in the simplest way.

2

The path of economic growth will also be new. No one can suppose that, in a generation, peasant societies will look very like

[1] Op. cit.

any developed country today. By the standards with which we now measure wealth, they cannot possibly be as rich. They will be using the techniques of the 1980s which may well suit them better than those of today. If their present mood is any guide, they will have built a society relatively rich in human services, far less rich in consumer goods. Because the developed countries will also have changed enormously by that time, the pattern of trade will have changed too—much of what the industrial countries now produce may be handed over to production in the 'third world', while the developed countries move on to new regions of social need and technical exploration. The current difficulties of the market will also have changed—the potential for human consumption is so enormous that the present muddle, analogous to the muddle in world monetary policy, cannot last. High population growth is an infinitely greater danger, for it cannot be cured by UNCTAD or GATT; it is change in physical circumstances which no political or administrative arrangement can wipe away.

It is because the world will be different, and the path to it new that it is so mistaken to suggest targets for peasant countries for 1980 which would bring them nearer to a developed country in 1960 terms: this is the process of reading history backwards so often condemned in this book.

Are there any signs today of the first steps towards this longer perspective? On the economic side they are certainly few, but these few are significant. First, the gloom about markets may well be lightening a little. Not only world trade but the export figures for developing countries took an upward swing in 1968. Cairncross, Mellor and Caine[1] have all pointed out that the rise in world consumption of commodities and the secular trend of prices is not nearly so discouraging to developing countries as is often supposed. Certainly, peasant countries will need an increasingly industrialized base to enable them both to supply more of their own needs and to take part in trade. In broad terms, it is metals and machines which they need most, especially in Africa. And this is not merely for industrial purposes. Successful development of

[1] Cairncross, op. cit.; Mellor, op. cit.; Sir Sidney Caine, *Prices for Primary Producers* (London, Institute for Economic Affairs, 1966). 'Far too much emphasis is put in current literature on the forces operating to limit or diminish the demand for primary produce, and far too little on the constant opening up of new requirements throughout the world as the standard of living rises' (Cairncross).

agriculture will multiply this need very fast indeed. The agricultural industry itself, as it modernizes, is an avid consumer of chemicals, power, transport, traction, pumps, metal tools and processing machinery. It will also be very difficult to prevent the incomes generated, both on the farm and in associated industries and services, from creating a heavy import demand for consumer goods. If these are going to be produced in increasing quantities locally (as they often should be, both to increase and diversify employment), machinery is again needed: there is no way to avoid the need for industrialization.

It therefore becomes more urgent to look for potential centres of engineering in large regions of the developing world and to build round them an economic community (unfortunately a Co-Prosperity Sphere has bad connotations!) which can specialize locally and trade within a single multi-lateral system. Some at least of the capital needed for this development can come from judicious local taxation of a more prosperous agriculture without totally destroying the farmers' incentive;[1] a small part could come through international funds. The prospect of creating such a system in the Indian subcontinent and in the Malaysia–Singapore–Indonesia–Hong Kong–Philippine zone are reasonably good in purely resource and skill terms, with Japan, New Zealand and Australia as developed neighbours. India and Pakistan with a base of heavy industry, under-used factory capacity and plenty of entrepreneurial and commercial skills, are particularly well placed. The prospects in Africa stretch far further ahead and are even more heavily clouded by political difficulty; white racialism in South Africa and Rhodesia and political collapse in the Congo are major economic catastrophes which will hold back the whole continent south of the Sahara for as long as they continue.

The prospects for more helpful international contact are also not unhopeful, even though there are periods of regression and discouragement, through one of which the world is now passing. There is still a great field for Technical Assistance in the scientific survey of resources—soils, water, marine development, minerals —and this is an area which both the United Nations and bilateral donors are still ready to cultivate. The reward for this work in economic growth may be slow in coming, but it can eventually be

[1] 50–80% of Japanese taxes were drawn from agriculture in the late 18th and early 19th centuries (Mellor, op. cit.).

very great. Probably a greater proportion of the funds available should go to this 'hard' area of scientific work, and less to the provision of experts in 'soft' subjects such as education or public administration: too often the expert in these subjects offers inapplicable experience from his own society to civil servants who well know what should be done if politics did not prevent them doing it.

It is through this hard-headed and technical work that the main accelerators—power, communications, relevant science and redesigned technology—will enter. An enormous work of translating the discoveries of industrial countries into new forms and uses needed in the developing world is waiting to be done. This is not only in the biological and physical sciences affecting tropical agriculture, where our ignorance is only beginning to be realized. It covers new methods in housing, storage, processing, new applications of mechanical power. The world's stock of scientific knowledge has not yet been half used. It may well be that Japan, Hong Kong, and India, with their experience of small-scale production and their resource of skills, will be a more likely source for such innovation than the older industrial countries whose experience is different and whose attention is elsewhere. Africa in particular is astonishingly ignorant of Asian progress: it is far more likely to find ideas there than in the high-technology/high-wage economies of the industrial giants.

In trade, the Delhi UNCTAD meeting of 1968 was certainly discouraging. The pattern of world trade is supported by an extraordinary conservatism—Lancashire fought for decades, by fair means and foul, to retain a textile trade as though by divine right. Yet not only technical changes but the slow growth of some signs of conscience in world affairs will add to the pressure for change. Countries which have accepted a duty to the poorer groups of their internal community cannot resist indefinitely a similar investment within the world economy. The word 'investment' is used advisedly; for in matters of trade, concessions which are not of mutual benefit will never be more than marginal. The distinction is between short-term advantage, which is sought by many donors through 'tied' aid and similar restrictive practices, and the longer-term investment in countries which will assuredly grow and provide expanding markets (they include two-thirds of world consumers) as their early difficulties are overcome.

Finally, the general expansion of international contact cannot be omitted from the economic balance. For the present moment the hard adjustment to the economic realities of their internal situation is turning attention more inwards in the developing countries. Simultaneously, the realization among the older Powers that the freedom of ex-colonies is real and includes the freedom to bite and kick has been a shock. But the development of closer contact goes on just as strongly beneath the surface and in many cases will re-emerge in new public relationships and with a new realism. The developing countries which have the self-confidence to develop these relations more fully and positively, with a better knowledge of the limitations of Aid and the central importance of self-development, are likely to gain most ground: there are signs that this awareness is growing.

This contact is likely to grow, and most valuably, not merely through governments but through organizations of the community in the developed world. A few years ago it would have been inconceivable that an ordinary Department of Electrical Engineering in a British college[1] would arrange to send groups of students to Ghana and Zambia to give them an idea of the nature and needs of rural communities in Africa, in relation to possible uses of electric power, or that groups of students from Wales would go overland to India to learn something of her agricultural problems.[2] Yet these are only two of many University schemes of varied types which involve research, or service, or simply experience of the developing world. 'Oxfam' and other relief organizations, charitable Trusts and Foundations, many religious organizations, both national and international, organizations for scientific research, public health, family planning, 'intermediate technology', educational planning—all these and more, in Britain alone, are stretching out a hand of friendship and common interest. This steadily growing interchange of ideas, techniques, channels of contact, minor but often critical financial help, has a value disproportionate to its cost. As it is met with growing education and resourcefulness in developing countries its fertilizing influence will constantly increase. A world culture is a flowing tide which is not stemmed at national frontiers.

---

[1] The Imperial College of Science, London.
[2] University College, Bangor.

('University classes must be of University standards') and the evident need for very simple adult education to which the University, to the credit of its heart at least, would like to contribute. It has not been possible to list and discuss all the many manifestations of this disease—the reader familiar with developing countries can add his own examples.[1] But in seeking to distinguish participation, representative Local Government, and local party political activity, and to relate them to the need for orderly and dynamic administration at local levels, perhaps these chapters will stimulate more and more accurate special studies. It is not merely that the British (or French or Dutch or American) models may be unsuitable in peasant societies; it is that each 'stage' may well need structures and institutions tailored to its needs. The large number of important variants between States in India shows at least that independent thought and judgement has been applied in each case —and that the All-India Government was wise enough not to insist on uniformity. This area of local participation and local decision is the most critical in the whole development process.

These concepts of organic sequence, of local variance, of multi-dimensional change, all firmly related to a time-scale which may be quite short—ten years is a long time in the developing world— are, alas, barely sketched here. But if the emphasis on them could provoke a wider recognition and a deeper study of the nature of developmental change, the sketch will have been worth while.

5

There is an intellectual trap in the very title of this book. For if 'modernizing' means bringing to the state of developed nations in 1969, the developing tortoise may reach it one day, but the developed hare will not be waiting there.

'Modernizing' might be described, as it has been in some of these chapters, in terms of achieving certain general changes. reform of land tenure; creating suitable institutions for agricultural development and marketing; building an honest bureaucracy and a stable political system centrally and locally. It might be described as a change from a traditional, custom-oriented society to an individualist or co-operative economic-oriented society; as the evolution of a system of values capable of mediating modern

[1] A number of other examples were discussed in *The Best of Both Worlds?*.

knowledge and techniques; as the mobilization of surplus manpower and under-used resources for economic growth; as the spread of higher education.

It might indeed include all these things, and more. But the question remains how far and how fast and by what means very different societies could do them. It is sometimes tempting to believe that 'modern' civilization—and that is apt to be defined roughly as the type created and spread from the industrial revolution in the West—is bound to spread all over the world. Certainly, some outward elements of it—from canned music to electric power—seem to spread irresistibly to the remotest corners of the world: Coca-Cola is available in tiny huts in the African bush. But in fact this is illusory: underneath these superficial signs utterly different cultures and ways of doing 'modern' tasks persist. Attitudes to politics and economics, ways of administrative action are totally different in Thailand, Bengal, Kenya, Sierra Leone. Each nation, in 1969, has a certain style and a certain capital of resources and skills, a certain capacity for making progress on this front or that. Even developed countries—Britain, France, U.S.A., Russia—have very greatly differing styles in the use of a knowledge and technology which in fact they share in common.

Modernization can in fact only mean following a path which is possible for each nation in its current circumstances, using to the best advantage the common stock of scientific knowledge which is available simultaneously to every country in the world. The impediments which may prevent a full use of knowledge lie in different planes. It may be a lack of natural resources; it may be a level of accumulated wealth too small to spread knowledge widely; it may be the persistence of social or religious customs, beliefs or values which preclude the use of knowledge in some fields; it may be a failure to discipline personal and social prejudices (racial feelings, for example), or personal ambition and greed (in both politics and economics), so that no political system can be built which is an adequate support for the development which knowledge could bring; it may be failure to control population growth, so that it outruns the resources which are available. The equations differ—Congo (Kinshasa) has great potential wealth, but remains poor; Switzerland, with few natural resources, has developed skills which make her very rich.

Certainly, some countries where the natural resources are poor and other impediments severe will not reach a high level of wealth in one generation or even two. But the inference of this book is certainly that, even in isolation, very great improvements in the daily life of their peoples can be made. But for the threat of too high population growth, land could produce more food and materials for each family; disease could be reduced; security from natural hazards could be improved. If we look more generally at Africa and Asia, the main impediments in Asia lie in population growth and the political/social systems; in Africa, in the sparseness of easily-worked resources and the huge land distances, with a population threat in the more favoured areas, and in the complex of traditional customs and values.

Discussion of politics has occupied a good part of this book. Thailand could be three times as rich if her political and administrative system allowed it. India could release a great volume of energy and skill if her agricultural social system encouraged it. But even deeper than politics lies the basis of religion, morals and education which can sterilize or fertilize human effort and give to society a unity of standards and values upon which a stable political and social system can be built. Within the older systems, whether in Buddhist, Hindu, Muslim, Christian or animist culture, there needs to come the steady, clear light of rational knowledge, a light which can shine in Primary schools as much as in Universities, for it is an attitude to the physical world at all its levels. Secondly, above the depths of true religious belief, in which the symbol stands in place of scientific knowledge—and the symbol can be in terms of any culture in the world—there needs to be a moral discipline and leadership without which no social action can gain the force and consistency needed for development. Both Hindu and African cultures are, in the main, religious rather than moral; and they produce religious rather than moral societies. Morality without a religious foundation tends to crumble; but religion without a moral guide to action is socially impotent. In some ways, it could be said that both Gandhi and Nehru began to moralize India; that Nyerere and Kaunda are seeking to moralize Tanzania and Zambia. It is very literally from their efforts that their societies —Asian or African—begin to gain the power of purposive, sustained action. The discipline of daily effort, care and patience in the peasant farming of much of Asia gives a basis, in character, for a disciplined society—in Africa, with her rougher methods, this is not yet so widely spread. But this discipline has to extend—as it did once in Europe—to honesty and thrift and loyalty in commercial and industrial life if a modern nation is to prosper.

This book makes no prophecies of the speed of growth in any country. It has pointed only to the possibilities—and they are great; to methods which have intrinsic logic; and to the need for a dynamic purpose and moral discipline, without which action runs out into the sand. Some peasant nations may well achieve a civilization which has qualities which the West will envy, even if their physical wealth is less. Some certainly will be pioneers in new experiments in social action. 'Europeans', in the widest sense, have much to give to these countries, if it is given modestly: they may also have much to learn from them.

INDEX OF AUTHORS AND WORKS QUOTED IN THE TEXT

Allan, W., *The African Husbandman*, 49, 135
All-India Credit Survey, 161
All-India Social Survey, 8th Round, 152
Anwaruzzaman Khan, *Introduction of Tractors in a Subsistence Farm Economy*, 118
Ayub Khan, President, 'Pakistan's Economic Progress', 17

Bachman, K. L., and Christensen, R. P., article in H. M. Southworth and B. F. Johnston (eds.), *Agricultural Development and Economic Growth*, 148
Bailey, F. G., *Caste and the Economic Frontier*, 37, 59, 64, 74; *Politics and Social Change*, 66, 67, 69–70; 'The Peasant View of the Bad Life', 42–3, 179–80
Balogh, T., 'Land Tenure, Education and Development in Latin America', 96
Banfield, E. C., *The Moral Basis of Backward Society*, 241
Beals, Alan R., *Gopalpur—a South Indian Village*, 42
Béteille, André, *Class, Caste and Power*, 63, 65
Bonney, R. S. P., *Relationship between Road Building and Economic and Social Development in Sabah*, 167
Bradfield, Dr. Richard, Presidential Address, Seventh International Congress of Soil Science (1960), 126, 128; 'Towards More and Better Food for the Filipino People and More Income for the Farmers', 132–3, 134
Brass, Paul K., *Factional Politics in an Indian State*, 66, 233–4
Brewster, John M., article in H. M. Southworth and B. F. Johnston (eds.), *Agricultural Development and Economic Growth*, 41–2, 241
British Broadcasting Corporation, 'Down Your Way', 170

Caine, Sir Sidney, *Prices for Primary Producers*, 287
Cairncross, Sir A., *Factors in Economic Development*, 114, 272, 287
Carroll, Thomas F., article in H. M. Southworth and B. F. Johnston (eds.), *Agricultural Development and Economic Growth*, 96–7
Chambers, Professor, 'Address to the Second International Conference of Economic History', 7
Charles, K. J., and Panika, P. G. K., *Education and Economic Development—A case study of Kerala*, 247

Dandekar, V. M., 'The Role of Small-Scale Industry in the Indian Experience', 271
Darling, Sir Malcolm, *The Punjab Peasant in Prosperity and Debt*, 37, 165
de Tocqueville, A., *Democracy in America*, 196, 283
de Wilde, John C., and others, *Experiences with Agricultural Development in Tropical Africa*, 84, 85, 121, 161, 167, 180
Dey, S. K., *Panchayati Raj*, 68
Duke, S. C., *India's Changing Villages*, 63–4, 68, 69
Dumont, René, *False Start in Africa*, 116, 117

Eliot, T. S., *Notes Towards the Definition of Culture*, 258; *The Rock*, 81
Epstein, T. S., *Economic Development and Social Change in South India*, 43, 47, 51, 58, 61
Etherington, D. M., 'Projected Changes in Urban and Rural Population in Kenya with Reference to Development Policy', 266, 271

Follett, Mary Parker, *Dynamic Administration*, 205–6
Fortes, Meyer, and Pritchard, E. E. Evans (eds.), *African Political Systems*, 219–20

Foster, Philip, *Education and Social Change in Ghana*, 12
Frankel, S. Herbert, *The Economic Impact on Under-developed Societies*, 139
Fukatake, T., Onchi, T., and Nakane, C., *The Socio-Economic Structure of the Indian Village*, 64, 266

Galetti, Baldwin and Dina, *Nigerian Cocoa Farmers*, 92
Garbett, D. Kingsley, 'Prestige, Status and Power in a Modern Valley Korekore Chiefdom, Rhodesia', 74
Geertz, Clifford, *The Social Context of Economic Change*, 50
Ghulam Mohammed, 'Development of Irrigated Agriculture in East Pakistan', 145
Gormeley, P. H., paper on Education, Employment and Rural Development, 99
Government of Kenya, Ministry of Economic Planning, Statistical Section, Nairobi, 101
Government of Madras, *The Intensive Agricultural Development Programme in Thanjavur*, 135
Government of Northern Rhodesia, Report of the Rural Working Party (1961), 268
Government of Pakistan, Central Statistical Office, Pakistan 2nd Plan, survey of credit sources, 161
Government of Tanzania, Ministry of Economic Affairs and Development Planning, *Labour Force Survey of Tanzania*, 102
Government of Thailand, Agricultural Economics Department, Ministry of Agriculture, report on Chainat Dam, 135
Gray, Hugh, 'Andhra Pradesh', 229
Griffiths, V. L., *The Contribution of General Education to Agricultural Development, Primarily in Africa*, 253

Harbison, Frederick, paper on Education, Employment and Rural Development, 99, 100
Harbison, Frederick, and Myers, Charles A., *Education, Manpower and Economic Growth*, 24
Haswell, Margaret, *Economics of Development in Village India*, 136, 137, 166-7, 182
Hill, Polly, 'A Plea for Indigenous Economics', 273-4

Hirschman, Albert O., *The Strategy of Economic Development*, 8-9, 114-15
Hla Myint, *The Economics of Developing Countries*, 46, 152
Hunter, Guy, *Manpower, Employment and Education in the Rural Economy of Tanzania*, 254-5; *The Best of Both Worlds?*, 4, 115, 295

International Labour Office, Paper MCYW 1967/2, 101; *Report to the Commission for Social Development of the United Nations Economic and Social Council*, 13

Jain, Dr. Sugan Chand, *Community Development and Panchayati Raj in India*, 208
Johnston, Bruce, F., *Agriculture and Economic Development: The Relevance of Japanese Experience*, 94, 97-100
Jorgensen, Dale W., 'Subsistence Agriculture and Economic Growth', 102

Kay, George, 'Agricultural Production in the Eastern Province of Zambia', 133
Kenyatta, President Jomo, *Facing Mount Kenya*, 53

Langland, William, *Piers Plowman*, 242
Lawson, Rowena, 'Innovation and Growth in Traditional Agriculture of the Lower Volta', 103; 'The Volta Resettlement Scheme', 127
Lewis, Sir Arthur, article in H. M. Southworth and B. F. Johnston (eds.), *Agricultural Development and Economic Growth*, 183, 248
Leys, Colin T., 'Notes on the Planning Process', 274
Lloyd, P. C., 'The Integration of the New Economic Classes into Local Government in Western Nigeria', 40; *The New Elites of Tropical Afrca*, 285-6
Lower Indus Survey, 151

MacMillan, A. A., *Aranjuez: Agricultural Development in a Suburban Setting*, 179
Matooka, Takeshi, 'The Conditions Governing Agricultural Development', 44, 169

INDEX OF AUTHORS AND WORKS QUOTED IN THE TEXT

Mayer, Adrian, C., *Caste and Kinship in Central India*, 61
Mellor, John W., article in *International Development*, 1966, 102, 126, 136; *The Economics of Agricultural Development*, 10, 85–6, 287, 288
Mettrick, Hal, *Aid in Uganda—Agriculture*, 128
Millikan, Max F., and Hapgood, David, *No Easy Harvest*, 108
Mukumoto, T., and Hosokawa, A., 'Changes and Mechanization in Agriculture in Japan', 105
Myrdal, Gunnar, *Asian Drama*, 115, 281

Nettl, J. P., 'Study in the Strategies of Political Development', 263
Norbye, O. D. K., paper on Education, Employment and Rural Development, 99
Nyerere, President J., Arusha Declaration, 17, 96

Oliver, Roland, *The Missionary Factor in East Africa*, 12

Paglin, Morton, article in *American Economic Review*, 143
Pande, B. M., 'Paddy Cultivation Practices in Community Development', 36
Pieper, Joseph, *Leisure the Basis of Culture*, 243
Pilgrim, J. W., 'Land Ownership in the Kipsigis Reserve', 122
Postan, M. M., 'Address to the Second International Conference on Economic History' (1962), 7

Ram Joshi, article in Myron Weiner (ed.), *State Politics in India*, 151
Rao, V. K. R. V., 'Educational Output in Relation to Employment Opportunities with Special Reference to India', 249; 'India's Long-Term Food Problem', 85
Retzlaff, R. H., *Village Government in India*, 62
Richards, Audrey I. (ed.), *East African Chiefs*, 197
Rostow, W. W., *The Stages of Economic Growth*, 24

Sen, S. R., 'Growth and Instability in Indian Agriculture', 87

Sheffield, J. R. (ed.), *Education, Employment and Rural Development*, 266
Shen, T. H., 'The Joint Commission on Rural Reconstruction, Taiwan', 105
Singer, Hans W., *International Development: Growth and Change*, 13, 92, 102, 203
Smith, M. G., *Malay Peasant Society in Jelebu*, 37
Southworth, Herman M., and Johnston, Bruce F. (eds.), *Agricultural Development and Economic Growth*, 8, 41–2, 96–7, 148, 183, 241, 248
Srinivas, M. N., *Caste in Modern India*, 60, 66, 223, 226, 233
Symonds, Richard, *The British and their Successors*, 12

Tarlok Singh, 'Agricultural Policy and Rural Economic Progress', 101, 213
Thirsk, Joan (ed.), *The Agrarian History of England and Wales*, 270
Thompson, F. M. L., 'The Second Agricultural Revolution', 109
Thorner, Daniel, *Agricultural Co-operation in India*, 158

United States A.I.D., *Agriculture in Pakistan*, 130

Wallman, Sandra, 'The Farmech Scheme—Basutoland (Lesotho)', 153–4
Weil, Simone, *The Need for Roots*, 218–19, 286
Weiner, Myron (ed.), *State Politics in India*, 151, 229, 232, 233
Wertheim, W. F., *East-West Parallels*, 50, 53
Wharton, Clifton R., *Research on Agricultural Development in Southeast Asia*, 24–5
Wilson, E. M. Carus (ed.), *Essays in Economic History*, p. 6.
Wilson, G. W., Bergman, B. K., Hirsch, L. V., and Klein, M. S., *The Impact of Highway Investment on Development*, 167
Wiser, W. H. and Charlotte, *Behind Mud Walls*, 41, 68, 240, 241, 266
Woods, George, 'The Development Decade in the Balance', 262
Wrigley, C. C., *African Farming in Buganda*, 48

Zaher Ahmed, *Dusk and Dawn in Village India*, 35

GENERAL INDEX

Achimota College, Ghana, 198
Addis Ababa Conference (1961), 255
Administration: Indian rural, 67–9, 206–13; paternalism in, 77, 202, 230, 241–2; development of, 191–6, 215–16; after Independence, 196–8, bureaucracy replaces traditional hierarchy, 197–8, 200; centralization of, 203; developing countries search for suitable, 204–6; farmers' participation in, 207, 210–11, 213, 215, 230; requirements for, 214–17; left strong by British in India, 221; and local politics, 230; and development, 230, 237; developing countries will not follow the West's example in, 281; and backward groups, 294
Administrators: training of, 198, 200–1; shortage of, 200, 201, 204; as 'Protectors of the Poor' in India and Pakistan, 229, 230
Ado, Nigeria, 39
Africa, Central: farmers in, 23; commercial agriculture in, 45, 47; village rankings in, 71; immigrant traders in, 168
Africa, East: farmers in, 23, 175, 182; Asians in, 38, 168, 272; commercial agriculture in, 45, 47; village rankings in, 71; land consolidated in, 75; local government in, 76; settlement schemes in, 85; trade in, 92; railway in, 111; and irrigation, 131; coffee in, 146, 205; land holdings in, 147; credit survey in, 161; immigrant traders in, 168, 272; Marketing Boards in, 169; Extension Officers in, 173; Plantation Companies in, 174; population of, 205; urbanization in, 266, 269; agriculture and industry in, 272; politics in, 286
Africa, North, Roman irrigation in, 124
Africa, Southern, 226 (see South Africa)

Africa, Tropical: agriculture in, 3, 11, 47–8, 81, 84, 103–4, 111–12, 185; fast growth needed in, 4; contrasted with mediaeval Europe, 6, 7–8; European expansion into, 6; peasant societies in, 7–8; spare land in, 7–8, 49; population of, 8, 49, 144, 205, Missions in, 12; education in, 12, 246, 249, 291–2, 293; technology in, 13, 245; developing countries in, 13; democracy in, 15; former authoritarian rulers in, 15; political systems in, 16–17; and self-reliance, 18, 278; and Asia, 20–4, 32, 49, 55, 72, 73–5, 77–8, 149, 284, 289; tribalism in, 21, 24; variety of groups in, 25; villages in, 30–1, 52, 71–4, 225; community effort in, 32; importance of social security in, 33–4; school fees in, 38; dummy chiefs in, 43; myth of 'old Africa', 53, 224, 238, 251; extended family in, 60; village rankings in, 71–2, 74; land tenure in, 73; modernization in, 75–8; areas of poor soil in, 88; local markets in, 92; farmers in, 95, 101, 118; non-farm employment in, 99; size of holdings in, 102–3; shortage of labour in, 103; Europeans' attitudes to, 111; tsetse fly in, 120, 133; barter in, 121; irrigation potential of, 131–2; oxen rarely used in, 133; potential of productivity in, 147–8; shortage of resources in, 148–9; political 'revolutions' in, 150; Co-operatives in, 154, 156; co-operative marketing in, 155, 169; credit in, 161, 162; storage, roads and markets in, 167–8; Extension Service in, 176; Administration in, 191, 200–6, 214, 236–7; suspicion of generals in, 192; rebellious provinces in, 197; indirect rule in, 198; training of administrators in, 198; shortage of trained staff in, 204; Provincial and District Teams in, 208; local

GENERAL INDEX 303

Africa, Tropical—*cont.*
government in, 217; Colonial peace in, 220; revolutionary politicians in, 221, 292-3; political changes in, 223-5; political will for development in, 231; no domination by landlords and merchants in, 231; local politics in, 233; faction in, 233-4, 236; one-party system in, 234-7, 284-6; attitude to officials in, 240-1; illiteracy in, 240; Indians mistrusted in, 241; socialization in, 245; animism in, 251; lacks common values and rules of conduct, 251; apprenticeship unsuitable for, 258; industry in, 262, 271, 288; big cities in, 267; food storage in, 271; engineering centres in, 272-3; and foreign aid, 276; European and American interest in, 277; new order in, 284; and contact with outer world, 292; obstacles to progress in, 297; purposive power in, 297-8

Africa, West: land in, 33; commercial agriculture in, 47; culture in, 72; local government in, 76; markets in, 92; palm-oil in, 93; effect of trade on farming in, 111; research into food-crops in, 112; cotton in, 116; rubber in, 120; Savannah belt of, 123; savings clubs in, 164; markets in, 166; indigenous traders of, 168; Marketing Boards in, 169; 'dash' in 194; industry in, 272

Agra, India, 68

Agricultural Colleges, 182, 249, 250

Agricultural development: stages in, 25, 46-7, 51-2, 114-15, 117, 120, 122-3, 138, 139-40, 163-4; conditions governing, 43, 45, 47; farmers and, 71, 146, 178-81; objectives of, 81-90; economics and, 82; politics and, 82-3; specialization and, 85, 91, 92, 94; and incomes, 85-6; big and small landholders and, 94-6; in Asia and Africa, 110-12; industry and, 112; 'package deals' for, 113, 115; plans for, 124; solution of problems in, 124-6; potential of, 129-30, 138; winter crops in Asia, 133-4; in developing countries and in Europe, 137-8; Village Level Workers and, 211; medium-size farming and, 227; in India, 229; and modernization, 295

Agricultural Development Corporations, 121, 172, 177, 183, 204

Agricultural Extension Service, 67, 69, 214, 216 (*see* Extension Services)
Agricultural Polytechnics, 256, 257
Agricultural Service: in India, 55; in Africa, 77
Agriculture: in Asia, 3, 22; in Africa, 3, 11; industry and, 9, 52, 173; role of, 9-10; labour for, 9-10; in 18th-century Britain, 9-10; in developing countries, 10-11; experiments in, 23, 36-7; classification of production in, 24-5; conservatism in, 34-5, 51; fragmentation of holdings, 89; in developing countries, 107-8; control of, 134; economics of, 136; Central Corporation and, 203-4; medium farmers in, 227; specialized, 264-5; tropical, 289 (*see* Crops: Cultivation: Farming)
Agronomy, 52, 102, 132, 138, 206, 273
Aguinaldo, Emilio, 221
Ahmadu Bello University, Nigeria, 248
Akhtar Hamid Khan, 158, 161, 205
Algeria, 111
Aluminium, 272
Alur people, Uganda, 21
Ammonium sulphate, 136
Anarchism, 282, 284
Andhra Pradesh, India: tobacco co-operative in, 45; caste-dominance in, 65; hybrid maize in, 119; grapes in, 130; rural administration of, 208, 212; panchayats in, 210-11
Angkor Wat, Cambodia, 124
Animal husbandry, 112, 113, 117, 148
Animals: draught, 32, 116, 267; depredations by, 35; compared with tractors, 35, 117-18; varied uses of, 117; underfed, 132 (*see* Cattle: Oxen)
Animateurs in French Africa, 178
Animism: in Africa, 55, 240, 251; in Asia, 251; and rational knowledge, 297
Ankole, Uganda, 153
Arabia, 116
Arabs in East Africa, 72
Aranjuez, Trinidad, 179
Artificial insemination of animals, 154; Centres for, 132
Arusha Declaration (1966), 17, 96
Ashanti, Ghana, 72, 192
Asia: agriculture in, 3, 81, 103-4, 110-12, 116, 185; fast growth needed in, 3-4; contrasted with mediaeval Europe, 6, 7-8; peasant societies in, 7-8, 32-42; population of, 8, 205; developing countries in,

Asia—*cont.*
13; former authoritarian rulers in, 15; searches for political systems, 16–17; and self-reliance, 18, 278; and Africa, 20–4, 32, 49, 55, 72, 73–5, 77–8, 149, 284; tribalism in, 24, 191; variety of groups in, 25; villages in, 30–1, 40–1, 42–8; social security in, 33–4; areas of poor soil in, 88; farmers in, 95–101; size of holdings in, 102–3; shortage of organized labour in, 103; managerial skills in, 109; Colonial Powers and, 110; barter in, 121; water control in, 129–30; mechanization in, 133; land tenure in, 148; political 'revolutions' in, 150; Co-operatives in, 154, 156; credit in, 161; savings societies in, 164; marketing in, 169; supply of trained staff in, 204; administration in, 205–6, 214; national politics in, 220–1; religious systems in, 225; development in, 230–1; local politics in, 233; modification of traditional society in, 237; education in, 240, 292; socialization in, 245; big cities in, 267; industry in, 262, 271–2; engineering in, 272–3; tourism in 276–8; capitalism in, 284; technical progress in, 289; obstacles to progress in, 297; purposive power in, 297–8

Asians, in East Africa, 38, 168, 272
Assam, India, panchayats in, 210
Australia: colonized from Europe, 6, 277; export standards in, 170; population of, 205; and engineering, 288
Authoritarianism, in Asia and Africa, 15, 214
Automation, 108
Awolowo, Chief Obafemi, 234
Ayub Khan, President, 17, 228, 229

Baluba tribe, Congo, 73
Bananas: in West Africa, 93; in Fiji, 93, 128; in Thailand, 135
Bangalore, India, 45
Bangkok, 72, 89, 192
Banks, 164–5, 285
Barbers in India, 44–5
Barotseland, 16, 73
Barter, 92, 121
Basic Democracy, Pakistan, 160, 178, 180, 213–14, 228
Bata Shoe Company, in Kenya, 271
Beans, 165; castor-beans, 132
Becket, Thomas à, 244

Beef, 132
Belgium, 111, 222, 269
Bemba people, Zambia, 21, 268
Bengal, India: overcrowding and poverty in, 50–1, 89; industry in, 109; and modernization, 296
Bengal, East, 30, 267–8
Bengal, West: food crops in, 84; panchayats in, 210; State politics in, 215, 234; education in, 247, 257; urbanization in, 266
Berseem, 36, 146
Biafra, 197
Bihar State, India: famine in, 87; and Western Uttar Pradesh, 123; irrigation in, 130; panchayats in, 210; agricultural study in, 274
Biology, 254, 289; marine, 277
Bisipara, Orissa, 67
'Block', in India, 56, 67, 159, 229; and development funds, 64–5; politics in, 65, 212–13, 229; delegation of authority to, 160; administration of, 173, 182, 208–13; planning by, 274
Block Development Officer (B.D.O.), 67, 173, 208–13, 229
Block Panchayats, 56, 64–6, 209–13, 227–9, 232
Blood feuds, 41
Boers, 111
Bolshevism, 15, 235, 238, 286 (*see* Communism)
Borgo a Mozzano, Italy, 164, 174–5
Borneo, 282
Botswana, diamond mine in, 176
Brahmins in India, 33, 56–8, 59–60, 62–3, 242
Bribery, 67, 70–1, 76, 95, 194, 202, 231
Brick-makers, 159, 270
Bridges, 113
British Broadcasting Corporation, 15, 170
British Road Research Laboratory, 167
Brookings Institution, Washington, 167
Buddhism: unifying influence of, 21; and other religions, 55; and social rankings, 71; in Thailand, 221; in a co-operative society, 225; suspicion of monks in, 242; and socialization, 250–1; and rational knowledge, 297
Buganda, 23, 48, 197, 221
Bulk buying, 155, 166
Bullocks, 137 (*see* Oxen)
Bureaucracy, 28; in Asia, 41; growth of, 194–7, 215–17, 283, 295; in British India, 198; kinship and, 199–200, 216; in Communism, 235, 286; in Tanzania, 285

GENERAL INDEX

Buret area, Kenya, 122
Burma: Kingdom of, 21; varying societies in, 24; savings in, 38; village rankings in, 71; one-party government in, 76, 222; Chinese and Indian traders in, 169; tribalism in, 171; radicalism in, 221, 226, 284; military government in, 222, 237; Chinese in, 241; religion in, 250-1

Cabbages, 165-6; Chinese, 135
Cairo, 272
California Company, 158
Cambodia: 'Le Camboge s'aide lui-même', 18, 263; population of, 20; village rankings in, 71; lakes and canals in, 191
Canada, 6, 205, 277
Canal Colonies in Punjab and Sind, 46, 90
Canals, in India and Pakistan, 110, 111, 129-30, 131
Canning factories, 155, 170
Capital: for development of waste land, 7-8; in developing countries, 8, 10, 117-18, 276; in 18th-century Britain, 9; gained through internal savings, 11; in Asia, 22; capital-intensive agriculture, 29, 97, 98, 145, 264; small peasants and, 37-8, 103; in Africa, 38, 103, 148-9; provided by the State, 53; and farming, 88, 121, 145, 152; for high-potential areas, 89; for small-scale industry, 98; return on, 118, 143-4 (*see* Investment)
Capital improvements, 88, 165
Capitalism: attitude of developing countries to, 15, 216; in India and Pakistan, 21; in Ghana, 23; capitalist agriculture, 152; and the farmer, 165; in Africa, 228, 238
Casa del Mezzogiorno, Italy, 169
Cash, 33, 37-8, 224; cash income, 38, 93, 121
Cash crops, 31, 84, 85, 89, 92, 121, 127, 146, 155, 162-3, 164, 167, 182, 224, 267; cash farming, 40, 123, 227, 228, 257
Cash economy, 24, 128; cash-and-subsistence economy, 25, 85, 92, 93, 121; change to, 86, 89, 161-4, 224; in 16th-century England, 109
Cassava, 84, 119
Caste: hampers change, 15, 22, 34-5; distinguishes Hinduism, 23, 31, 55-9; Africa and, 23, 55, 74; division of labour under, 33; discrimination based on, 34, 59, 61, 69; effects of wealth on, 37, 74; in villages, 40-1, 56-9; Pakistan and, 55, 71; modernization and, 59-60, 63-4; provides security, 60, 70-1; and politics, 65-6, 227, 232; Gandhi and, 221
Cattle, 74; diseases of, 35; industrial societies, 38; in Pakistan, 46; underfed, 118, 132; in Kenya, 119-20, 121, 147; and rotation of crops, 146 (*see* Animals: Bullocks: Cows: Oxen)
Cauvery River, 110
Central Nyanza, Kenya, 122
Central Province, Kenya, 89, 120, 187
Certified Seed factories, 45
Ceylon, 20, 110
Chainat Dam, Thailand, 135
Chao Phya Delta, Thailand, 89, 153, 232
Cheating: education and, 240-3, 253
Chemicals: as fertilizers, 112; for pest-control, 112, 120, 121, 167; agriculture needs, 288
Chiefs, 34, 75, 40, 41, 42-3, 61, 73-4, 231; in Tanzania, 201
Chiengmai, Thailand, 25, 271; University at, 185
China: civil service under Empire of, 192; Communism in, 238
Chinese: in South-East Asia, 38-9, 71, 168-9, 241; managerial skills of, 109
Christianity: and education in mediaeval Europe, 11-12, 244; in Africa, 74, 111, 238, 242, 245, 251; in the West, 238; in Asia, 245; and socialization, 250; and rational knowledge, 297
Chulalongkorn University, Thailand, 198
Church Missionary Society, 205
Cities, growth of, 266 (*see* Towns)
Civil service: politicians and, 77, 230, 236; creation of, 192-3; in China, 192; in India, 198; Nyerere and, 285 (*see* Administration: District Administration: Officials)
Clans, 16, 21, 30, 41, 139, 194
Climate, 167-8, 169
Cloth, buying of, 166
Clothes, in developing countries, 261
Cocoa, in Ghana, 23, 47, 92, 111
Coffee: in Africa, 92, 118, 146; prices of, 132, 165; credit for, 161; in Uganda, 171; and co-operatives in East Africa, 175; in Kilimanjaro, 205

Collectors, in India, 208, 215, 229 (see Deputy Commissioners)
Colonial Administration: and education, 12; constitutions left by, 16; and local agricultural development, 84, 88, 110–11; provided foreign markets, 93; industry under, 108–9; introduced Law, 192–3; growth of bureaucracy in, 194; and problem of modernization, 196; in India, 198; establishment's rigidity under, 206; imposed peace, 220; in Africa, 221, 222–3, 241–2; British model of Local Government in developing countries, 294
Comilla, East Pakistan: study of tractor economics at, 118; population density in, 143; Rural Academy in, 158–61, 178, 182, 205, 216, 257
Commercialization: of India, 21, 22, 226; of Pakistan, 21, 226, 228; of Philippines, 221; of South-Eas Asia, 228; of Africa, 272
Communications, 20, 22, 85, 110, 166–8, 261, 267, 268
Communism: in South India, 65–6; and the landlord system, 149; avoided by Africa, 226, 235, 238; and the Western World, 281, 283–4; 1848 Manifesto of, 282–3
Community, 32, 33–4, 243; and administration, 194
Community Development, 59, 62, 182, 189, 213
Community Development Department, 55, 67, 177, 182, 208–10, 243, 255
Community Development Training College, 258
Compost, 69, 135
Congo, 21; Baluba culture in, 73; Belgium's economic motives in, 111; *paysannat* experiment in, 127; political collapse of, 222, 288; growth of cities in, 266; agriculture in, 272; its natural resources, 296
Congress Party, India, 65, 76, 226–7, 229
Consumer goods: in developing countries, 18, 261; manufacture of, 19, 272; cash-crops and demand for, 85, 121, 264–5; as stimulus to indirect employment, 89, 154; in West Africa, 92; local markets and, 166; growth in world demand for, 287
Consumer services, 261
Convention People's Party (C.P.P.),

Ghana, 76, 180
Co-operative farming, 45, 96, 122, 127, 145, 147
Co-operatives, 16, 18, 28, 46, 122, 216, 285; loans by, 26, 70, 162, 164, 165; in the third stage of agricultural development, 47; village politics and, 62, 158; national 'drives' for, 69, 124; and the farmer, 78, 155–6, 162; rivals of private enterprise, 82, 155, 175; and cultivation of large acreages, 96; and agricultural development, 113, 149; and villagers, 122, 140–1, 155, 178; marketing by, 127, 228; pre-requisites for, 140–1; favour varied sizes of holdings, 148; causes of failure or success of, 154–8, 165, 168, 169, 206; distribute fertilizers, 158; Comilla Rural Academy and, 158–61; management of, 159; rates of interest charged by, 162; and savings schemes, 165; suitable agency for agricultural development, 172; and Extension Services, 174, 181; extended families and, 225; and small-scale industry, 271; and modernization, 285, 295
Co-operatives Department, 182, 208–10, 255
Co-operative stores, 90
Copper, in Zambia, 10, 264
Copperbelt, Zambia, 23, 111, 268, 272
Cotton, 225; in Gezira, 90, 183; a cash-crop, 92, 132; early sowing of, 116–17; group-farming of, 122; East African co-operatives for, 155, 175, 205; prices for, 165; in Uganda, 171; financing companies and, 174
County Councils in Africa, 75, 76, 201, 207, 217, 236
Cowpeas, 127
Cows, 35, 132; India bans slaughter of, 31 (see Cattle)
Craft skill: in Europe, 3, 11, 14, 244, 258, 271–2; and education, 12; in India, 22, 110, 266
Craftsmen: absorbed by factories, 6, 7, 14, 270; in Indian villages, 33, 48; and food prices, 228; education for, 255
Credit, 119, 138, 161–5; institutions for, 18; in Africa, 23, 161–2; for fertilizers, 34, 38, 116; state-provided, 38, 161; progressive farmers and, 53; Extension Services and cheap, 95; in Ford 'package deal', 113; co-operatives and, 122, 156; subsidized, 153; in

GENERAL INDEX

Credit—*cont.*
  Lesotho, 154; in the change from subsistence to cash economy, 161-4; credit surveys, 161; for social expenditure, 164; flexibility of, 165; landlords and, 174; exchange system and, 264
Credit Services, 182
'Critical Path' in project planning, 27-8
Crop genetics, 148 (*see* Plant genetics)
Crops: failure of, 32, 37, 185; high-yielding, 34, 45, 132, 135, 140, 153, 275; traditional, 34, 36, 130, 136, 291; new and improved varieties of, 34, 36-7, 45, 52, 89, 116, 117, 118; drought-resistant, 34, 126, 130, 132, 137; experiments with, 36-7; caste attitude towards new, 64; rotation of, 90, 109, 113, 126, 132, 134-5, 146; plant protection for new, 119; staple, 85, 136, 149, 166 (*see* Cash crops: Export crops: Food crops: Storage)
Cuba, 220
Cultivation: intensive, 19, 50, 92, 97, 102, 135, 147, 151, 210, 212; shifting, 49, 50, 111, 135, 141 (*see* Agriculture: Farming)
Custom, 36, 37, 51, 52, 56, 74, 148, 295, 296
Czechoslovakia, 238, 283-4

Dacca District, East Pakistan, 122
Dairying, 132; dairy farmers, 25; co-operatives and machinery for, 155; dairy unit in co-operatives, 159
Dar-es Salaam, Tanzania, 77
Daska, West Pakistan, 97, 228
Debt, 116; repayment of, 162, 164; in settlement schemes, 163
Deccan, India, 130, 135
Delamere, Lord, 120; 'delameres', 153
Delegation of authority, 21, 197, 200, 202-3, 204, 211-12, 285; in agriculture, 197, 204-5; in planning, 274
Delhi, 72, 73, 197, 221, 227, 228-9, 231
Democracy: in Europe and America, 14; industry and, 14; Africa and, 15, 221, 224; in developing countries, 16; local, 18; and stages of development, 25; world forces behind, 53; in panchayats, 63, 65; a collection of values, 82; and exercise of power, 197; in India, 214; and faction, 233; compared with other systems, 235

Demonstration farms, 34, 135
Departmental rule, 55, 67, 200, 202, 206, 208, 212; Department of Agriculture, 67, 119, 208-10, 255
Deputy Commissioners, in India, 209, 212-13 (*see* Collectors)
Developed countries: compared with developing, 4, 6, 186, 260-1; contacts with developing countries, 290 (*see* Europe: West, the)
Developing countries: and developed countries, 4, 6, 186, 260-1; and the West, 7, 17-18, 226, 281-2, 286, 290, 298; handicapped, 7-9, 18-20; and problems of development, 196; shortages in, 261-2, 263-4; and self-reliance, 263 (*see* Africa: Asia)
Development, 139; brutal in the West, 7, 17, 19; its stages defined, 25-6, 293-5; funds for, 62, 64; participation in, 216-17; political will for, 230-1, 233; Administration and, 237 (*see* Agricultural development)
Development Committees, 140-1, 178, 181
Dictatorship, 28, 235, 241
Director of Agriculture, 184-5, 208, 212
Director of Co-operatives, 208
Diseases: in crops, 34, 117, 119, 178; of cattle, 35, 133; control of, 176
Distribution in marketing, 168, 169-71
District Administration: (a) in India: and agriculture, 84; and loans, 162; as a development agency, 172; co-ordinates work in agricultural development, 185; and technical officers, 206-7, 213; (b) in Africa: political control of, 202, 236-7
District Boards in India, 75-6, 201, 211, 217
District Commissioners, 75, 77, 186, 193, 201, 205, 207
District Councils: in Africa, 78, 201; in India, 211, 213
District Magistrates, in British India, 193
District Officers, and rural development, 222
District Panchayats, in India, 56, 65, 209, 211-13, 229, 232
District Training Centres, in Kenya, 256
Divisional Commissioners, in India, 209
Djakarta, Java, 72
Double- and treble-cropping, 39, 89, 102, 113, 117, 131, 132, 134, 265

Drought, 34, 36, 39, 84, 87–8, 108, 116, 133; loans and, 162, 164
Dung: undigested grain retrieved from, 35–6, 52; as a fertilizer, 109, 117–18
Dusi, Madras, 166–7
Dyaks, in Borneo, 282

East African Community, 205
Economic growth: education and employment and, 11–13; stages in, 24–5; strength of economic life, 195; in Africa, 224, 225; in developing countries, 275, 278
Economics, 3, 4; and agriculture, 82, 136; of developing peasant societies, 263–5, 283, 286–7; mobilization of local resources, 262, 264, 275–8; and the exchange system, 262–5, 275
Economy: education and, 12–13; diversified, 99
Education: mass, 8, 11, 17–18, 19, 258; and economic growth, 11; and employment, 11, 12–13, 246–7, 252; in mediaeval Europe, 11, 244–5; primary, 11, 100, 153, 202, 243, 246–7, 248, 252, 253, 258, 291–2; Missions and, 12, 251; grammar school, 12, 245, 252, 258; as a means to wealth, 12; in developing countries, 12–13, 240–59, 261–2; often irrelevant, 13, 19, 245, 247, 281, 291, 294; more valuable than consumer goods, 18; in Asia, 22; secondary, 23, 100, 246, 248, 257, 258, 291; higher, 23, 246–50, 258, 291, 292–3, 296; weakens caste, 60, 64; in Africa, 73–4, 246, 291, 292–3; in overcrowded areas, 89; of farmers, 113, 122, 256; of women, 159, 292; in backward areas, 176; in villages, 240, 242–3, 246, 252; buys power, 243, 250, 252; socialization through, 245, 250, 252, 253; in crafts, 245, 256; technical, 245, 246, 248, 252, 253, 254, 255, 258; in Arts, 245, 247, 249, 251, 257; as Truth, 250, 252, 257; children without, 254–5; further study for the young, 255–6; evening classes, 258 (*see* Schools)
Education Department, 208–10
Egg-plant, 135
Eggs, 165
Egypt, 150
Elders, village, 34, 44, 61, 73, 75
Electricity: in developing countries, 5, 8, 20, 53; and agricultural development, 10, 113–14, 118; in Japan, 97; for pumps, 131, 137; in the West, 261; and settlement schemes, 268; and industry, 272
11-plus examinations, 107
Elgeyo-Marakwet area, Kenya, 121
Elgon, Mount, Uganda, 148
Employment: education and, 11, 12–13, 246–7, 252, 291; wage-paid, 13, 96, 99, 101, 103, 247; non-farm, 19, 44, 48, 89, 98, 99–102, 104–5, 144, 146, 147, 247, 266; diversification of, 83, 89, 93, 97; agricultural development and, 86, 265–6; for school-leavers, 100–1, 246, 249, 292; self-, 101–2, 104; in overcrowded areas, 147; indirect, in farming areas, 154; co-operatives and, 159; economics of, 260; in towns, 267; part-time, 269–70 (*see* Labour)
Enahoro, Chief Anthony, 234
Enclosure of land: in England, 6, 109; and the poor, 36; in Kenya, 122
Endicott House, Massachusetts Institute of Technology, 108, 114
Engineering: under Colonial Administrations, 111; and co-ordination of expert services, 206; unemployment in, 247; training in, 249, 252; centres for, 272, 288
England, mediaeval: culture and expansion in, 5–6; population of, 6, 206; industrial changes in, 26, 272; Saints' Days in, 39; four-course rotation of crops in, 109, 134
England, modern: agricultural revolution in, 6, 9, 109; and rust-resistant wheat, 119; Co-operatives in, 157; Funeral Clubs in, 164; size of farm holdings in, 174; law in, 193; aristocratic factionalism in, 233 (*see* Great Britain)
Entrepreneurs: and Western industry, 14; in Asia, 22, 48; in Ghana, 23, 47, 53; in Mysore, 44; and village elections in India, 62; farmers as, 152; and growth, 216; education and, 247 (*see* Private enterprise)
Enugu University, Nigeria, 248
Environment: control of, 138, 276; traditional society based on, 140
Erosion, 176
Eruvellipet, Madras State, India, 167
Esusu societies, in West Africa, 164
Ethiopia, 21, 221, 222
Europe, mediaeval: Asia and Africa compared with peasant society of, 3–7, 98–9; education in, 11, 244–5; technology in, 13, 245; slow rate of

GENERAL INDEX

Europe, mediaeval—*cont.*
  development in, 20, 28–9, 31, 120; agricultural revolution in, 109, 114, 137; bureaucracy in, 202; religion in, 219–20; monks in, 242; part-time occupations in, 269–70
Europe, modern, as model for developing countries, 4, 8–9, 16–19, 26, 203, 216, 226; industrial development in, 7, 17–18, 19, 281–2; democracy in, 14, 220; slow rate of development in, 20, 31; technology in, 107; agricultural development in, 109, 114; religion in, 251; education in, 258–9; overseas development studied in universities of, 277; 'Study and Serve' schemes in, 278; purposive power in, 298
Europeans: in India and South-East Asia, 72, 268; in Africa, 72, 111, 268; in Kenya, 84–5, 111, 136, 147; mistrust of, 241
Experimental farms and stations, 119, 126
Export crops, 10, 83, 155, 156, 165–6, 168, 169–70; tropical, 262, 264
Exports, 137, 262–3, 264, 265
Extended family, in Africa, 60, 139, 225
Extension Services, 172–81; and agricultural development, 47, 113; roads help work of, 121; help voluntary schemes, 122; and rotation of crops, 135–6; as a substitute for landlords, 149; Co-operatives and, 158; distribute fertilizers, 158; give training, 159; attitude to mortgages in Africa, 162; collect debts, 163; training personnel for, 182; finance for, 182–3; and the Universities, 184–5; problems of, 186, 250, 256; foreign aid to, 200–1, 256–7; need to expand, 201; in Pakistan, 204; Village Level Workers and, 210; Block Panchayats and staff of, 211; and intensive cultivation, 212; creation of, 213; and further education of the young, 255 (*see* Agricultural Extension Service)

Faction: in villages, 40–2, 46, 59, 61; in politics, 233–4, 236, 239
Factories: absorb craftsmen, 6–7, 14, 270; processing, 168, 170
Families: limitation on, 51, 89–90, 101, 264, 296; Family Planning, 68, 69; labour of, 89, 142–4, 152; firms belonging to, 241; and education, 292

Famine, 116; in primitive societies, 32–3, 35–6, 49; and strategy of rural development, 82–91 *passim*; government relief measures against, 84, 110, 111; in India and Pakistan, 85, 87–8, 91; in Bihar, 87, 131; and population growth, 100; insurances against, 146
Farmech Scheme, in Basutoland, 153–4
Farmers: progressive, 18, 31, 51, 52, 62, 78, 95–6, 178–9; competing interests of, 36, 53, 82–3, 94–5, 105, 142–6; varied duties of, 107, 112, 138; training of, 113, 122, 243–4, 256; response to innovation, 118, 129; and economists, 137, 243; need help, 138, 149; prosperous, 228, 230
Farmers' Associations, 96, 172, 181, 216, 285
Farmers' Clubs, 254, 256, 292
Farmers' Training Centres, in East Africa, 182, 244, 256
Farm implements and tools, 32, 38, 53, 97–8, 113, 116, 117, 145–6, 244, 271
Farming: commercial, 31, 45–7, 48, 51, 86, 89, 91, 98, 112, 121, 122, 125, 136, 138, 152–3, 164, 224, 268; co-operative, 45, 118, 147, 225; labour-intensive, 142; innovations in, 256 (*see* Agriculture: Cultivation)
Farms: innovations on, 18, 256; size of, 86, 90, 102–3, 113, 132, 141; management of, 112, 134, 136, 137, 257; planning for, 135–6, 141–3; Indian studies on, 142–3 (*see* Holdings)
Fascism, 235, 241, 284
Feasts and festivals, 33, 37, 38, 39, 54, 56, 58, 251
Federal Land Development Authority (F.L.D.A.), Malaysia, 82–3
Fertilizers: important for development, 31, 112, 265; irrigation and, 34, 52–3, 119, 126, 131, 132, 138; bought on credit, 34, 38, 161; modern government and, 62; subsidized, 66, 95, 153, 275; Village Level Workers and, 68; in 19th-century England, 109; in 'package deals', 113; improved seed and, 121, in Pakistan, 121; cost and efficiency of, 139; distribution of, 156, 158; landlords and, 174
Fibres, 37, 265

Fiji: exemption from community rights and duties in, 40; banana trade in, 93, 128; jobs for school-leavers in, 100; education in, 248
Floods, 108, 110, 130, 133, 134, 164
Fodder, 35, 36, 52, 118, 120–1, 132
Food: demand for, 9; in 18th-century Britain, 9–10; in India, 32; caste and, 56, 58, 60; policies on, 84–5; and producers of cash crops, 92, 121, 224; prices of, 137, 228; storage of, 159, 271; in developing countries, 261–2, 265; production and consumption, 265
Food crops, 84–5, 112, 121, 132, 136, 165
Food-grains, 84, 85, 86, 87, 137
Ford Foundation programme, in India, 113
Foreign aid, 19, 111; for technical surveys, 53, 288; American, 150, 264; and cost of development administration, 187, 200–1, 256–7; exchange system in, 262–4, 289; repayment of, 276; limitations of, 290; administration of, 293
Foreign capital, 224, 278
Foreign exchange: means of earning, 11, 265; and simple modern technology, 98, 104; shortage of, 114, 202; Aid loans repayable in foreign currency, 262; and internal mobilization of resources, 276
France: French Revolution, 15; attitude to colonial peasant farming, 110; mediaeval England exported wood to, 270; 1968 upheaval in, 284; limitations as model for developing peasant societies, 295, 296
Free enterprise, 16, 18 (see Private enterprise)
French North Africa, 111
French West Africa, 49, 200
'Friendship Highway', Thailand, 167
Fruit, 37, 132, 163, 165
Fulani Empire, in Nigeria, 72, 221
Fundamental Human Rights, 12, 16, 17, 219, 223
Funeral Clubs, in 19th-century England, 164
Funerals, cost of, 248

Ganda people, Uganda, 16, 21
Gandhi Memorial Centre, Madras State, 90, 257
Gandhi, Mohandas Karamchand, 150, 221, 271, 297
Gangkaiondan, Madras State, 167

Ganges, River, 110, 123, 130
Geography, improved teaching of, 254
Gezira, Sudan, 90, 124, 173, 183
Ghana: peasants' incomes in, 22; cocoa in, 23, 47, 153; commercial agriculture in, 45; classification of farmers in, 48; C.P.P. in, 76, 180; Volta Dam in, 125, 126–7, 128; markets in, 166; training for administrators in, 198; rural administration in, 201, 214; political control of district administration in, 236; politics in, 286; British students visit, 290
Government: peasants' attitude to, 25, 68–9, 179–80; and credit schemes, 161, 165; and repayment of debts, 162; and agricultural development, 174–5, 183–5, 186–7, 257; and rule by civil services, 192–4; and urbanization, 268–9; and finance for small-scale industry, 271–2; and representation in Africa, 285 (see Officials)
Graduates, 246–8, 258, 291, 292
Gram Sabha, 210
Gramsewak, 55, 67–8, 210 (see Village Level Workers)
Grapes, 45, 86, 130, 135
Great Britain: growth of population in, 6; labour in, 9–10; administration of India, 21, 193, 198, 221; non-farm employment in, 105; attitude to colonial peasant farming, 110; motives in Africa, 110–11; use of fertilizers in, 136; cereal yields in, 142; Local Government in, 195; Postal Corporation in, 203; 'Study and Serve' scheme, 277–8; contacts with developing countries, 290; has planted her institutions in Asia and Africa, 294–5; has her own outlook, 296 (see England)
Greece, Ancient, 83, 159, 216, 233, 235, 245
Gross National Product (G.N.P.), 99–100
Groundnuts, 127, 165
Group effort, 32, 47, 128, 147, 225 (see Farming, co-operative)
Gujarat State, India, 87, 210–11, 266
Guyana, 111

Hanumanthayya, Shri, 226
Harambee Schools, Kenya, 68
Harijans, in Indian caste system, 48, 56, 58, 59, 61, 62–3, 64, 65
Hausa people, Nigeria, 21
Headmen, in India, 35, 41, 42, 55, 62

GENERAL INDEX

Health, 17–18, 261–2
Health Department, 176
Himalayas, tribes in, 191
Hinduism: under British rule, 21–2, 221; and politics, 23; division of labour in, 33; has survived, 53–4, 73, 221; joint family in, 64; Gandhi and, 221; weakening, 225; and fear of change, 241; Brahmins, 242; and socialization, 250; and rational knowledge, 297 (*see* Caste)
History: as a guide to the future, 4–5; teaching of, 254
Hobbes, Thomas, 16
Hoes, principal farm tools in Africa, 22, 97, 103, 116, 154
Holdings, size and shape of, 139, 141–8, 149–50; reduction in, 147, 152 (*see* Farms)
Holland, 72, 110, 136, 142, 295
Hong Kong, 272, 288, 289
Horticulture, 25, 132, 166
Housing: of wealthy villagers, 44, 45; in developing countries, 261; employment in construction of, 267; on plantations, 268; in mediaeval England, 270; new methods of, 289
Hutu tribe, Rwanda, 71
Hyderabad State, India, 45, 131, 132

Ibo people, Nigeria, 21, 247, 268
Idealism: international, 12; inspired by Independence, 17–18, 286; of political leaders, 223–4, 230; and social growth, 225–6; of the young, 256
Illiteracy, 240, 243, 255
Imperial College of Science, London, 290
Incomes: non-farm employment and agricultural, 11, 19, 102, 147, 266; raising agricultural, 83, 85–6; greater equality of, 96–7; and size of holdings, 141–2; in Kerala, 247; National, 260 (*see* Standard of living)
India: conditions of progress in, 4; compared with mediaeval England, 5; European countries expand into, 6; agriculture in, 11, 45–6, 47, 84, 85, 113, 120, 136, 141–5, 185; industrialization in, 15, 271, 272, 289; native authoritarian rulers in, 15–16; Princes of, 16, 193, 197, 198; population of, 20, 205; empires in, 21; British rule in, 21, 72, 193, 198, 221; and Africa, 21–3, 77–8; commercialization of, 21, 22, 226; personal incomes in, 22; politics in, 23, 65–7, 220–1, 226–8, 230, 232–3; tribal societies in, 24, 191; village system in, 32–8; Land Reform in, 46, 147, 149–51; types of peasants in, 48; changes in villages in, 52; conservatism in, 53–4; caste in, 56–60, 65–6; unemployment in, 101; Japan's rice-growing methods compared with those of, 102; size of holdings in, 103, 147, 152–3; managerial skill in, 109; Europeans' attitudes to, 111; irrigation in, 111, 129; geographical homogeneity in, 123; as an agricultural exporter, 131; climate of, 133; Farm Management studies in, 136, 142–3; use of fertilizers in, 136; government's price policy in, 136–7, 275; Japanese farmers in, 145; potential productivity of, 147–8; political 'revolution' in, 150; Co-operatives in, 156, 158; credit surveys in, 161; loans in, 162; natural catastrophes in, 164; markets in south of, 166–7; storage in, 167, 271; indigenous traders in, 168; landlords' help for tenants in, 174; panchayats and agricultural progress in, 180; taxation in, 182; administration in, 194, 198, 207–14, 228–30, 237; and Nagas, 197; discipline weakened by litigation in, 199; delegation of authority in, 205; political crises in, 215; development in, 217, 237; Colonial Administration ended wars in, 220; democracy in, 222, 235; influence of medium farmers in, 227; Peasants' Party in, 227, 230; States' rivalry with Centre in, 229–30; universal suffrage in, 232; political will for development in, 233; faction in States of, 234; illiteracy in, 240; education in, 247, 292; apprenticeship unsuitable for, 258; modernization in, 266; planning in, 274; capitalism in, 284; engineering centre in, 288; British students visit, 290; States vary considerably in, 295; Nehru and, 297
Indian Administrative Service, 162, 206
Indian Civil Service, 72, 198
Indians: in Burma, 169; in Africa, 243
Indo-China, 72, 110, 221
Indonesia: population of, 20; various societies in, 24; Muslim culture in, 71, 72, 73; Hindu influence in, 71, 72; one-party government in, 76,

Indonesia—*cont.*
222; agricultural development in, 94; plantations in, 110; tribal culture in, 191; indirect rule in, 193; violent politics in, 220–1, 228, 284; military coup in, 222; industry in, 272; engineering centre in, 288

Indus, River, 110

Industrialization: as a means of wealth, 9, 12; in developing countries, 18–19, 26, 91, 272–3; internal division of labour under, 94; and mass markets, 96; non-farm employment increased by, 98; competes with agriculture, 173; Nehru and, 221; for the domestic market, 264

Industry: labour in Great Britain for, 6–7, 9–10; labour in developing countries for, 9; disastrous investment in, 11; personal liberty and, 14–15; in Asia, 22; cottage, 37, 270–1; and agriculture, 52, 112, 228; small-scale, 97–9, 100, 101, 104, 269–72, 289; dual pattern of, 98; transfer to developing countries, 107–8; administration uses practices based on, 203–4, 206–7, 212, 216; teams in, 206; family firms in, 241; Asia and Africa lack heavy, 262; the West criticizes its own development in, 281–2 (*see* Trade)

Insects, 121; insecticide, 254

Institutes of Rural Technology, 257

Institutions: borrowed from Europe, 9; for production, marketing and credit, 18, 168; affecting agriculture, 25, 112, 138, 213; villages and, 30; to help modernization, 52; defined, 139; need for new, 139–40; increase in economic, 195; early empires and, 197; representative, 217

Insurance: social, 17; against famine, 88; against crop failure, 146; in developing countries, 261

Interest, rates of, 33, 156, 162, 164

Intermediate technology, 265, 269, 290

International Labour Organization (I.L.O.), 13

Investment: in villages, 44; in overcrowded areas, 50–1, 89; and famine, 87; in market economy, 91; and non-farm employment, 100; in irrigation, 111; progressive, 114–15, 121; in scientific efficiency, 119; in revolutionary big schemes, 138; and shifting cultivation, 141; in farms of different sizes, 143;
African agriculture short of, 148; credit and, 161, 164; in roads, 167; in backward areas, 175–6; in Kenya, 187; foreign, 278; within the world economy, 289 (*see* Capital)

Iran, 150

Irrigation: in Asia, 22, 134; helps fertilizers, 34, 52–3, 119, 126, 131, 132, 138; and agricultural progress, 43–4, 45, 52; and medium farmers in the Punjab, 46, 71; by tubewells, 46; in Sind, 50; in Bengal, 50; to prevent famine, 87; as a public relief scheme, 88; in high-potential areas, 89; in India, 110; by pumps, 114, 131; on hard ground, 116; needs to be well organized, 119; in hills, 120; large schemes of, 124–5, 127–8, 138, 273, 285; effects of, 126, 128; potential of, 129–32, 148, 165; and rice, 133; and traditional society, 140; Co-operatives and, 154; to combat drought, 162; by dams, 265, 273; small schemes of, 273

Irrigation Department, 208–9

Islam: and social order of Pakistan, 17, 53–4, 251; opposed to change in Asia, 21–2; and caste, 55, 71; in Africa, 238, 251; and rational knowledge, 296 (*see* Muslims)

Israel, 16

Italy: agricultural development scheme in, 164, 174–5; commercial experiment in, 169–70; faction in Renaissance times in, 233; effect of education in, 241

Jamaica, 101

Jammu State, India, 211

Japan: not a developing country, 13; and research in India, 64, 266; agricultural progress in, 94–5; small-scale industry in, 97, 98, 289; growth of non-farm employment in, 100, 101, 105–6; raising of incomes in, 102; rice-growing methods in, 102, 132–3; size of holdings in, 103; use and cost of fertilizers in, 136; cereal yields in, 142; farmers in India from, 145; Land Reform in, 150; and tools, 271; engineering in, 272, 288; taxation in, 288

Java, 22, 50–1, 72

Jewellery, investment in, 38

Jinja Dam, Uganda, 111

Jogjakarta, Sultanate of, 193

GENERAL INDEX

Justice, social, 82 (see Fundamental Human Rights)
Jute, in India, 116

Kafue River, 131
Kariba Dam, Rhodesia, 111
Karimpur, Agra District, India, 68
Kasetsart University, Thailand, 185
Kashmir State, India, 87, 211
Katanga, Congo, 222, 272
Katsina College, Nigeria, 198
Kaunda, President Kenneth, 16, 223, 297
Kenya: no common bond of culture in, 21; peasant incomes in, 22; school-fees in, 38; commercial agriculture in, 47; Mau Mau in, 53, 241; K.A.N.U. in, 76; private Secondary schools in, 78; 'outgrower' system for tea in, 83; ex-European farms in, 84–5, 111, 136, 147; insistence on food crops in, 84–5; overcrowding in, 89; non-farm employment in, 99; jobs for school-leavers in, 100; survey on self-employment in, 101–2; cattle-breeding in, 119–20, 121; wheat introduced into, 120; progressive investment in, 121; group-farming in, 122; water in, 131; land consolidation in, 135–6; price of maize in, 137; farms for civil servants in, 153; Co-operatives in, 156; credit in, 161; settlement schemes in, 163; and export market, 170; expenditure on 'close administration' in, 187; tribal societies in, 197, 231; local government in, 202, 294; population of, 205; rural administration in, 214; politics in, 223–4; Polytechnics in, 256; small-scale industry in, 271; engineering in, 272; has its own outlook, 296
Kenya African National Union (K.A.N.U.), 76
Kenya, Mount, 148
Kenyatta, President Jomo, 52, 223–4
Kerala State, India: co-operative farming in, 122; cattle-breeding in, 132; no formal panchayats in, 211; political crisis in, 215; education in, 247, 257; towns in, 267
Khalapur, Uttar Pradesh, India, 62
Khartoum, 90
Khon-Khaen University, Thailand, 185
Kikuyu people, Kenya, 21, 53, 75, 197
Kilimanjaro, Mount, 148, 205
Kinshasa, Congo, 269, 296

Kinship: in Africa, 74, 199, 200, 215 216; kinship groups, 225
Kipsigis tribe, Kenya, 122
Korat Plateau, Thailand, 232
Krishna District, Andhra State, India, 45
Krishnarajasagar reservoir, Mysore State, India, 133
Krishna River, 110
Kshatryas in Indian caste-system, 56
Kumaon District, Uttar Pradesh, India, 36
Kumasi, Ghana, 166; University at, 248

Labour: for industry in England, 6–7, 10; surplus in developing countries, 8, 10, 11, 97–9; size of labour force in Asia and Africa, 13, 19, 20; labour-intensive methods, 86, 97, 105, 142, 262, 264; family, 89, 142–4, 152; for non-farm employment, 89; for Indian agriculture, 101, 103, 151; non-family, 103–4, 224; scarcity of, 146; forced, 192; communal, 225; for industry, 262; in towns, 267
Lam Pao Dam, Thailand, 273
Lam Pung Dam, Thailand, 273
Land: in Africa, 7–8, 32, 33, 49, 148; intensive use of, 19; potential of underdeveloped, 20, 99; consolidation of, 31, 48, 75, 77, 118, 122, 135–6, 141, 148; clearance of, 36, 49–50, 62, 83, 163; in India, 46, 64, 103; open market in, 48; fragmentation of, 50–1, 52, 73, 141; pressure on, 50–1, 73; sequestered, 151; debts secured on, 162
Landless peasants, 32–3, 46, 47, 48, 53, 88, 103, 104, 151, 153, 163, 227–8, 232
Landlords: (a) in Asia: authoritarian, 15; system of, 22, 284; opposed to progress, 148, 150; regularization of position towards tenants, 193; (b) in India: power over tenants, 26, 55, 70, 140, 150, 215; types of, 46; and Land Reform, 46, 68, 147, 151–2; *patwaris* and, 67–8; as moneylenders, 70, 116, 149, 151, 161; and political power, 140, 148, 150; services to tenants, 151, 154, 174; Co-operatives as an alternative to, 157–8; (c) in Africa, 47, 73, 77; (d) in Pakistan, 231–2
Land Reform: in India, 46, 52, 68, 147, 149–52; in Asia, 149–50
Land Revenue, in India, 182, 193, 197

314 MODERNIZING PEASANT SOCIETIES

Land tenure: undemocratic, 15; African customary, 31, 33, 148, 149, 224, 231; by usufruct, 73; reform of, 112, 113, 122, 233, 295; in Asia, 148, 231; regularization of, 193
Laos, 20
Latin America, 7–8, 13, 81, 96
Law: development of, 192–3; in backward areas, 215
Leadership: local, 18, 25, 62, 69, 76; traditional, 40, 55, 63–4, 74–5, 77, 78, 228, 232; in agriculture, 46; in Africa, 73–8; new, 73, 140; of Co-operatives, 159; of panchayats, 228; needed for development, 297
Legume hay, 127; legume plants, 135
Leopoldville (Kinshasa), Congo, 269
Lesotho, 153–4
Lineage system in Africa, 39, 60, 71, 75, 77
Literacy, 243, 245, 247, 249, 257; certificates of, 243 (*see* Illiteracy)
Litigation, 35, 68, 151, 199
Loans: given by landlords to tenants, 70, 116, 149, 151, 161; Co-operatives and, 70, 156, 164; security for, 156, 162; for marriages, 156, 164; repayment of, 160; to African farmers, 224 (*see* Credit: Debt: Moneylenders)
Local Committees, 172, 181, 230
Local Government: peasants' attitude to, 25; in Africa, 75–6; and the farmer, 172; development of, 194–5; delegation of power to, 201–3; politics in, 202, 217; in rural areas, 207, 211–17; and single-party systems, 236; world spread of, 283; developing countries and British model of, 294–5 (*see* Panchayats)
Locusts, as food, 36
Lomaivuna, Fiji, 128
Lower Indus Basin, credit survey in, 151, 161
Lozi people: in Barotseland, 16; in Zambia, 21
Lumpa Church, in Zambia, 53
Lumumba, Patrice, 222
Luo people, Kenya, 21, 197

Machinery, developing countries need, 261, 287–8
Madras State, India: failure of monsoon in, 87; social survey in, 90; 'tanks' in, 131; plans for farms in, 135; effect of transport on prices in, 166–7; Union Council Panchayats in, 210; rural training in, 256, 257; towns in, 267–8; planning in, 274

Madurai District, Madras State, India, 256, 257
Madya Pradesh, India, 61, 210–11
Magic, in Africa, 31, 71, 74
Magistrates, in India, 67, 193, 208, 215
Maharashtra State, India, 151, 210–11, 232
Maize: in Kenya, 85, 137; hybrid, 119, 132, 135; in rotation in Volta Dam scheme, 127; prices for, 137, 157; in rotation in India, 146; marketing of, 156
Malawi, 53, 200, 281
Malaya: Sultans of, 16; rice land in, 37; rubber in, 37, 120, 136, 163; plantations in, 83, 110; research on food crops in, 112; primitive peoples in, 191; continuity in politics of, 220–1; modernized Muslim order in, 221; slow democratization of, 222; commercialization in, 226
Malay Rulers, 16, 199
Malaysia: population of, 20; varying societies in, 24; F.L.D.A. in, 82–3; unemployment in, 101; agricultural economists in, 136; settlement schemes in, 163; prejudice against Chinese in, 241; capitalism in, 284; engineering centre in, 288
Malay States, indirect rule in, 193
Malnutrition, 85, 147 (*see* Nutrition)
Malthusian theories, 49, 50, 88, 92, 103
Management: of factories, 5; managerial society, 14; of farms, 27, 112, 121, 134, 136, 137, 146–7, 243, 257; contrast between agricultural and industrial, 108; of a Co-operative, 159, 178; in settlement schemes, 163; in Development Corporations, 177
Mandya District, Mysore, India, 89
Manpower, 25, 170, 172, 186, 205, 215, 246, 250, 252, 255, 285, 296
Market economy, 86, 88–9, 90, 91–3, 140; domestic market, 19, 102, 108–9, 264; individuals and, 26; nation-wide markets, 92–3; mass markets, 276
Marketing, 165–71; institutions for, 18, 113, 139, 295; Co-operatives and, 82, 122, 155, 159, 225, 228; and famine, 84; encourages specialization, 85–6, 168; need for, 113, 138, 139; irrigation and, 126; information and intermediaries needed for, 166, 170; buying for, 168; landlords and, 174; economics of, 260

GENERAL INDEX

Marketing Boards, 149, 155, 162, 169
Markets for exports: for 15th-century Europe, 6–7, 10; for developing countries, 10, 11, 19, 264, 265; and local markets, 93–4; search for new, 170–1
Markets, local, 165–6; importance of roads to, 5, 166–7; can alter traditional society, 140
Marriage: expenditure on, 33, 38, 156, 164; feast at, 33, 38, 39; village Elders can obstruct, 34; saving for, 37; in Hinduism, 56; intercaste, 60; in Asia, 134; in Africa, 238
Marx, Karl, 220, 282–3; Marxist theory, 75
Masai people, Kenya, 21, 231
Mass communication, 20, 261
Mau Mau, in Kenya, 53, 241
Mboya, Tom, 223–4
Meat, production of, 117–18
Mechanical maintenance, 182, 256
Mechanization: effect on the poor, 36; in West Pakistan, 95; farming and, 96, 112; productivity of smallholders and, 97, 145–6; in Japan, 102; modernization and, 109; cattle needed even after, 117–18; forms a stage in improvement of cultivation, 120; potential of, 133–4, 138; landlords and, 174; urbanization and, 266; labour shortage and, 267 (*see* Tractors)
Medical Colleges, 249
Medicine, 261
Mekong River, 125, 131
Members of State Legislative Assemblies (M.L.A.s), 66, 211, 212
Merchants: in mediaeval Europe, 3; abound in India and South-East Asia, 22; and power in villages, 62; compete successfully with Co-operatives, 155–6, 168–9; at local markets, 165; can help farmers, 172; compared with Extension Services, 174–5
Messianic revivalism, in Malawi, 53
Mexico: agricultural development in, 94–5, 120; growth of non-farm employment in, 100, 101; raising of incomes in, 102; wheat from, 116; and guarantees against crop failure, 146
Middle-class: in Asia, 22, 284; in the Copperbelt, 23; among farmers in India and South-East Asia, 45, 46, 153; family limitation among, 89–90; in East Pakistan, 228

Milk: cows provide, 35, 117; for family consumption, 91; low production of, 118, 132; processing of, 166
Millennial movements, 241
Millet, 36
Milling factories, 155
Mill, John Stuart, 14, 193
Mills, grain, 166
Minerals: in Africa, 110, 111; export of, 263, 265; survey of, 288
Mining, 6, 10, 83, 111, 176, 267
Ministers, 199–200, 203
Ministry of Agriculture, 176–7, 183, 206; in Thailand, 177, 185; in Africa, 200–1
Ministry of Education, in Africa, 200–1
Ministry of Planning, in Africa, 200–1
Missionaries: and education, 12, 250, 251; their zeal in Africa, 110; and agricultural progress, 205; respect for, 242
Model farms, 145
Modernization: defined, 4, 43–5, 295–6; of agriculture, 19, 83, 109; in Africa, 21–2, 71–8, 231; in India and Pakistan, 21–2; speed of, 26–9; of traditional societies, 30–1, 40, 140, 293–4; stages of, 31–2, 46–7, 146; agencies of, 42; by individuals, 51; Hinduism and, 55; and caste, 60, 64; panchayats and, 63; the choice for Indian villagers, 70–1; and marketing, 114; and food prices, 228; and urbanization, 266, 268
Moghul Empire, in India, 21, 72, 192
Money, not usually saved by villagers, 37–9 (*see* Cash)
Moneylenders: peasants dependent on, 26, 37, 38, 55, 67, 70, 149; charge exorbitant interest, 33, 162, 164; not prominent in Africa, 73, 77; oppose agricultural progress, 148; rivals of Co-operatives, 156; and repayment of debts, 162; lend for marriages, 164
Monks, 242, 251
Monsoon, 125, 149; failure of, 87–8; novel attitude to, 133–4
Morogoro Agricultural College, Tanzania, 248
Muhuroni Sugar Scheme, Kenya, 163
Municipal Councils in Africa, 75
Mushrooms, 135
Muslims: in Asia, 21, 225; in India, 21–2, 23; in West Africa, 23, 251; priests among, 33; their culture, 55; and caste, 55, 71; in South-East

Muslims—*cont.*
  Asia, 71; their women in agriculture, 104; modernized in Malaya, 221; fear change, 241; and socialization, 250; in Pakistan, 251; and rational knowledge, 297 (*see* Islam)
Mwanza District, Tanzania, 155, 205
Mymensingh, East Pakistan, 117, 160
Mysore State, India: agricultural progress needed in, 24; village changes in, 43–4, 47, 48, 51; caste in, 59, 65–6; population density in, 89, 144; canal schemes in, 130; grapes grown in, 130; rice-growing in, 131; Taluk Boards in, 210–11; voters in, 226, 233; election to panchayats in, 232
Myths, 238, 250

Nagas, 197
Nairobi, 272; University College at, 248
Natural catastrophes, 37, 39, 84, 162, 164
Natural resources, 86, 296–7
Nehru, Jawaharlal, 150, 221, 229, 251, 297
New Zealand, 6, 93, 277
Nigeria: no common bond of ancient culture in, 21; jobs for school-leavers in, 100–1; railway in, 111; markets in, 166; training of administrators in, 201; oil in, 272
Nigeria, Eastern: densely crowded areas in, 148; political control of District Administration in, 236; unemployment in, 247
Nigeria, Northern: Emirs of, 16, 197; indirect rule in, 196, 198; training of administrators in, 198; slow democratization of, 222
Nigeria, Southern: classification of farmers in, 48; rebellion in, 197
Nigeria, Western: successful traders in, 39; Fulani Empire in, 72, 221; settlement schemes in, 163; faction in, 234; old order in, 238; unemployment in, 247; towns in, 267
Niger, River, 111, 131
Nilo-Hamitic pastoralists, 73
Nitrogen in fertilizers, 136
Nkrumah, President Kwame, 251
Non-agricultural goods, marketing of, 166
Nong Wai Dam, Thailand, 273
Nutrition, improvement in, 83–4, 85, 86, 105, 257 (*see* Malnutrition)
Nyakashaka, Uganda, 205
Nyasaland, 53

Nyerere, President Julius, 22–3; political idealism of, 16, 17, 223, 235–6; egalitarian, 96; and civil servants, 153, 285; seeks to moralize Tanzania, 297
Nyeri District, Kenya, 161

Officials, 56; peasants' attitude to, 41, 42, 70, 179–80, 202; in India, 67–9; in Africa, 75, 77; sponsor private Secondary schools in Kenya, 78; and landlords, 150, 151–2; and marketing, 170; increase in number of, 194; poor quality of lower, 194, 199, 202 (*see* Administration: Civil service: District Administration: District Commissioners: Government)
Oil: Sheikhdoms and, 264; in Nigeria, 272 (*see* Palm-oil)
Oilpressers, 58, 61–2
Olives, 169–70
Onitsha, Nigeria, 166, 171
Order: and politics, 218; religion and, 218–19; in Africa, 238; revolt against traditional, 282
Orissa State, India: caste strong in, 59; politics in, 66, 67; advance of trading frontier in, 74; savings scheme in, 164; peasants' attitude to officials in, 179; panchayats in, 210–11
'Outgrower' system, for tea in Kenya, 83, 183
Overcrowding: in Africa, 33, 103; Malthusian theory about, 49, 50, 88, 92; in high-potential areas, 91, 92; non-farm employment and, 147; settlement schemes and, 163; in the West, 286
Oxen: for ploughing, 22, 116–18, 145; debt incurred in buying, 33; for transport, 117, 166–7; rare in Africa, 133 (*see* Animals: Cattle)
'Oxfam', 290

Packaging, of food, 166, 169–70
Paddy: new method of transplanting, 36; in Malaya, 37; irrigation of, 132–3; rattoon crops of, 135 (*see* Rice)
Pakistan: industrialization in, 15; a Muslim State, 17, 251; population of, 20; commercialization in, 21, 226, 284; contrasted with Africa, 21–2; agriculture in, 45, 47, 131, 136, 141, 182–3, 185; tribalism in, 47, 191; conservatism in, 53–4; village rankings in, 71; food crisis

GENERAL INDEX

Pakistan—*cont.*
in, 85; Agricultural Development Corporation in, 121, 177, 204; irrigation possibilities in, 129–30; climate of, 133; reduction in size of holdings in, 147; potential productivity of, 147–8; political 'revolution' in, 150, 234, 237; Co-operatives in, 156, 158; Basic Democracy in, 160, 180, 214, 228; indigenous traders of, 168; landlords in, 174; slow democratization of, 222; District Administration in, 229; engineering in, 272, 288
Pakistan Civil Service, 206
Pakistan, East: tractors in, 117, 118; co-operative farming in, 122; irrigation potential of, 130; winter crops in, 134; small pumps in, 145; Comilla Rural Academy in, 158–61, 182; Basic Democracy in, 160; politics in, 228; illiteracy in, 240
Pakistan, West: big and middle farmers' success in, 46, 53, 95, 228; wheat in, 46, 275; small-scale industry in, 97; agricultural problems in, 121; irrigation potential of, 130; winter crops in, 134; credit for tubewells in, 161, credit survey in, 161; agricultural training in, 182; local politics in, 228, 231–2; illiteracy in, 240; price control in, 275
Palakkurichi, Madras State, India, 167
Palm fruit, 165
Palm-oil: in Malaysia, 82; in Africa, 92, 93, 110, 111
Pan-Africanism, 224
Panchayati Raj, 61, 62, 63, 210, 213, 215, 229–30
Panchayats in India: and traditional society, 56, 60–1, 64–5, 70, 216; elected, 56, 61–2, 63–4, 227, 229, 231, 232–3; and democracy, 63–4, 75–6, 78; and politics, 65–6, 152, 158, 228, 229–30, 233; pre-requisites for, 140, 214–15; and the farmer, 172, 178, 180–1; system of, 210–13
Panchayat Samiti, 56, 210–11, 229 (*see* Block Panchayats)
Participation: world support for, 53; democracy and, 82; in development, 216–17, 231; in politics, 230, 285; bureaucracy and, 283; in industry, 284, 286
Pastoral tribes, 24, 30, 73, 231, 240
Pasture, improvement of, 117
Patronage: bought, 38; villagers and, 70; Councils and, 75; political, 76, 226, 233, 235; old system of, 139, 200, 216, 234; Ministers', 199–200
Patwaris, 35, 55, 67, 198, 208–9, 242
Paysannat experiment, in the Congo, 127
Peasants: conservative, 34, 36, 43, 51; diversified, 48; and imposed progress, 71
Peasant societies: in mediaeval Europe, 4; in developed and developing countries, 3–7; in Africa and Asia, 20–4; conservative, 51–2; research into the agriculture of, 110–13; Development Corporations in, 204; and crisis in administration, 205–6; economics of, 260–8 (*see* Traditional society: Villages)
Peasants' Party, 227, 230
Peru, 96
Peshawar, West Pakistan, 41, 182
Pests: storage against, 37, 167, 271; control of, 127, 257, 275
Philippine Islands: population of, 20; landlords' attitude to tenants in, 110; rice from, 116; climate of, 133; winter crops in, 134; agricultural economists in, 136; and Land Reform, 150; tribal cultures in, 191; Ministers and officials in, 199; continuity in politics in, 220–1; no tenancy reform in, 232; education in, 247, 257; capitalism in, 284; engineering centre in, 288
Pigs, 135, 269
Planning, 113, 124, 137; initial steps in, 115; vision in, 125; for farms, 135–6, 141; and Indian Land Reform, 150; for education, 170; and delegation, 202–3; politics and, 215; of towns, 268–9; developing countries' economic, 273–5; for big schemes, 285; in Africa, 286
Planning Commission, India, 229
Planning Departments, 136
Plantations, 183; in Malaysia, 82, 83; and marketing, 84; European-owned in colonial times, 110, 111; in Africa, 111, 112; plantation companies, 149, 174; and settlement schemes, 163; can be managed by Corporations, 203; housing on, 268
Plant genetics, 109, 112, 132, 138, 277
Plant protection, 112, 113, 119 (*see* Spraying)
Plastic, 270–1
Plato, 16, 243
Ploughing: ox-ploughs, 22, 116, 118, 133, 145; counter-ploughing, 120; cost of, 137

Political parties: and panchayats, 65–6, 212, 215, 228, 232–3; peasants and, 75, 77–8; single-party system, 75, 76, 214, 215, 216–17, 222, 234–5, 236, 284–6; objects of, 76, 223; after Independence, 76–7; and agricultural progress, 172, 178, 234; in villages, 180; District Councils and, 211; in Africa, 231
Politics, 3, 218, 225, 239; and history, 4; individual rights and, 14; authoritarianism and, 15; developing countries and Western political systems, 19, 281; in Asia, 22, 23, 220–1, 231; in Africa, 23, 221–2; in villages, 27, 42, 139–40, 231, 234; caste and, 65–6; vote-catching in, 66–7, 76, 77, 223, 233–4; and the voter, 69, 223, 226, 233; mobilization of local energies by, 75, 77, 150, 216–17, 255; and military dictatorships, 76, 222, 234, 237, 285; and development, 82–3, 104–5, 216–17, 230–1, 233, 239; and will for reform, 150, 152, 230, 233, 234; at local level, 202, 229–30, 232, 233, 237, 247–8, 283, 285, 286; after Independence, 220–1; Peasants' Party and, 230; middle farmers in, 230; reforms needed in, 297
Population: in 19th-century Britain, 6; in developing countries, 8, 13, 19, 98–9; labour force and, 9, 11, 99–100, 147, 247, 275, 276; of Africa and Asia compared, 20–1, 49; in Africa, 33, 49; and wealth, 44; pressure on land and density of, 49–50, 81; control of, 51, 296; and land tenure and size of holdings, 83, 141–5; and choice of crops, 85; agricultural, 99, 101; growth in Uganda, 99; agricultural progress affected by growth of, 129, 131, 265, 297; Extension Services and density of, 172; and urbanization, 266, 267
Potatoes, 121; sweet, 127; seed, 159
Potters, 33, 58, 159
Poverty: and social services, 17, 215; and politics, 23–4, 224; in Bengal, 50; through overcrowding, 50; 'shared', 50, 52; increased production helps, 147; in Africa, 147–8; Co-operatives as a partial remedy for, 157; Indian rural development and, 214; District Administrators as 'Protectors of the Poor', 229–30; wins trust, 242; education and, 243, 247, 291, 292; the poor are getting richer, 261; and urban growth, 269; self-perpetuating, 291; and natural resources, 296
Prices: of land, 47, 89; agricultural and non-agricultural, 85; of produce, 113–14, 137, 151, 166–7, 168, 275; of food, 165, 228; of crops for export, 165; storage and, 166; and distance from markets, 166–7; fluctuations in, 167–8; guaranteed, 168; stabilization of, 169, 275; world, 287
Priests, and respect, 242
Private enterprise: and 'managerial society', 14; in developing countries, 16, 18; of agricultural corporations, 47; among young villagers, 70; agricultural policy and, 96; in small-scale industry, 98; and development, 139; for engineering in Asia, 272
Processing: employment in, 19, 89; factories for, 155, 170; of milk, 166; and marketing, 166, 168; increases a crop's value, 169; of sugar-cane, 174; training in, 182, 257; in single high-value crop areas, 183; growth of towns and, 268; in East Africa, 272; machinery for, 288; research into, 289
Production: institutions for, 18; economics of, 260; in developing countries, 261–2; rural, 264; of food, 265
Productivity: and variations in supply, 88; mechanization and, 97; and labour, 103; potential, 130–2, 147–8, 265; improved implements increase, 145–6, 271; and Land Reform in India, 147, 151; and development, 264
Profit, mechanization and, 145
Progressive Farmers' Clubs, India, 181
Proteins, 85
Provence, France, Roman irrigation in, 124
Provincial Administration, 202, 206
Provincial Commissioners, India, 75, 201
Public Corporations, 183
Public Service Commission, 139, 199
Pumps, 50, 119, 122, 130–1, 137, 145
Punjab: improved wheat in, 116; irrigation scheme in, 124
Punjab, East India: progressive farmers in, 71; panchayats in, 201–11; prices stabilized in, 275

GENERAL INDEX

Punjab, West, Pakistan: prosperous farmers in, 45, 46, 230; market economy in, 90; tubewells in, 130, 205; politics in, 230
Purdah, in India, 31, 159
Puri, Orissa State, India, 54
Pyrethrum, 85, 86, 121

Racialism, 169, 241, 272, 283, 288, 296
Radicalism, 76, 221, 222, 292–3
Railways, 111, 272
Rain: employment independent of, 88; monsoon rains in Asia, 125; in Africa, 131; uncertainty of, 132; winter, 134 (see Monsoon)
Rajasthan State, India, 87, 130, 146
Ramayana, 242
Ranching, in Uganda, 153
Rats: as food, 36; as a pest, 121, 167
Rayalaseema, India, 87
Ray, Robert, 101–2
Reaping, 34, 126, 129–30; machines for, 43–4
Refrigeration, Co-operatives and, 155
Relief, loans as, 162
Religion: and democracy, 15; Islam, 17; contrasted in Asia and Africa, 21–2, 23; in India, 23; in traditional society, 30, 31, 52, 56; conservatism of, 36, 40, 53–4, 73; caste and, 58; in Africa, 74, 238; order brought about by, 218–20, 237; in Asia, 237; and education, 243, 245; and the socializing process, 250–1; and morality, 297; and political and social stability, 297
Renaissance, in Europe, 233, 245
Rent, remission of, 180
Research: institutions for, 113; on developing countries' problems, 117, 289; on storage, 117, 167; into tractor economy, 118; on crops, 118; on plant-breeding and seeds, 119; on tsetse fly, 120; on agricultural development, 121, 148, 185; in Africa, 148; on social and economic conditions, 159; on market prices and roads, 166–7
Revenue, 201
Revenue Department, 208
Revenue Officers, 67, 69, 208, 212
Rhodesia, 40, 74, 111, 288
Rice, 86; in Asia, 36–7; in Malaya, 37; high-yielding, 45; in Java, 50–1; cultivation in Japan, 68, 102, 132–3; in India, 102; in the Philippines, 116; co-operative farming and, 122; 'puddling' of, 132; water for cultivation of, 133; Thai export levy on, 137; in Burma, 169; commercialized by Chinese in South-East Asia, 169 (see Paddy)
Rickshaw-pullers, Co-operative for, 159
Roads: important for markets, 5, 166–8, 169; and higher productivity, 37, 148; as relief works, 88; and agricultural progress, 113–14, 121; national 'drives' for increase in, 124; and traditional society, 140; and town growth, 267
Rome, Ancient: and irrigation in France and North Africa, 124; her administration, 245
Rotation of crops, 36, 90, 109, 113, 126, 132, 134–5, 146; four-course in mediaeval England, 109, 134
Rousseau, Jean-Jacques, 16
Rubber, 37, 82, 92, 120, 136, 163, 183
Rufigi River, 131
Rural Academies, 182, 256
Russia: Revolution, 15, 282–3; agricultural development in, 149; rigid discipline in, 238; planning in, 273; doctrinal lies in, 284; has her own outlook, 296
Rwanda, 16, 272

Sabah, 39, 167, 191, 281
Sahara, 131
Samburu people, Kenya, 231
Sanitation, in African new towns, 269
Sarawak, 39, 191
Savings, 11, 37, 38; schemes for, 88; savings clubs, 164
School fees, in Africa, 38, 85, 89, 258
School-leavers, jobs for, 12–13, 100–1, 246, 249, 292
Schoolmasters, 55, 68, 78, 242, 243 (see Teachers)
Schools: private, 78, 246, 247, 258; Secondary, 78, 254–5, 256–7, 268, 291; denominational, 250, 252; Primary, 250, 253, 254–5, 291, 297 (See Education)
Schumacher, Dr., 269
Science: in developing countries, 8, 20; in mediaeval Europe, 11, 246–7; in industrialized countries, 11–12; and pest control, 187; truth of, 243; training in, 245, 249, 257, 258; and modernization, 289, 296; religion and, 297
Scotland, education in, 258–9
Secularism, 64; Nehru and, 221, 251

Seed: improved, 34, 113; bought on credit, 34, 38, 161; by bid, 38, 68; research into, 119; high-yielding, 121, 171, 184; need for, 138; landlords and improved, 174 (*see* Crops)
Sekou Touré, President, 235
Senegal, 23
Senghor, President Léopold Sédar, 16, 235
Servants, village, 33, 48, 52, 58
Services: and political blackmail in Africa, 77; of landlords, 151, 154; and feudal governments, 192–3; in towns, 194, 266–7; government and, 194, 195; in India, 198; in developing countries, 261
Settlement Boards, 163
Settlement schemes: in East Africa, 85; on new land, 90, 140; in Sudan and India, 90; wholesale changes caused by, 126–7, 138; in Tanzania, 127, 163; in Kenya, 135–6, 156, 163; credit granted in, 163; in Malaysia, 163; in West Africa, 163; Extension Officers and, 173
Sewing-machines, Singer, 271
Share-cropping, 32, 68, 154, 165, 166
Shell experiment, at Borgo a Mozzano, Italy, 164, 174–5
Shoemakers, 271
Shops, 266, 269, 271
Sialkot, West Punjab, 97, 228
Sierra Leone, 296
Silk-weaving, 271
Silos, 271
Sind, West Pakistan, 45, 50, 90, 130
Singapore, 20, 226, 272, 288
Slums, 269
Smallholders: aims of, 39; freehold for, 48; in Africa, 48–9; in Malaysian settlement schemes, 82, 163; irrigation and, 122; in Kenya, 136; in modernized areas, 143; in overcrowded areas, 144, 147; output of, 146; increased skill of, 147; Land Reform and, 151; in East Pakistan, 228
Snakes: as food, 36; snake-bite, 36
Socialism: State, 15, 16, 231; and trade, 170; and entrepreneurial initiative, 216; Nehru and, 221, 231; in Africa, 221, 238
Socialization, 245, 250, 252, 258
Social life: traditional social order, 15; of peasants, 39; social support for village communities, 139; effect of social institutions on population, 147; problems of land ownership and tenure in, 148; loans for social expenditure, 164; growth and changes in Africa, 221–2, 224, 225
Sociology, 3, 245
Soils: in Sind, 50; in areas of adequate rainfall, 88; research into, 115, 290; new variants of, 120; conservation of, 120; effect of irrigation on, 126; in Kenya and Uganda, 148; in Africa and Asia, 149; soil chemistry, 257
Sorghum, 132
South America, 6 (*see* Latin America)
South Africa, Republic of, 13; and European expansion, 6; minerals in, 111; engineering centre in, 272; racialism in, 283, 288
South-East Asia: European expansion into, 6, 72; population of, 20; and change, 22; Chinese traders in, 38, 168–9; village rankings in, 71; commercialization in, 169, 221, 226; politics in, 226
Sowing: line-sowing, 69, 120; of wheat, 69; early, 116–17; broadcast, 120, 132–3; of rice, 132–3
Spain, and the Philippines, 110, 221
Specialist advice: Universities and, 183–4; District Administration and, 185, 194, 206–7, 213, 252–3
Specialization: examples of, 37; as a cure for poverty, 52; and agricultural development, 86, 264; and agricultural management, 109; and marketing, 166; threatened by irrelevant politics, 225; in education, 248; and exports, 265
Spices, 92, 165
Spraying: of weeds, 52; of crops, 119, 176; in West Pakistan, 121; aerial, 137
Standard of living, 11, 18, 133, 287 (*see* Incomes)
Standards, commercial and agricultural, 170
Statistics, unreliability of, 101–2, 145, 274
Steelworks, 27–8, 115
Storage: and pests, 37, 167, 271; and famine, 88; and agricultural advance, 113, 116, 261; research into, 117, 167, 271; roads and, 121; by Co-operatives, 155, 159, 182; and marketing, 166, 167–8, 169; training in, 257, 289
Sub-divisional Officers, India, 208–9
Subsidies, 69, 95; for seed, 38, 69; for fertilizers, 69, 95, 153, 275; for plant-protection, 95; for credit, 95,

GENERAL INDEX

Subsidies—*cont.*
153; American aid to South-East Asia, 150, 264; for savings schemes, 164; for agricultural produce, 168
Subsistence economy: in Africa, 21; and cash economy, 25, 31, 47, 91, 92, 93, 95, 121, 161–5, 224; in overcrowded areas, 90, 144; Colonial policy towards, 84–5, 112; and the farmer, 84, 123, 127; in Mexico, 94; conditions that prolong, 95; and industry, 115; in India, 136; economics of, 137; shifting cultivation and, 141; and food prices, 228; and urbanization, 267
Sudan: Gezira scheme in, 90, 124, 173; and field-work for women, 104; irrigation in, 111, 124, 131; Extension Services in, 173
Sudras, in India, 56, 58
Suffrage, universal adult, 16, 61, 65, 214, 222, 231–2, 236, 285
Sugar cane: in Mysore, 44; in West Africa, 47, 93; as cattle-feed, 120; processing factories for, 155, 170, 174; in Uganda, 171
Sunlight, necessary in agriculture, 125, 133, 138, 263
Superstition: among peasants, 26, 53; in India, 35, 36; truth and, 250, 252; and education, 253; and traditional skills, 291
Surveys: on employment in Tanzania, 100–1; Lower Indus survey on land, 151; of credit, 161; of manpower, 170
Sweden, 36
Switzerland, 296

Taccavi (*taqavi*) system, in India, 162
Taiwan, 100, 101, 105, 120, 150, 264
Taluka, in South India, 56, 208–9
Tanganyika African National Union (T.A.N.U.), 214, 234–5, 285
Tanjore (Thanjavur) District, Madras, India, 135, 137, 267–8
'Tanks' in India, 30, 129, 131
Tanzania: Nyerere and, 17, 22–3, 297; honey-gathering in, 36; Village Development Committees in, 76, 214; village mobilization in, 77; settlement schemes in, 100, 127, 163; jobs for school-leavers in, 101; employment survey in, 101–2; irrigation in, 131; civil servants in, 153; Co-operatives in, 155, 157; wheat-growing scheme in, 173; mines in, 176; local government in, 201; cotton in, 205; population of, 205; rural administration in, 214; 'Ujamaa' in, 224; politics in, 225, 234; political control of district administration in, 236; education in, 246, 248, 254–5; railway for, 272; industry in, 272
Taxation: to raise capital, 11, 288; of land, 150, 152–3, 154, 182–3, 256, 288; local, 183; government and, 192
Tea, 47, 83, 118, 155, 170, 174, 183
Teachers, 243–4, 251; training of, 249, 254, 292 (*see* Schoolmasters)
Technical Colleges, 257
Technology: and modernization, 3, 4, 281; in Europe, 6–7, 11, 13, 107, 244–5; and developing countries, 8, 19, 20, 26, 261; and agriculture, 25, 53, 104, 112; in village communities, 139; and Extension Services, 177; problem of accelerating technology compared with that of administrative changes, 204; training, 243, 246, 247, 248, 249; 'intermediate', 265, 269, 290; and economic expansion, 276
Tehsil, 56, 208–9
Tehsildar, 55, 208–9
Tenancy reform, 150; in India, 227; Philippines and, 232; in Thailand, 232
Tenants: in lowest layer of peasant life, 32–3, 48; displacement of, 46, 47, 227; market economy of, 100; landlords' power over, 140, 150, 151–2; incomes of, 141; increase in acreage held by, 147, 149, 150, 151; get help from landlords, 149, 151, 154, 161; want security, 150; in Thailand, 153; in settlement schemes, 183; their position in relation to landlords regularized, 193; and food prices, 228
Textile industry, in England, 270
Thailand: population of, 20; old kingdom in, 21, 72; agriculture in, 22, 45, 135, 136, 177, 185; varying societies in, 24, 25; village rankings in, 71; dam and irrigation schemes in, 127, 273; 'tanks' in, 131; winter crops in, 133–4; fertilizers in, 136, 158; export levy on rice in, 137; middle-class farming in, 153; 'Friendship Highway' in, 167; tribes in, 191; restrictions on Governors in, 192; administrators trained at universities in, 198; Ministers and officials in, 199; continuity of politics in, 220–1; Buddhism and monarchy in, 221; slow

Thailand—*cont.*
democratization of, 222; commercialization of, 226; no elected government in, 232, 237; land tenure in, 232; criticism of monks in, 242; education in, 248; religion in, 250–1; American subsidies to, 264; small-scale industry in, 271; capitalism in, 284; has its own outlook, 296; potential of, 297
Thana, in Pakistan, 159, 160
Threshing, 117–18; use of small threshers, 97; Co-operatives and hiring of threshers, 154–5
Tillers, use of small, 145, 271
Tiu people, Nigeria, 21
Tobacco, 45, 47, 127, 132, 162, 170, 174, 183
Tomatoes, 170
Tourism, 262, 263, 264, 276–8
Town Boards, India, 75–6
Towns: in Asia, 22; jobs in, 44; growth of, 89, 93, 266–8; services in, 193; starting-point for self-government, 193–4; in Europe, 221; squalor of, 269 (*see* Cities: Urbanization)
Toynbee, Arnold Joseph, 108
Tractors: their use contrasted with that of cattle, 35, 117–18; Java and, 51; and the poor, 52; in group-farming, 96, 122, 127, 128; fuel for, 113–14; and early sowing, 116; cost of ploughing by, 137; small, 145; hiring of, 145, 154; Co-operatives and, 159; tractor-factory, 165
Trade: growth of European, 6; in developing countries, 8, 26, 168, 265; international, 8, 92–3, 165, 260, 289; its openings for industry and agriculture, 9; in West Africa, 23, 111; interdependent with agriculture and industry, 52; and agricultural development, 86; British colonial motives in, 110–11; in world commodities, 165, 170–1; peasant communities and, 168; widens a nation's outlook, 244, 245; Africa and, 245; and exchange system, 263; regional, 265; with developed countries, 278; future, 287 (*see* Marketing)
Traders, 39, 168–9; and planned trading centres, 268
Trade Schools, 245
Trade Unions, 14, 16, 294
Traditional society: yields to modernization, 5, 9, 12, 15–16, 30–1, 42–8, 139–41, 224–5, 241, 291; education and, 12; peasant economies in, 32; African and Asian compared, 32; provides security, 32, 33–4, 35–6, 40, 140, 224, 293; in Indian villages, 32–3, 40–5; money in, 33, 37–8; honour in, 33–4, 39; conservatism of, 34, 36–7; poverty in, 35–6, 291; aim of peasants in, 39; in Africa, 41, 74, 225; hierarchy in, 55, 74, 78, 140, 197, 215–16; the choice in Asia, 71; gradual reform in, 137–8, 152, 187; and change, 141, 220, 241; credit given in transition from, 161–5; marketing in, 170; and religion in Asia, 237, 291; stifles development, 291 (*see* Developing countries: Peasant societies: Villages)
Training: of farmers, 113, 122, 176, 182, 243–4, 256; of Extension Services, 173, 181–2; concentration of agricultural, 182; in heavy industry, 262 (*see* Education)
Training Colleges, futile upgrading of, 248
Transport: its effect on markets, 4, 166–7; in Japan, 97; by animals, 117–18, 267; Co-operatives and, 154; developing countries need to improve, 261; and growth of urbanization, 267
Tribalism: in Africa, 21, 75, 191, 220, 221, 231, 234; in India and Pakistan, 24, 47, 191; in South-East Asia, 24, 191; may be found near rich peasants, 31; European Administrations and, 43, 72; and agriculture, 47, 148; experiments in modernization possible with, 73, 77; and markets, 92; yields to bureaucracy, 200, 216; politics and, 222–3, 224; education and, 240; universal suffrage and, 285
Trinidad, 179
Tsetse fly, 120, 133
Tubewells: in Punjab, 46, 130, 205; small, 97, 130; large-scale public schemes for, 98; in Sind and India, 130; and winter crops, 134; sharing of, 145; Co-operatives and, 154; credit for, 161
Tungabhadra River, 130
Tutsi tribe, Rwanda, 71
Typhoons, 162

Uganda: tribes in, 21; development needed in, 24; commercial agriculture in, 47; population of, 99, 205; tractorized group farming in, 128; ranching scheme in, 153; and search for new markets, 171;

GENERAL INDEX 323

Uganda—*cont.*
 conflict with Buganda, 197; Youth Settlement in, 205; industry in, 272
Unemployment: in 19th-century England, 7; in developing countries, 8, 12–13, 19; large-scale farming may cause, 94, 144–5; among school-leavers, 100–1, 292; proposals for reducing, 104; education and, 246; among graduates, 247, 292 (*see* Employment)
Union Councils, Pakistan, 213–14
United National Independence Party (UNIP), Zambia, 235
United Nations, 288; UNCTAD, 262, 287, 289
United States: European expansion into, 6, 277; education in, 13, 259; democracy in, 14; American Revolution, 15; Founding Fathers of, 16; development often brutal in, 19; politics in, 23, 227; growth of non-farm employment in, 105; U.S.A.I.D., 108; and Philippines, 110, 221; linked stages of agricultural development in, 114; her Reclamation Bureau and the Mekong project, 124; fertilizers in, 136; cereal yields in, 142; financial aid to South-East Asia, 150, 264; Universities and agricultural extension work, 184–5; early Puritan Societies in, 227; alliances with Thailand and South Vietnam, 237; 19th-century growth of towns in the West of, 269; overseas development studied in, 277; service overseas from, 278; revolt against old prescriptions for progress, 281–3; limitations as model for developing peasant societies, 295; has her own outlook, 296
Universities: in England, 11; in Colonies, 12; in developing countries, 16, 246; farms run by, 117, 132; and Extension work, 176, 183–5, 187; and agricultural training, 182; as training-grounds for administrators, 198, 200–1, 213; African leaders attend Western, 222; Arts subjects in, 245; excessive use of, 247–8, 249–50; debasing of, 248, 258; raising of standards in, 257, 258; overseas development studied in foreign, 277; revolt in Western, 284; extramural functions of, 294–5; and rational knowledge, 297
University College, Bangor, 290

University of Sussex, 263, 274
University of the South Pacific, Fiji, 248
Upper Kitete, Tanzania, 173
Urbanization: in developing countries, 26; in overcrowded areas, 51; weakens caste, 60, 64; and high-potential areas, 88–9; and internal division of labour, 93–4; in Kenya, 99; likely to follow increase in agricultural productivity, 265; non-farm employment and growth of, 266; reasons for, 267–8 (*see* Towns)
Uttar Pradesh, India: superstition in, 36; caste faction in, 62, 233; influence of caste in panchayat elections in, 66; villagers' attitude to Village Level Workers in, 68; differs from Bihar, 123; panchayats in, 210–11; political crisis in, 215

Vadamalaipuram, Madras State, India, 167
Vaisyas, in Indian caste-system, 56
Vegetables, 91, 135, 166
Vegetarianism, 60
Victoria, Lake, 33, 111, 272
Vietnam, 71, 191; North, 20, 222, 284; South, 20, 237, 264
Vijayawada, Andhra Pradesh, India, 119
Village Development Committees, Tanzania, 76, 214, 216
Village elders, 34, 44, 61, 73, 75
Village Level Workers (V.L.W.), 67–9, 70, 173, 209–10, 212; training college for, 256
Village Panchayats, 41, 56, 58, 60–6, 70, 76, 78, 158, 209–11, 227, 231, 232 (*see* Panchayats)
Villages, 30, 32–5, 40, 51, 52, 58; in Asia and Africa, 3, 201; power in, 18, 22, 55; modernization and, 22, 23, 31, 43–7, 51–3, 63, 292; servants of, 33, 48; honour in, 34, 39; economy of, 35–6; resist progress, 36, 39, 42–3, 69, 241; enclosed communities, 37, 40–1, 51, 240, 252, 256; suspicious of outsiders, 40, 41, 68, 240–1; factions in, 40–2, 46, 59, 61–2, 64, 69, 233; hierarchy of, 55, 62, 63–4; ranking system in, 55, 56, 58, 71; main units in feudal times, 192; politics and, 222–3, 225, 226, 228, 231, 232–3; their attitude to government, 257; agricultural villages and urbanization, 266–7 (*see* Peasant societies: Traditional society)

Viti Levu, Fiji, 93
Volta River Dam, Ghana, 125, 126-7, 128, 268

Wages, 36, 88, 99, 103, 105; wage-labour, 38, 96, 152, 225; regulation of, 194; wage-paid jobs, 246; rural, 267
Waidina Valley, Fiji, 93
Wakamba people, Kenya, 271
Water: supply of, 113-14; control of, 129-30, 261, 273, 276; sharing of, 145, 154 (see Irrigation)
Weddings, cost of, 33, 248 (see Marriage)
Weeds, 35, 52, 116, 126; weeding, 163
Welfare, 14, 17-18, 19, 111, 215-16, 220
Welfare Services, 176
Welfare State, 195-6
Wells, 45, 129-30 (see Tubewells)
West, the: contrasted with developing countries, 5-6, 9; advantage of, 7; its limitations as model for developing countries, 7, 8-9, 13, 17-18, 226, 278, 286-7, 292, 295, 297; decline of Christianity in, 238; education borrowed from, 244, 292; graduates emigrate from developing countries to, 248; planning in, 273; its growth compared with that of developing countries, 281-2, 284; revolt in, 282-4, 286; Local Government in, 285; can learn from developing countries, 286, 298; and closer ties with developing countries, 290 (see Developed countries: England: Europe: United States)
Wheat: in Punjab, 46, 116, 275; line-sowing of, 69; Japanese and Indian yields compared, 102; Mexican, 116; introduced into Kenya Highlands, 120; in sandy soil, 146; Tanzania scheme for, 173
White ants, as food, 36
Wine, in Italy, 169
Winnowing, 117
Witchcraft, 40

Wolsey, Cardinal, 244
Women: inherit rice land in Malaya, 37; and cottage industries, 37; harvest rice in Java, 50-1; more conservative than men, 60; seats on panchayats for, 61; older practices of work for, 73; modernization and the position of, 83; and agricultural work, 103-4; petty trading by, 165-6; classes for, 159, 256; education of, 292
Wood, 271; in European crafts, 269-70
Woollen industry, in England, 270
Works Departments, in India, 208-9
World Bank, 201
World War II, 112, 116

Yields: of wheat, 102, 142, 146; by labour-intensive methods, 142; higher on smaller units, 146
Young Farmers' Clubs, 181, 255, 256
Yoruba people, Nigeria, 21, 39, 72, 238, 267
Yugoslavia, 238, 283-4

Zambesi, River, 111
Zambia: mining in, 10; tribes in, 21; personal incomes in, 22; middle class in, 23; clearing of land in, 49-50; Lumpa Church in, 53; areas of malnutrition in, 88; irrigation in, 131; plough-oxen in, 133; and political control of District Administration, 202, 236; single-party politics in, 234-5; education in, 246; foreign exchange in, 264; towns in, 268; engineering in, 272; new pattern of politics and development planning in, 286; British students visit, 290; Kaunda and, 297
Zamindars, in India, 69-70, 197 (see Landlords)
Zaria, Nigeria, 248
Zilla Parishad, 56, 211, 212 (see District Panchayats)